Marmalade Boy

By

Wataru Yoshizumi

TOKYOPOP®
Los Angeles • Tokyo

Story and Art – Wataru Yoshizumi
Translator – Jack Niida
English Adaptation – Deb Baer
Retouch and Lettering – Monalisa de Asis
Graphic Designer – Anna Kernbaum
Senior Editor – Julie Taylor

Production Manager – Joaquin Reyes
Art Director – Matthew Alford
Brand Manager – Joel Baral
VP of Production – Ron Klamert
Publisher – Stuart Levy

Email: editor@tokyopop.com
Come visit us online at www.TOKYOPOP.com

A  manga

TOKYOPOP® is an imprint of Mixx Entertainment, Inc.
5900 Wilshire Blvd. Ste 2000, Los Angeles, CA 90036

ISBN: 1-931514-56-9

First TOKYOPOP® printing: September 2002

10 9 8 7 6 5 4

Printed in Canada

Main Characters

ARIMI SUZUKI: PERSUADED YUU TO GO OUT WITH HER ON A BET. YUU DUMPED HER, BUT SHE STILL LIKES HIM. SHE GOES TO A NEARBY SCHOOL.

YUU MATSUURA: MIKI'S STEP-BROTHER...KINDA. HE'S GOOD LOOKING, BUT TEASES MIKI. KISSED MIKI WHEN HE THOUGHT SHE WAS SLEEPING.

MIKI KOISHIKAWA: ALWAYS CHEERFUL, BUT SLOW ON THE UPTAKE. HAS A HARD TIME ADJUSTING TO HER CRAZY FAMILY.

MEIKO AKIZUKI: MIKI'S BEST FRIEND. MEMBER OF THE LITERARY CLUB. HAS AN AIR OF MYSTERY ABOUT HER.

GINTA SUOU: MIKI HAD A CRUSH ON HIM. HE LIKED HER BUT DIDN'T ADMIT IT 'TIL NOW. HE'S ON THE TENNIS TEAM WITH MIKI.

THE STORY SO FAR...

DURING BREAKFAST ONE DAY, MIKI'S PARENTS BREAK IT TO HER THAT THEY'RE GETTING DIVORCED AND SWAPPING SPOUSES WITH ANOTHER COUPLE! NOW MIKI HAS FOUR PARENTS AND A NEW STEPBROTHER, YUU, WHO KEEPS TEASING HER. YUU'S SWEET ON THE OUTSIDE, BUT HE'S GOT A BITTER STREAK - HE'S A MARMALADE BOY! AS MIKI GETS TO KNOW YUU, SHE STARTS TO FORM A CRUSH ON HIM.

THINGS GET COMPLICATED WHEN MIKI'S OLD CRUSH, THE TENNIS CHAMP, GINTA, CONFESSES HIS LOVE FOR HER. MIKI WROTE HIM A LOVE LETTER BACK IN JUNIOR HIGH, BUT WHEN HE SHOWED IT TO HIS FRIENDS, SHE WOULDN'T SPEAK TO HIM FOR A WHOLE YEAR. SINCE THEN, THEY'VE JUST BEEN GOOD FRIENDS. AND THINGS GET EVEN MORE CONFUSING WHEN YUU'S EX-GIRLFRIEND, ARMINI, TRANSFERS TO MIKI'S SCHOOL AND TRIES TO WIN HIM BACK. DRAMA-RAMA!

WHEN GINTA'S DOUBLES PARTNER GETS INJURED, YUU TEAMS UP WITH GINTA FOR THE TENNIS INVITATIONAL AT THE SCHOOL FESTIVAL. ODDLY ENOUGH, THEY ARE MATCHED UP AGAINST YUU'S OLD CLASSMATE AND ARCH RIVAL, TSUTOMU ROKUTANDA. IN THE PAST, TSUTOMO AND YUU HAD FOUGHT OVER ARMINI'S AFFECTIONS—AND IT TURNS OUT THAT TSUTOMO IS STILL IN LOVE WITH HER. UNFORTUNATELY, ARMINI IS STILL IN LOVE WITH YUU—BUT THE FEELING IS NOT MUTUAL. ARMINI DECIDES TO GO OUT WITH GINTA TO MAKE YUU AND MIKI JEALOUS...AND IT WORKS! MIKI DOESN'T KNOW WHO SHE LIKES...YUU OR GINTA. HER CONFUSION SKYROCKETS WHEN THE 'RENTS JET OFF ON A TWO-WEEK HONEYMOON, LEAVING MIKI AND YUU TOTALLY AND COMPLETELY ALONE. IS THIS A RECIPE FOR LOVE...OR DISASTER?!

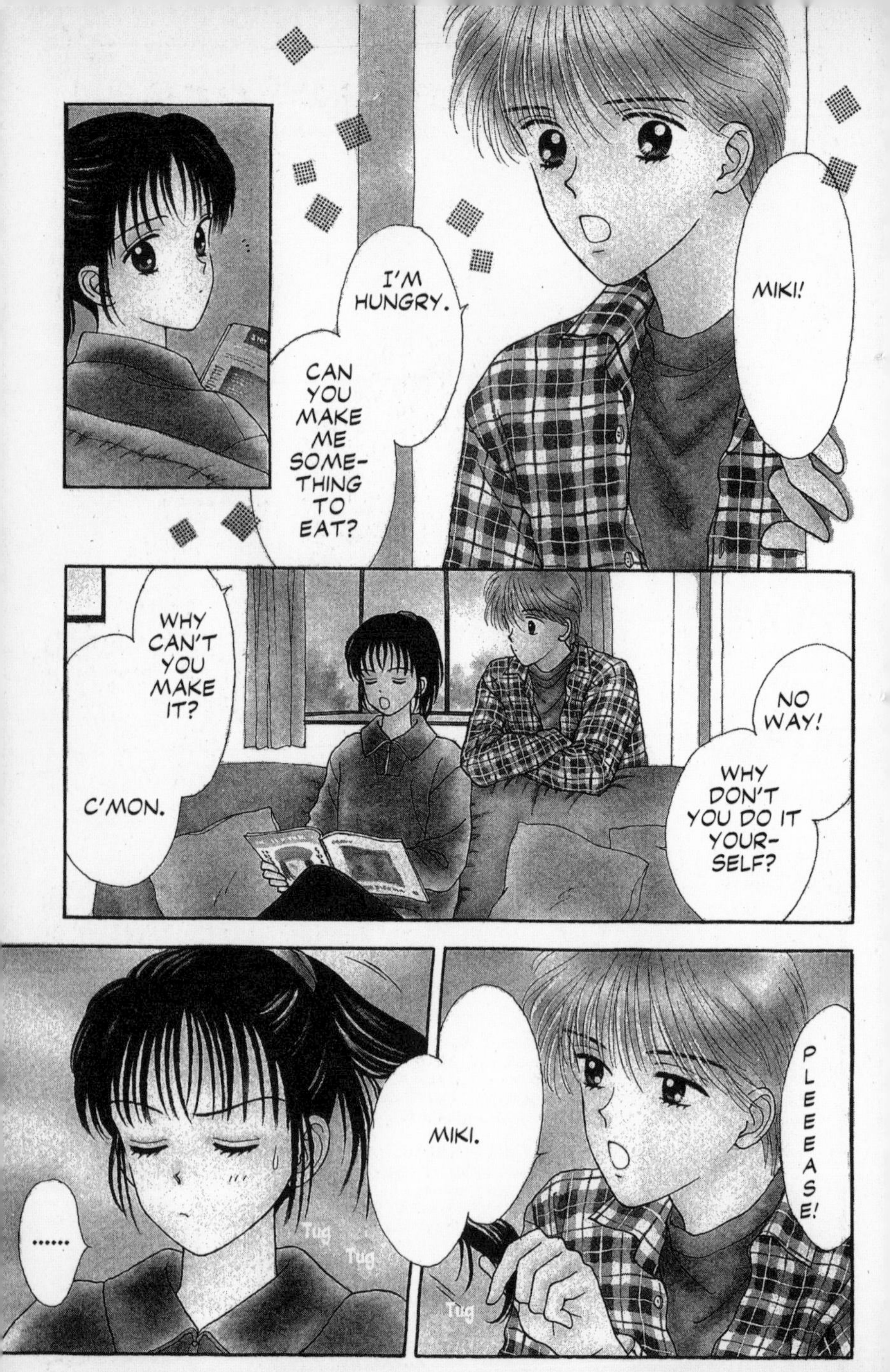
MIKI!
I'M HUNGRY.
CAN YOU MAKE ME SOME-THING TO EAT?
NO WAY!
WHY DON'T YOU DO IT YOUR-SELF?
WHY CAN'T YOU MAKE IT?
C'MON.
PLEEEASE!
MIKI.
Tug
Tug
Tug
......

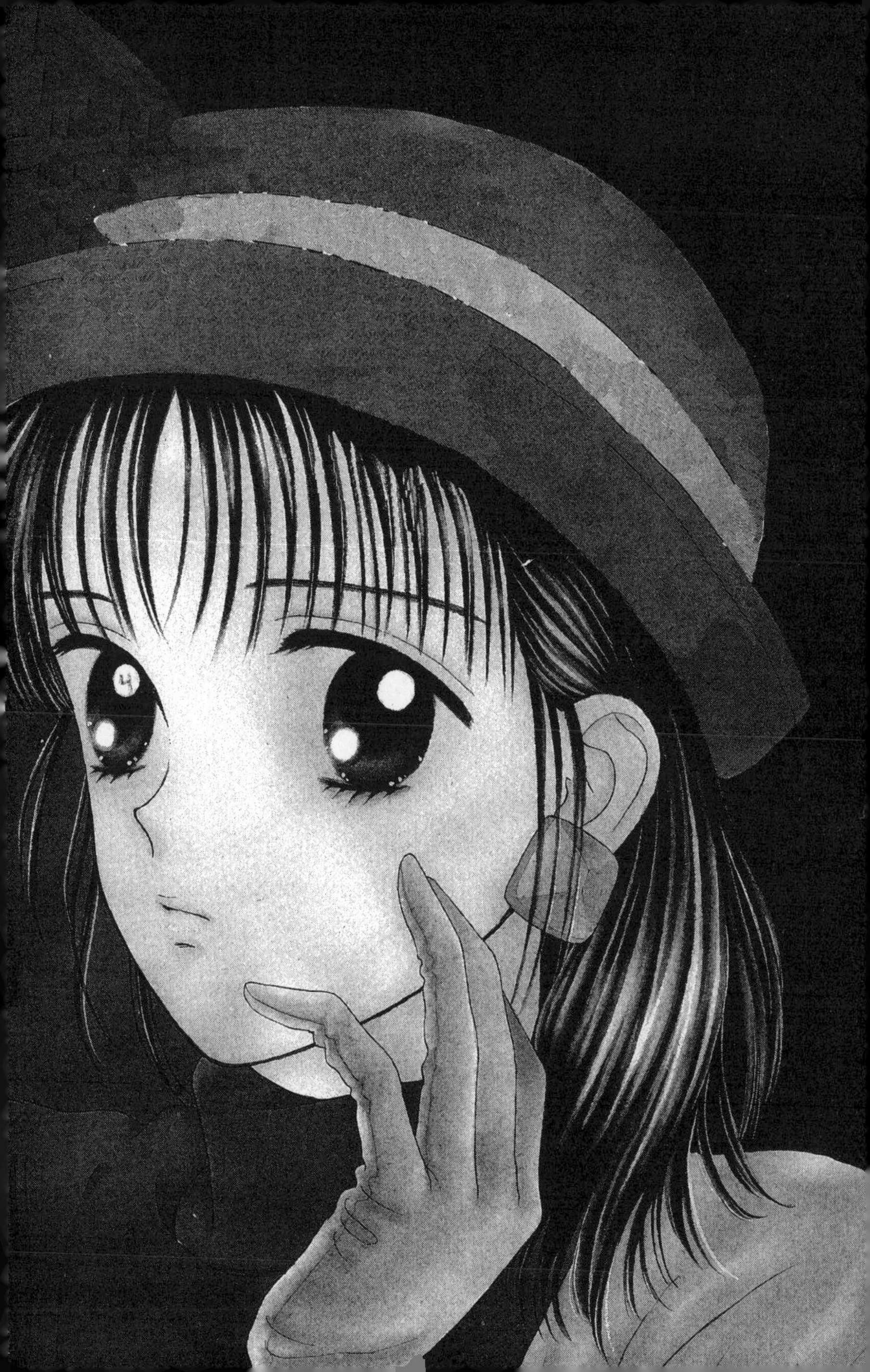

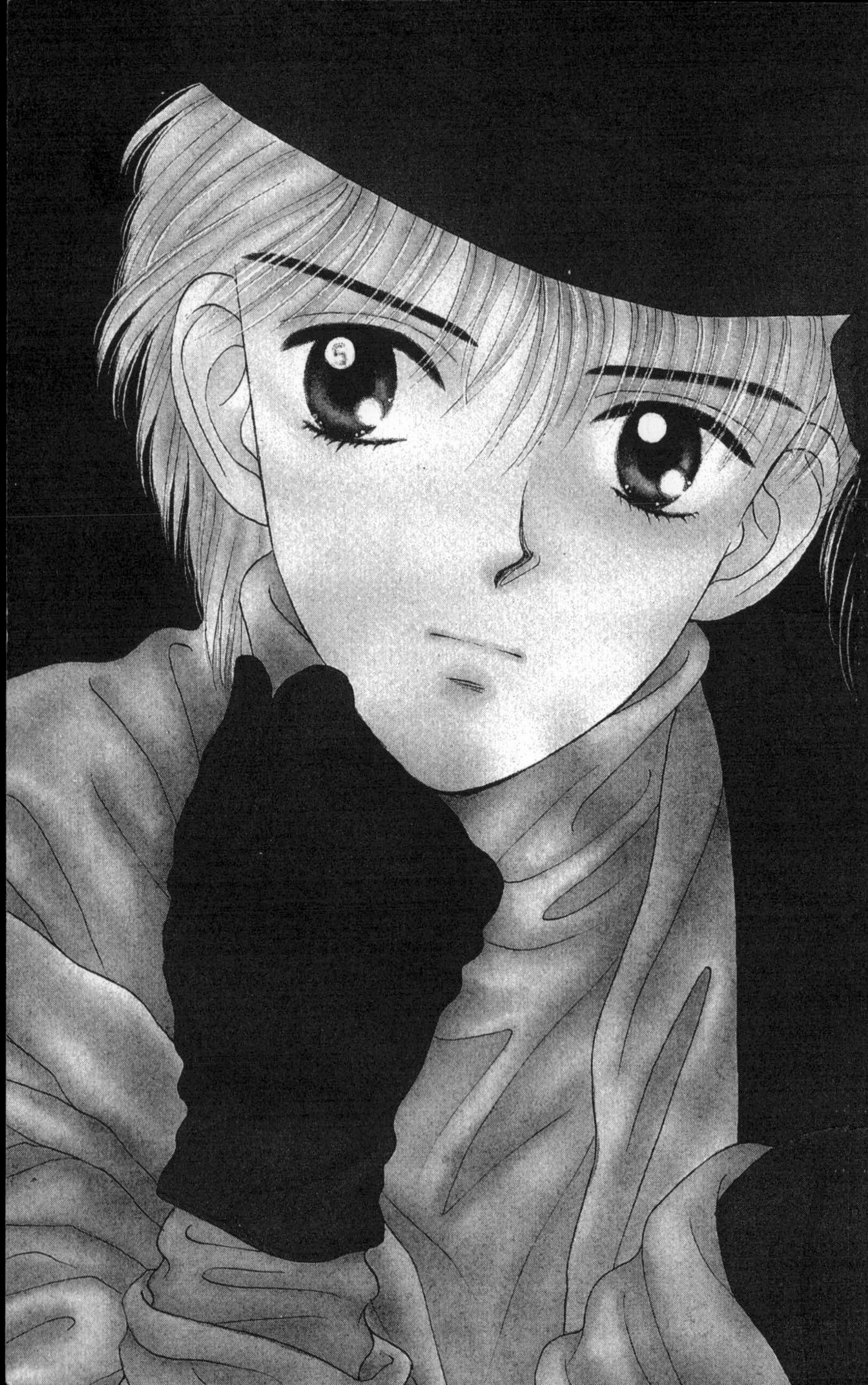

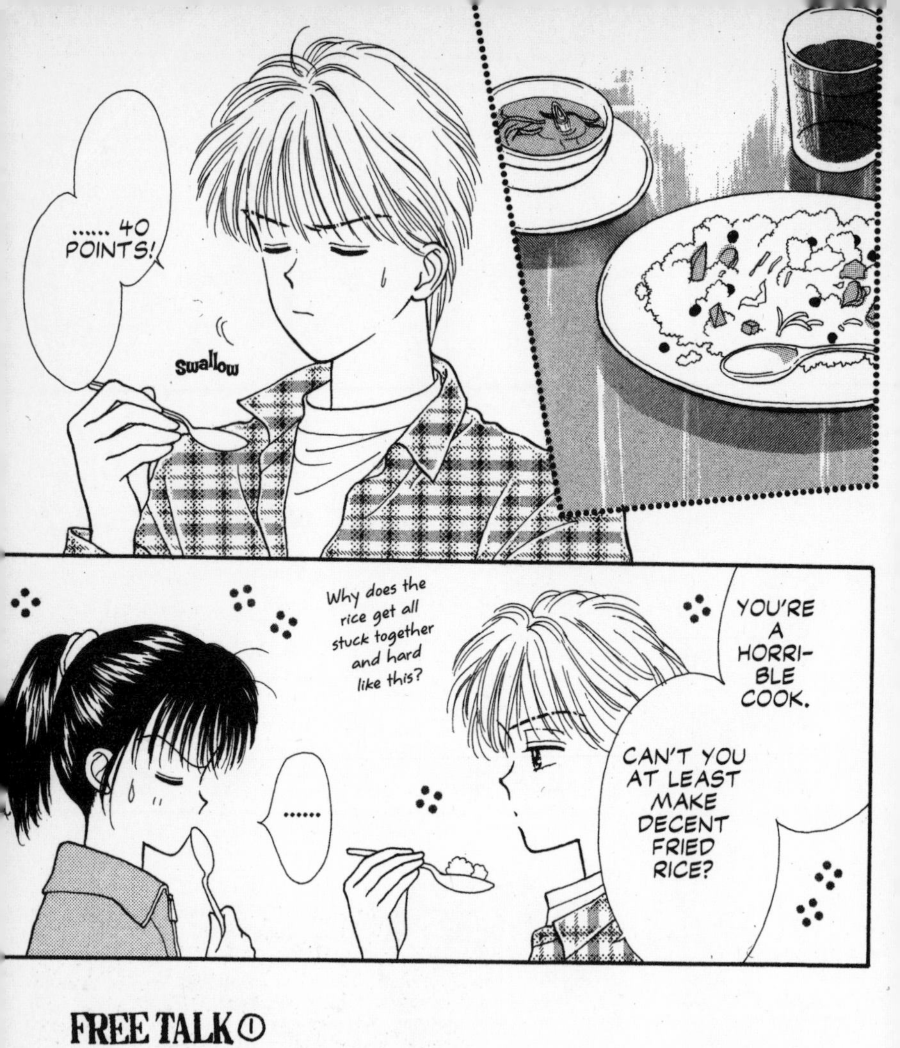
...... 40 POINTS!
swallow
YOU'RE A HORRI-BLE COOK.
CAN'T YOU AT LEAST MAKE DECENT FRIED RICE?
......
Why does the rice get all stuck together and hard like this?

FREE TALK ①

Hello, it's Yoshizumi. Thank you so much for reading Volume 3. In Marmalade Boy 2, I wrote that I am collecting angel marks. Lots of you generous readers sent them in. In fact, I received over fifty! Thank you so much. I'll definitely write thank-you cards when I find the time, so please wait patiently, okay? Thanks to all those who sent me a birthday present, too!

Here's the Can of Toys! It looks like an ordinary can with a cap on it. In fact, it has the same design as a can of Choco-Balls. But inside, there's a surprise! This one contained: a) a Kyoro-chan keychain, b) a pair of sunglasses, c) some sketch sheets and) a few other goodies. Cool!

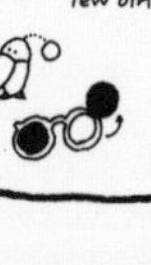

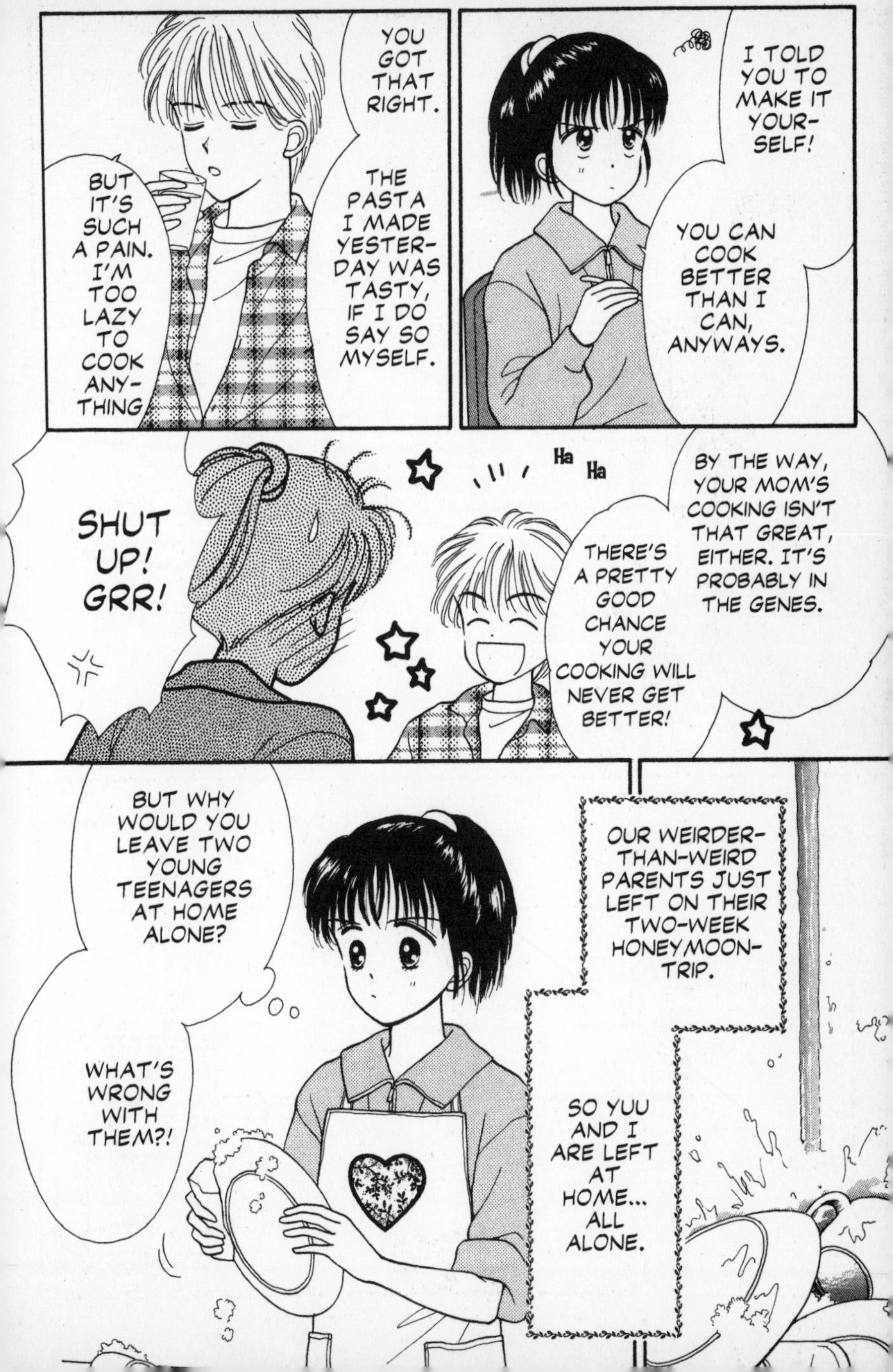
I TOLD YOU TO MAKE IT YOURSELF!
YOU CAN COOK BETTER THAN I CAN, ANYWAYS.
YOU GOT THAT RIGHT.
THE PASTA I MADE YESTERDAY WAS TASTY, IF I DO SAY SO MYSELF.
BUT IT'S SUCH A PAIN. I'M TOO LAZY TO COOK ANYTHING
BY THE WAY, YOUR MOM'S COOKING ISN'T THAT GREAT, EITHER. IT'S PROBABLY IN THE GENES.
THERE'S A PRETTY GOOD CHANCE YOUR COOKING WILL NEVER GET BETTER!
Ha Ha
SHUT UP! GRR!
OUR WEIRDER-THAN-WEIRD PARENTS JUST LEFT ON THEIR TWO-WEEK HONEYMOON-TRIP.
SO YUU AND I ARE LEFT AT HOME... ALL ALONE.
BUT WHY WOULD YOU LEAVE TWO YOUNG TEENAGERS AT HOME ALONE?
WHAT'S WRONG WITH THEM?!

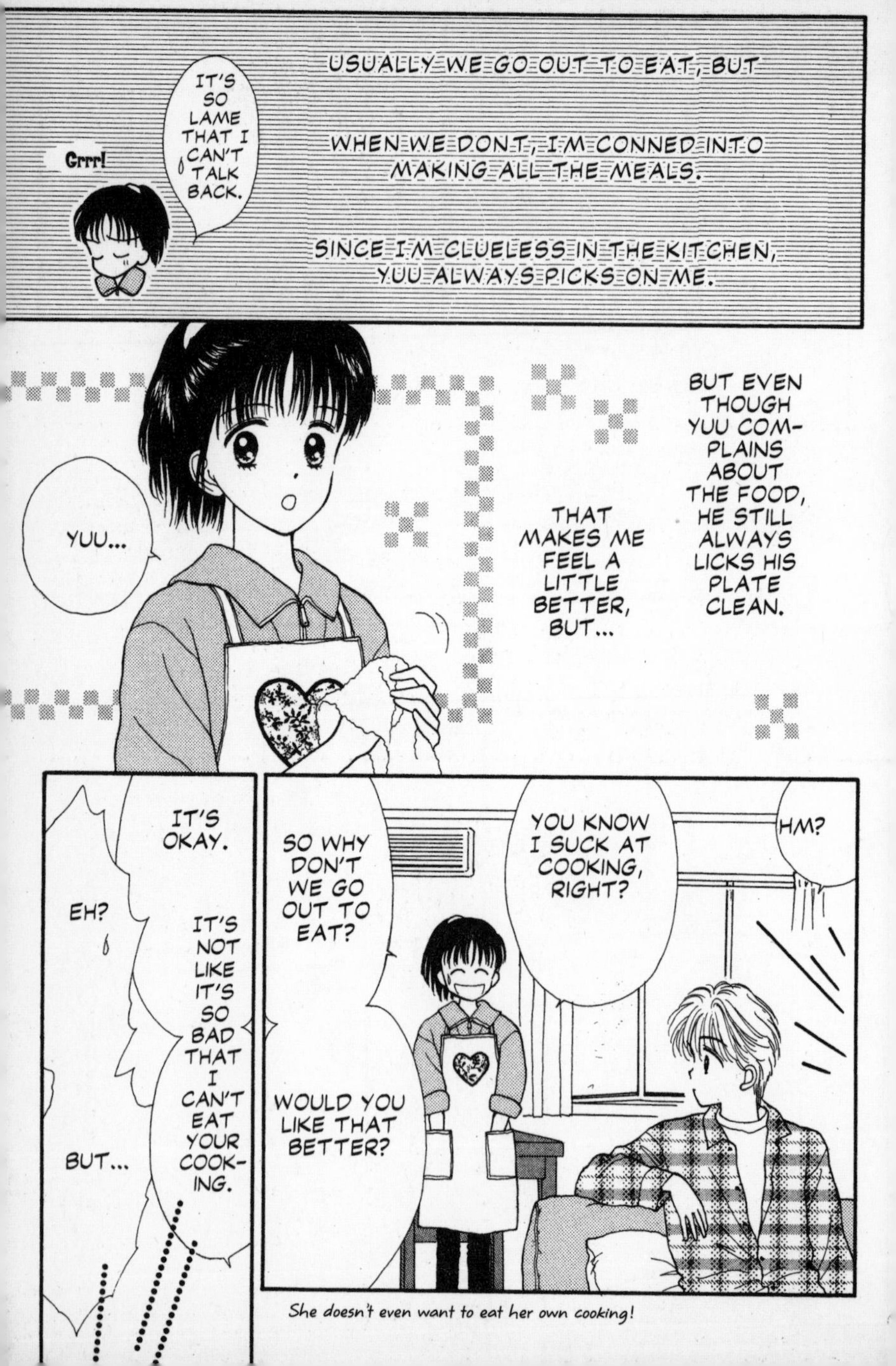
USUALLY WE GO OUT TO EAT, BUT
WHEN WE DONT, I'M CONNED INTO MAKING ALL THE MEALS.
SINCE I'M CLUELESS IN THE KITCHEN, YUU ALWAYS PICKS ON ME.
IT'S SO LAME THAT I CAN'T TALK BACK.
Grrr!
BUT EVEN THOUGH YUU COM-PLAINS ABOUT THE FOOD, HE STILL ALWAYS LICKS HIS PLATE CLEAN.
THAT MAKES ME FEEL A LITTLE BETTER, BUT...
YUU...
HM?
YOU KNOW I SUCK AT COOKING, RIGHT?
SO WHY DON'T WE GO OUT TO EAT?
WOULD YOU LIKE THAT BETTER?
IT'S OKAY.
IT'S NOT LIKE IT'S SO BAD THAT I CAN'T EAT YOUR COOK-ING.
EH?
BUT...
She doesn't even want to eat her own cooking!

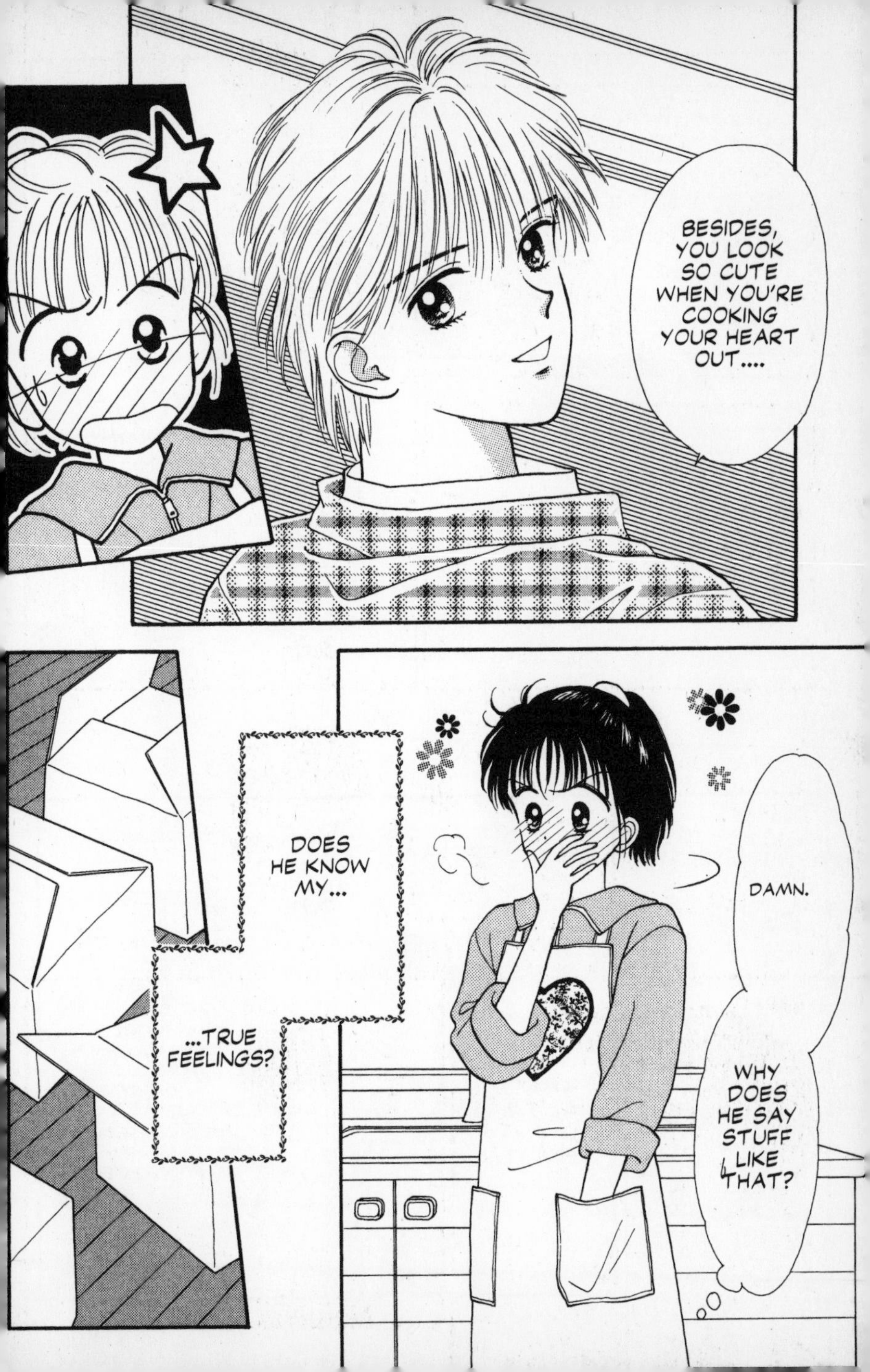
BESIDES, YOU LOOK SO CUTE WHEN YOU'RE COOKING YOUR HEART OUT....
DAMN.
WHY DOES HE SAY STUFF LIKE THAT?
DOES HE KNOW MY...
...TRUE FEELINGS?

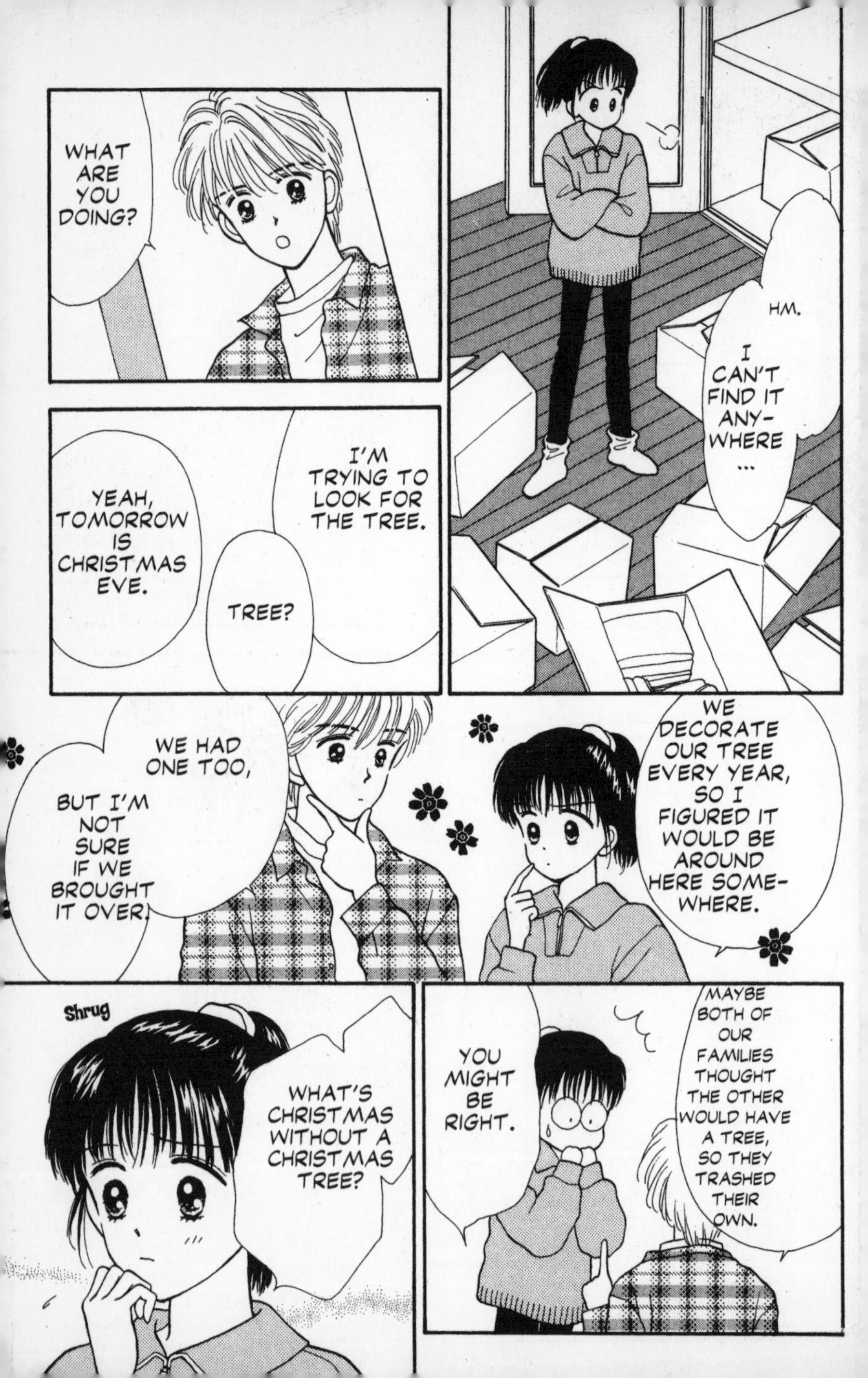
HM.
I CAN'T FIND IT ANYWHERE ...
WHAT ARE YOU DOING?
I'M TRYING TO LOOK FOR THE TREE.
TREE?
YEAH, TOMORROW IS CHRISTMAS EVE.
WE DECORATE OUR TREE EVERY YEAR, SO I FIGURED IT WOULD BE AROUND HERE SOMEWHERE.
WE HAD ONE TOO,
BUT I'M NOT SURE IF WE BROUGHT IT OVER.
MAYBE BOTH OF OUR FAMILIES THOUGHT THE OTHER WOULD HAVE A TREE, SO THEY TRASHED THEIR OWN.
YOU MIGHT BE RIGHT.
Shrug
WHAT'S CHRISTMAS WITHOUT A CHRISTMAS TREE?

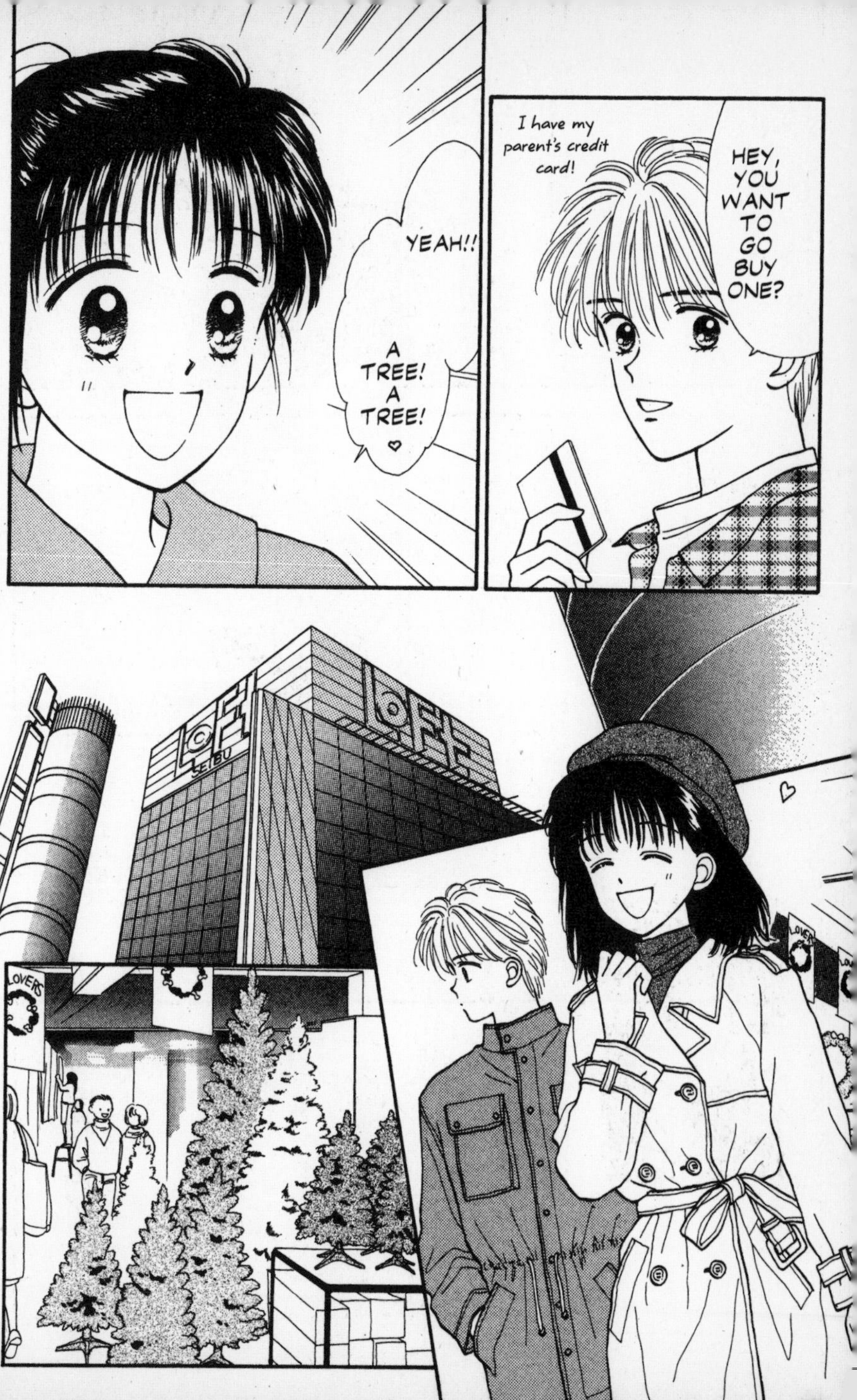
HEY, YOU WANT TO GO BUY ONE?
I have my parent's credit card!
YEAH!!
A TREE! A TREE!
LOVERS

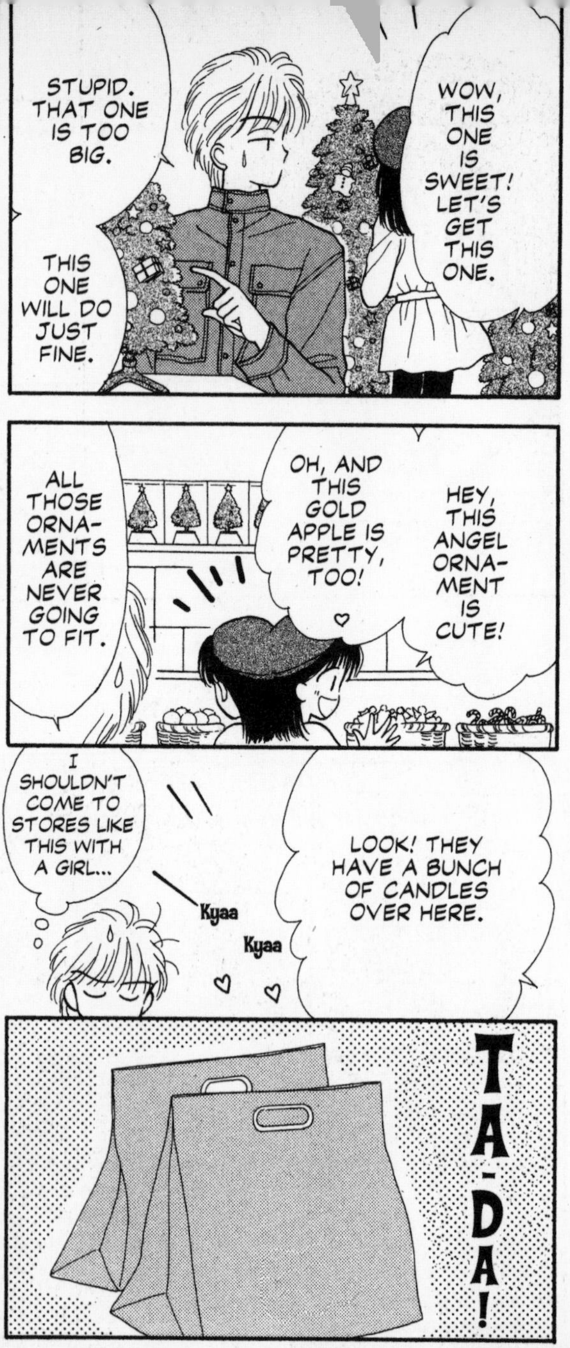
WOW, THIS ONE IS SWEET! LET'S GET THIS ONE.
STUPID. THAT ONE IS TOO BIG.
THIS ONE WILL DO JUST FINE.
HEY, THIS ANGEL ORNAMENT IS CUTE!
OH, AND THIS GOLD APPLE IS PRETTY, TOO!
ALL THOSE ORNAMENTS ARE NEVER GOING TO FIT.
LOOK! THEY HAVE A BUNCH OF CANDLES OVER HERE.
Kyaa
Kyaa
I SHOULDN'T COME TO STORES LIKE THIS WITH A GIRL...
TA-DA!

Miki Koishikawa

HOROSCOPE: ARIES

BLOODTYPE: A

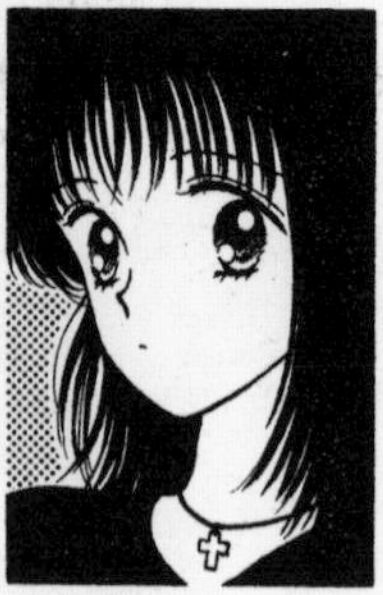

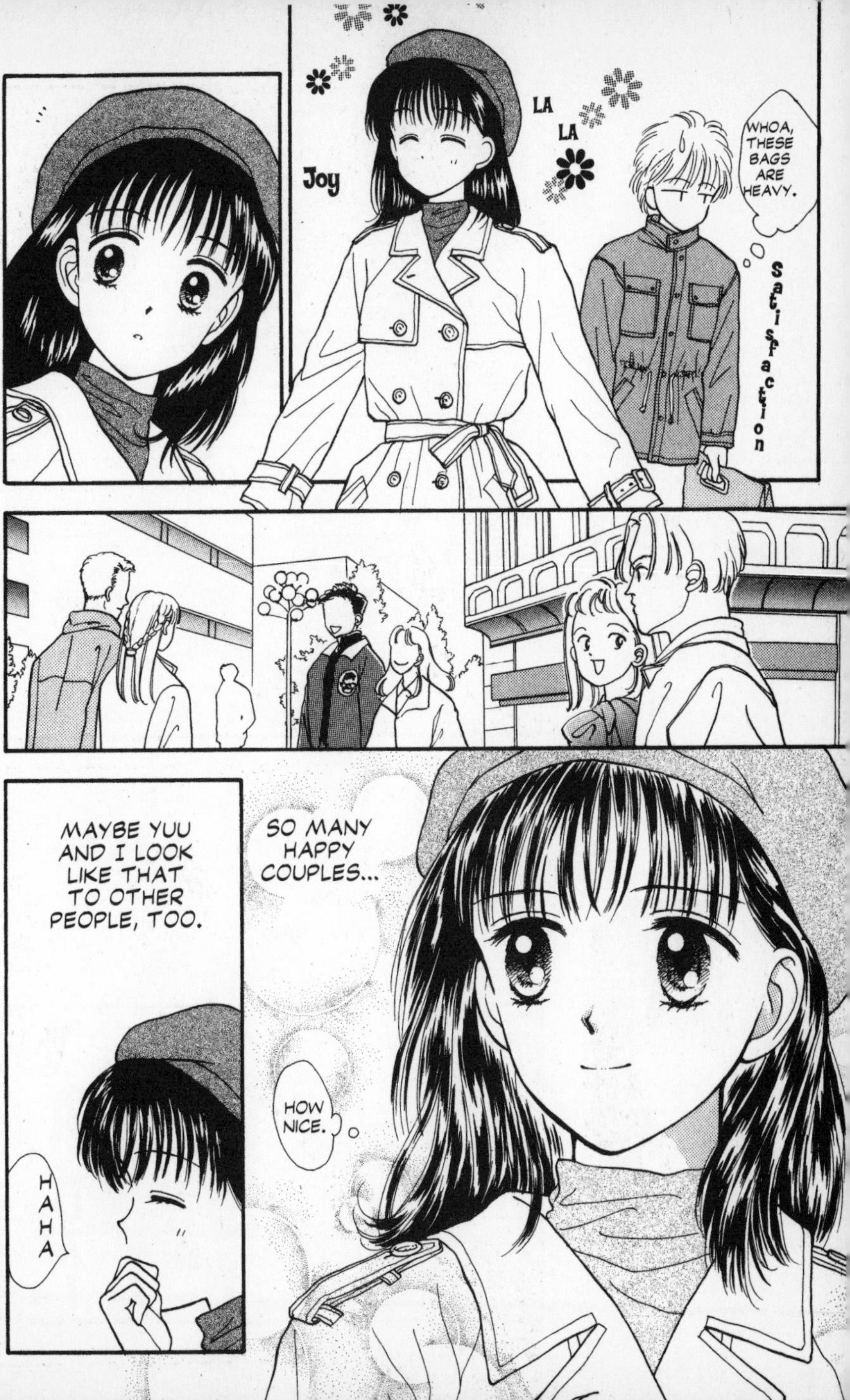
WHOA, THESE BAGS ARE HEAVY.
Satisfaction
LA LA
Joy
SO MANY HAPPY COUPLES...
HOW NICE.
MAYBE YUU AND I LOOK LIKE THAT TO OTHER PEOPLE, TOO.
HAHA

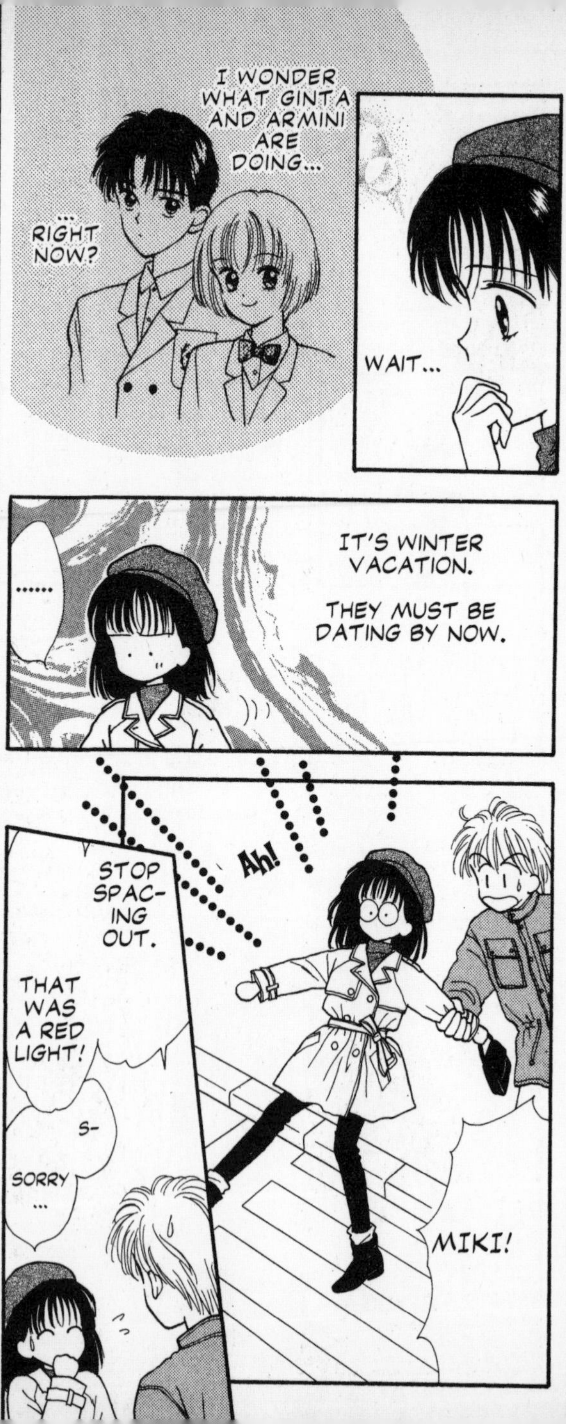
WAIT...
I WONDER WHAT GINTA AND ARMINI ARE DOING...
...RIGHT NOW?
IT'S WINTER VACATION.
THEY MUST BE DATING BY NOW.
......
MIKI!
Ah!
STOP SPAC-ING OUT.
THAT WAS A RED LIGHT!
S- SORRY...

Yuu Matsuura

HOROSCOPE : GEMINI

BLOODTYPE : B

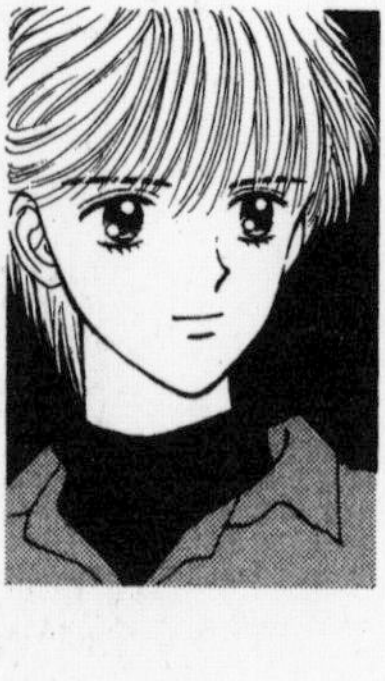

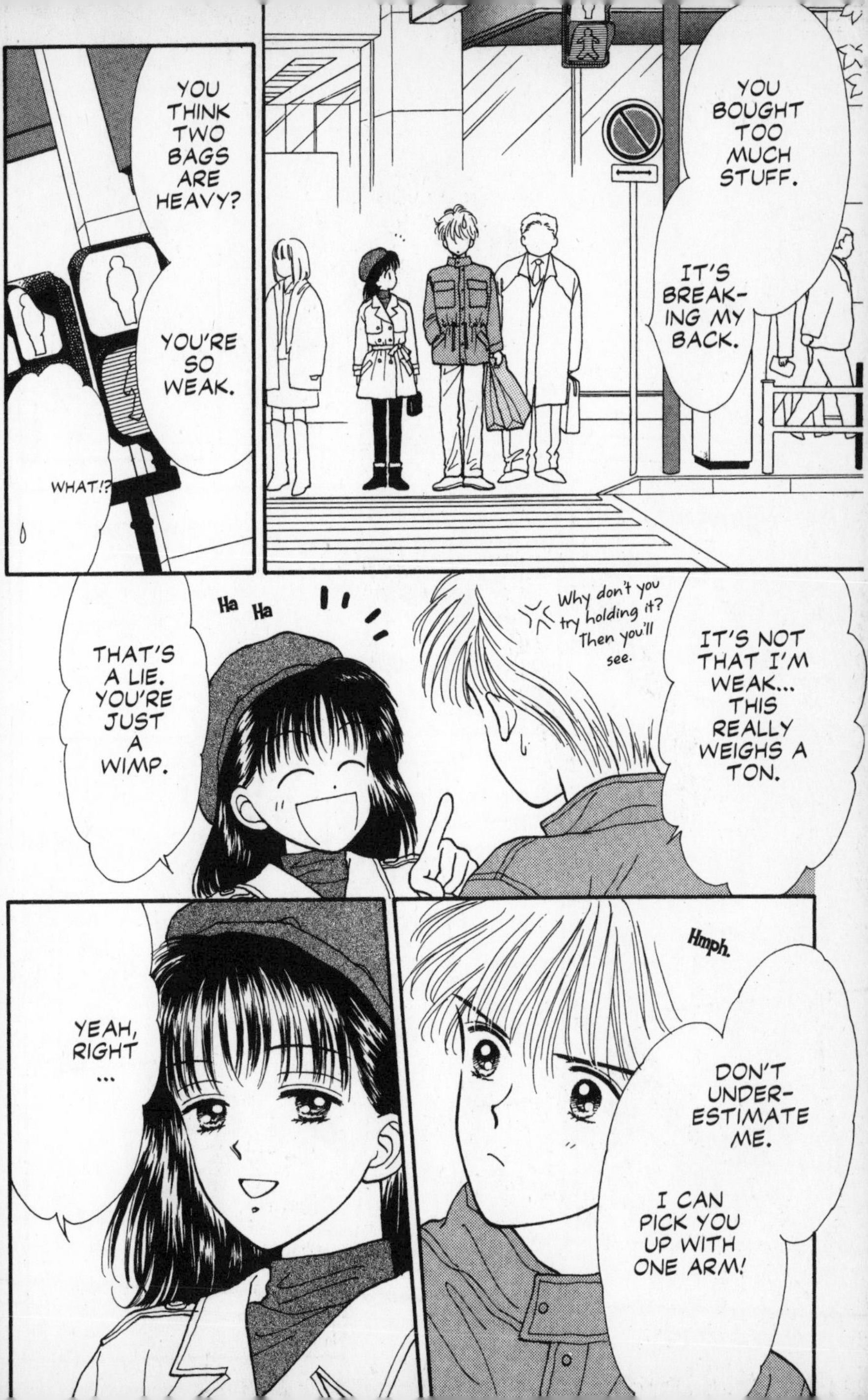
YOU BOUGHT TOO MUCH STUFF.
IT'S BREAKING MY BACK.
YOU THINK TWO BAGS ARE HEAVY?
YOU'RE SO WEAK.
WHAT!?
IT'S NOT THAT I'M WEAK... THIS REALLY WEIGHS A TON.
Why don't you try holding it? Then you'll see.
Ha Ha
THAT'S A LIE. YOU'RE JUST A WIMP.
Hmph.
DON'T UNDER-ESTIMATE ME.
I CAN PICK YOU UP WITH ONE ARM!
YEAH, RIGHT ...

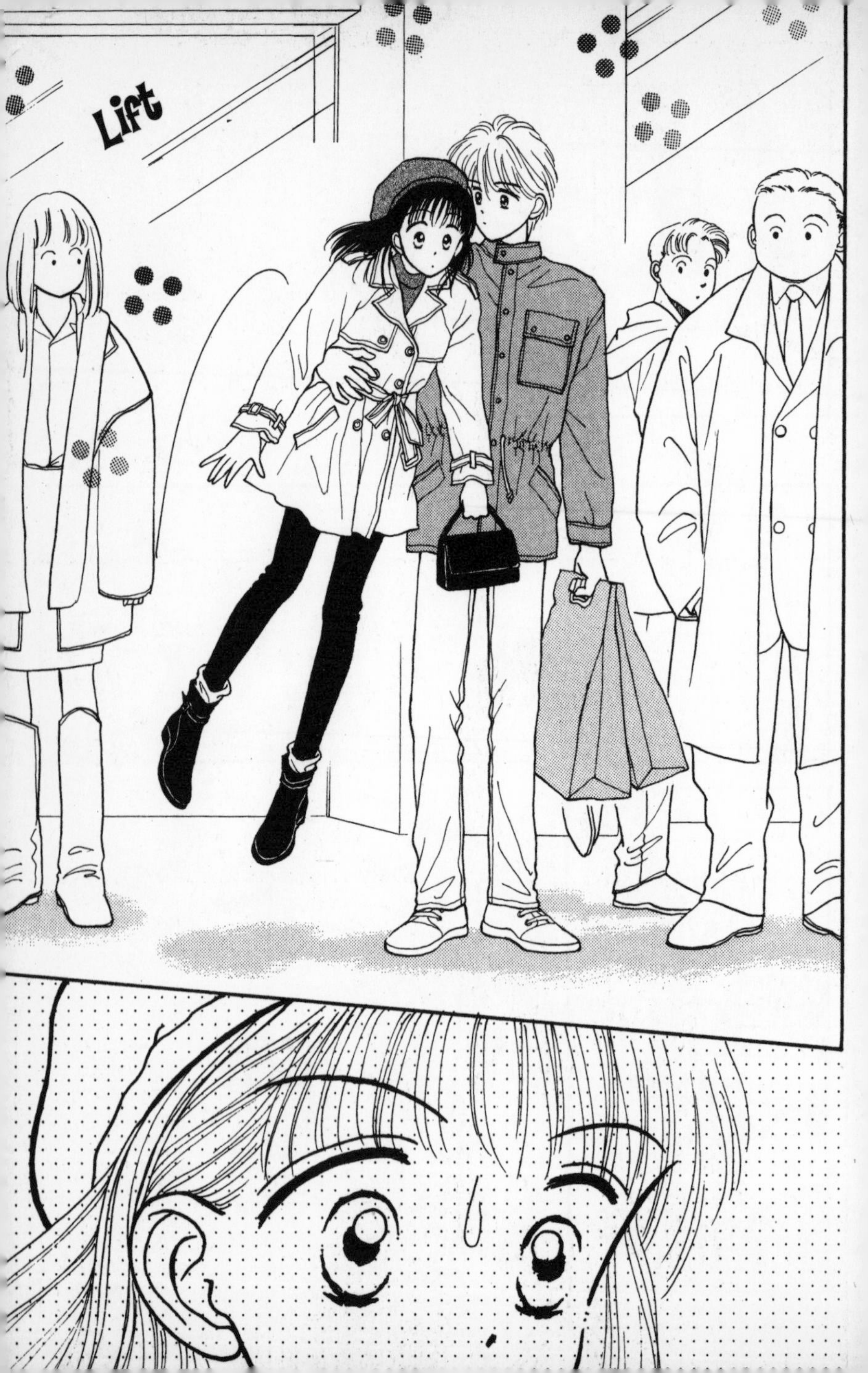
Lift

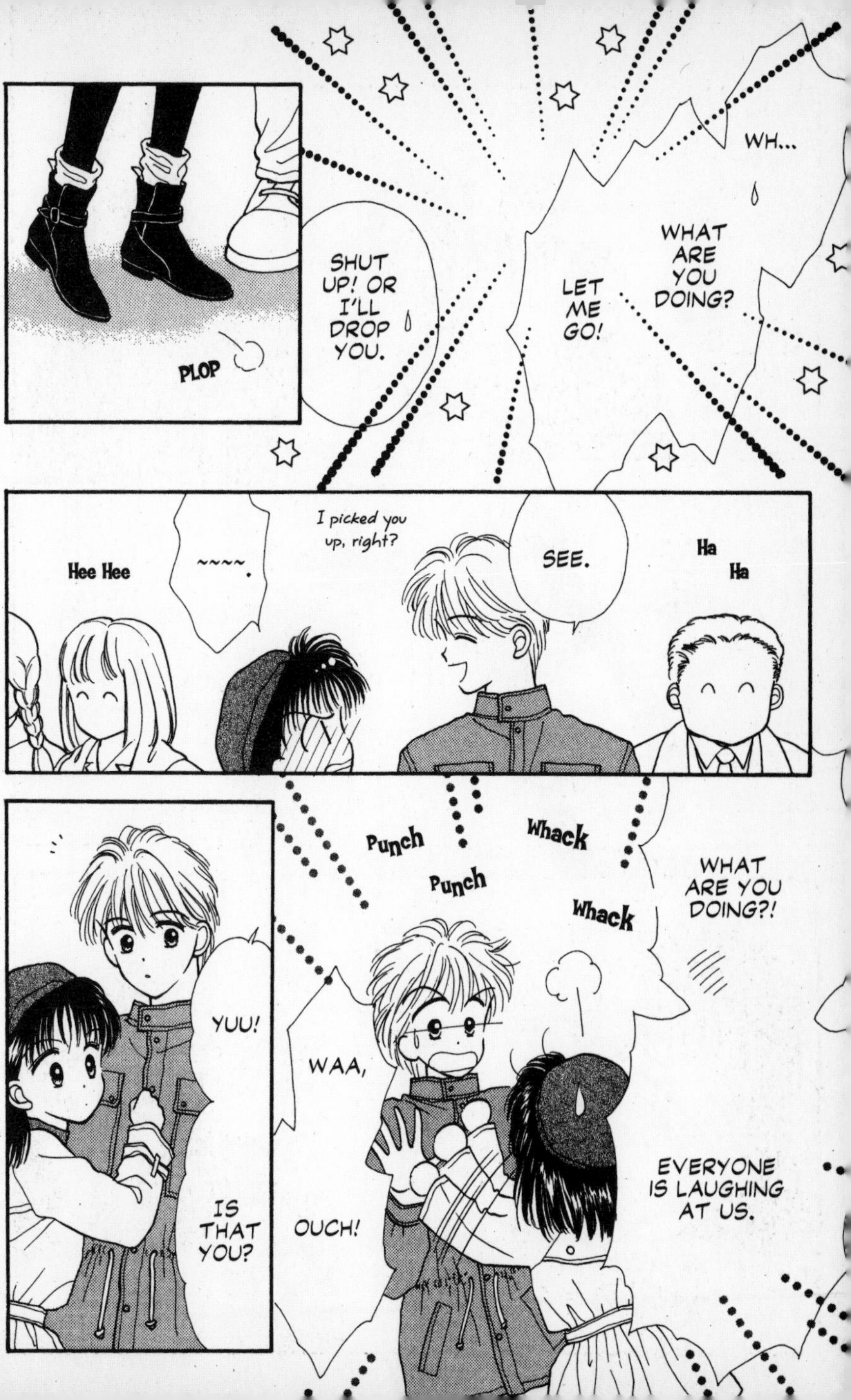
WH...
WHAT ARE YOU DOING?
LET ME GO!
SHUT UP! OR I'LL DROP YOU.
PLOP
Ha Ha
SEE.
I picked you up, right?
~~~~.
Hee Hee
WHAT ARE YOU DOING?!
Whack
Whack
Punch
Punch
EVERYONE IS LAUGHING AT US.
WAA,
OUCH!
YUU!
IS THAT YOU?
~~~~

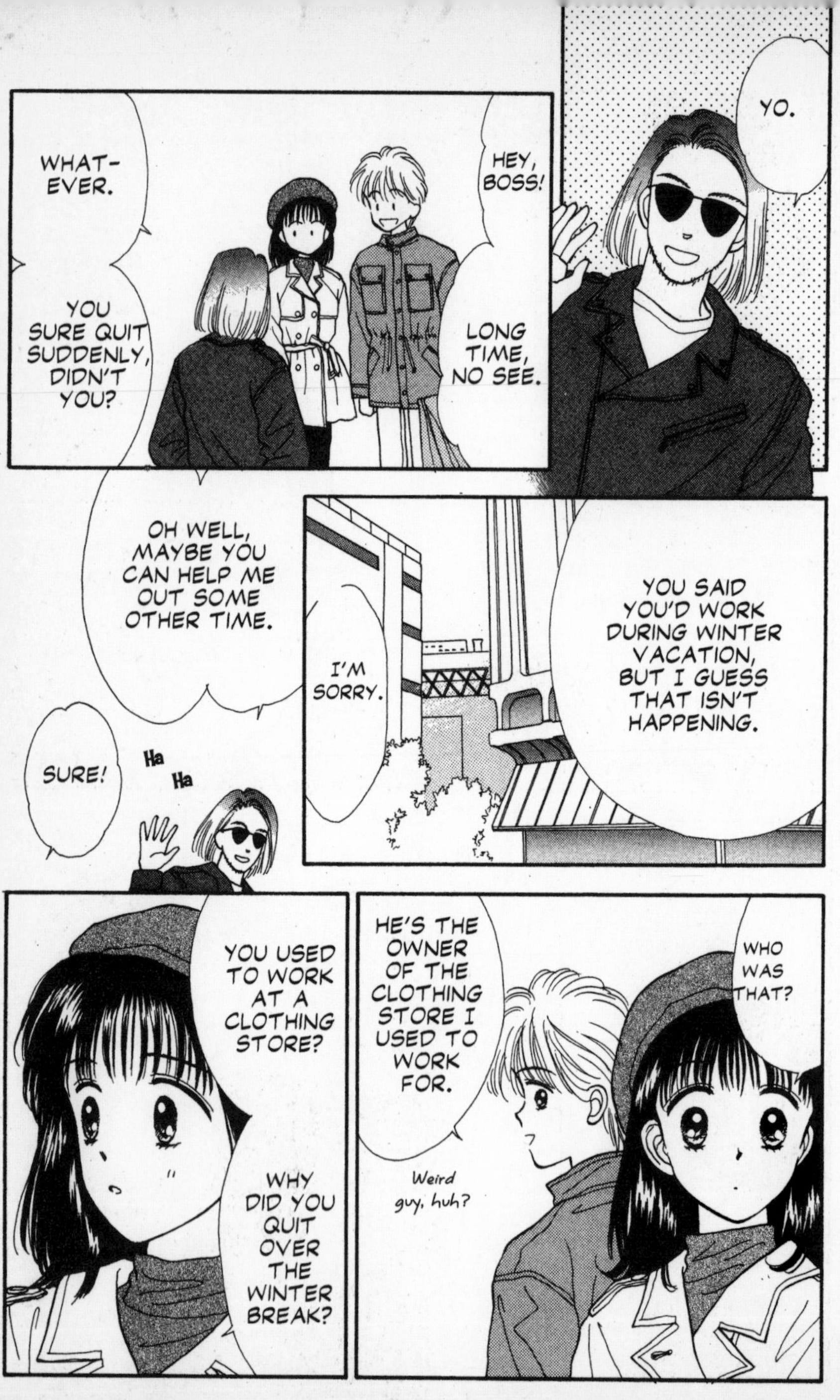
YO.
HEY, BOSS!
LONG TIME, NO SEE.
WHAT-EVER.
YOU SURE QUIT SUDDENLY, DIDN'T YOU?
YOU SAID YOU'D WORK DURING WINTER VACATION, BUT I GUESS THAT ISN'T HAPPENING.
I'M SORRY.
OH WELL, MAYBE YOU CAN HELP ME OUT SOME OTHER TIME.
SURE!
Ha Ha
WHO WAS THAT?
HE'S THE OWNER OF THE CLOTHING STORE I USED TO WORK FOR.
Weird guy, huh?
YOU USED TO WORK AT A CLOTHING STORE?
WHY DID YOU QUIT OVER THE WINTER BREAK?

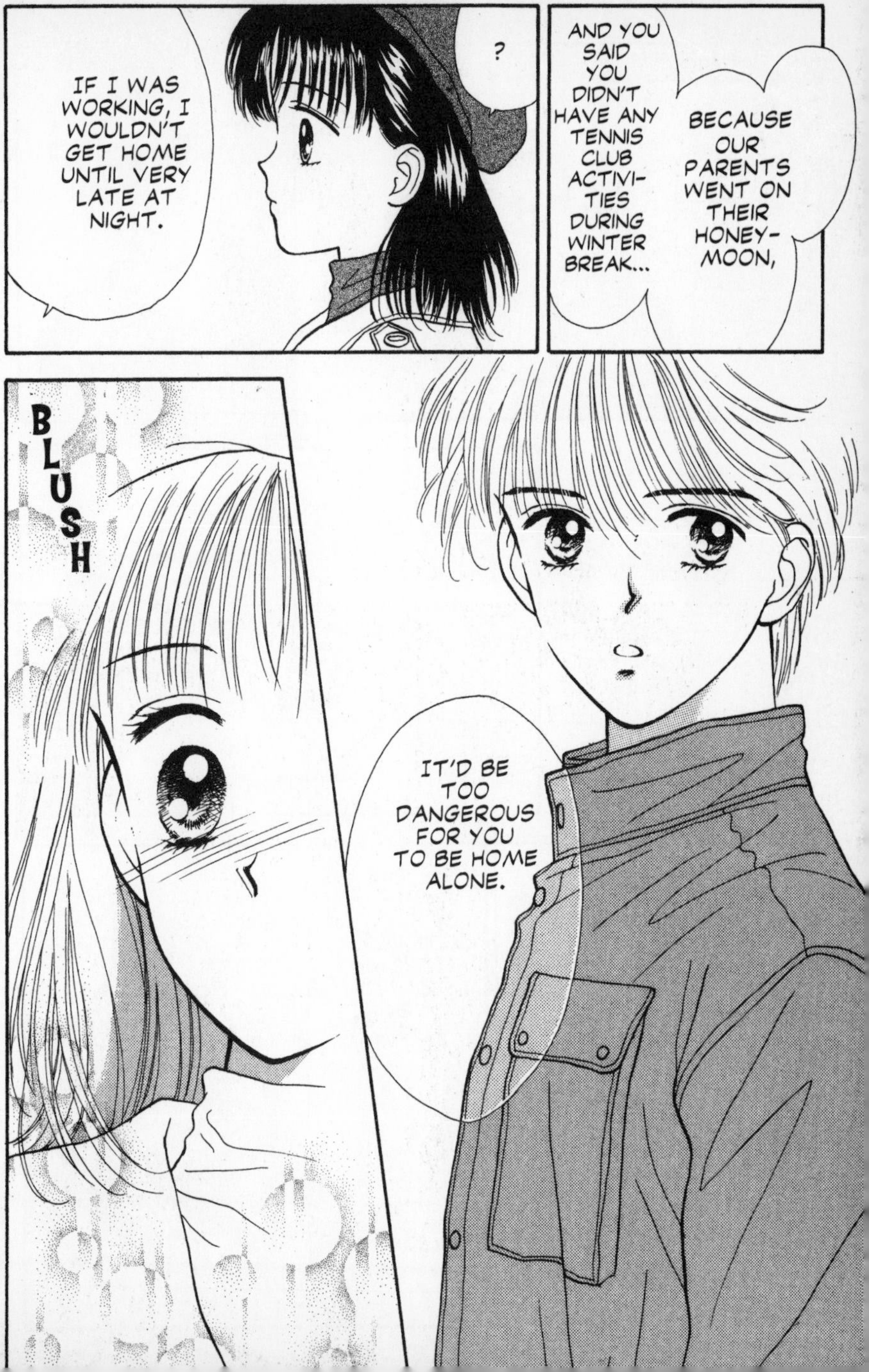
BECAUSE OUR PARENTS WENT ON THEIR HONEY-MOON,
AND YOU SAID YOU DIDN'T HAVE ANY TENNIS CLUB ACTIVI-TIES DURING WINTER BREAK...
?
IF I WAS WORKING, I WOULDN'T GET HOME UNTIL VERY LATE AT NIGHT.
IT'D BE TOO DANGEROUS FOR YOU TO BE HOME ALONE.
BLUSH

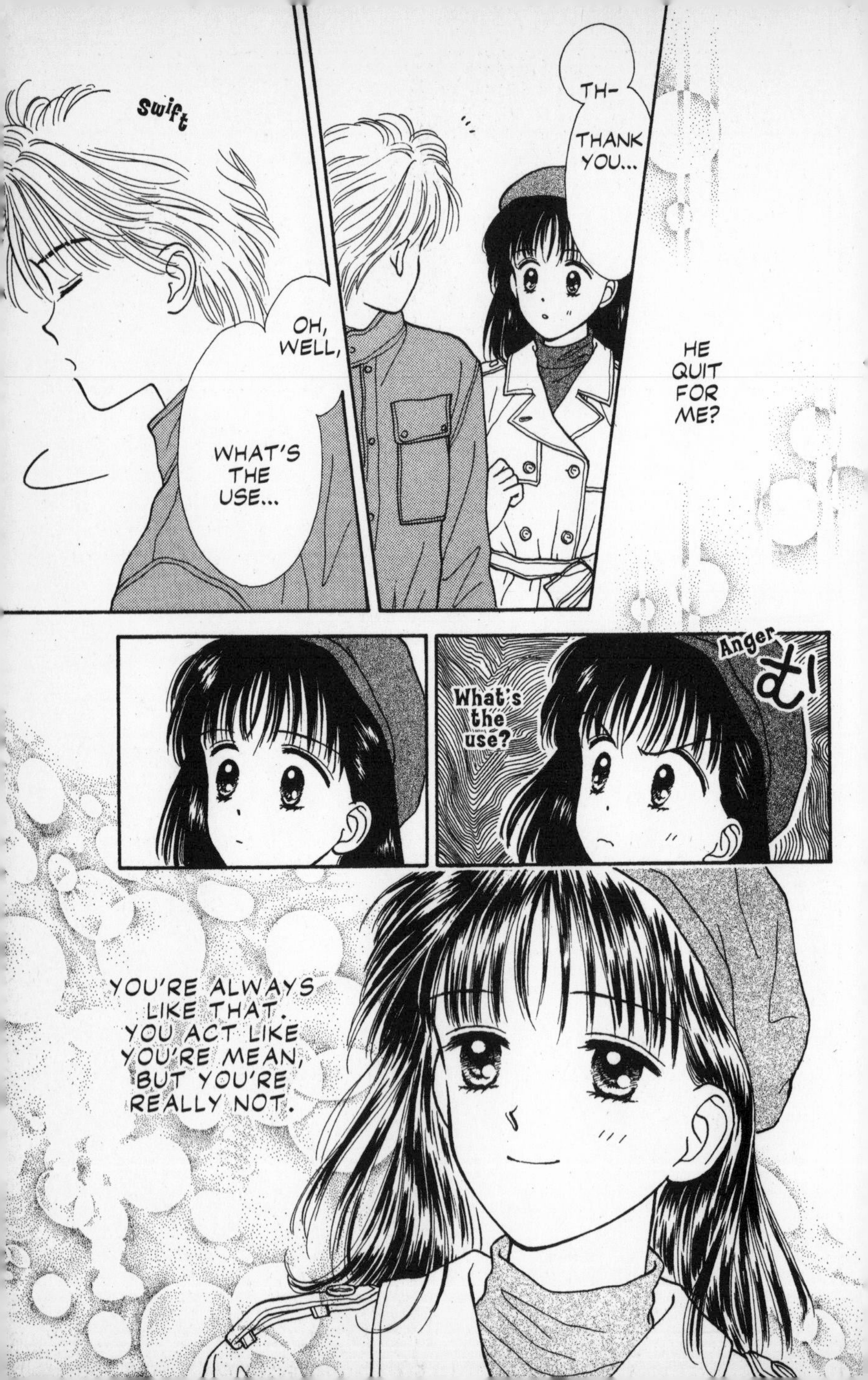
TH-
THANK YOU...
HE QUIT FOR ME?
swift
OH, WELL,
WHAT'S THE USE...
Anger
What's the use?
YOU'RE ALWAYS LIKE THAT. YOU ACT LIKE YOU'RE MEAN, BUT YOU'RE REALLY NOT.

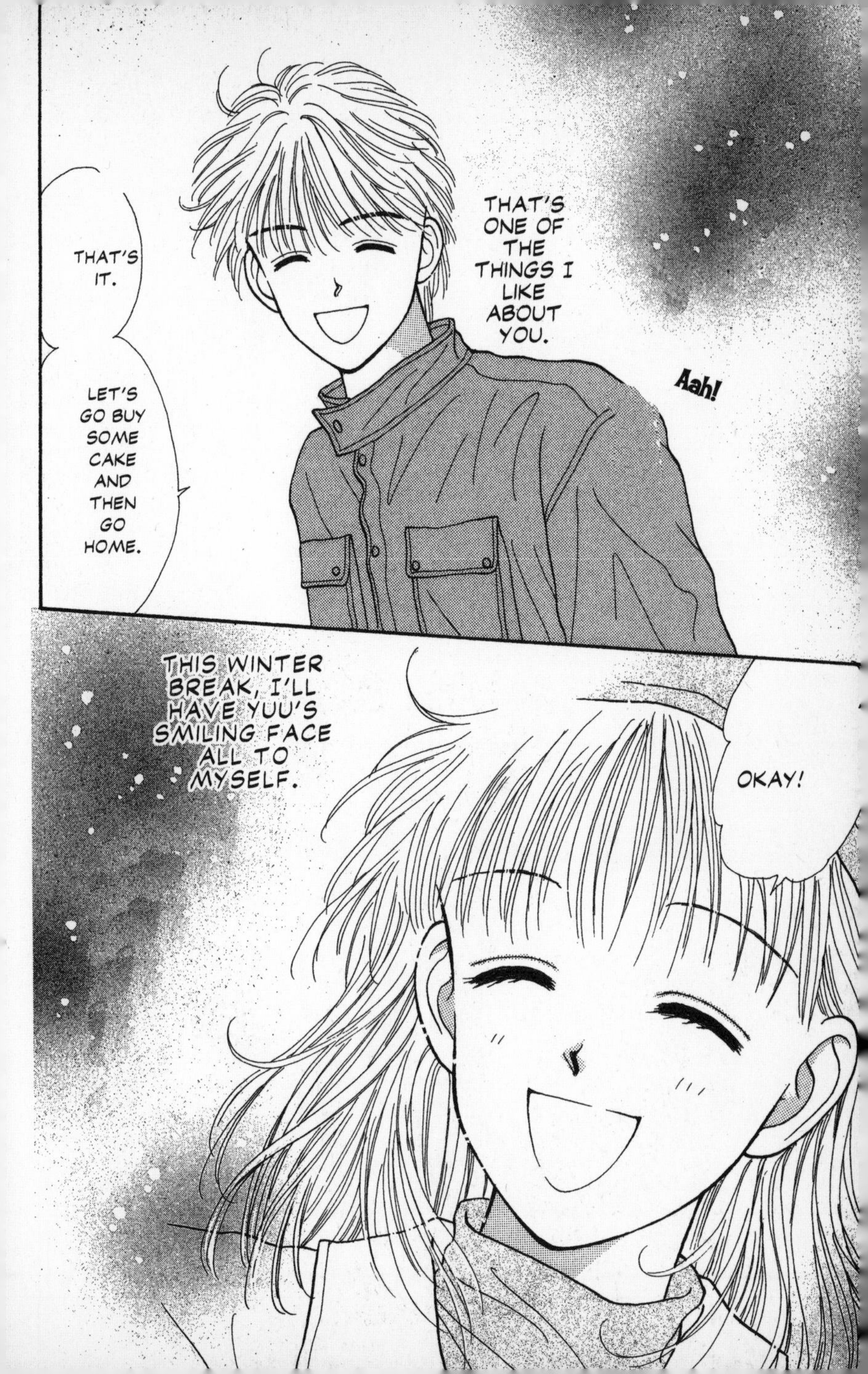
THAT'S ONE OF THE THINGS I LIKE ABOUT YOU.
Aah!
THAT'S IT.
LET'S GO BUY SOME CAKE AND THEN GO HOME.
OKAY!
THIS WINTER BREAK, I'LL HAVE YUU'S SMILING FACE ALL TO MYSELF.

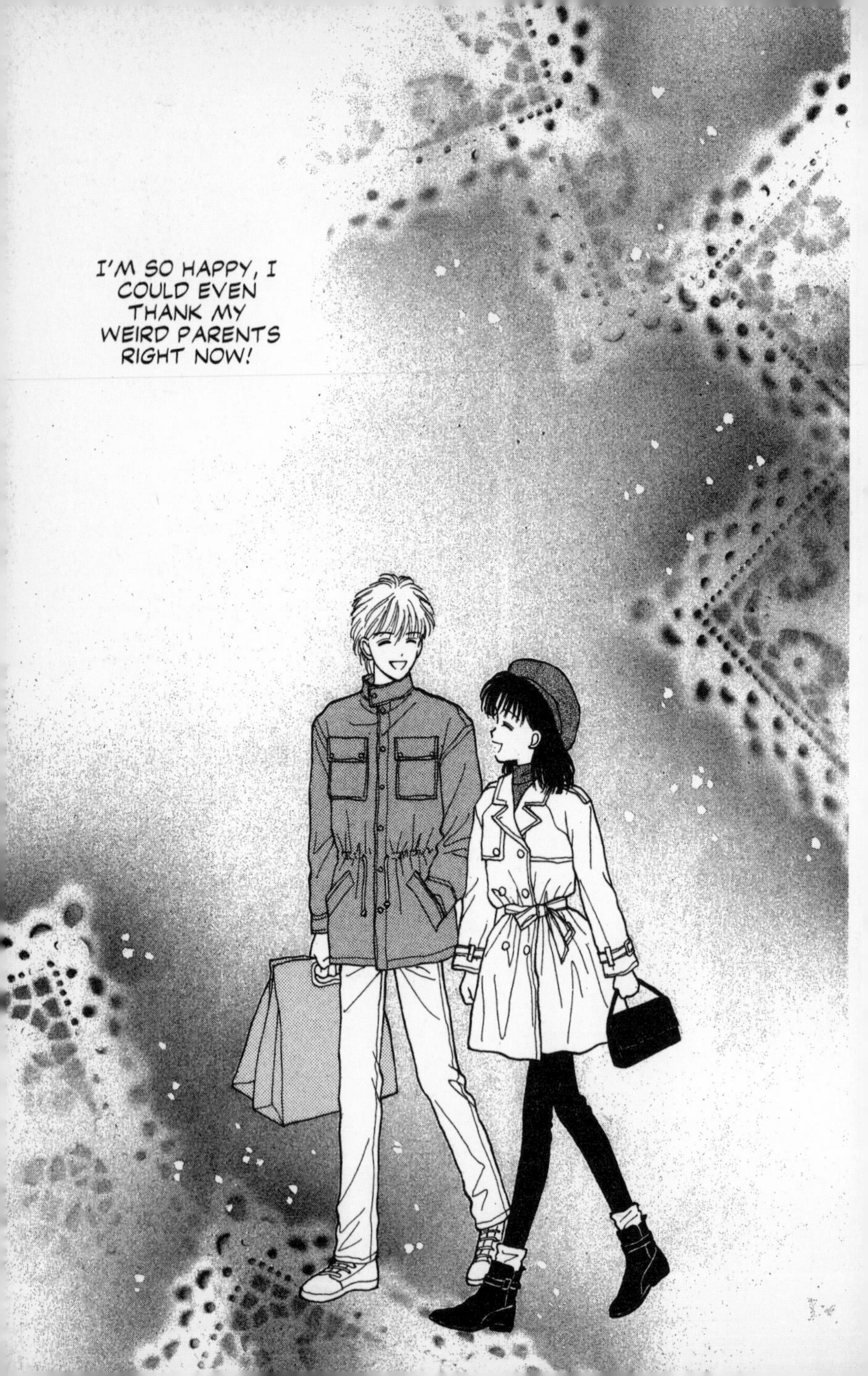
I'M SO HAPPY, I COULD EVEN THANK MY WEIRD PARENTS RIGHT NOW!

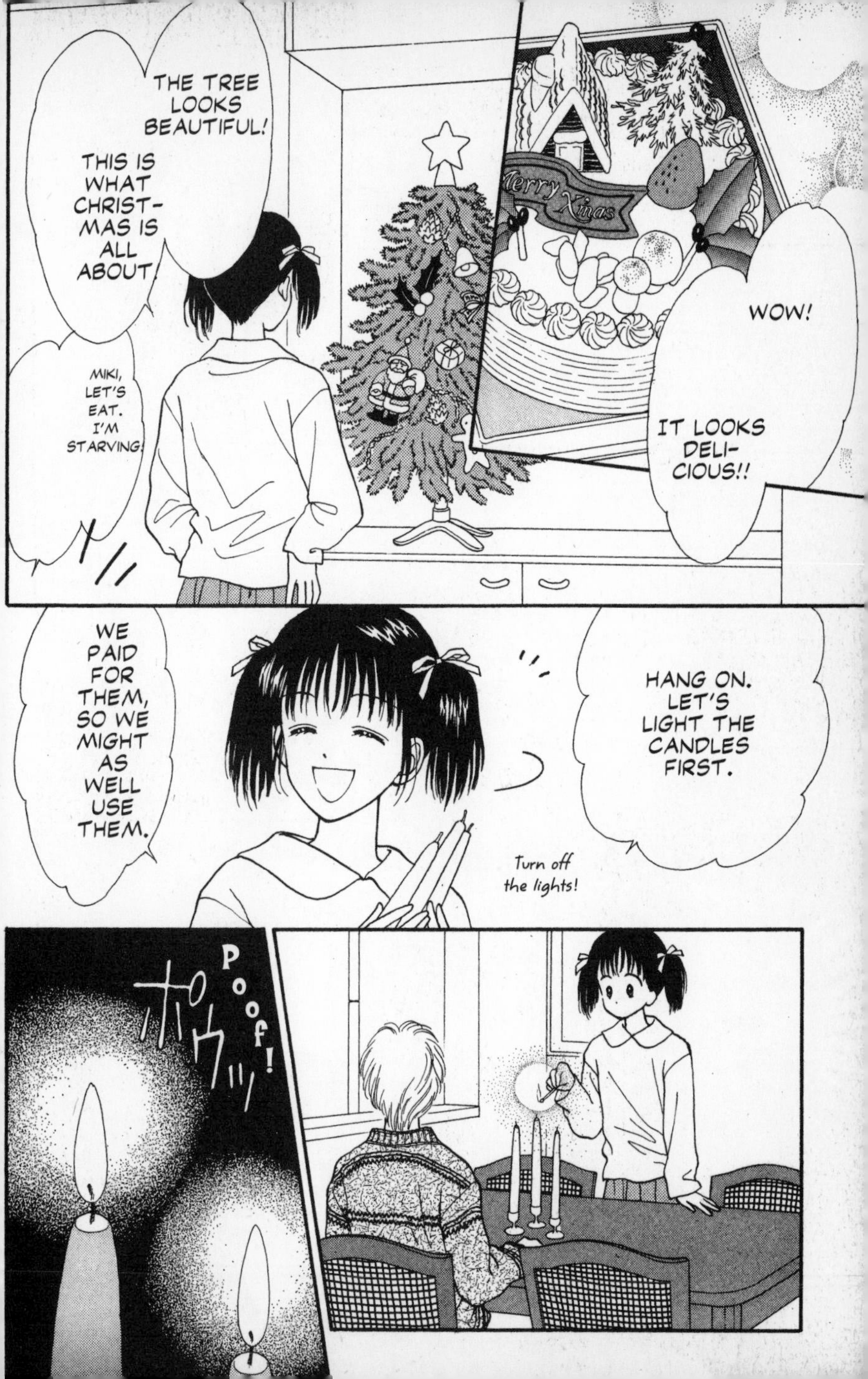
WOW!
IT LOOKS DELI-CIOUS!!
THE TREE LOOKS BEAUTIFUL!
THIS IS WHAT CHRIST-MAS IS ALL ABOUT!
MIKI, LET'S EAT. I'M STARVING!
HANG ON. LET'S LIGHT THE CANDLES FIRST.
WE PAID FOR THEM, SO WE MIGHT AS WELL USE THEM.
Turn off the lights!
Poof!

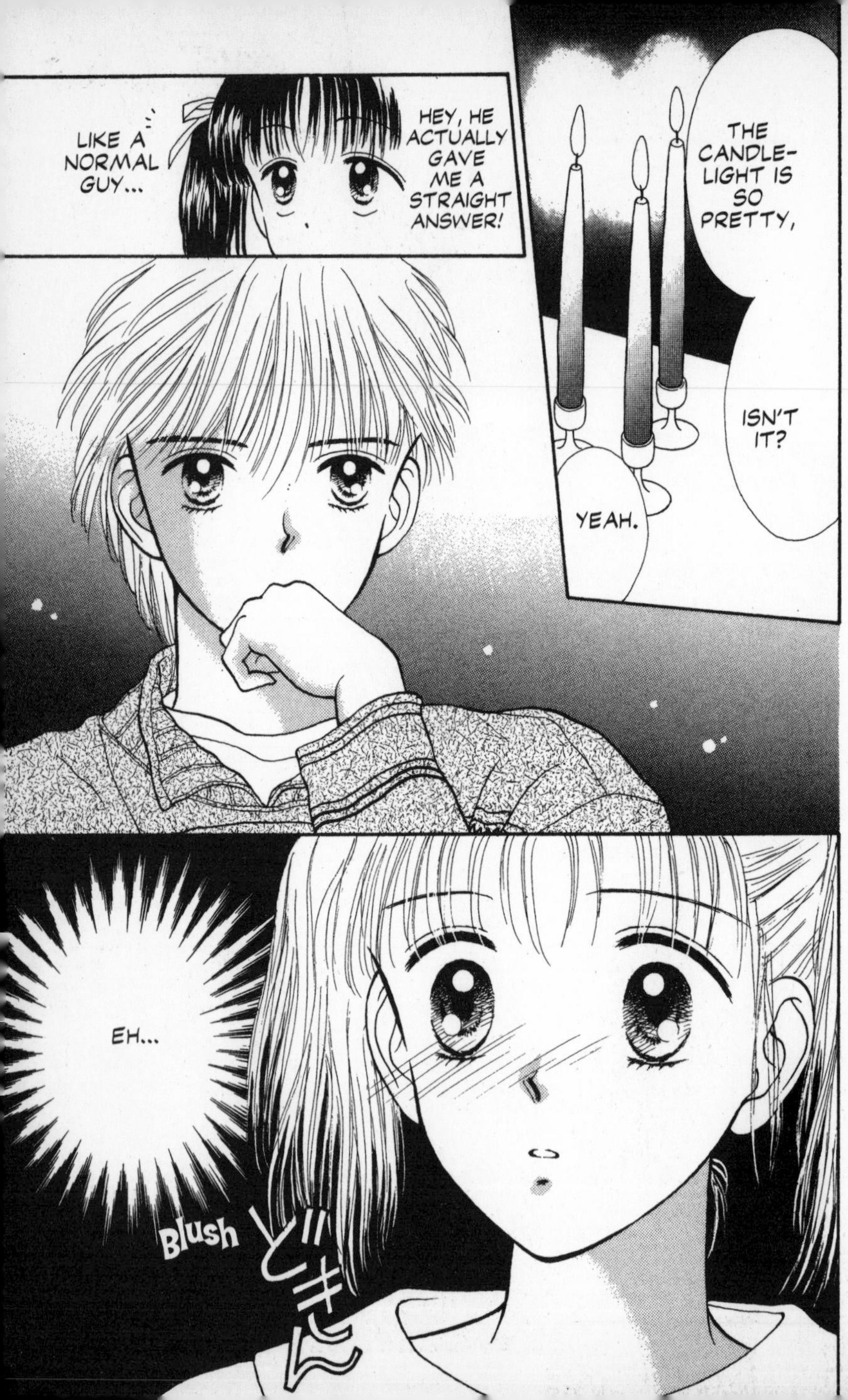

THE CANDLE-LIGHT IS SO PRETTY,
ISN'T IT?
YEAH.
HEY, HE ACTUALLY GAVE ME A STRAIGHT ANSWER!
LIKE A NORMAL GUY...
EH...
Blush
どきん

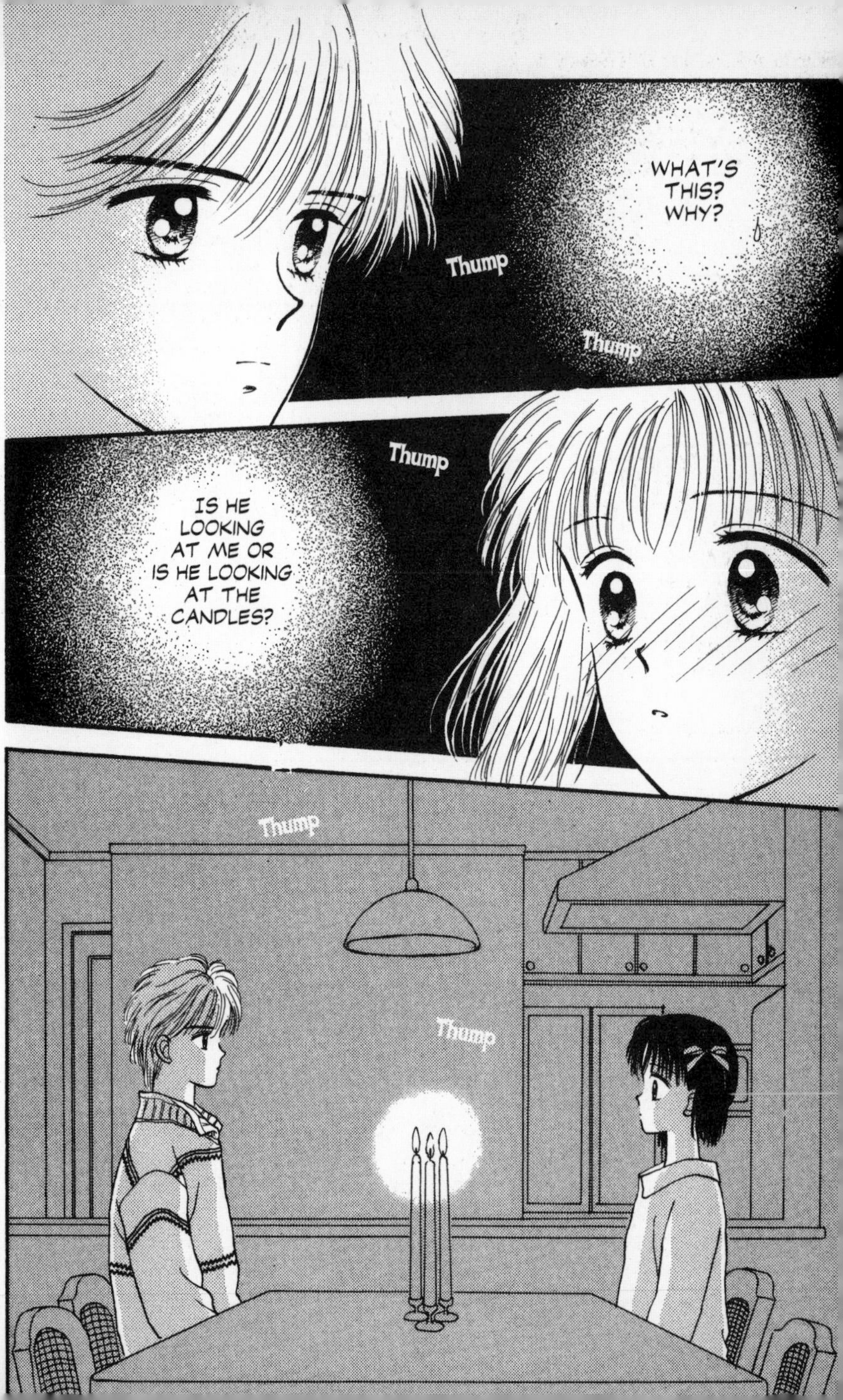
WHAT'S THIS? WHY?
Thump
Thump
Thump
IS HE LOOKING AT ME OR IS HE LOOKING AT THE CANDLES?
Thump
Thump

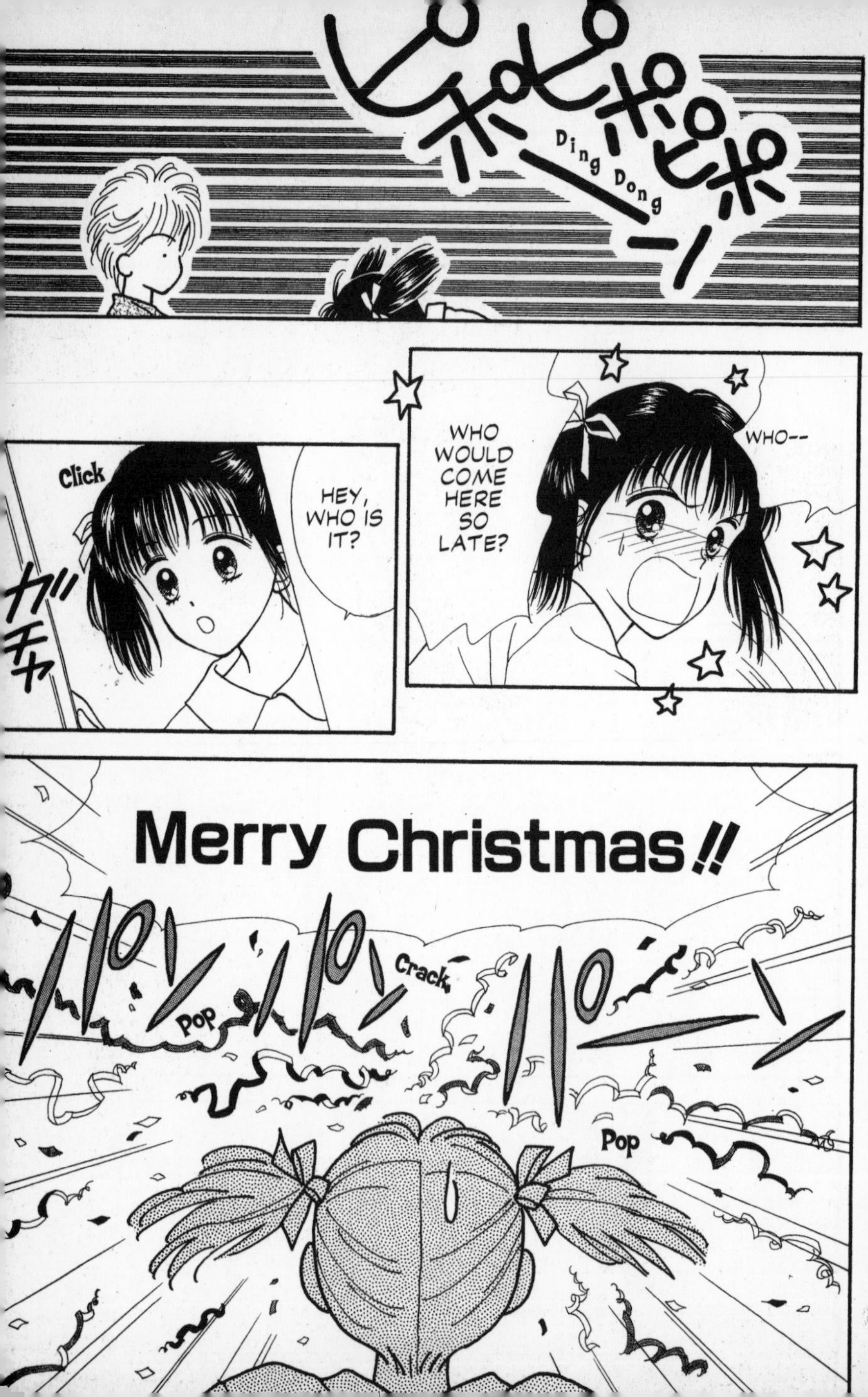
Ding Dong
WHO--
WHO WOULD COME HERE SO LATE?
HEY, WHO IS IT?
Click
ガチャ
Merry Christmas!!
パン
Pop
パン
Crack
パン
Pop

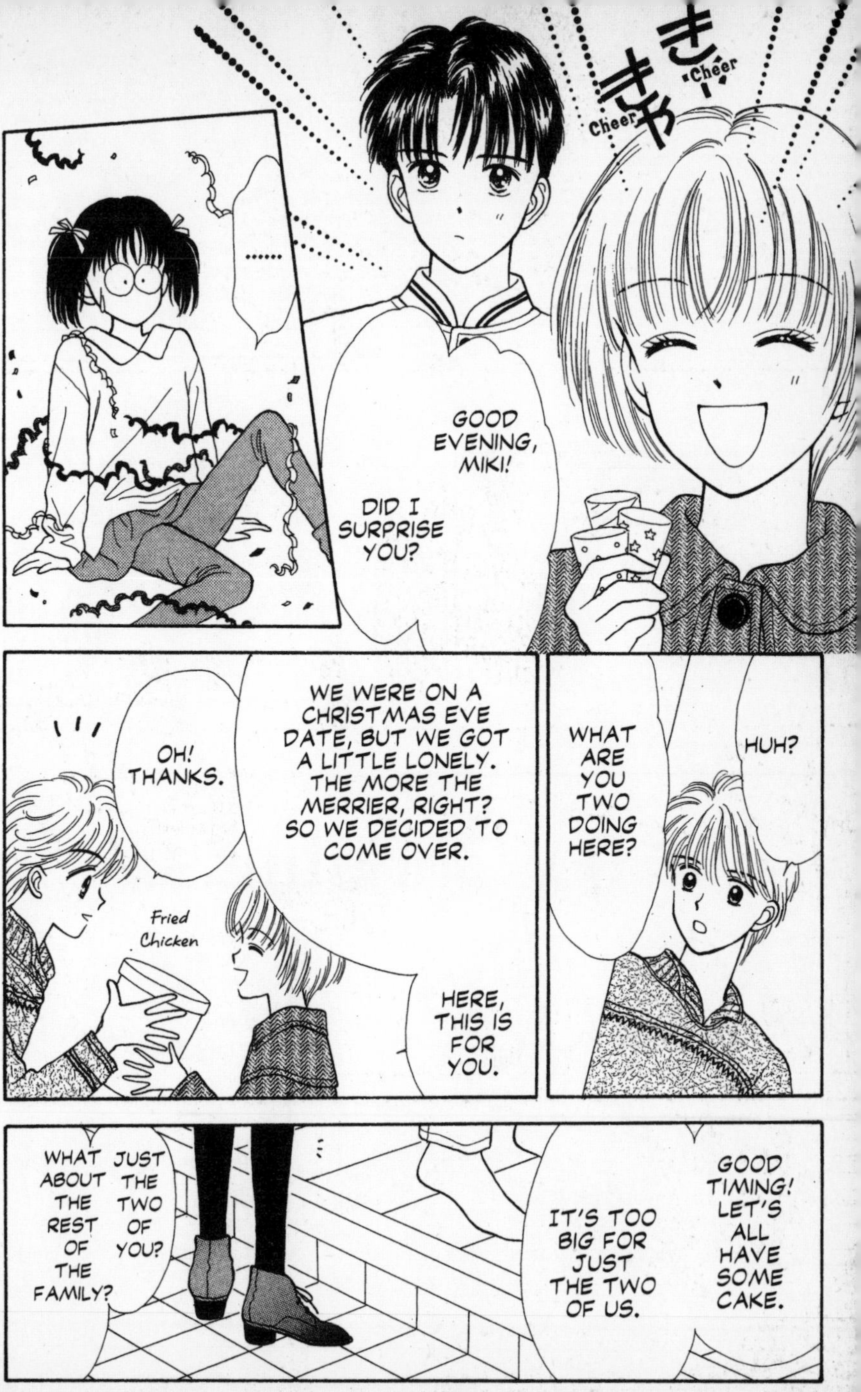

きゃー
Cheer Cheer
GOOD EVENING, MIKI!
DID I SURPRISE YOU?
......
HUH?
WHAT ARE YOU TWO DOING HERE?
WE WERE ON A CHRISTMAS EVE DATE, BUT WE GOT A LITTLE LONELY. THE MORE THE MERRIER, RIGHT? SO WE DECIDED TO COME OVER.
HERE, THIS IS FOR YOU.
OH! THANKS.
Fried Chicken
GOOD TIMING! LET'S ALL HAVE SOME CAKE.
IT'S TOO BIG FOR JUST THE TWO OF US.
JUST THE TWO OF YOU?
WHAT ABOUT THE REST OF THE FAMILY?

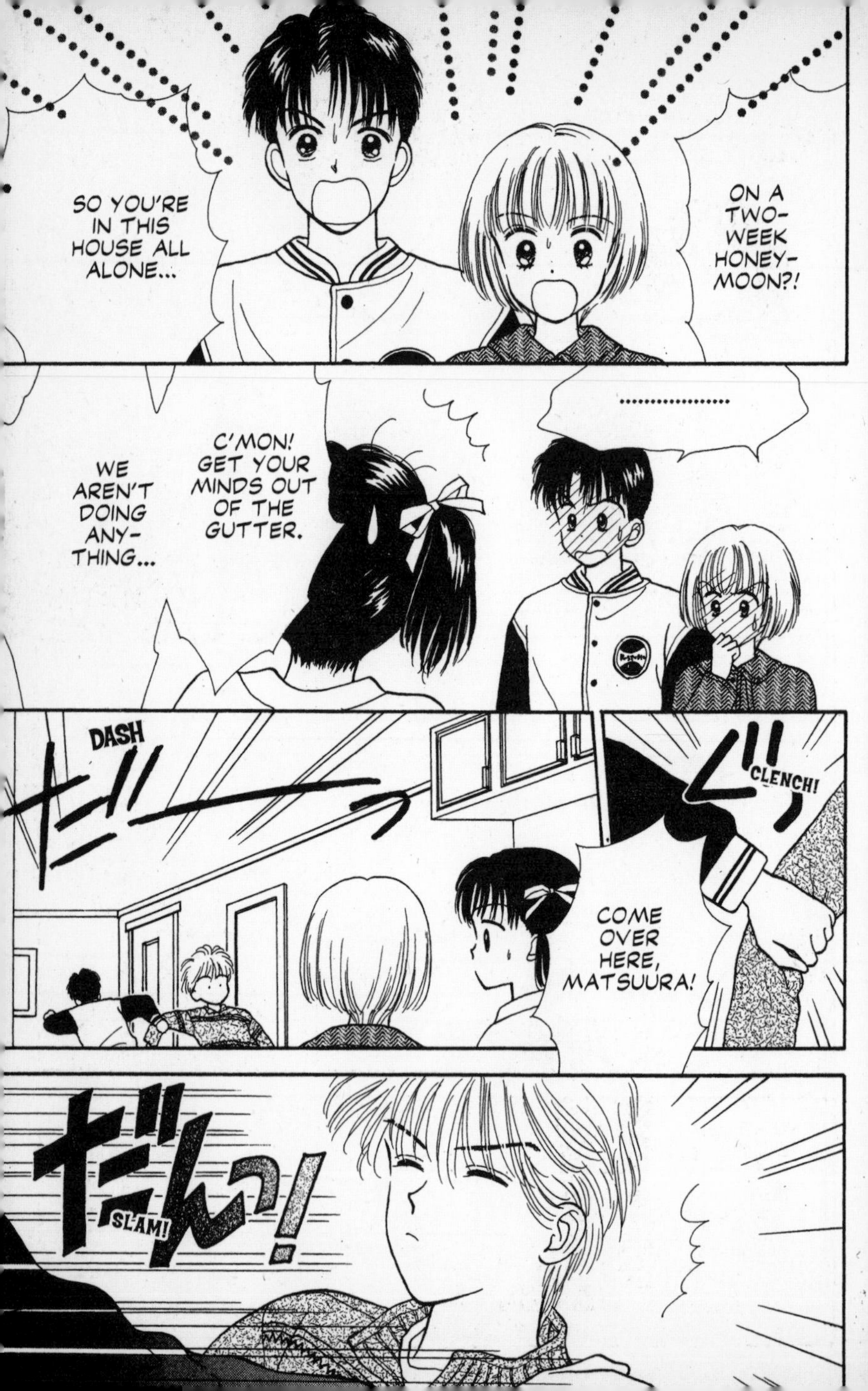
SO YOU'RE IN THIS HOUSE ALL ALONE...
ON A TWO-WEEK HONEYMOON?!
....
C'MON! GET YOUR MINDS OUT OF THE GUTTER.
WE AREN'T DOING ANYTHING...
CLENCH!
COME OVER HERE, MATSUURA!
DASH
SLAM!

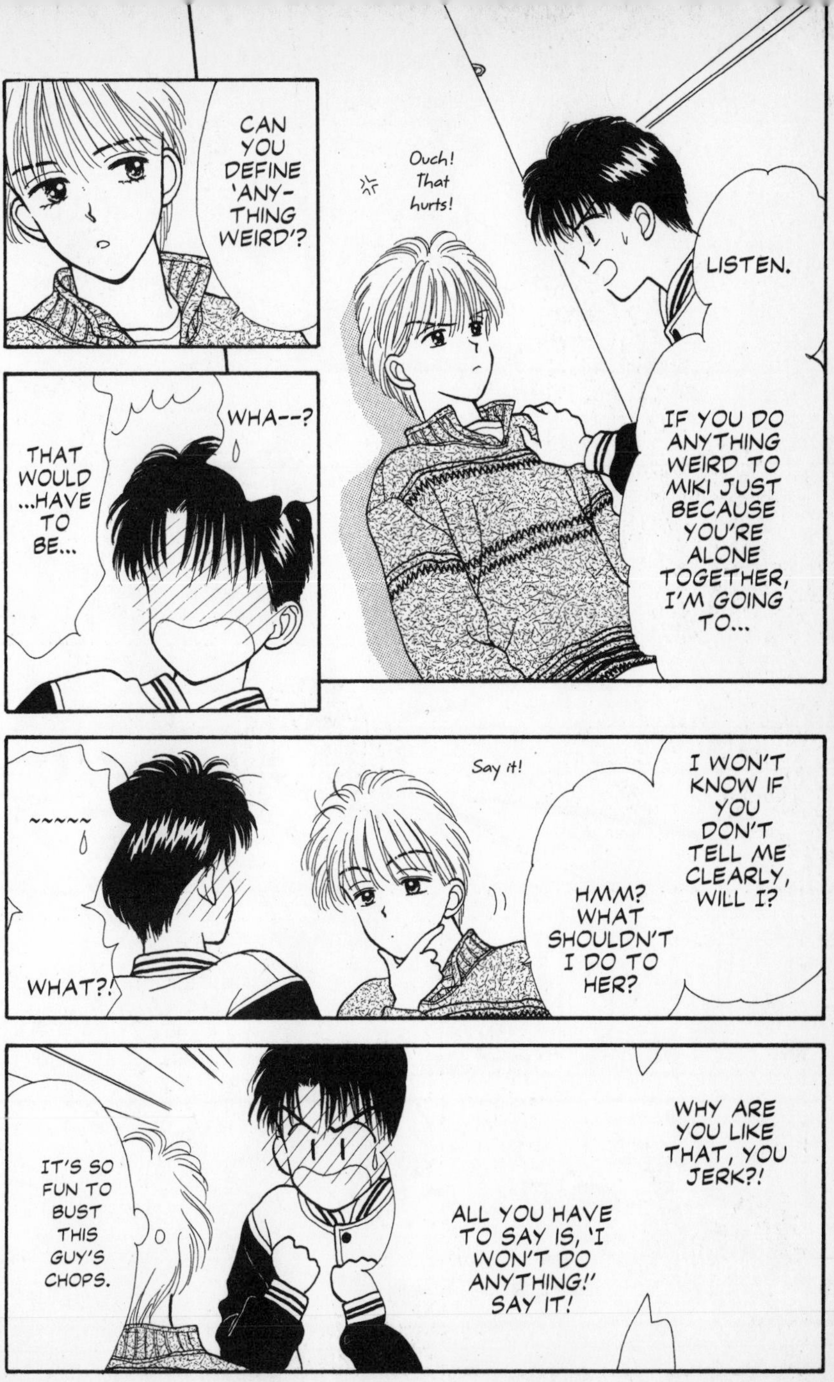
LISTEN.
IF YOU DO ANYTHING WEIRD TO MIKI JUST BECAUSE YOU'RE ALONE TOGETHER, I'M GOING TO...
Ouch! That hurts!
CAN YOU DEFINE 'ANY-THING WEIRD'?
WHA--?
THAT WOULD ...HAVE TO BE...
I WON'T KNOW IF YOU DON'T TELL ME CLEARLY, WILL I?
Say it!
HMM? WHAT SHOULDN'T I DO TO HER?
~~~~~
WHAT?!
WHY ARE YOU LIKE THAT, YOU JERK?!
ALL YOU HAVE TO SAY IS, 'I WON'T DO ANYTHING!' SAY IT!
IT'S SO FUN TO BUST THIS GUY'S CHOPS.
~~~~~

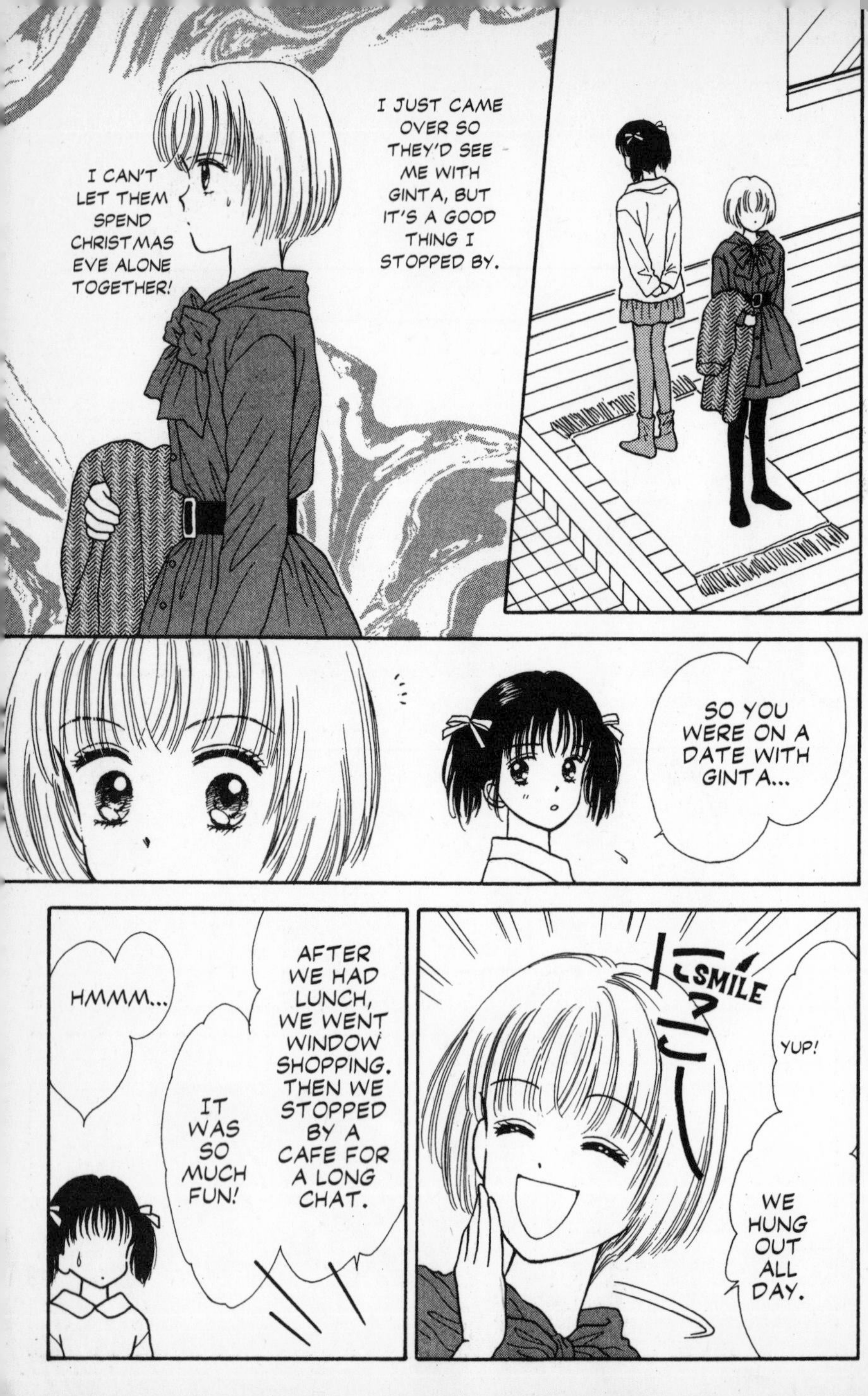
I JUST CAME OVER SO THEY'D SEE ME WITH GINTA, BUT IT'S A GOOD THING I STOPPED BY.
I CAN'T LET THEM SPEND CHRISTMAS EVE ALONE TOGETHER!
SO YOU WERE ON A DATE WITH GINTA...
SMILE
YUP!
WE HUNG OUT ALL DAY.
AFTER WE HAD LUNCH, WE WENT WINDOW SHOPPING. THEN WE STOPPED BY A CAFE FOR A LONG CHAT.
IT WAS SO MUCH FUN!
HMMM...

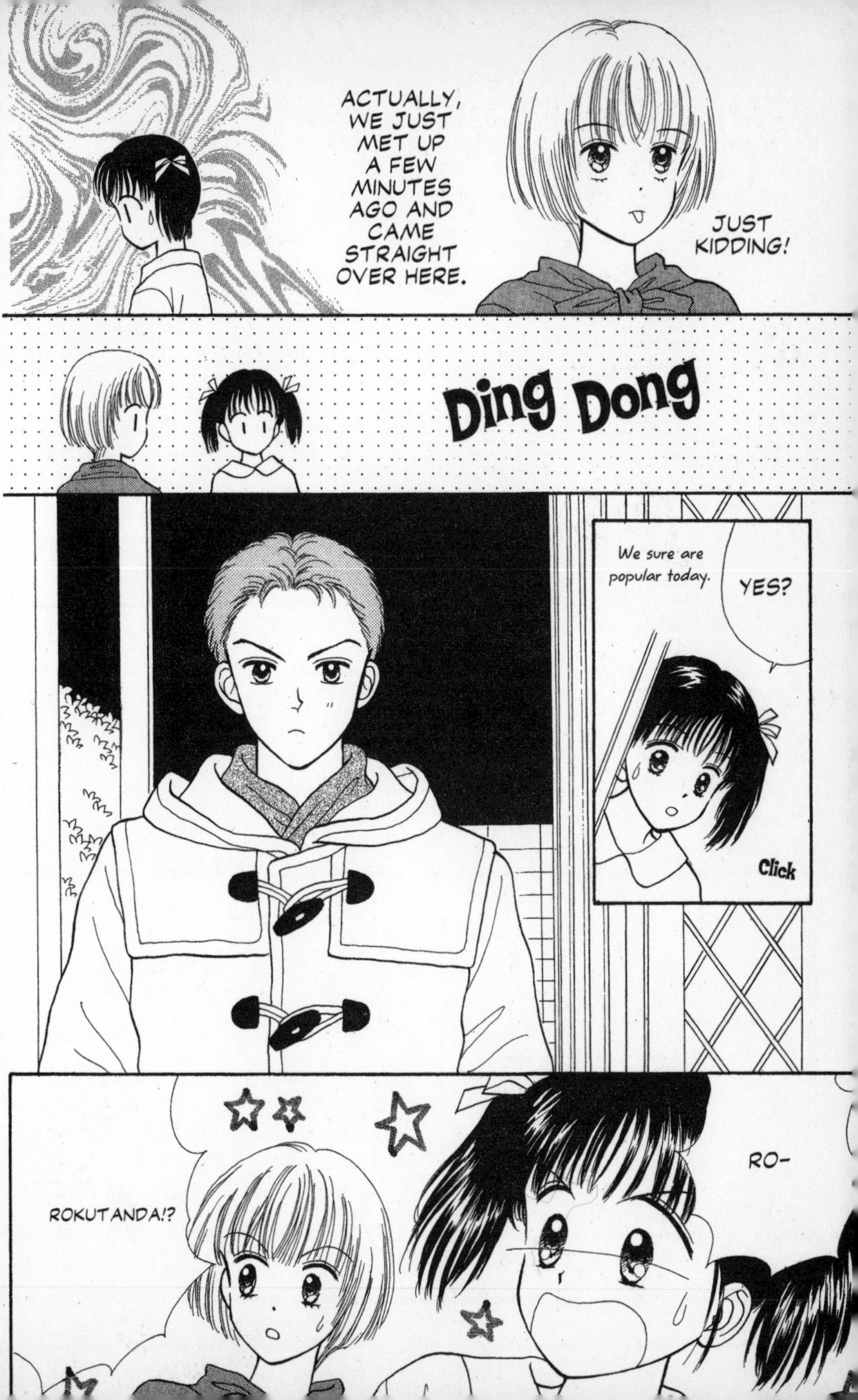
JUST KIDDING!
ACTUALLY, WE JUST MET UP A FEW MINUTES AGO AND CAME STRAIGHT OVER HERE.
Ding Dong
YES?
We sure are popular today.
Click
RO-
ROKUTANDA!?

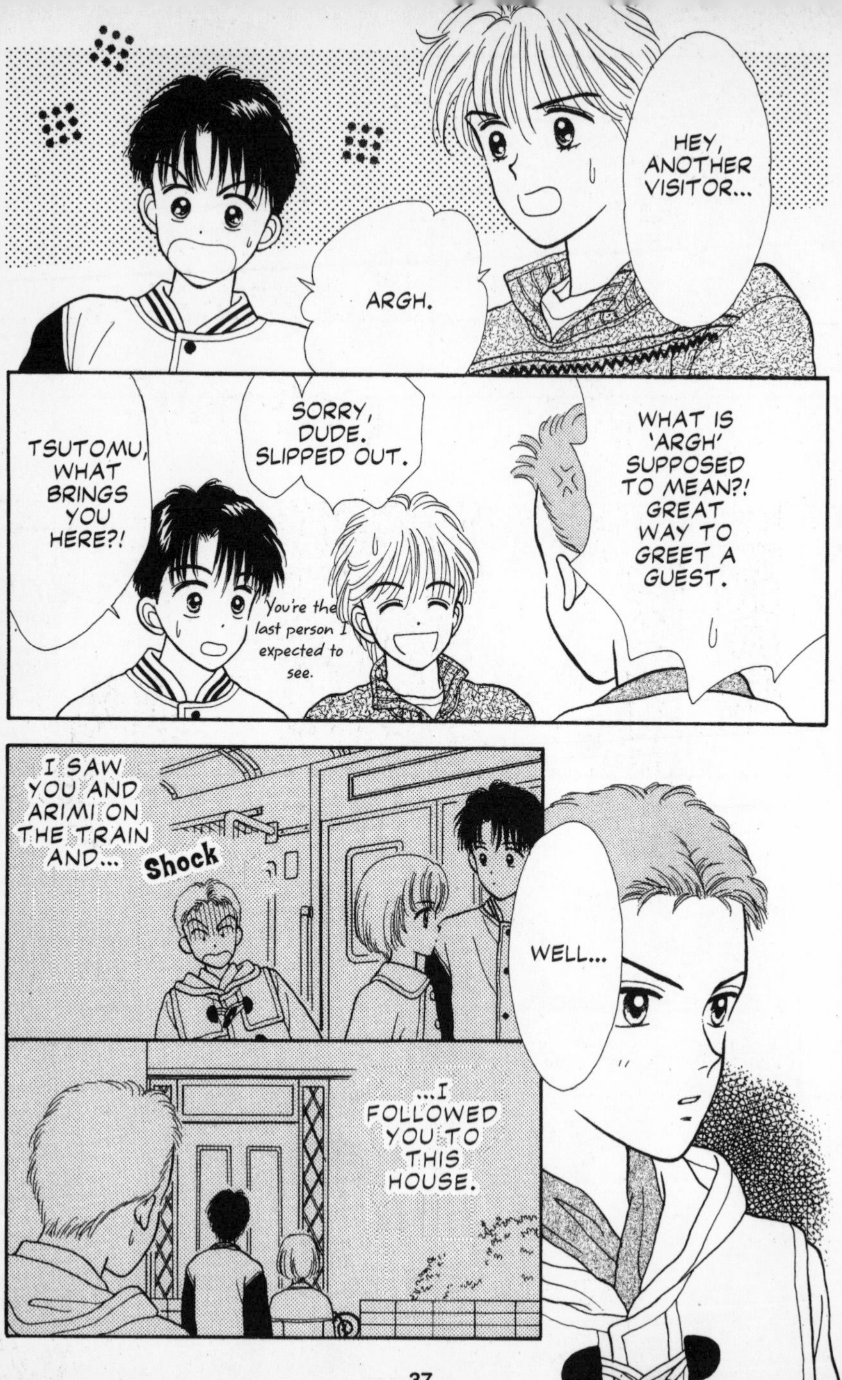
HEY, ANOTHER VISITOR...
ARGH.
WHAT IS 'ARGH' SUPPOSED TO MEAN?! GREAT WAY TO GREET A GUEST.
SORRY, DUDE. SLIPPED OUT.
TSUTOMU, WHAT BRINGS YOU HERE?!
You're the last person I expected to see.
WELL...
I SAW YOU AND ARIMI ON THE TRAIN AND...
Shock
...I FOLLOWED YOU TO THIS HOUSE.

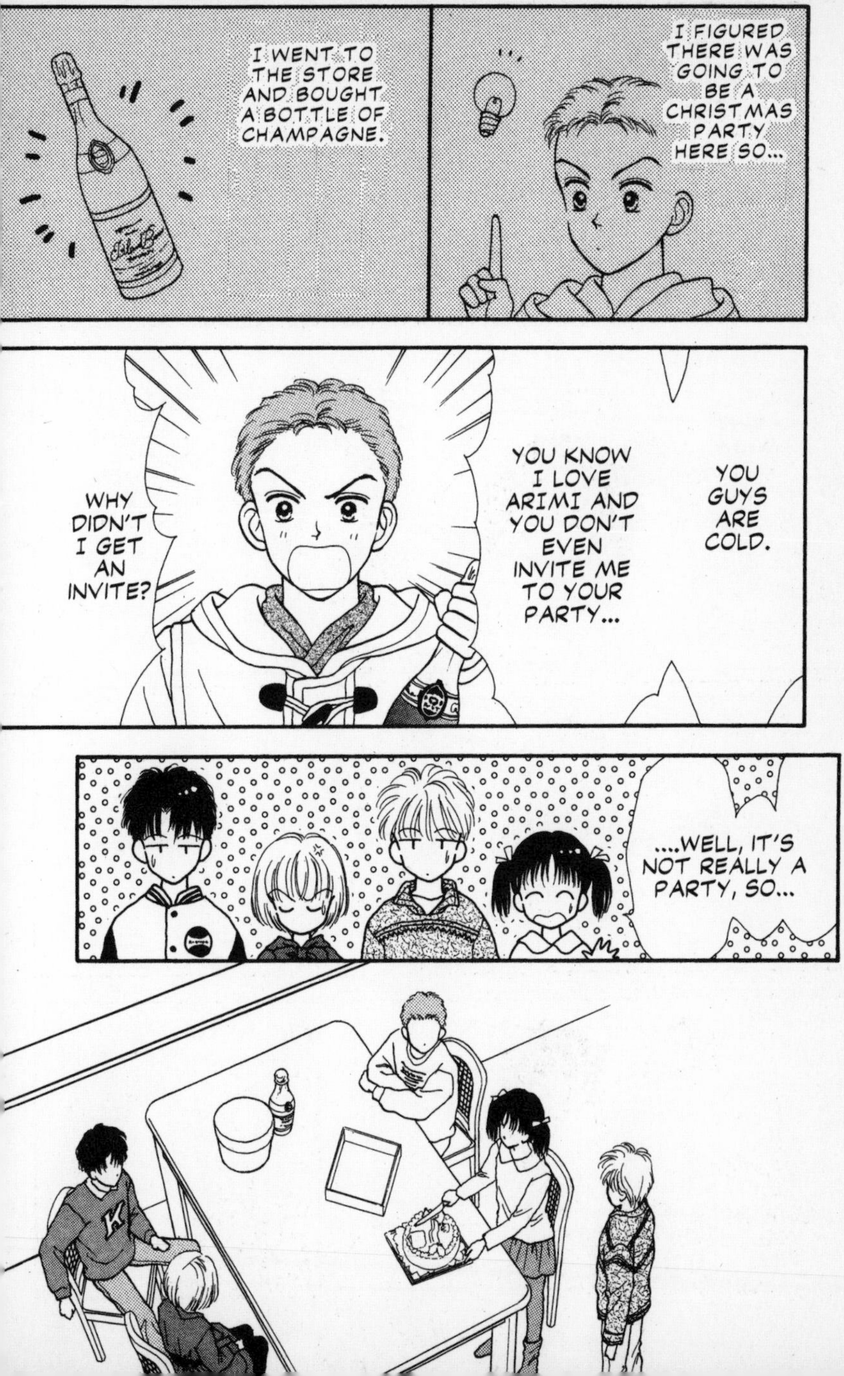
I FIGURED THERE WAS GOING TO BE A CHRISTMAS PARTY HERE SO...
I WENT TO THE STORE AND BOUGHT A BOTTLE OF CHAMPAGNE.
YOU GUYS ARE COLD.
YOU KNOW I LOVE ARIMI AND YOU DON'T EVEN INVITE ME TO YOUR PARTY...
WHY DIDN'T I GET AN INVITE?
....WELL, IT'S NOT REALLY A PARTY, SO...

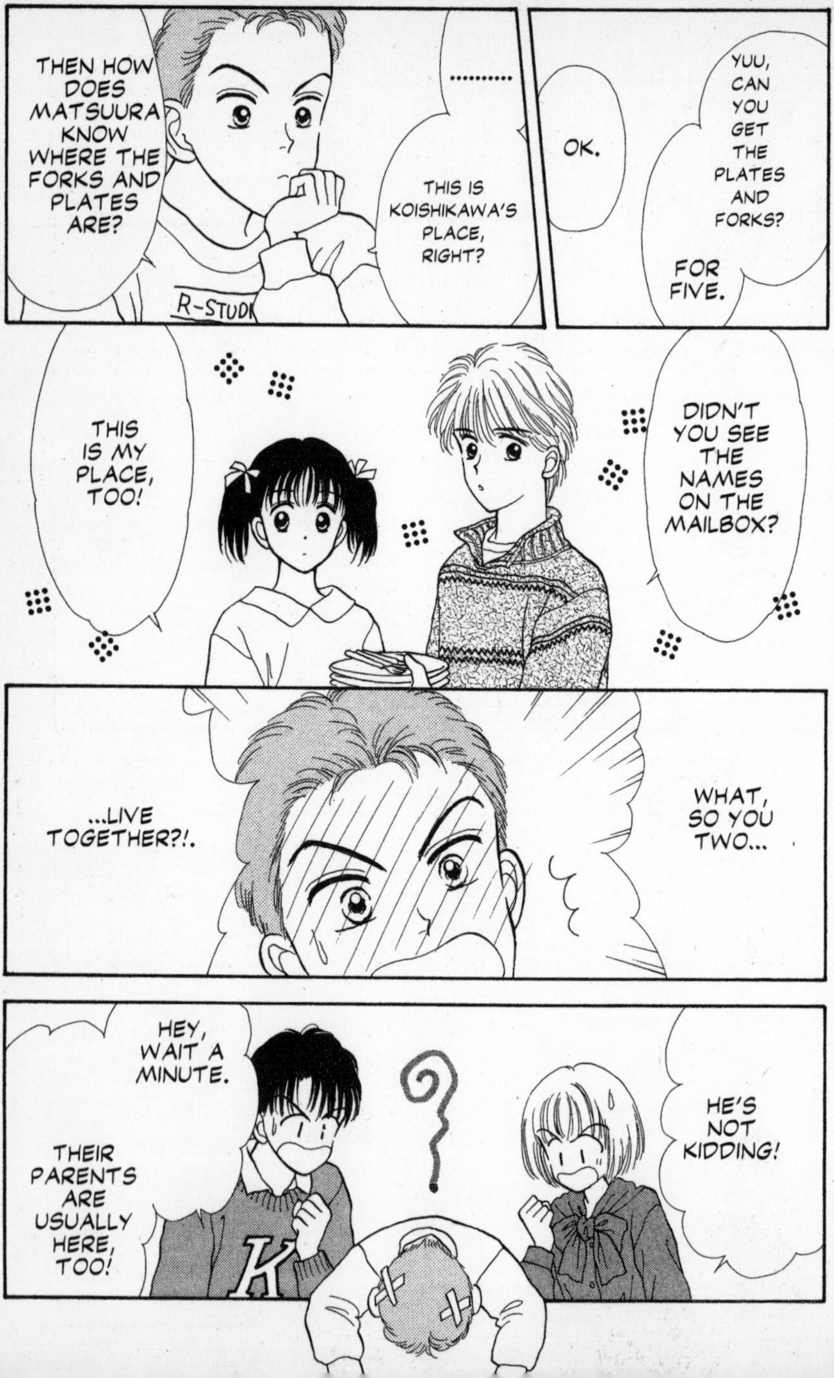
YUU, CAN YOU GET THE PLATES AND FORKS?
FOR FIVE.
OK.
....
THIS IS KOISHIKAWA'S PLACE, RIGHT?
THEN HOW DOES MATSUURA KNOW WHERE THE FORKS AND PLATES ARE?
DIDN'T YOU SEE THE NAMES ON THE MAILBOX?
THIS IS MY PLACE, TOO!
WHAT, SO YOU TWO...
...LIVE TOGETHER?!.
HE'S NOT KIDDING!
HEY, WAIT A MINUTE.
THEIR PARENTS ARE USUALLY HERE, TOO!

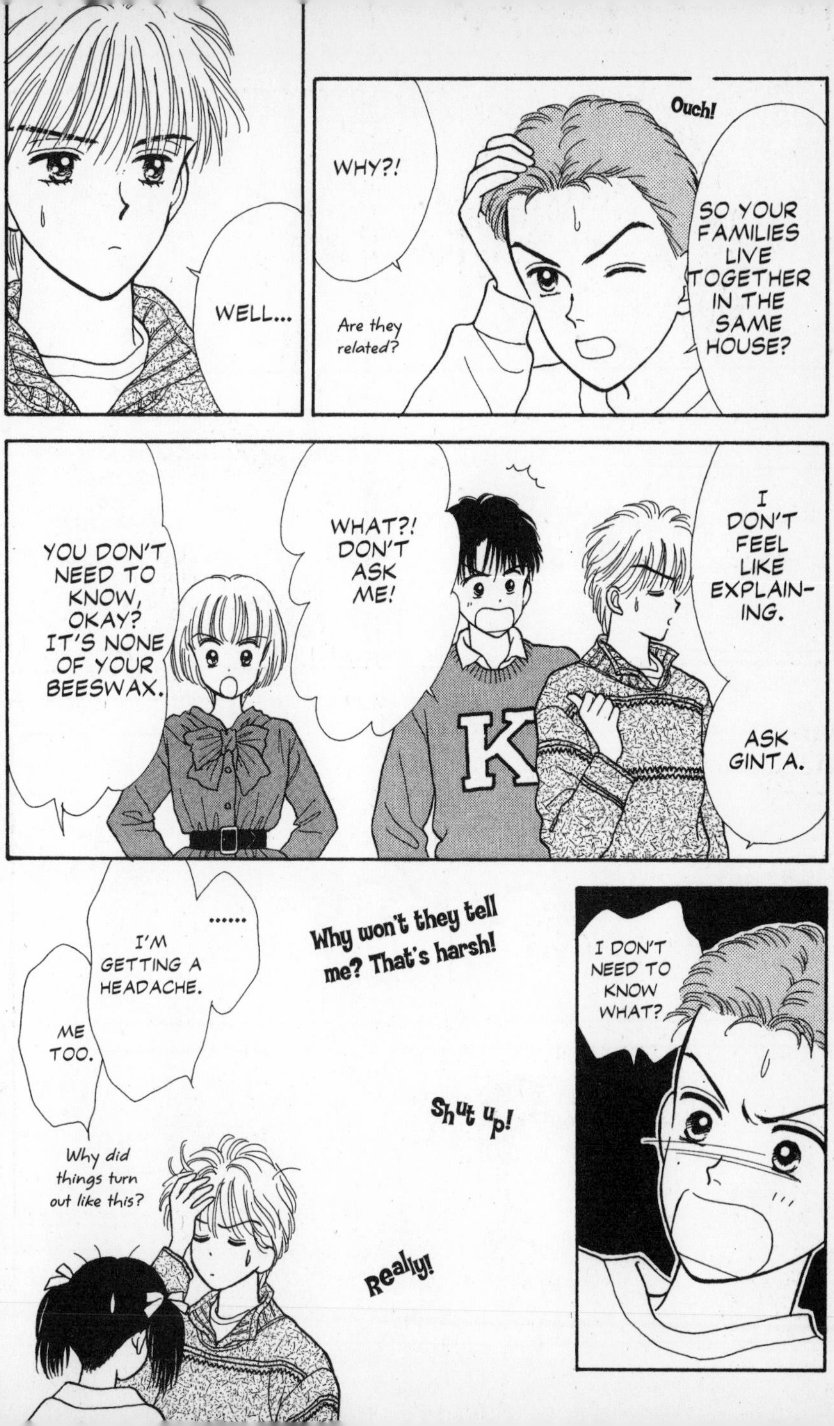

Ouch!
SO YOUR FAMILIES LIVE TOGETHER IN THE SAME HOUSE?
WHY?!
Are they related?
WELL...
I DON'T FEEL LIKE EXPLAIN-ING.
ASK GINTA.
WHAT?! DON'T ASK ME!
YOU DON'T NEED TO KNOW, OKAY? IT'S NONE OF YOUR BEESWAX.
I DON'T NEED TO KNOW WHAT?
Why won't they tell me? That's harsh!
Shut up!
Really!
......
I'M GETTING A HEADACHE.
ME TOO.
Why did things turn out like this?

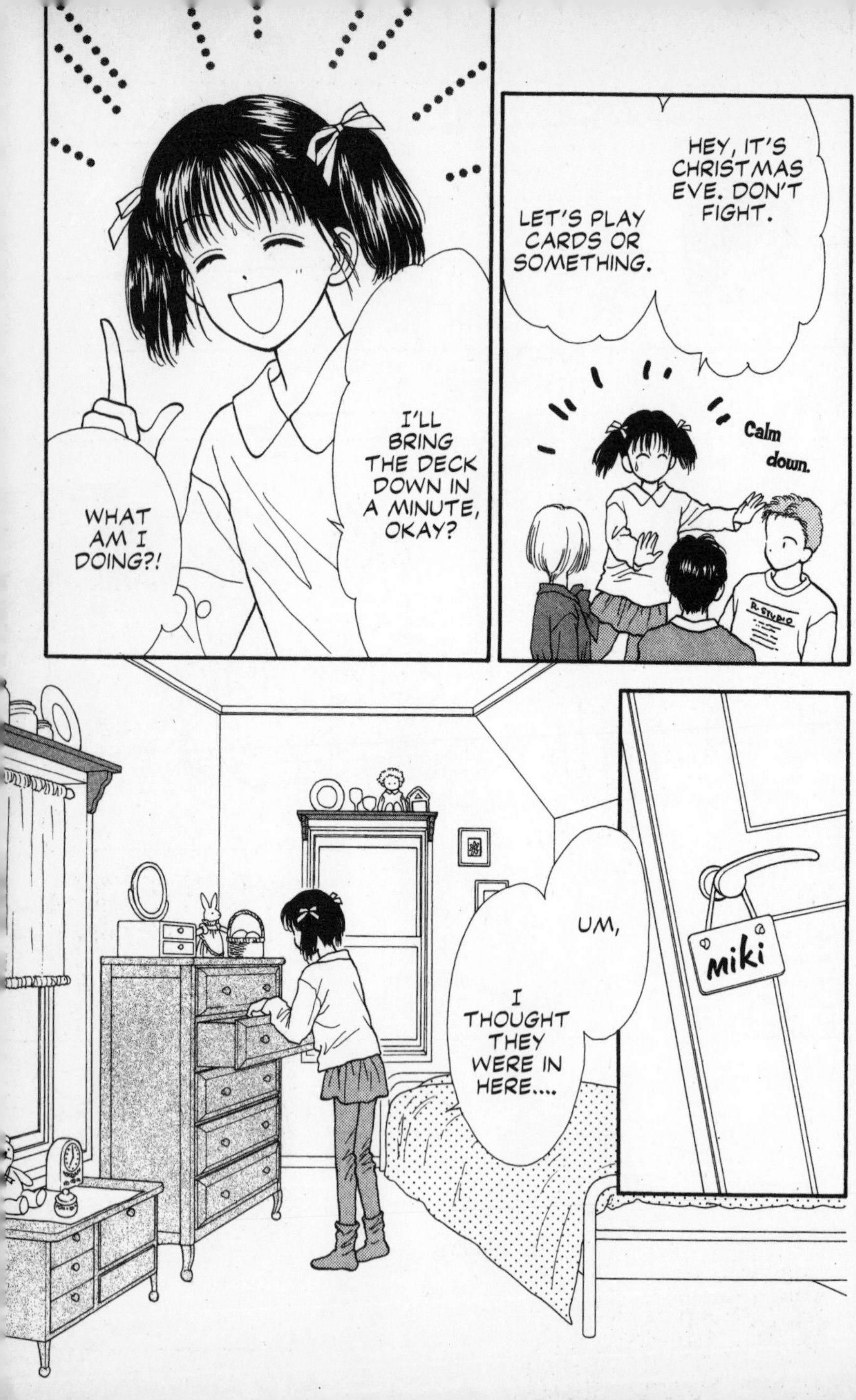
HEY, IT'S CHRISTMAS EVE. DON'T FIGHT.
LET'S PLAY CARDS OR SOMETHING.
Calm down.
I'LL BRING THE DECK DOWN IN A MINUTE, OKAY?
WHAT AM I DOING?!
miki
UM,
I THOUGHT THEY WERE IN HERE....

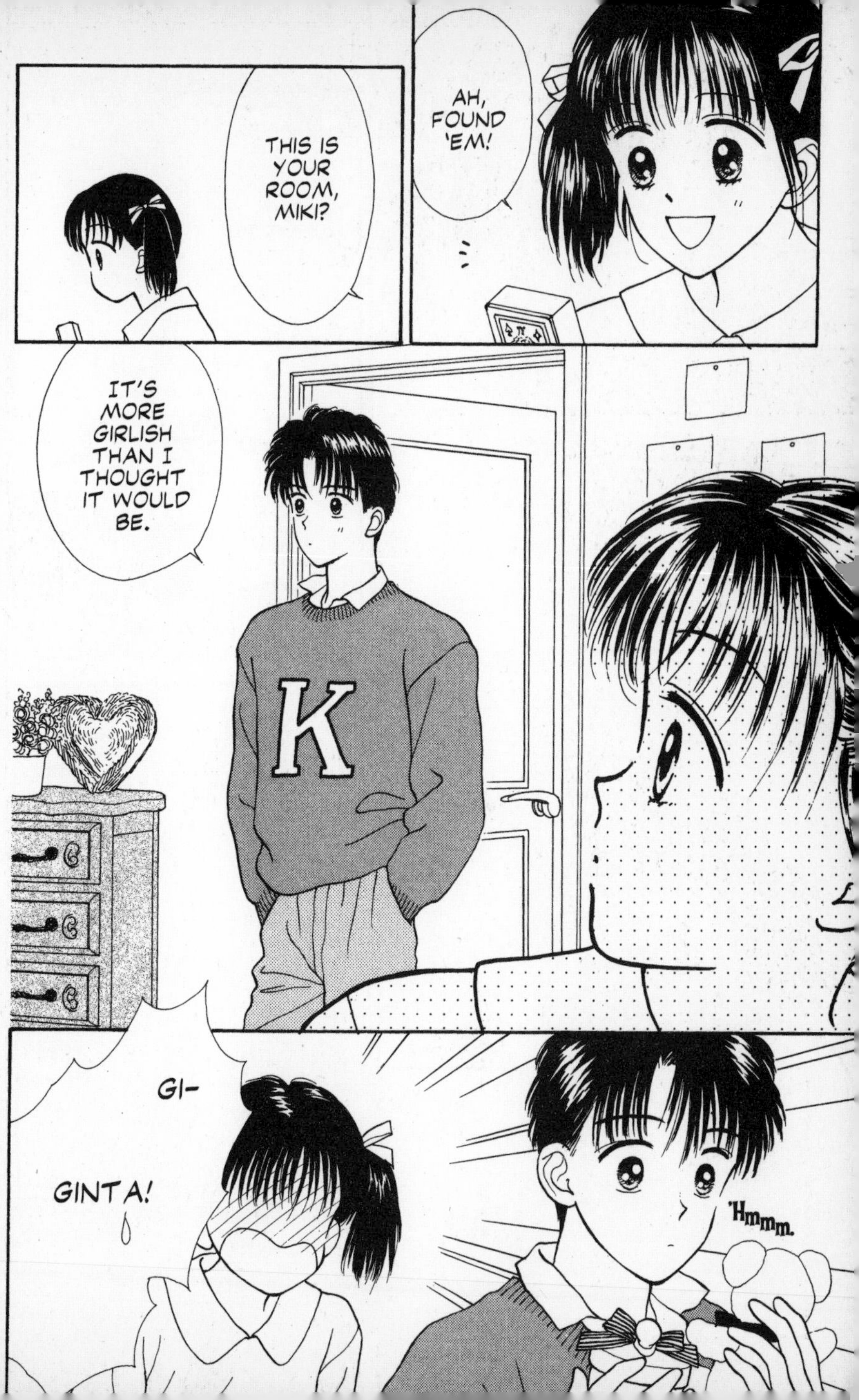
AH, FOUND 'EM!
THIS IS YOUR ROOM, MIKI?
IT'S MORE GIRLISH THAN I THOUGHT IT WOULD BE.
'Hmmm.
GI-
GINTA!

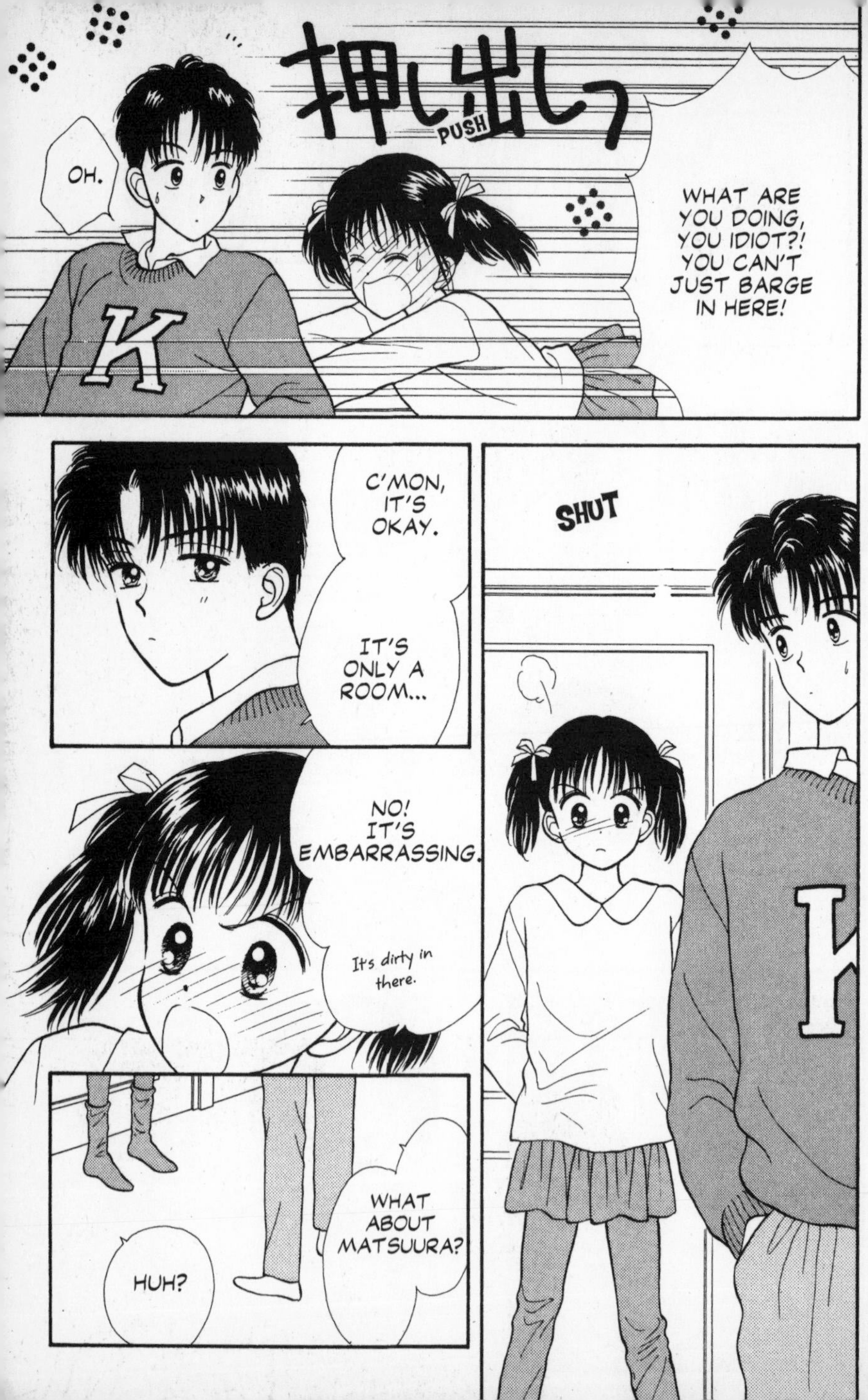
押し出しっ
PUSH
WHAT ARE YOU DOING, YOU IDIOT?! YOU CAN'T JUST BARGE IN HERE!
OH.
SHUT
C'MON, IT'S OKAY.
IT'S ONLY A ROOM...
NO! IT'S EMBARRASSING.
It's dirty in there.
WHAT ABOUT MATSUURA?
HUH?

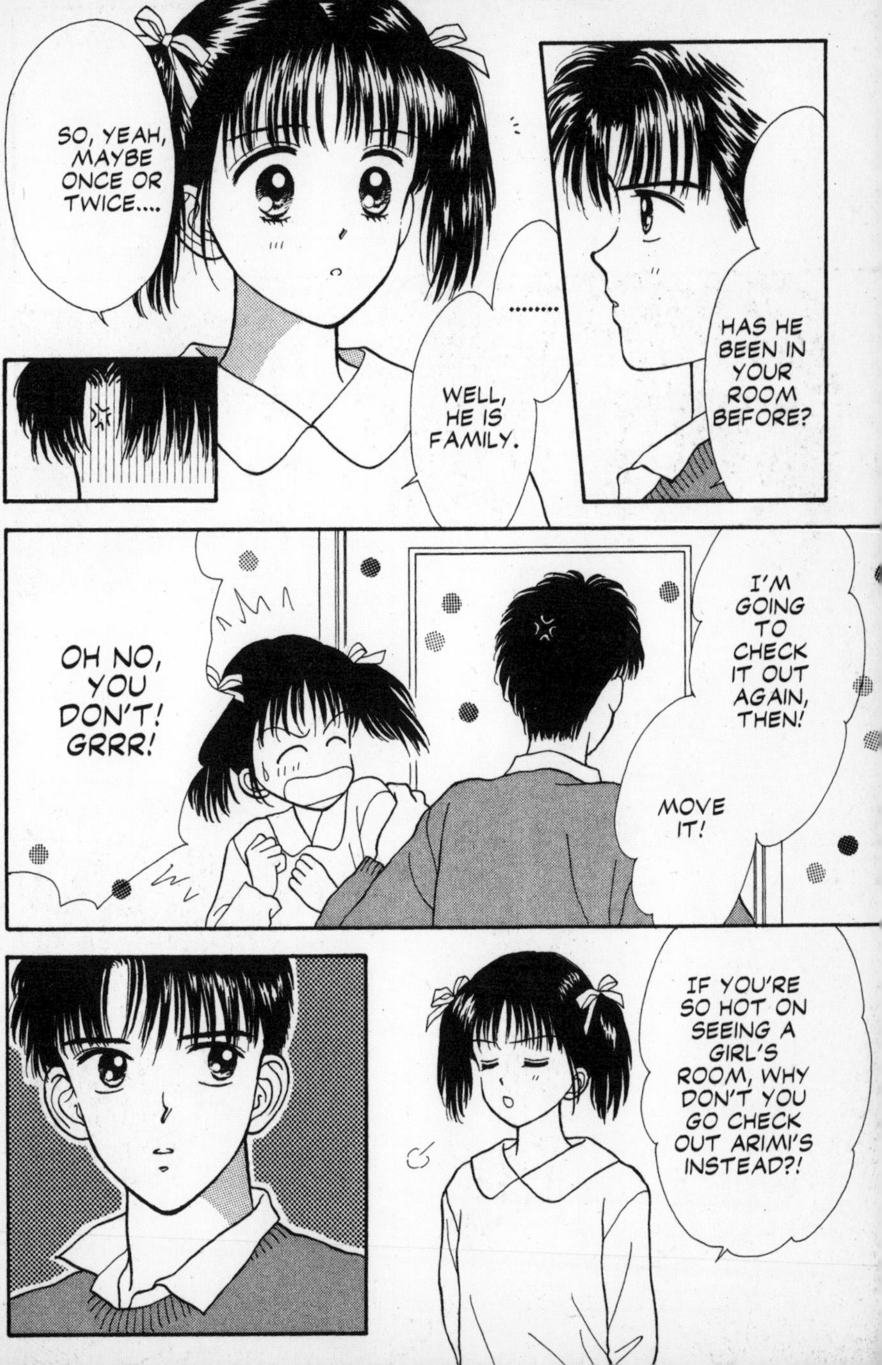
HAS HE BEEN IN YOUR ROOM BEFORE?
....
WELL, HE IS FAMILY.
SO, YEAH, MAYBE ONCE OR TWICE....
I'M GOING TO CHECK IT OUT AGAIN, THEN!
MOVE IT!
OH NO, YOU DON'T! GRRR!
IF YOU'RE SO HOT ON SEEING A GIRL'S ROOM, WHY DON'T YOU GO CHECK OUT ARIMI'S INSTEAD?!

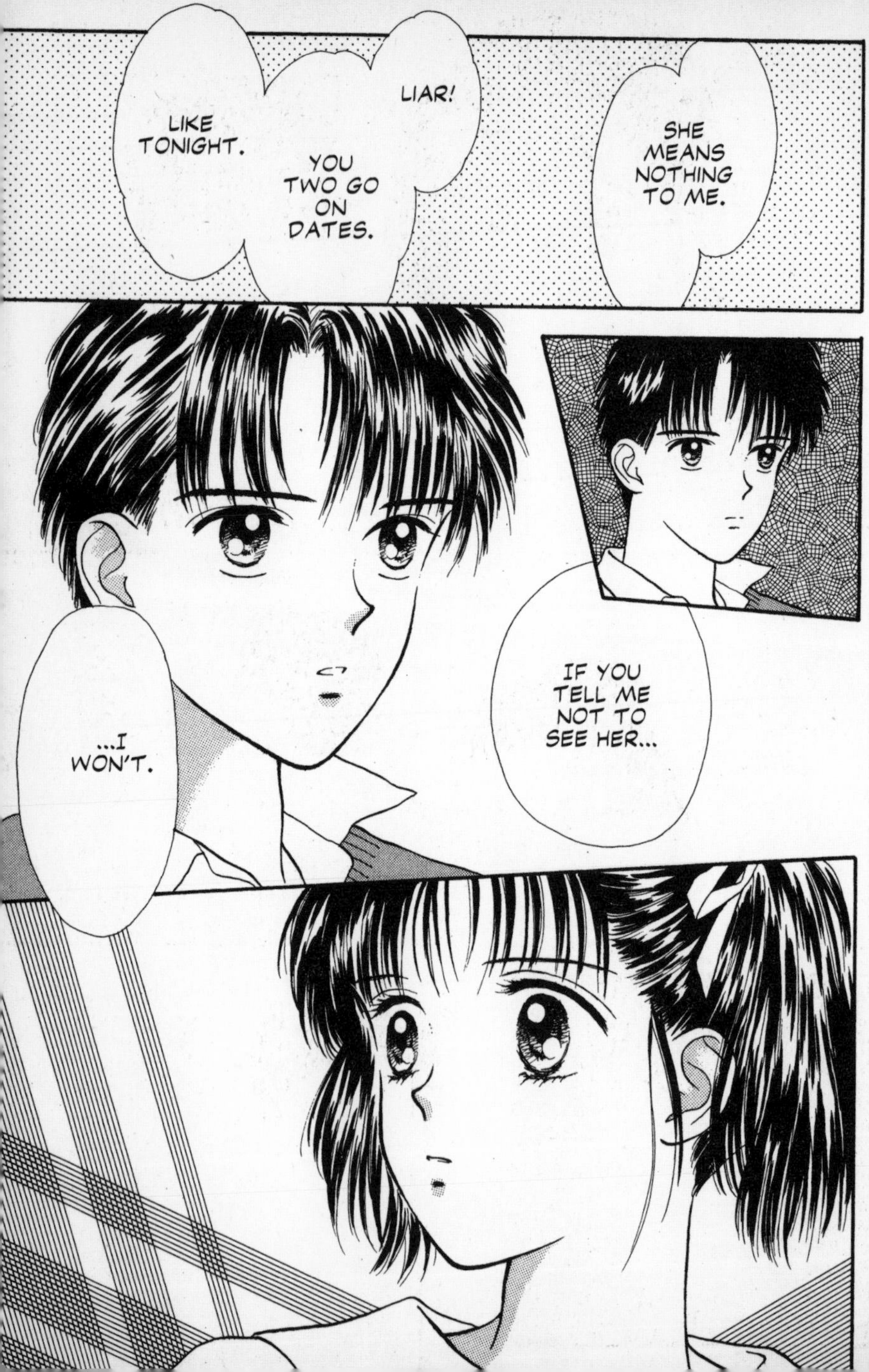
SHE MEANS NOTHING TO ME.
LIAR!
YOU TWO GO ON DATES.
LIKE TONIGHT.
IF YOU TELL ME NOT TO SEE HER...
...I WON'T.

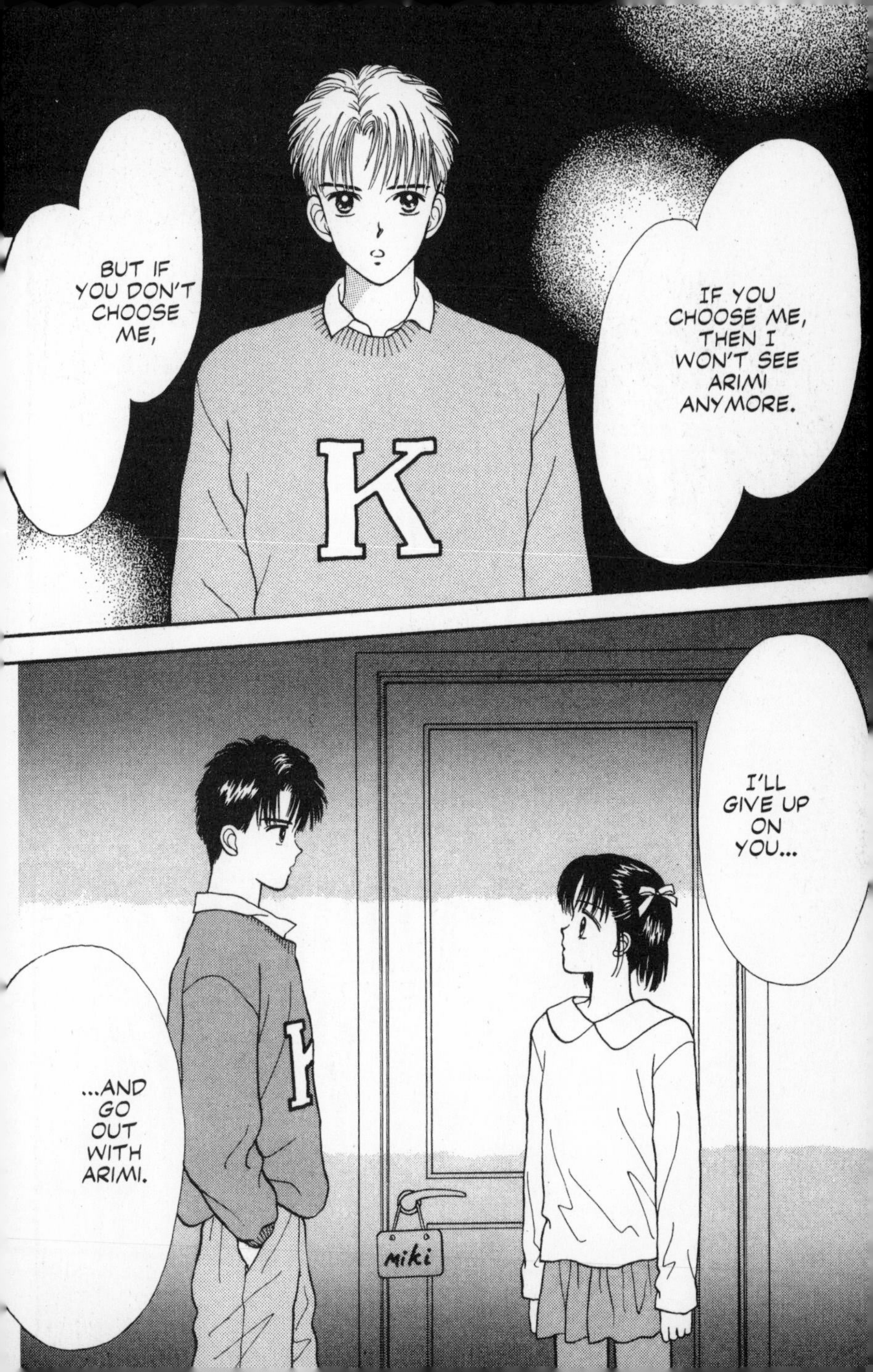
IF YOU CHOOSE ME, THEN I WON'T SEE ARIMI ANYMORE.
BUT IF YOU DON'T CHOOSE ME,
I'LL GIVE UP ON YOU...
...AND GO OUT WITH ARIMI.
miki

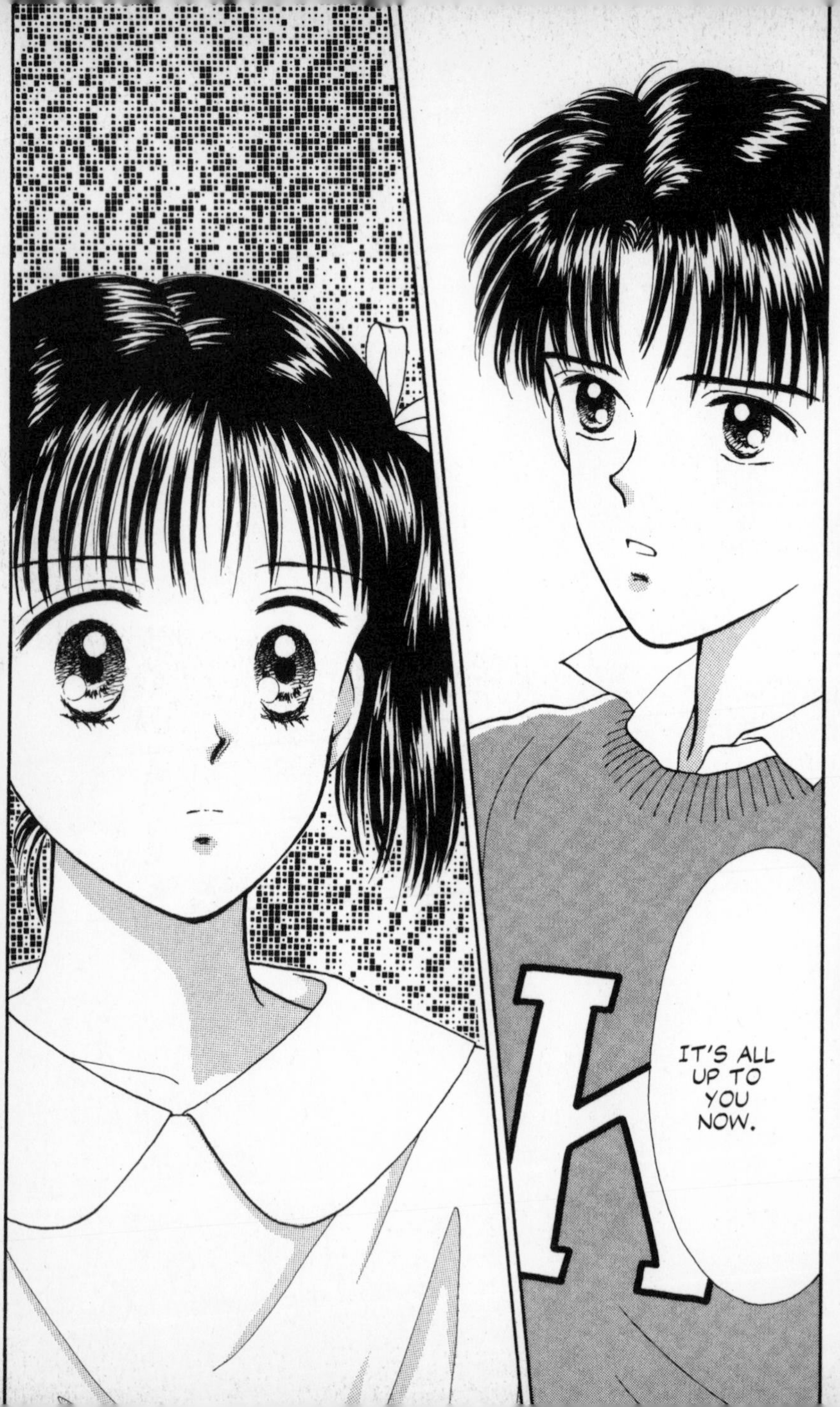
IT'S ALL UP TO YOU NOW.

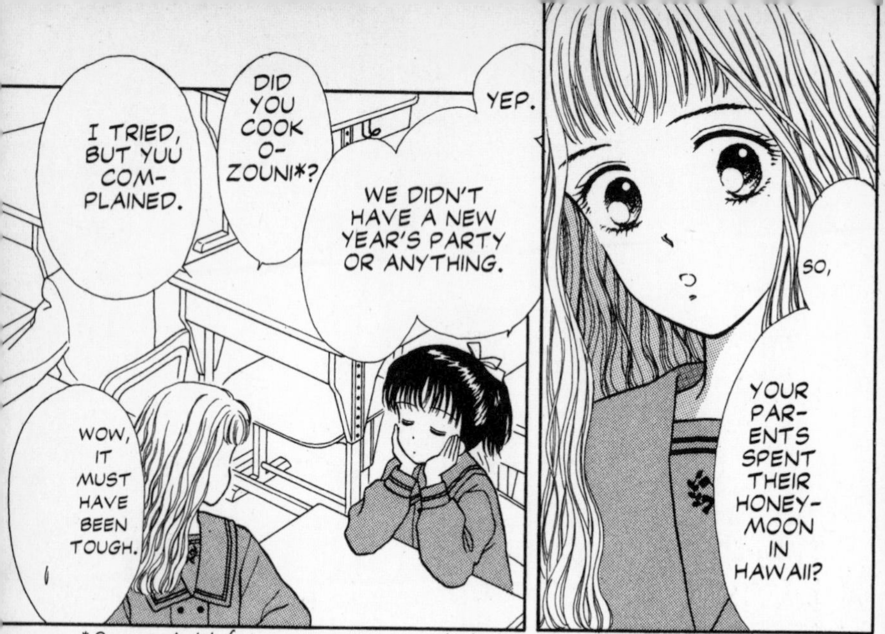
SO,
YOUR PARENTS SPENT THEIR HONEYMOON IN HAWAII?
YEP.
WE DIDN'T HAVE A NEW YEAR'S PARTY OR ANYTHING.
DID YOU COOK O-ZOUNI*?
I TRIED, BUT YUU COMPLAINED.
WOW, IT MUST HAVE BEEN TOUGH.

* O-zouni - A dish featuring rice cakes in vegetable broth that is traditionally served on New Year's.

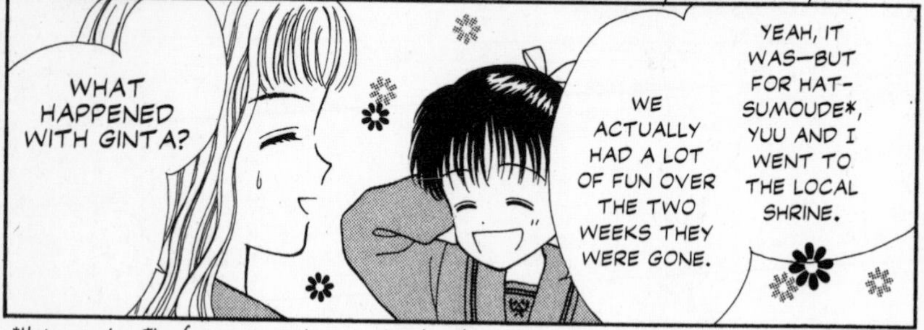
YEAH, IT WAS—BUT FOR HATSUMOUDE*, YUU AND I WENT TO THE LOCAL SHRINE.
WE ACTUALLY HAD A LOT OF FUN OVER THE TWO WEEKS THEY WERE GONE.
WHAT HAPPENED WITH GINTA?

*Hatsumoude - The first visit to a shrine in the New Year.

FREE TALK ②

When I'm hanging out with my friends, we sometimes talk about video games. But since I don't like RPG (Role-Playing Games), I don't always take part in the conversation. But I really like Tetris-type games and ones that involve action and shooting even though I'm no good at them. When I want to take my mind off work, I play my GameBoy. I'm not that great at that, either. I like the Tom and Jerry and Crayon Shin-chan games, but I can never make it to the end. If anyone has any pointers about clearing all levels to the end, please give me some tips!

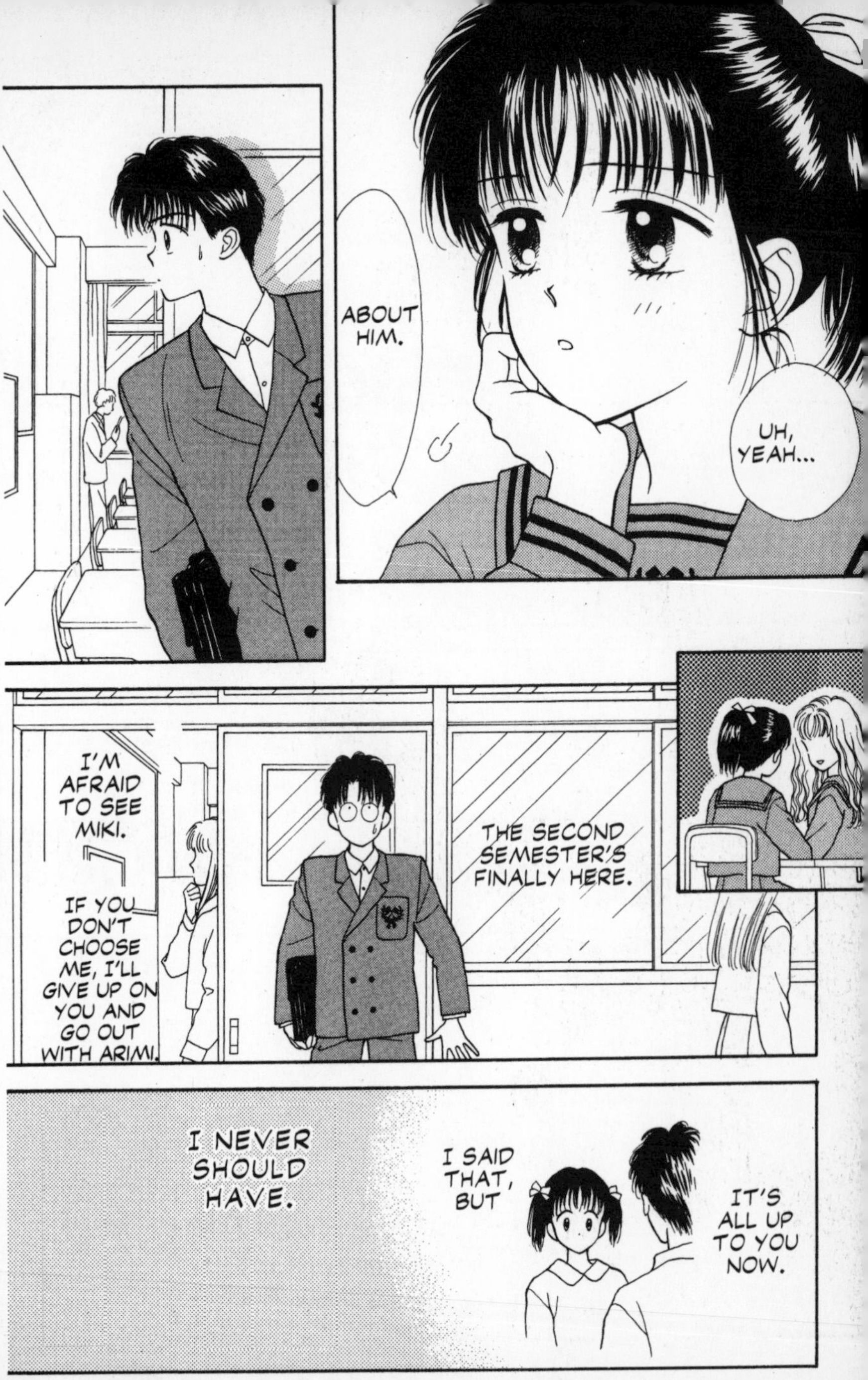
UH, YEAH...
ABOUT HIM.
THE SECOND SEMESTER'S FINALLY HERE.
I'M AFRAID TO SEE MIKI.
IF YOU DON'T CHOOSE ME, I'LL GIVE UP ON YOU AND GO OUT WITH ARIMI.
IT'S ALL UP TO YOU NOW.
I SAID THAT, BUT
I NEVER SHOULD HAVE.

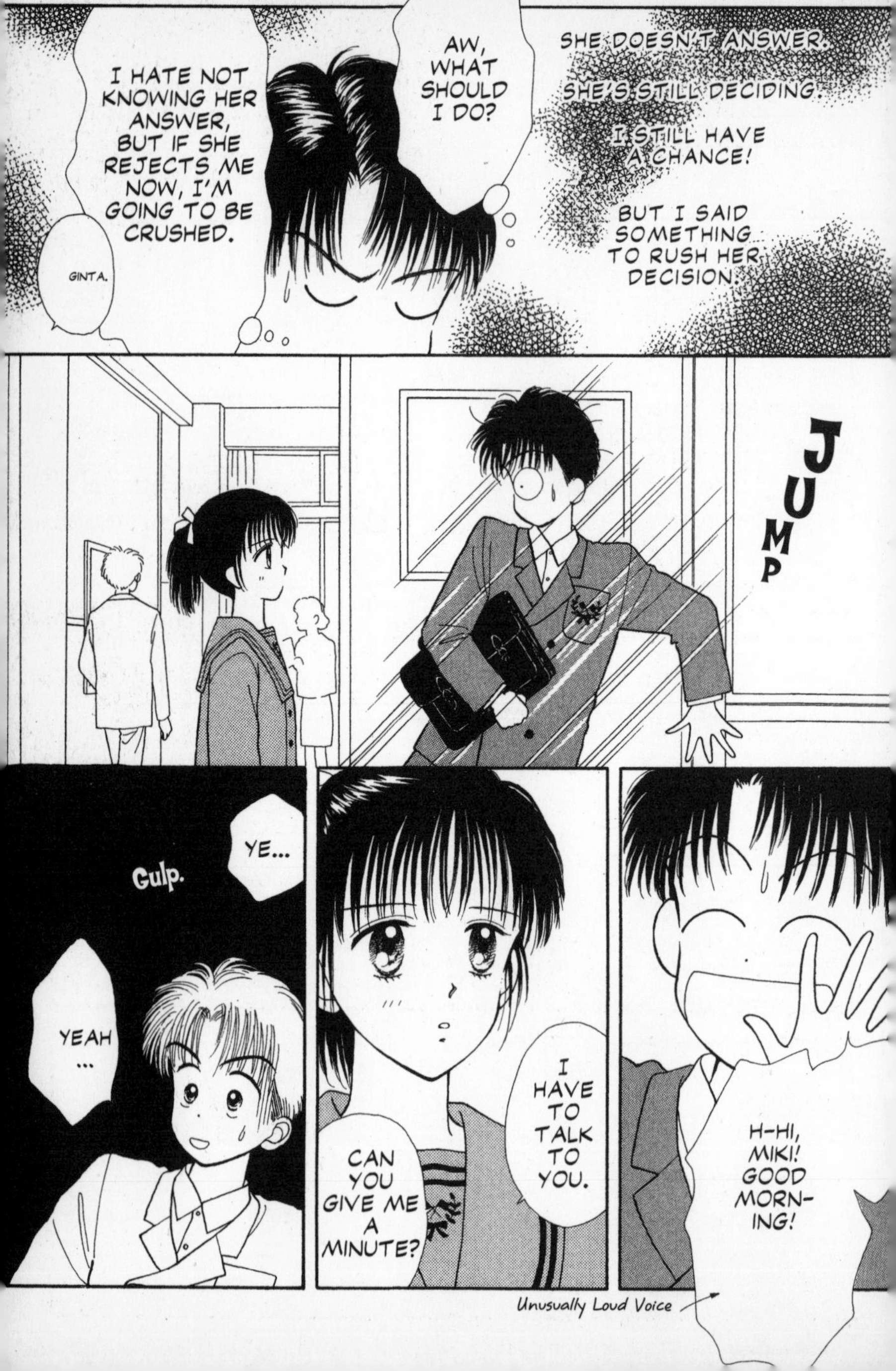
SHE DOESN'T ANSWER.
SHE'S STILL DECIDING.
I STILL HAVE A CHANCE!
BUT I SAID SOMETHING TO RUSH HER DECISION.
AW, WHAT SHOULD I DO?
I HATE NOT KNOWING HER ANSWER, BUT IF SHE REJECTS ME NOW, I'M GOING TO BE CRUSHED.
GINTA.
JUMP
H-HI, MIKI! GOOD MORNING!
Unusually Loud Voice
I HAVE TO TALK TO YOU.
CAN YOU GIVE ME A MINUTE?
YE...
Gulp.
YEAH ...

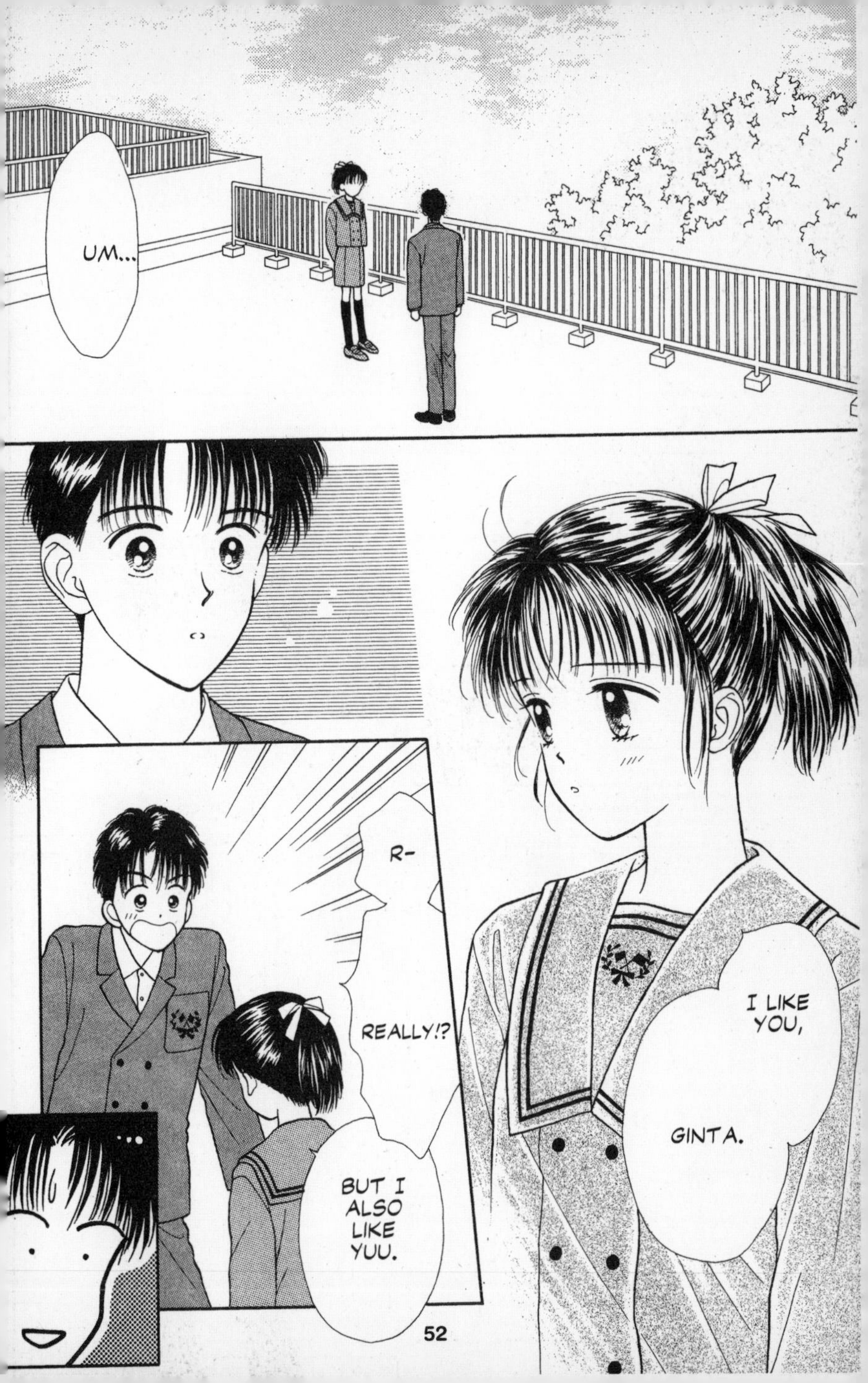
UM...
I LIKE YOU,
GINTA.
R-
REALLY!?
BUT I ALSO LIKE YUU.

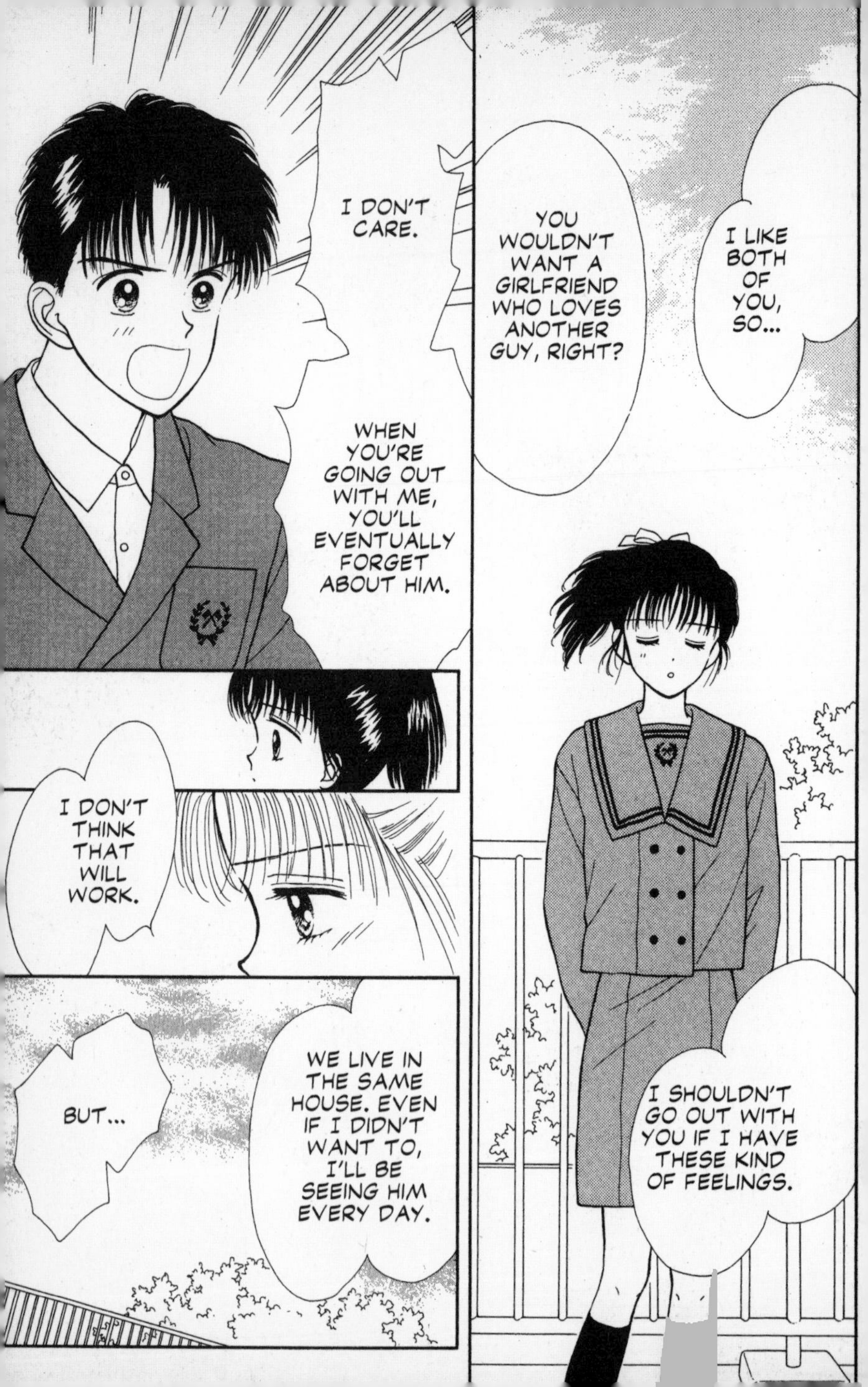
I LIKE BOTH OF YOU, SO...
YOU WOULDN'T WANT A GIRLFRIEND WHO LOVES ANOTHER GUY, RIGHT?
I SHOULDN'T GO OUT WITH YOU IF I HAVE THESE KIND OF FEELINGS.
I DON'T CARE.
WHEN YOU'RE GOING OUT WITH ME, YOU'LL EVENTUALLY FORGET ABOUT HIM.
I DON'T THINK THAT WILL WORK.
WE LIVE IN THE SAME HOUSE. EVEN IF I DIDN'T WANT TO, I'LL BE SEEING HIM EVERY DAY.
BUT...

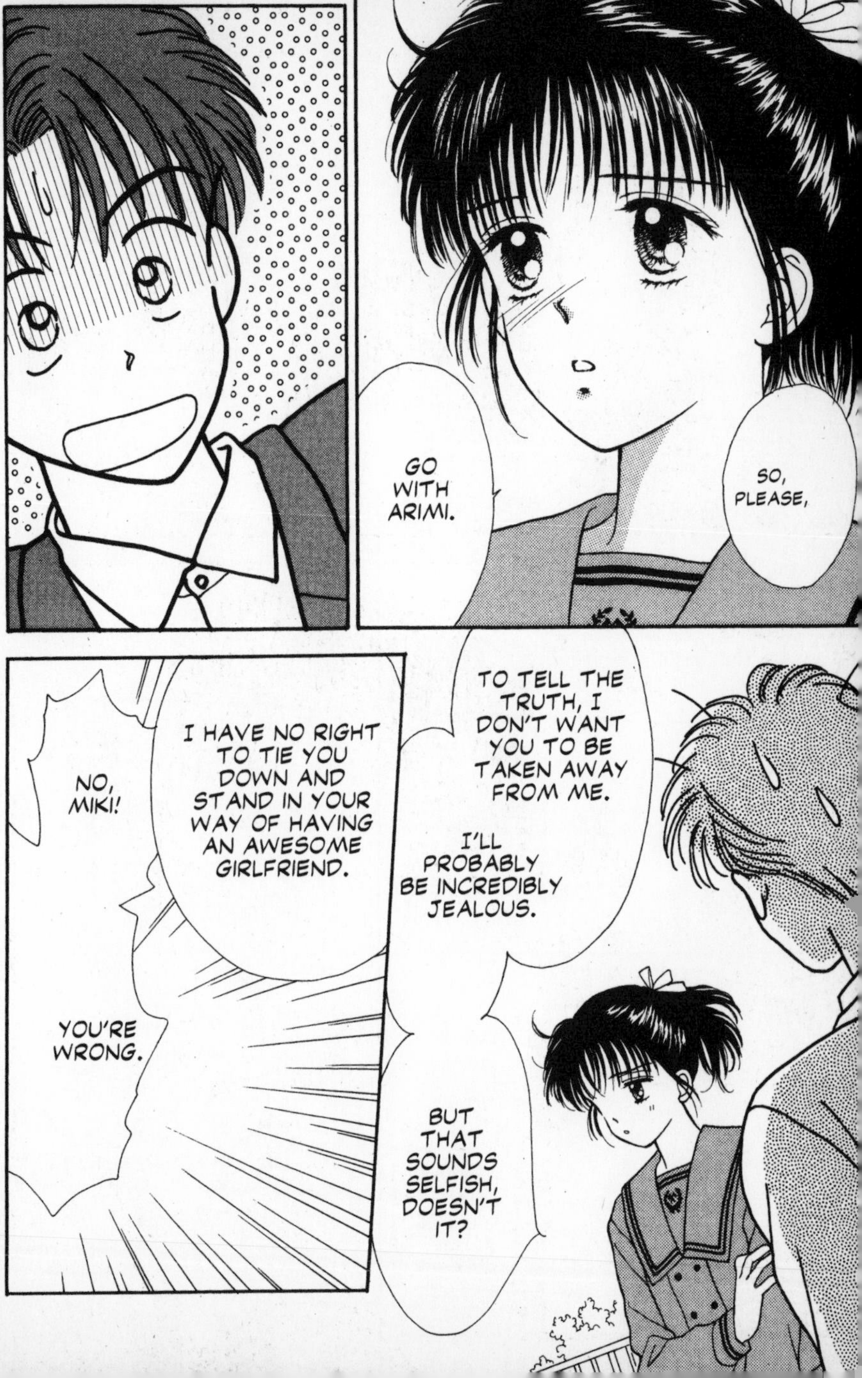
SO, PLEASE,
GO WITH ARIMI.
TO TELL THE TRUTH, I DON'T WANT YOU TO BE TAKEN AWAY FROM ME.
I'LL PROBABLY BE INCREDIBLY JEALOUS.
BUT THAT SOUNDS SELFISH, DOESN'T IT?
I HAVE NO RIGHT TO TIE YOU DOWN AND STAND IN YOUR WAY OF HAVING AN AWESOME GIRLFRIEND.
NO, MIKI!
YOU'RE WRONG.

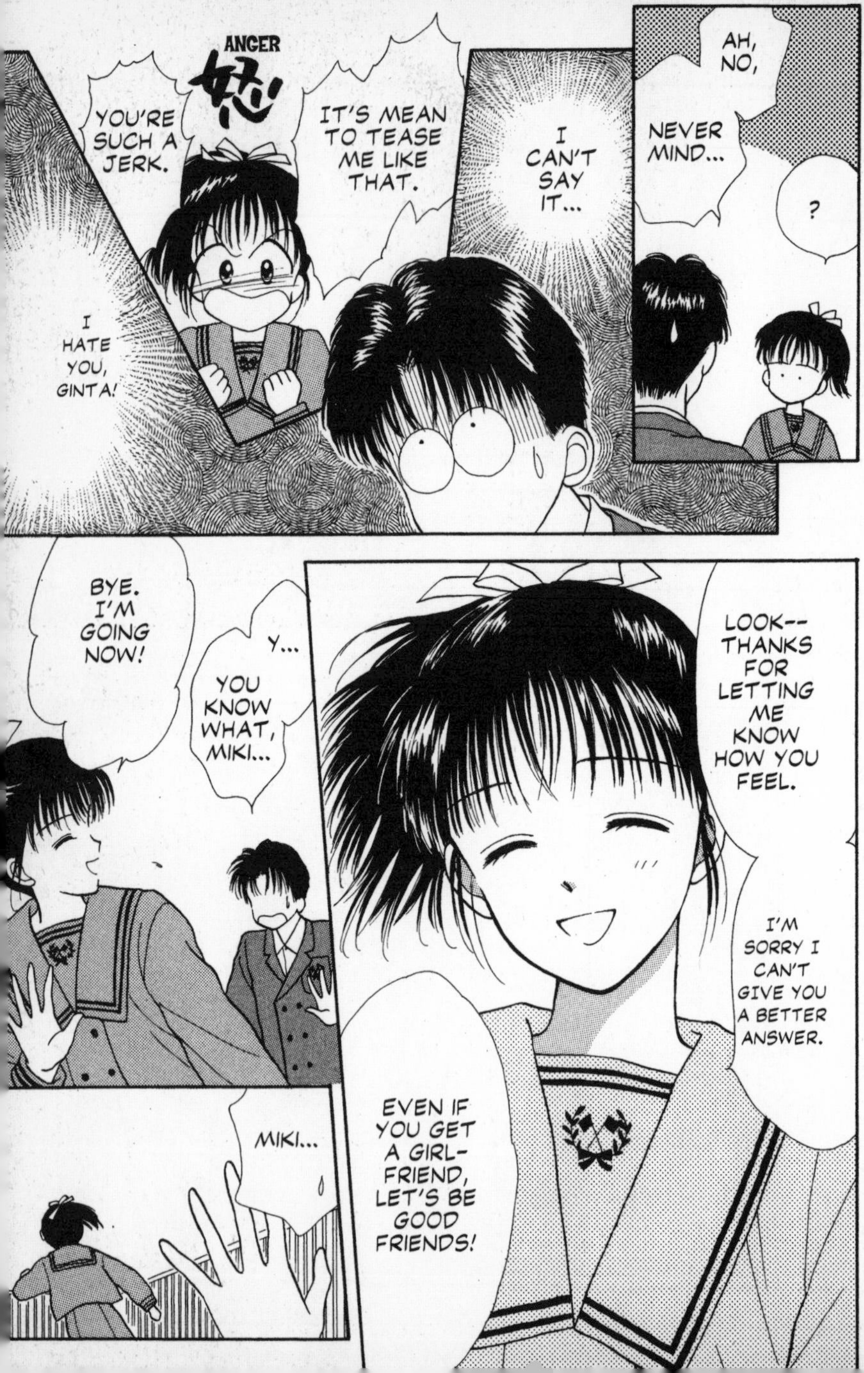
AH, NO,
NEVER MIND...
?
I CAN'T SAY IT...
IT'S MEAN TO TEASE ME LIKE THAT.
ANGER
YOU'RE SUCH A JERK.
I HATE YOU, GINTA!
LOOK-- THANKS FOR LETTING ME KNOW HOW YOU FEEL.
I'M SORRY I CAN'T GIVE YOU A BETTER ANSWER.
EVEN IF YOU GET A GIRL-FRIEND, LET'S BE GOOD FRIENDS!
BYE. I'M GOING NOW!
Y...
YOU KNOW WHAT, MIKI...
MIKI...

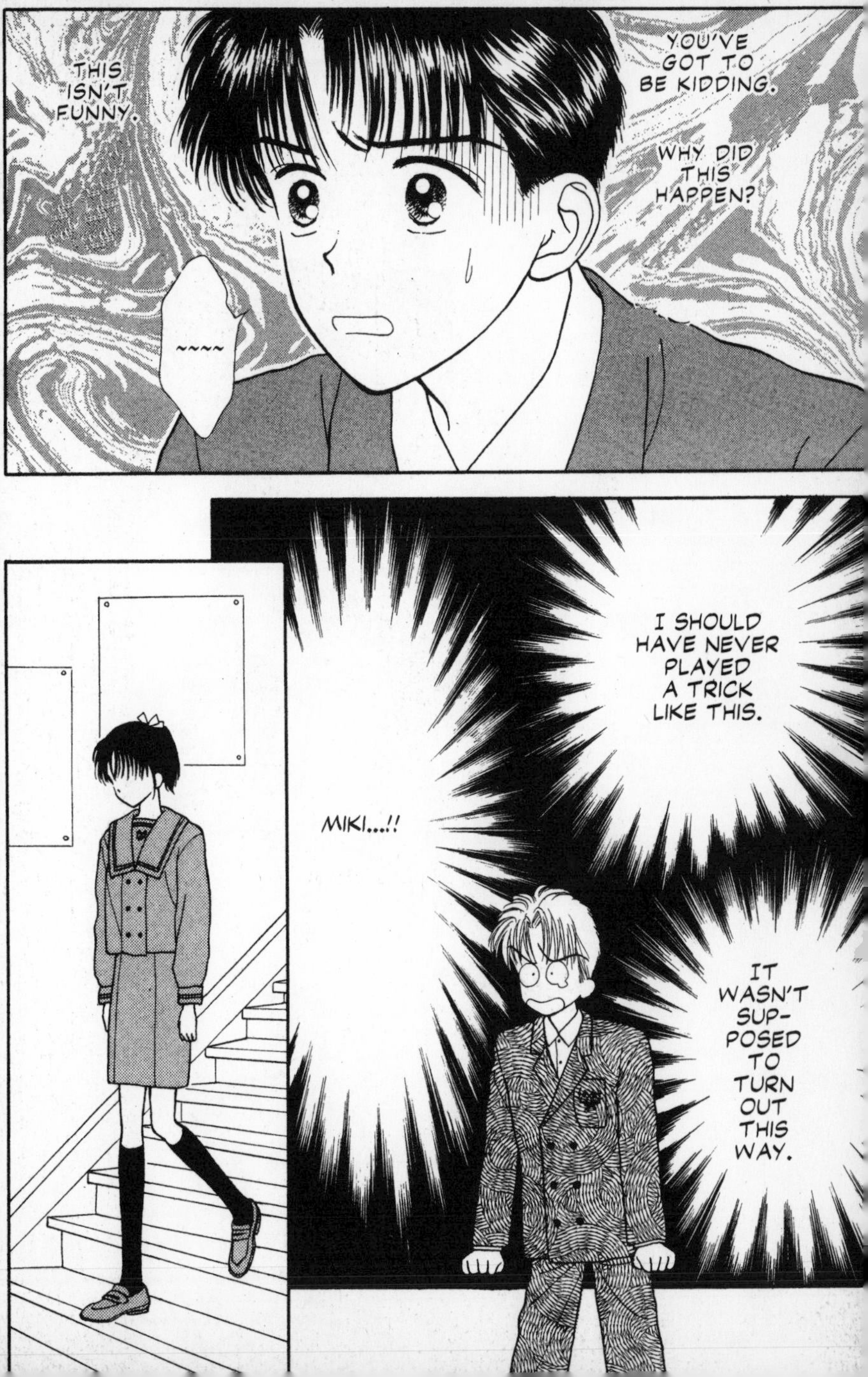
YOU'VE GOT TO BE KIDDING.
WHY DID THIS HAPPEN?
THIS ISN'T FUNNY.
~~~~
I SHOULD HAVE NEVER PLAYED A TRICK LIKE THIS.
MIKI...!!
IT WASN'T SUP-POSED TO TURN OUT THIS WAY.
~~~~

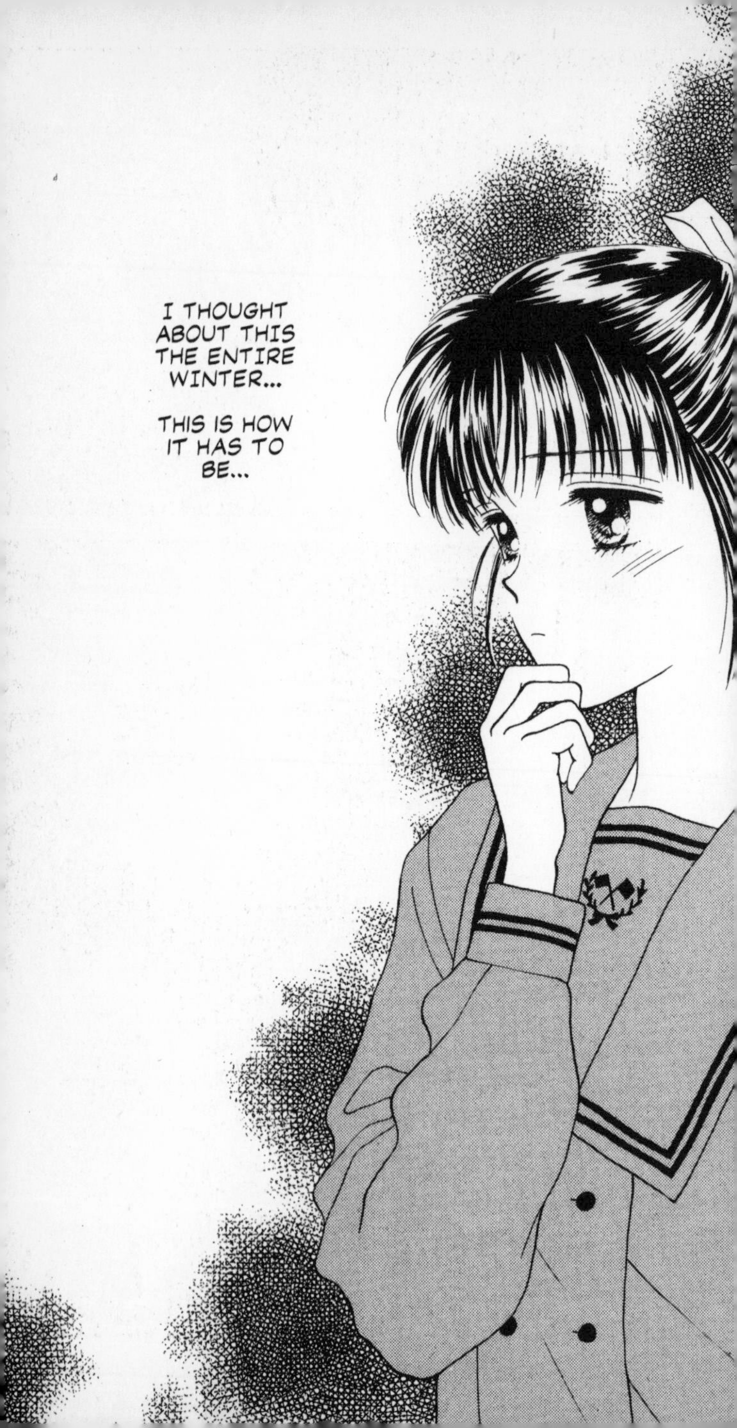
I THOUGHT ABOUT THIS THE ENTIRE WINTER...
THIS IS HOW IT HAS TO BE...

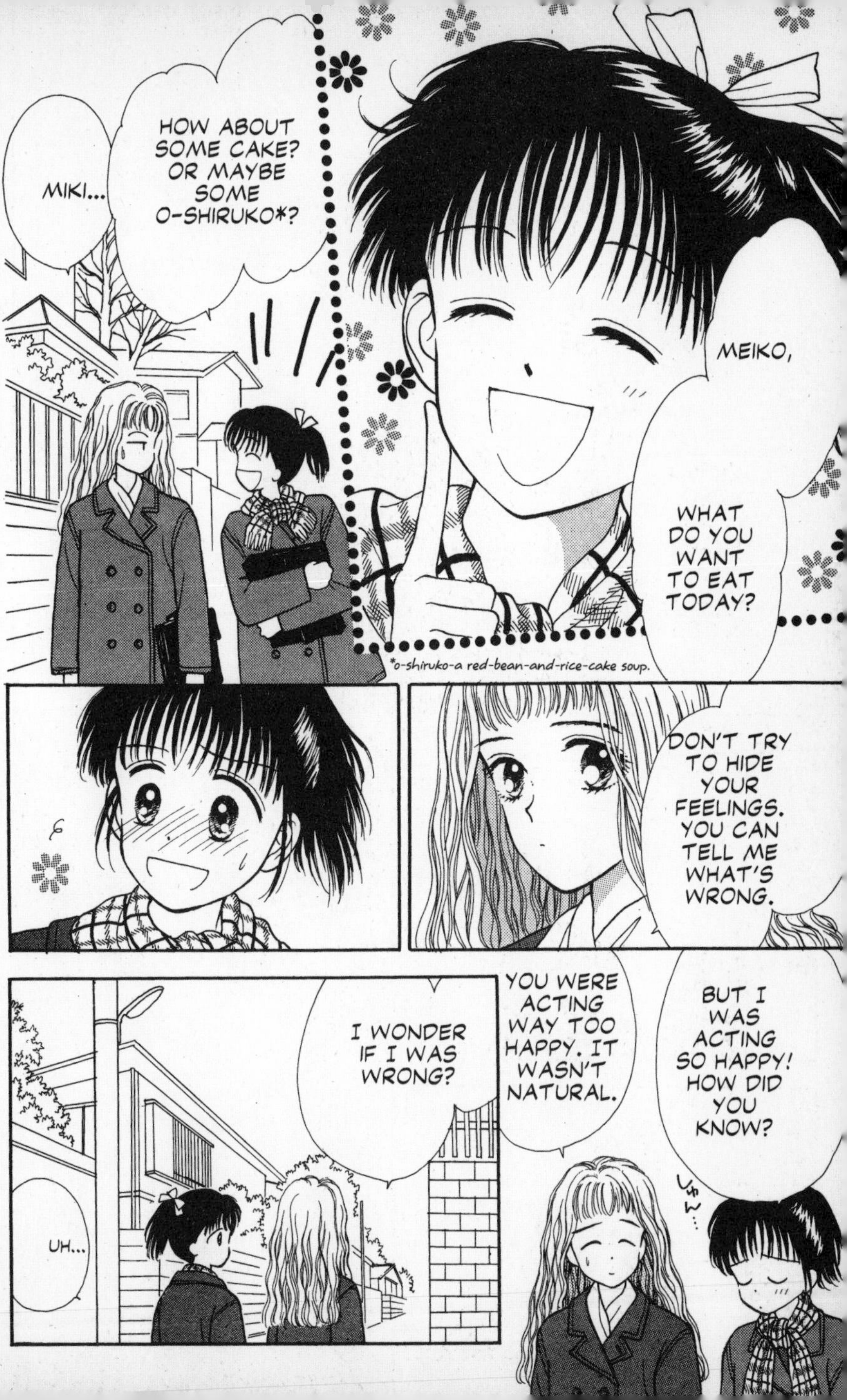
MEIKO,
WHAT DO YOU WANT TO EAT TODAY?
HOW ABOUT SOME CAKE? OR MAYBE SOME O-SHIRUKO*?
MIKI...
DON'T TRY TO HIDE YOUR FEELINGS. YOU CAN TELL ME WHAT'S WRONG.
BUT I WAS ACTING SO HAPPY! HOW DID YOU KNOW?
YOU WERE ACTING WAY TOO HAPPY. IT WASN'T NATURAL.
I WONDER IF I WAS WRONG?
UH...
*o-shiruko-a red-bean-and-rice-cake soup.

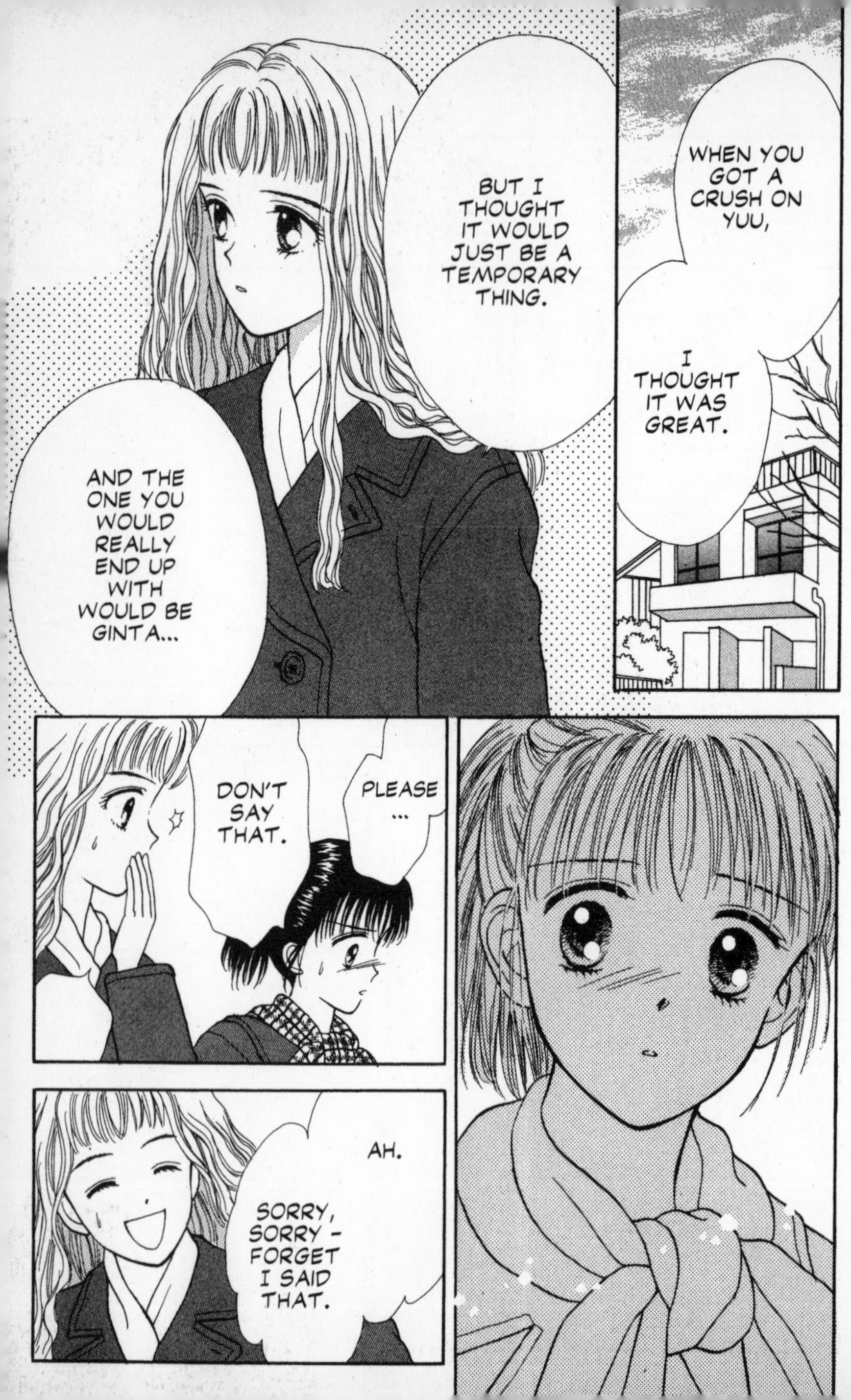
WHEN YOU GOT A CRUSH ON YUU,
I THOUGHT IT WAS GREAT.
BUT I THOUGHT IT WOULD JUST BE A TEMPORARY THING.
AND THE ONE YOU WOULD REALLY END UP WITH WOULD BE GINTA...
PLEASE...
DON'T SAY THAT.
AH.
SORRY, SORRY - FORGET I SAID THAT.

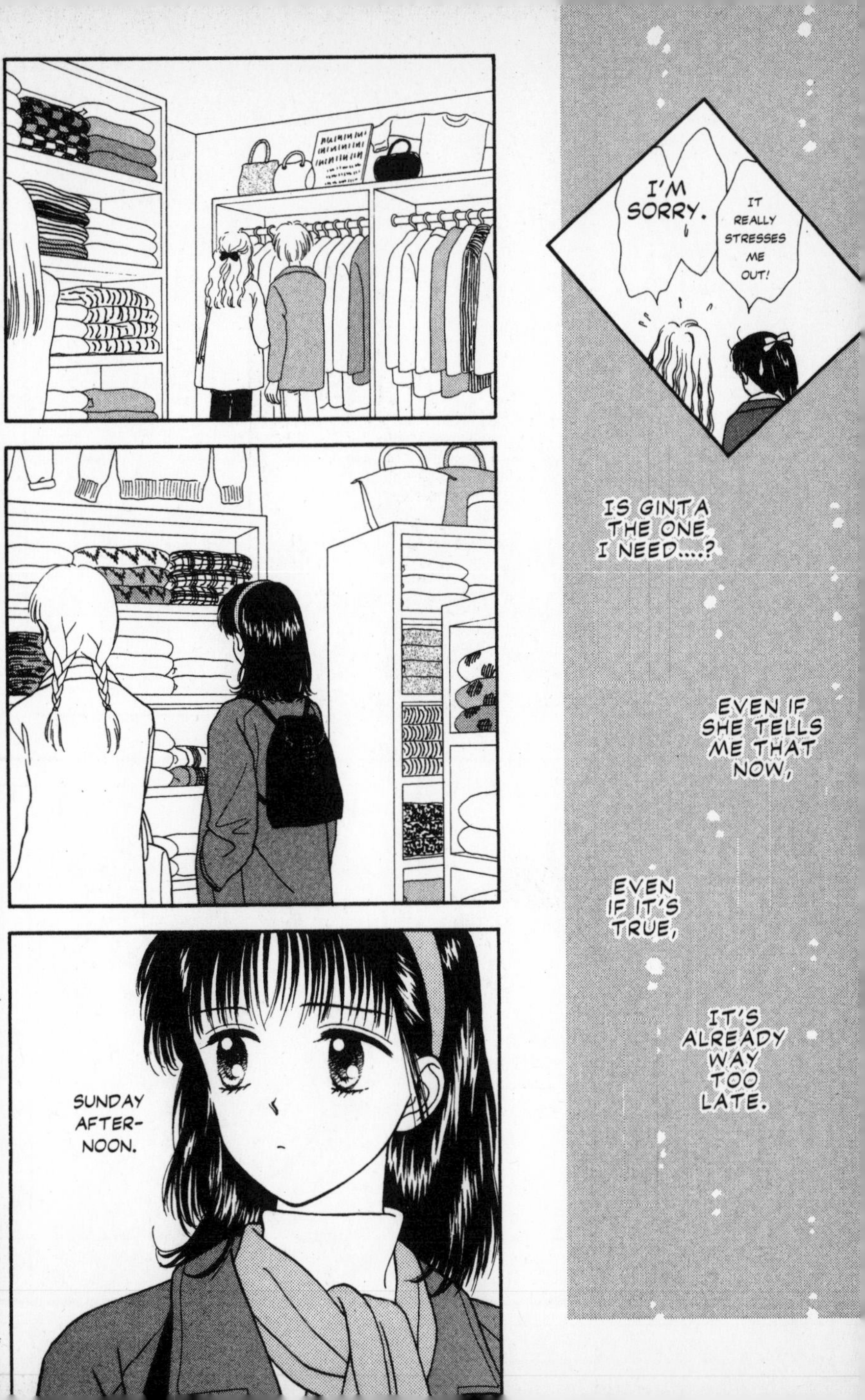
I'M SORRY.
IT REALLY STRESSES ME OUT!
IS GINTA THE ONE I NEED....?
EVEN IF SHE TELLS ME THAT NOW,
EVEN IF IT'S TRUE,
IT'S ALREADY WAY TOO LATE.
SUNDAY AFTER-NOON.

FREE TALK ③

Recently, my friends have been inviting me to see plays done by a theater group called Caramel Box here in Japan. They are simple plays that are really funny and easy to understand. They are full of jokes and always end up with a happy ending. The only problem is that some of the plays have a few flaws in the script. Some scenes aren't very believable, and the character development leaves something to be desired. But I did enjoy the acting and I think they're a great troupe. I definitely want to go see their next performance. I especially liked Uekawa Tatsuya, an actor in "When it Becomes April, She Will." He's so good, isn't he?

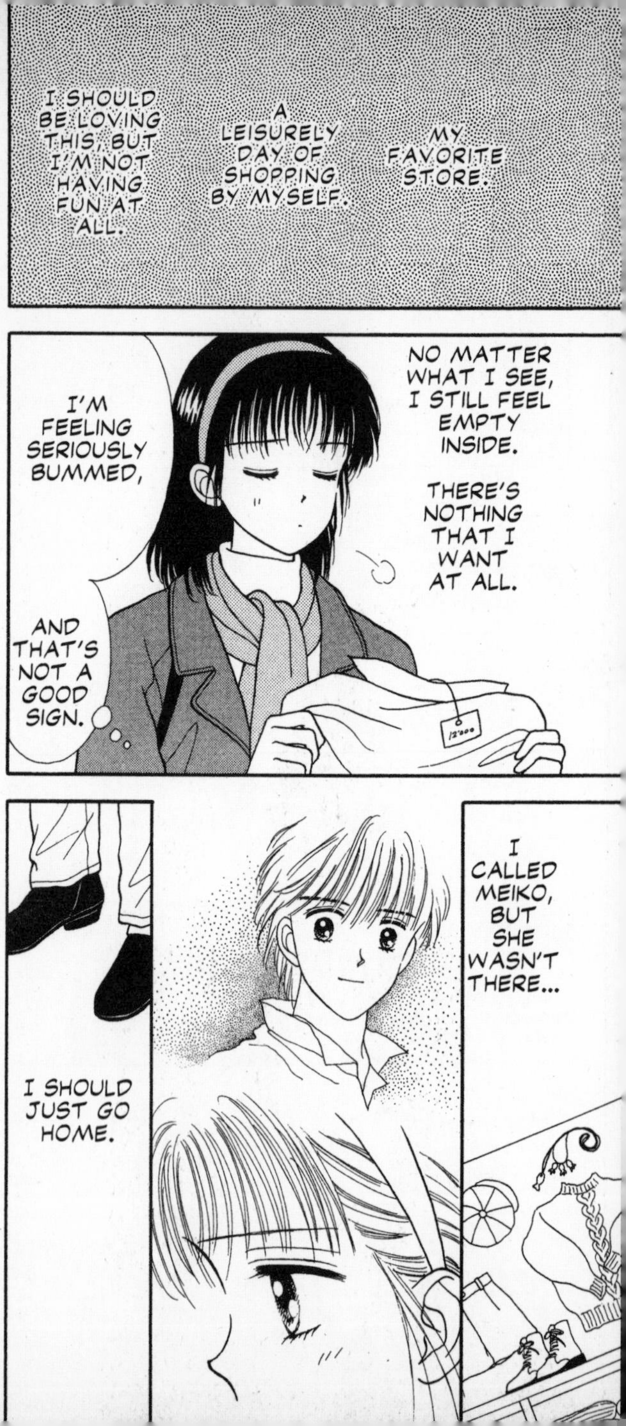
MY FAVORITE STORE.
A LEISURELY DAY OF SHOPPING BY MYSELF.
I SHOULD BE LOVING THIS, BUT I'M NOT HAVING FUN AT ALL.
NO MATTER WHAT I SEE, I STILL FEEL EMPTY INSIDE.
THERE'S NOTHING THAT I WANT AT ALL.
I'M FEELING SERIOUSLY BUMMED,
AND THAT'S NOT A GOOD SIGN.
I CALLED MEIKO, BUT SHE WASN'T THERE...
I SHOULD JUST GO HOME.

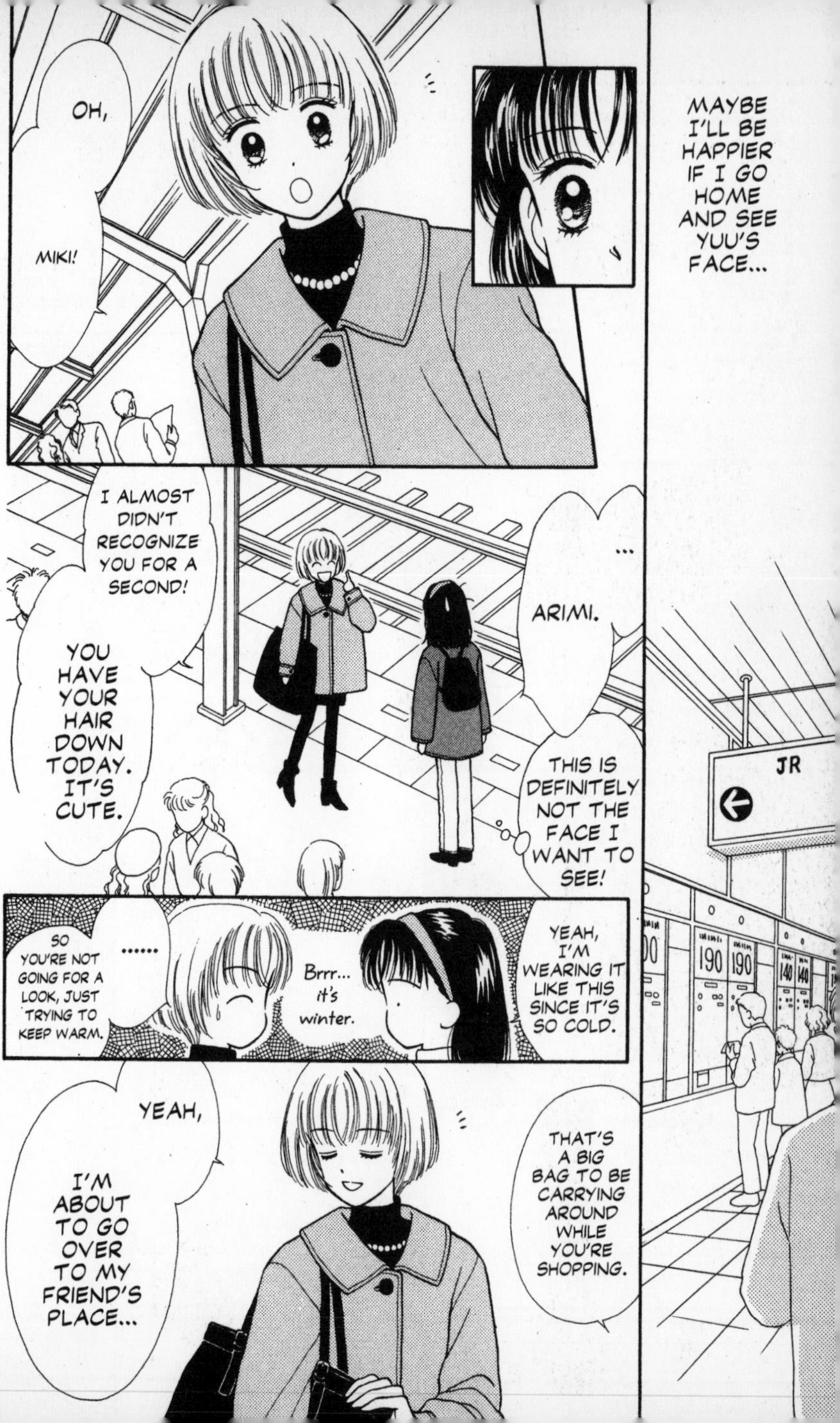
MAYBE I'LL BE HAPPIER IF I GO HOME AND SEE YUU'S FACE...
JR
190
190
140
140
OH,
MIKI!
...
ARIMI.
THIS IS DEFINITELY NOT THE FACE I WANT TO SEE!
I ALMOST DIDN'T RECOGNIZE YOU FOR A SECOND!
YOU HAVE YOUR HAIR DOWN TODAY. IT'S CUTE.
YEAH, I'M WEARING IT LIKE THIS SINCE IT'S SO COLD.
Brrr... it's winter.
......
SO YOU'RE NOT GOING FOR A LOOK, JUST TRYING TO KEEP WARM.
THAT'S A BIG BAG TO BE CARRYING AROUND WHILE YOU'RE SHOPPING.
YEAH,
I'M ABOUT TO GO OVER TO MY FRIEND'S PLACE...

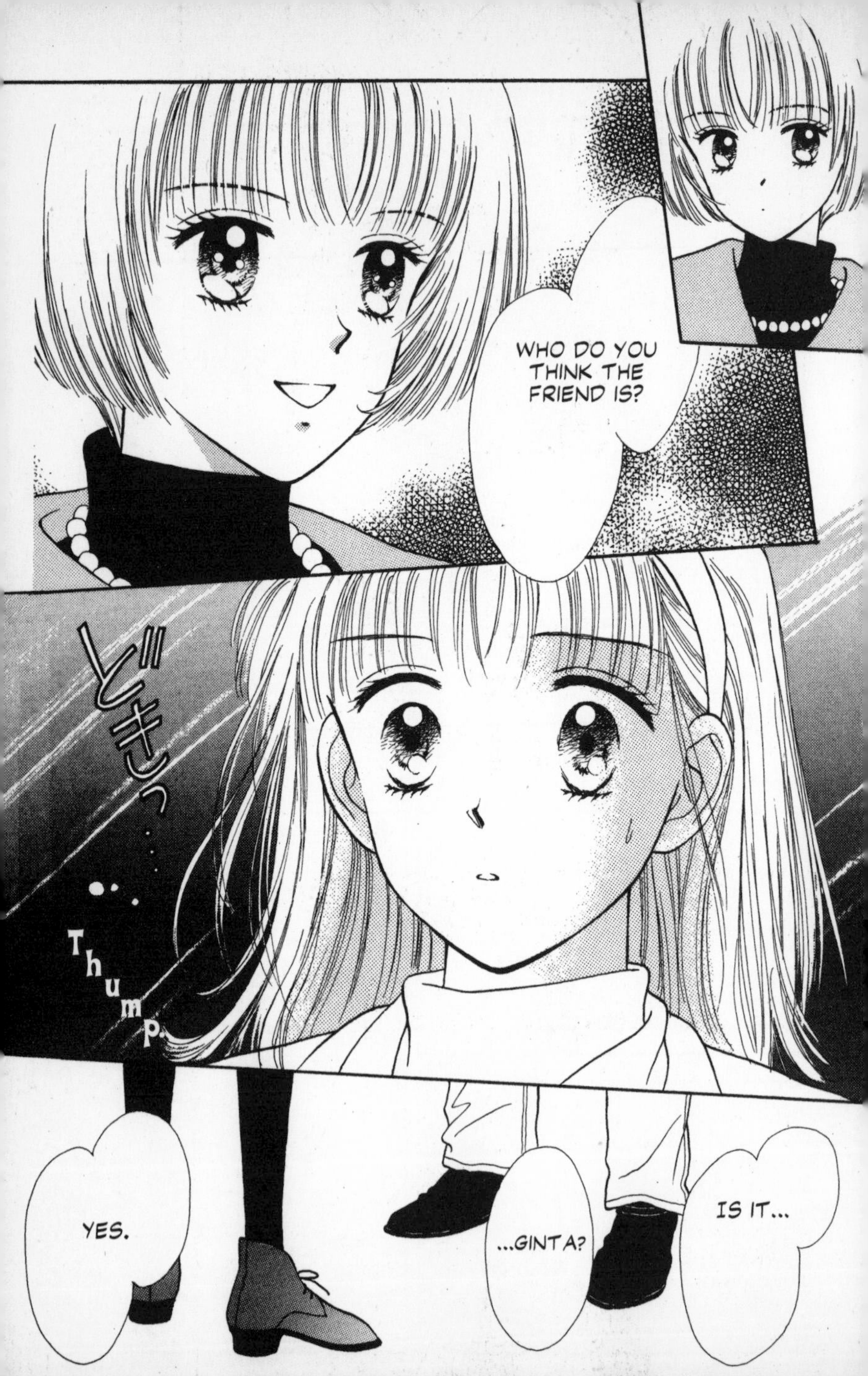
WHO DO YOU THINK THE FRIEND IS?
どきっ…
Thump.
IS IT...
...GINTA?
YES.

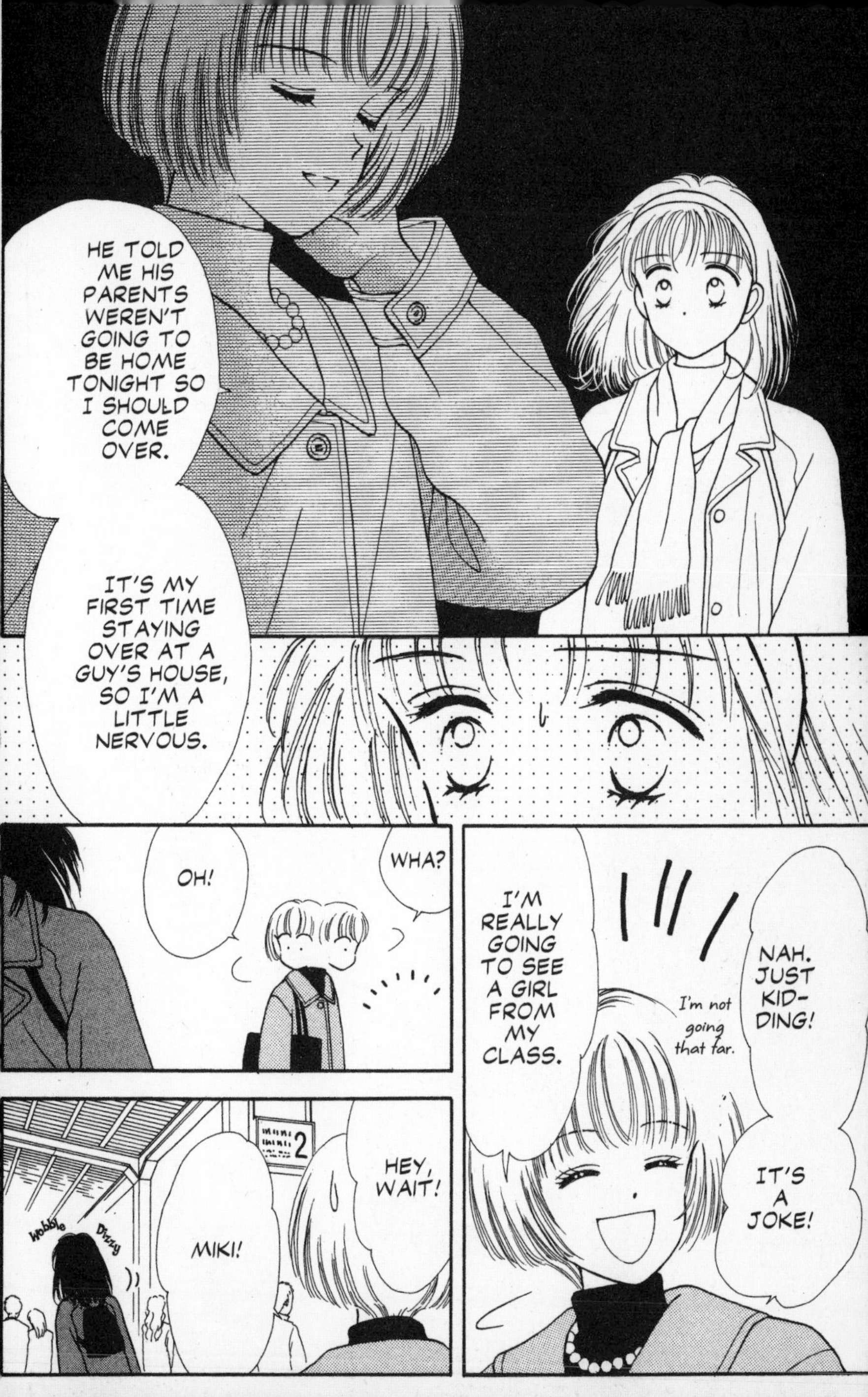
HE TOLD ME HIS PARENTS WEREN'T GOING TO BE HOME TONIGHT SO I SHOULD COME OVER.
IT'S MY FIRST TIME STAYING OVER AT A GUY'S HOUSE, SO I'M A LITTLE NERVOUS.
NAH. JUST KID-DING!
I'm not going that far.
IT'S A JOKE!
I'M REALLY GOING TO SEE A GIRL FROM MY CLASS.
WHA?
OH!
HEY, WAIT!
MIKI!
Dizzy
Wobble

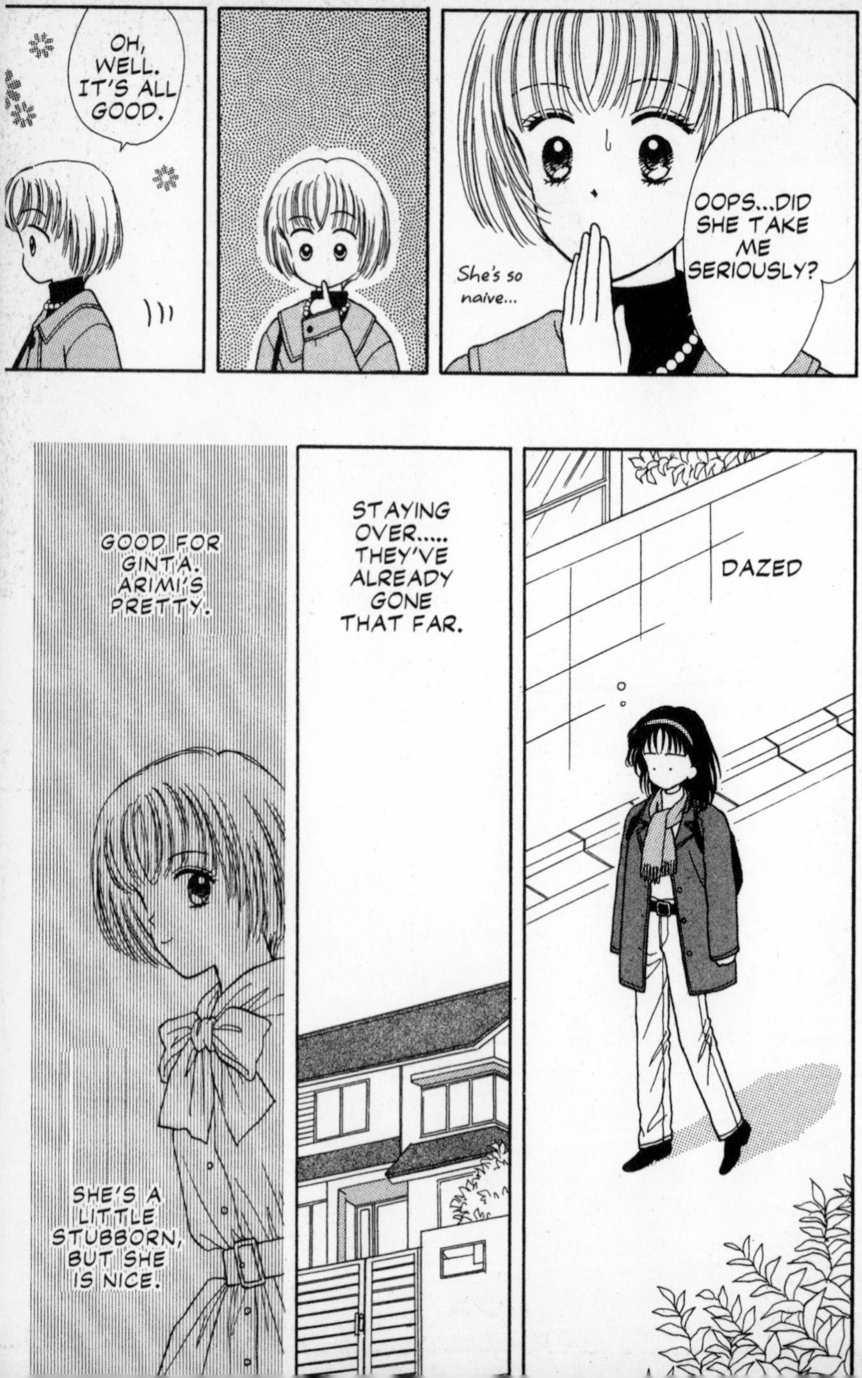
OOPS...DID SHE TAKE ME SERIOUSLY?
She's so naive...
OH, WELL. IT'S ALL GOOD.
DAZED
STAYING OVER..... THEY'VE ALREADY GONE THAT FAR.
GOOD FOR GINTA. ARIMI'S PRETTY.
SHE'S A LITTLE STUBBORN, BUT SHE IS NICE.

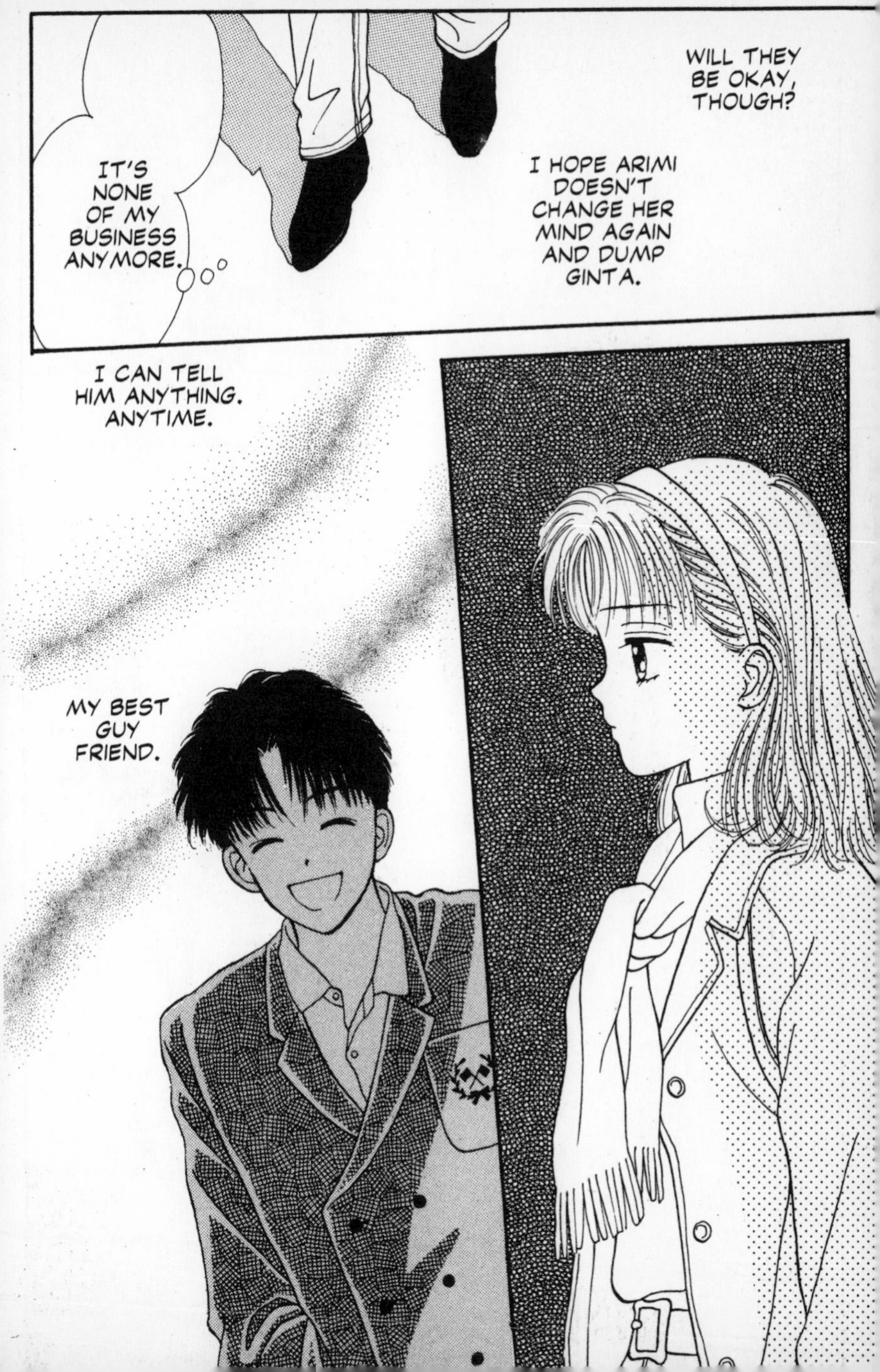
WILL THEY BE OKAY, THOUGH?
I HOPE ARIMI DOESN'T CHANGE HER MIND AGAIN AND DUMP GINTA.
IT'S NONE OF MY BUSINESS ANYMORE.
I CAN TELL HIM ANYTHING. ANYTIME.
MY BEST GUY FRIEND.

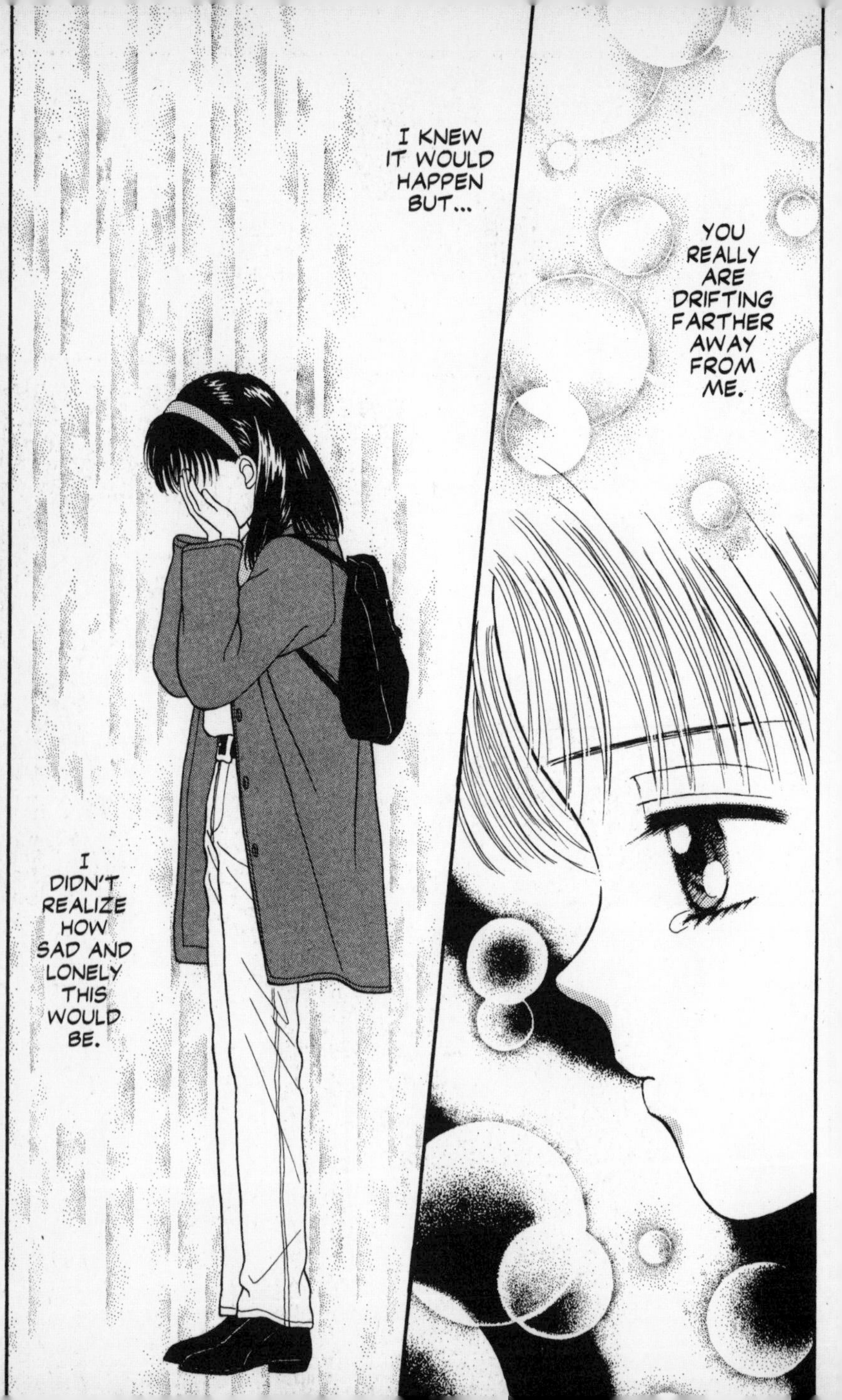
YOU REALLY ARE DRIFTING FARTHER AWAY FROM ME.
I KNEW IT WOULD HAPPEN BUT...
I DIDN'T REALIZE HOW SAD AND LONELY THIS WOULD BE.

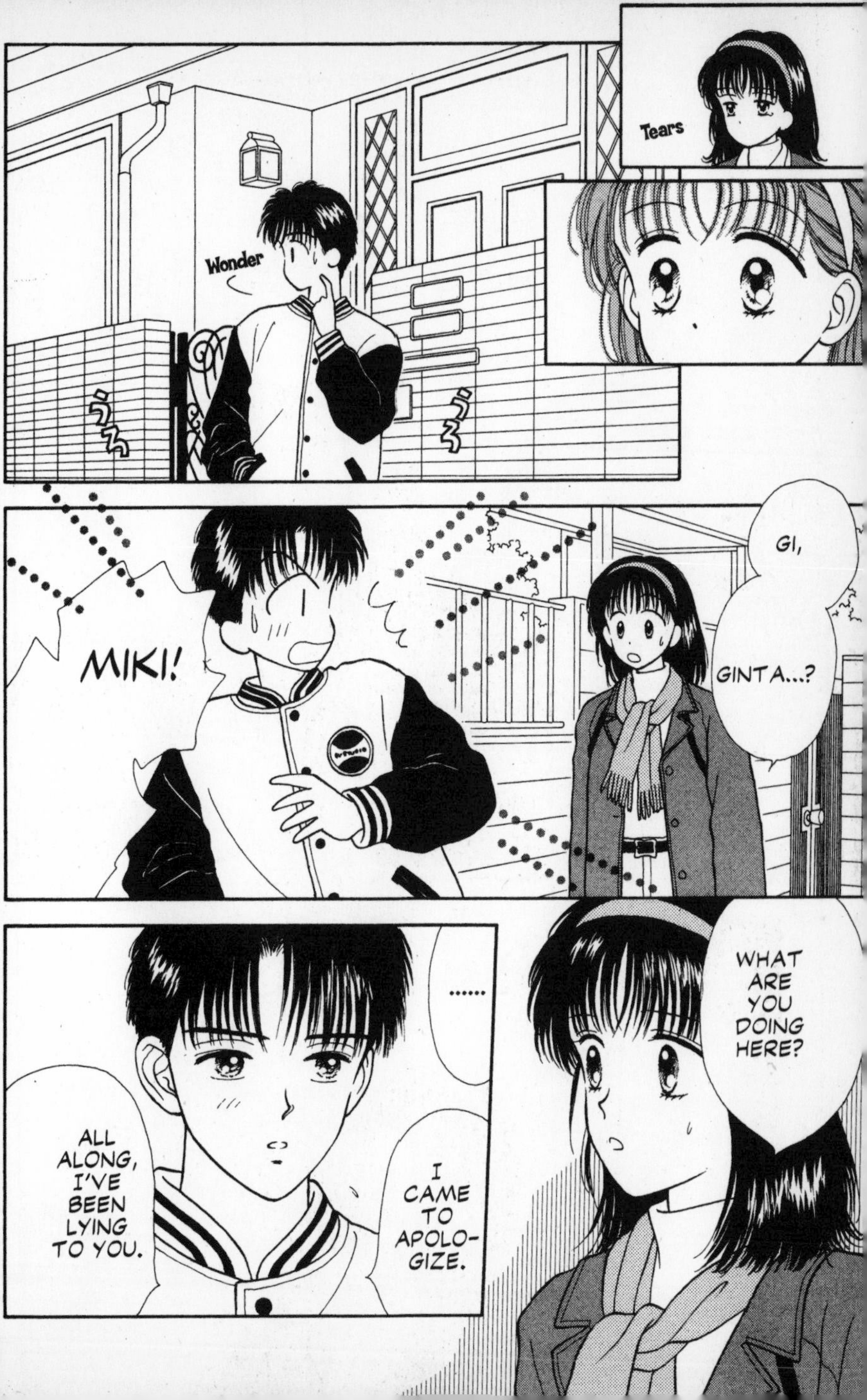
Tears
Wonder
うろ
うろ
GI,
GINTA...?
MIKI!
WHAT ARE YOU DOING HERE?
......
I CAME TO APOLO-GIZE.
ALL ALONG, I'VE BEEN LYING TO YOU.

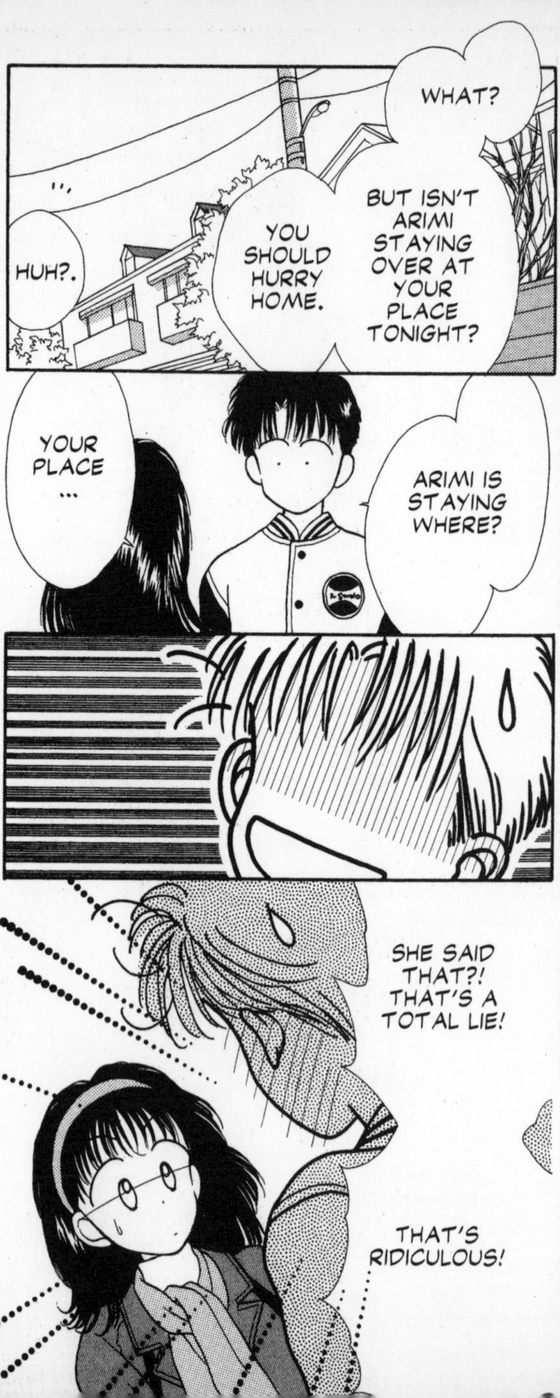
WHAT?
BUT ISN'T ARIMI STAYING OVER AT YOUR PLACE TONIGHT?
YOU SHOULD HURRY HOME.
...
HUH?.
ARIMI IS STAYING WHERE?
YOUR PLACE ...
SHE SAID THAT?! THAT'S A TOTAL LIE!
THAT'S RIDICULOUS!

Ginta Suou

HOROSCOPE: ARIES

BLOODTYPE: O

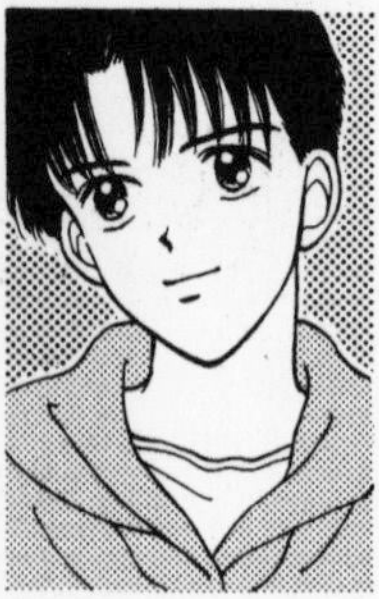

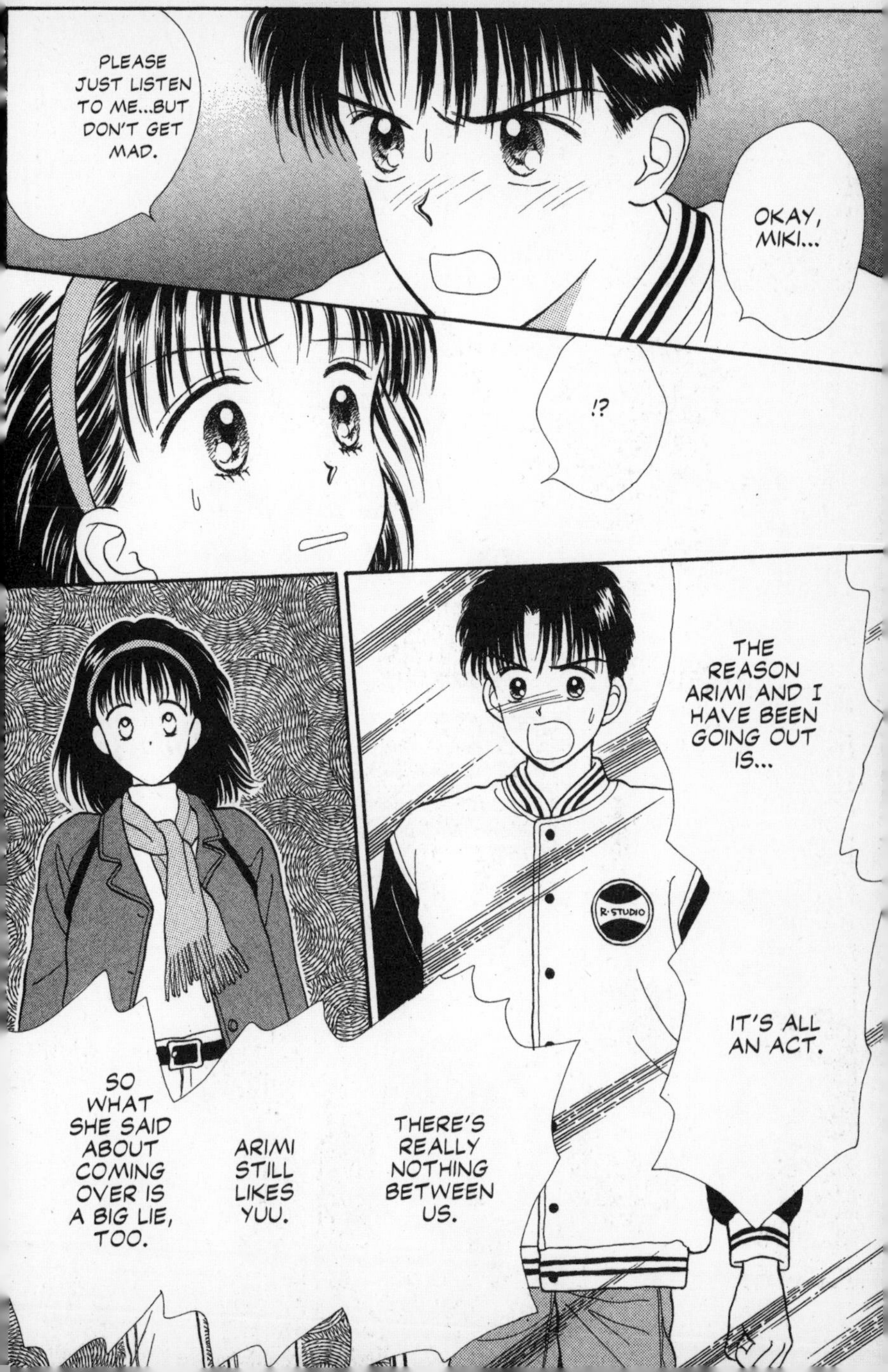
OKAY, MIKI...
PLEASE JUST LISTEN TO ME...BUT DON'T GET MAD.
!?
THE REASON ARIMI AND I HAVE BEEN GOING OUT IS...
IT'S ALL AN ACT.
THERE'S REALLY NOTHING BETWEEN US.
ARIMI STILL LIKES YUU.
SO WHAT SHE SAID ABOUT COMING OVER IS A BIG LIE, TOO.
R·STUDIO

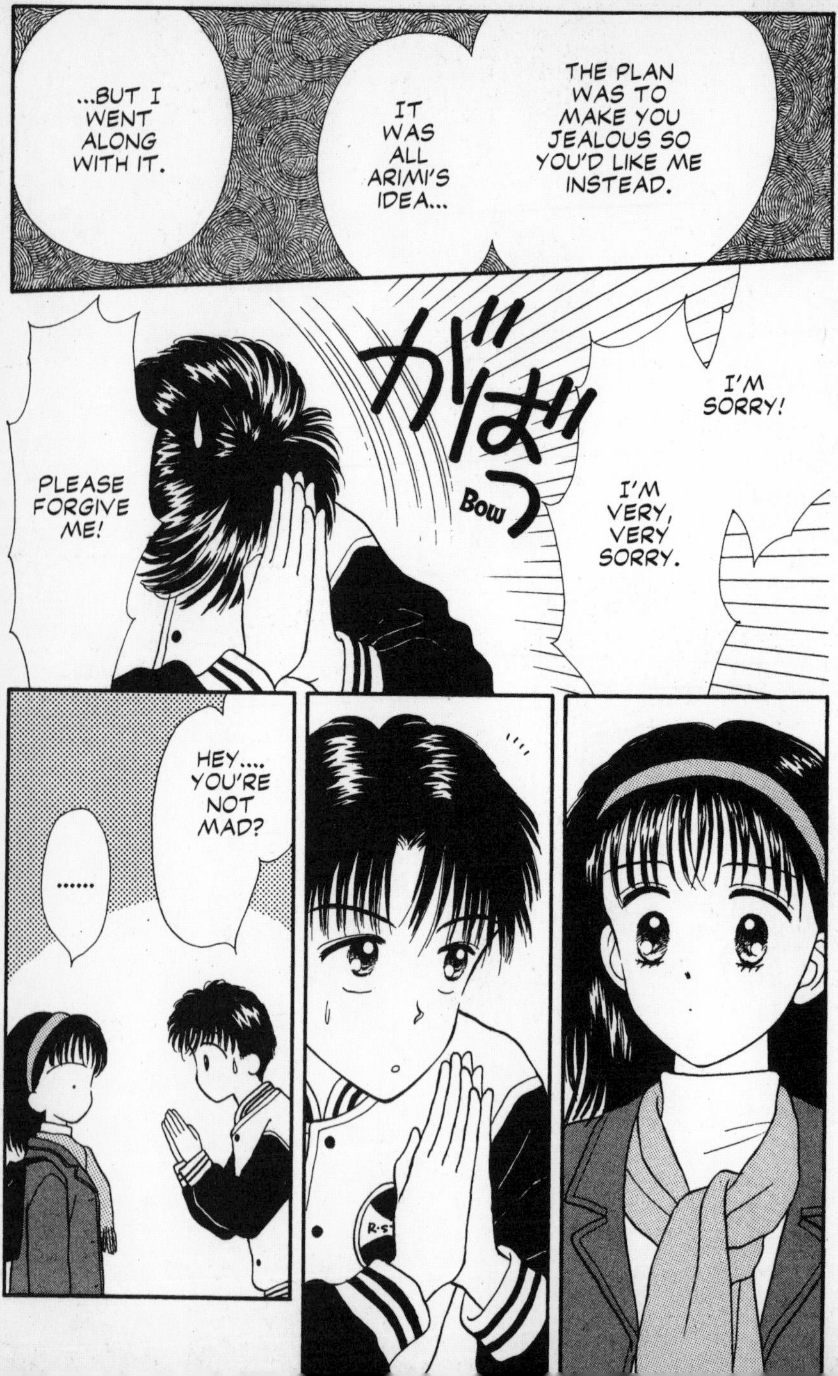
THE PLAN WAS TO MAKE YOU JEALOUS SO YOU'D LIKE ME INSTEAD.
IT WAS ALL ARIMI'S IDEA...
...BUT I WENT ALONG WITH IT.
がばっ
BOW
I'M SORRY!
I'M VERY, VERY SORRY.
PLEASE FORGIVE ME!
HEY.... YOU'RE NOT MAD?
......

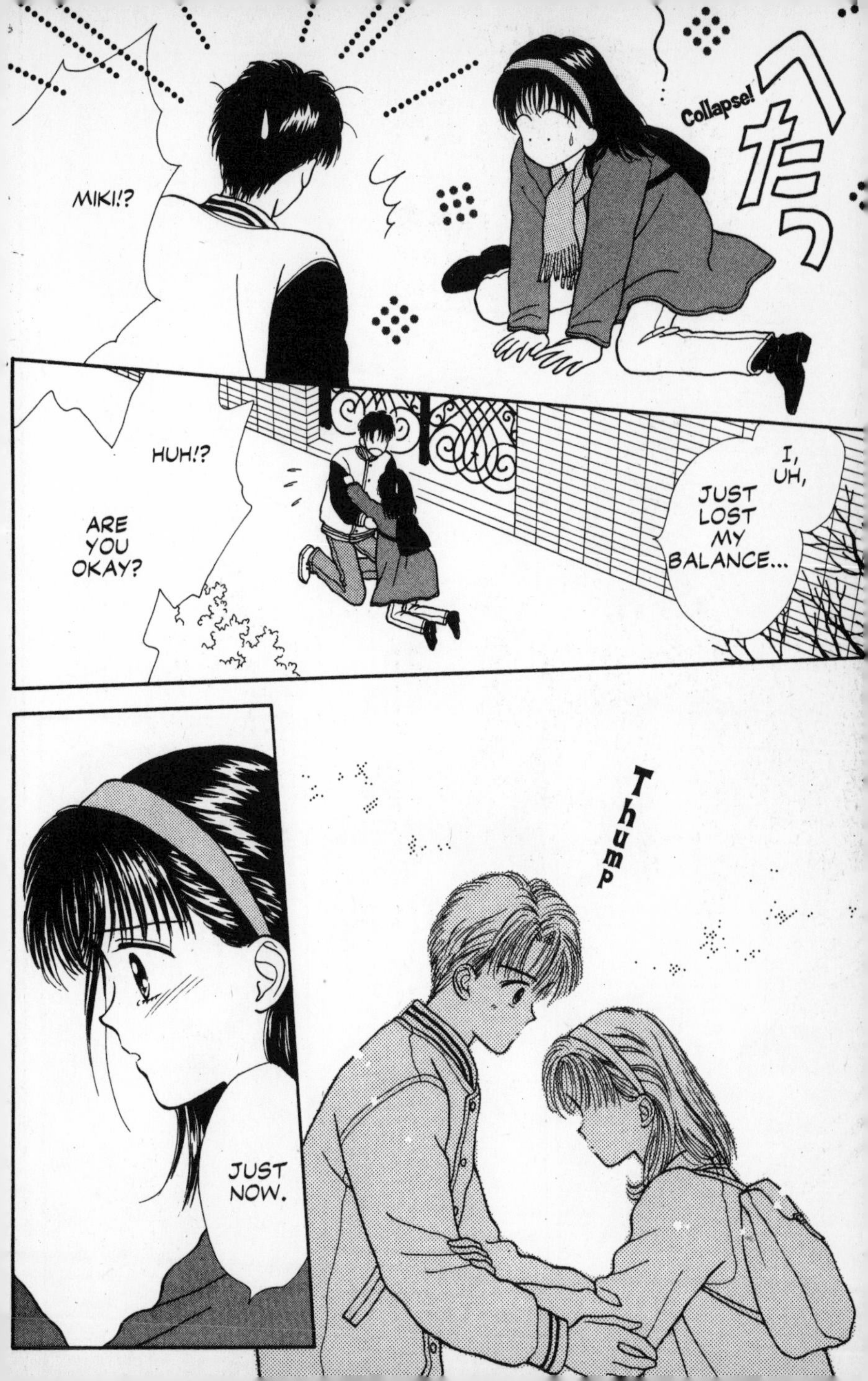
Collapse!
へたっ
MIKI!?
I, UH, JUST LOST MY BALANCE...
HUH!?
ARE YOU OKAY?
Thump
JUST NOW.

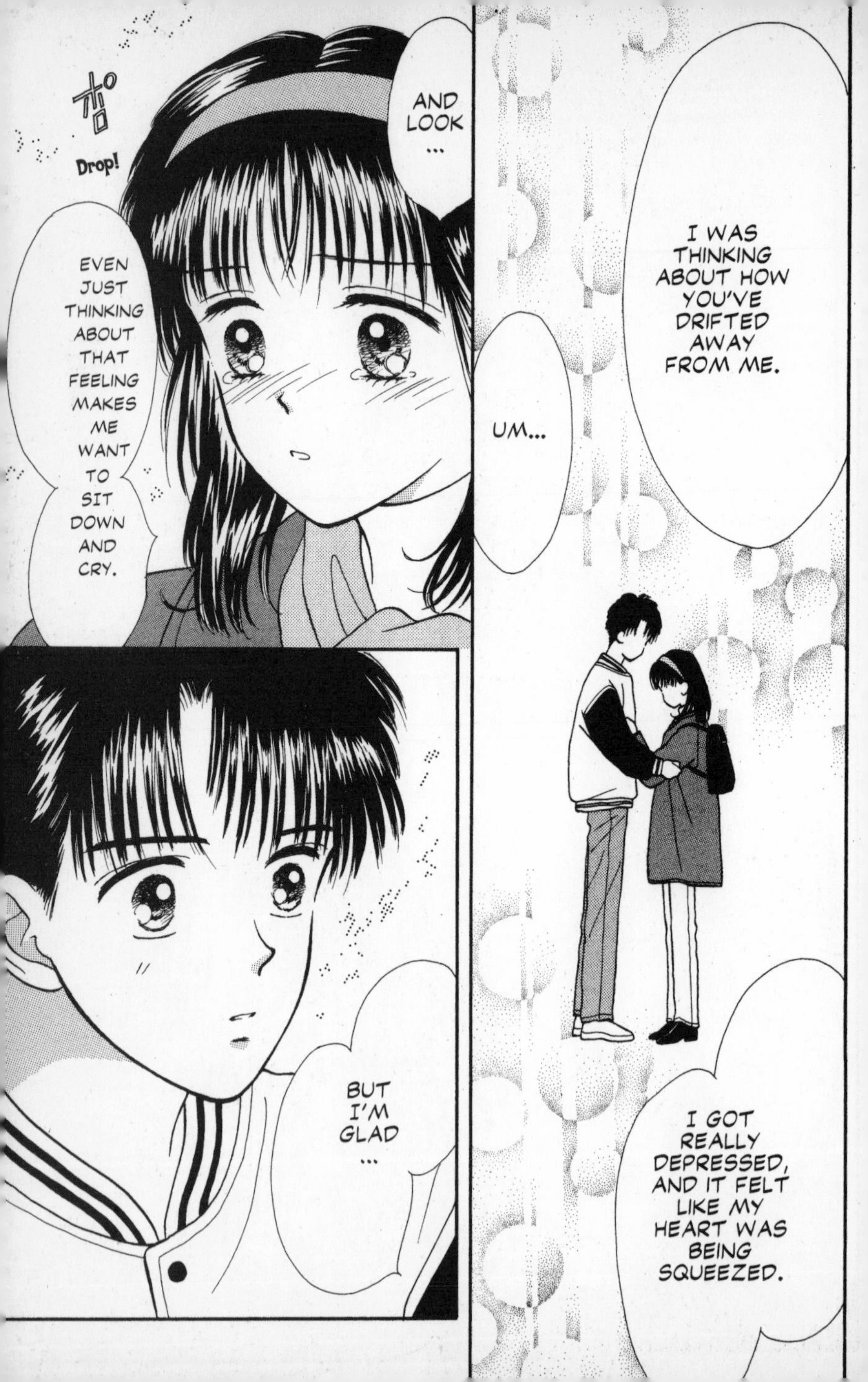
I WAS THINKING ABOUT HOW YOU'VE DRIFTED AWAY FROM ME.
UM...
I GOT REALLY DEPRESSED, AND IT FELT LIKE MY HEART WAS BEING SQUEEZED.
AND LOOK ...
ポロ
Drop!
EVEN JUST THINKING ABOUT THAT FEELING MAKES ME WANT TO SIT DOWN AND CRY.
BUT I'M GLAD ...

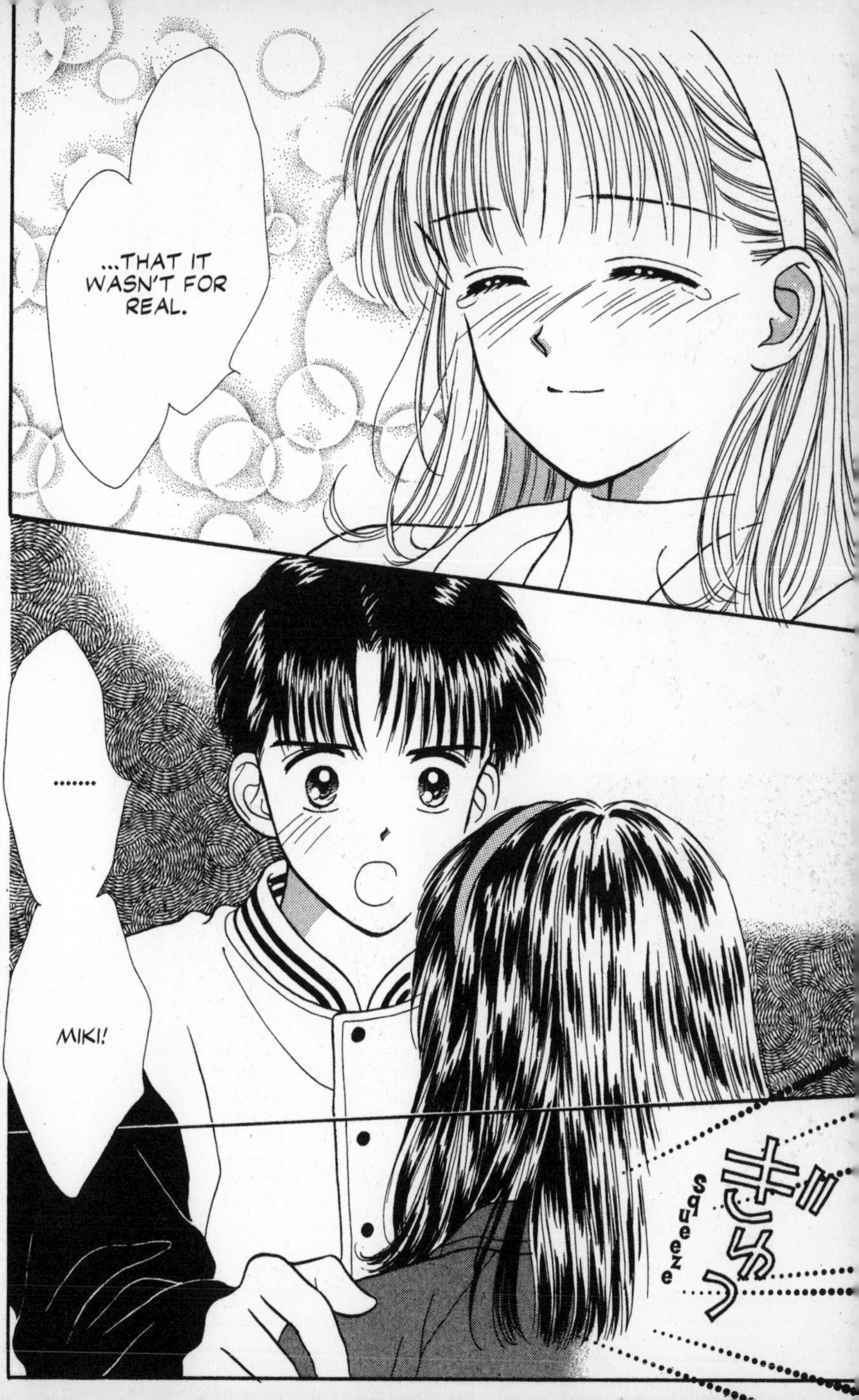
...THAT IT WASN'T FOR REAL.
....
MIKI!
ぎゅっ
squeeze

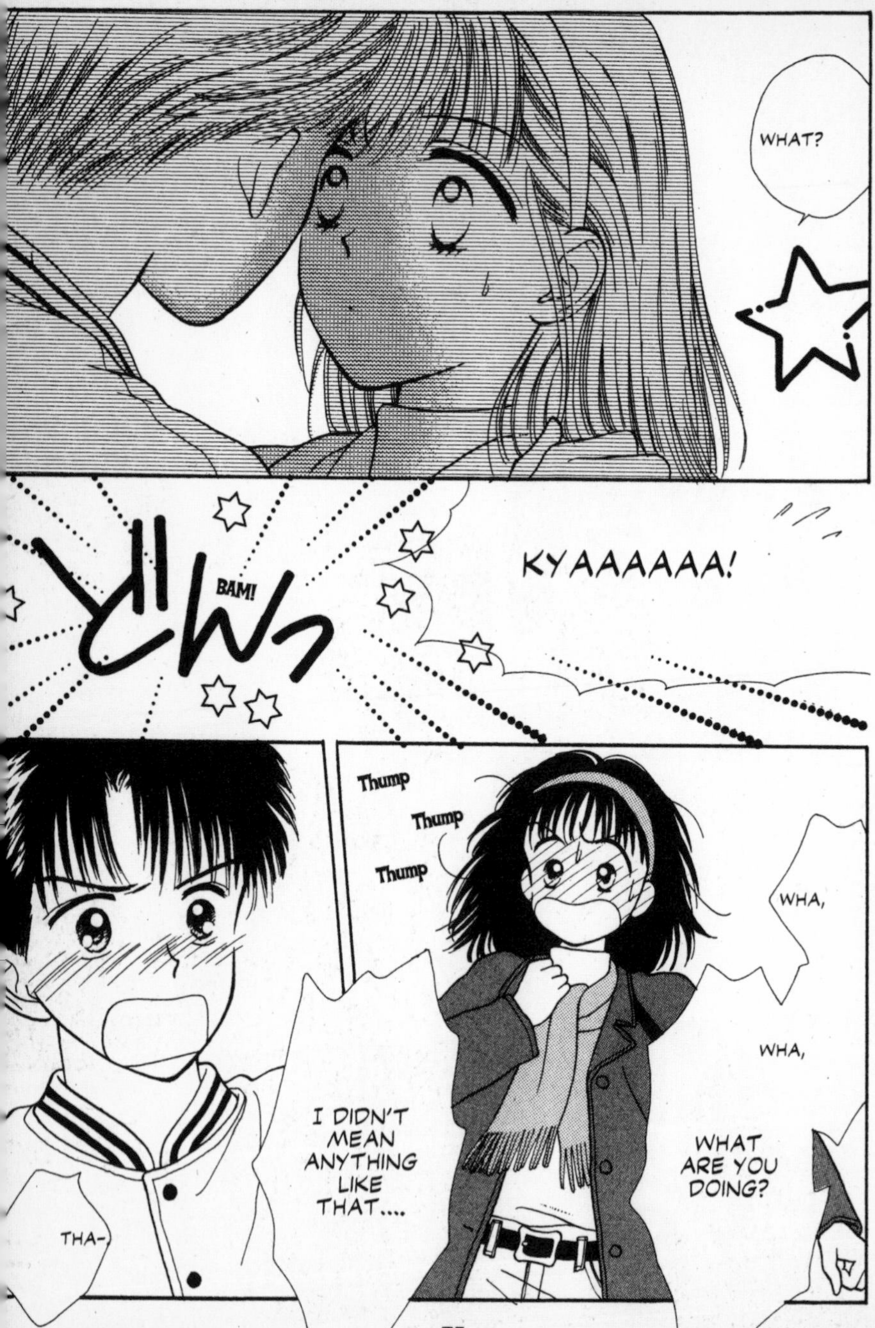
WHAT?
KYAAAAAA!
BAM!
どんっ
Thump
Thump
Thump
WHA,
WHA,
WHAT ARE YOU DOING?
THA-
I DIDN'T MEAN ANYTHING LIKE THAT....

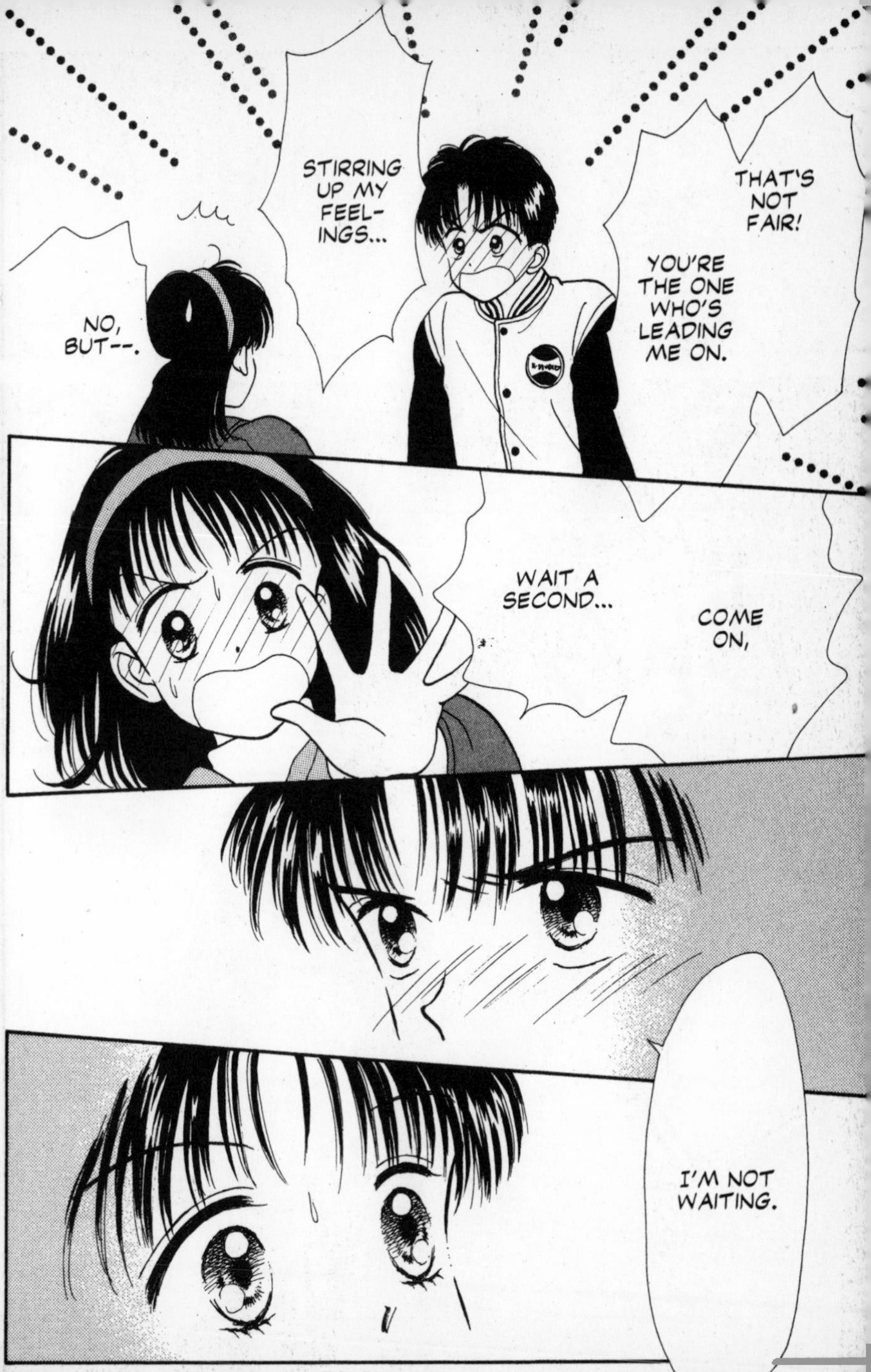
THAT'S NOT FAIR!
YOU'RE THE ONE WHO'S LEADING ME ON.
STIRRING UP MY FEELINGS...
NO, BUT--.
COME ON,
WAIT A SECOND...
I'M NOT WAITING.

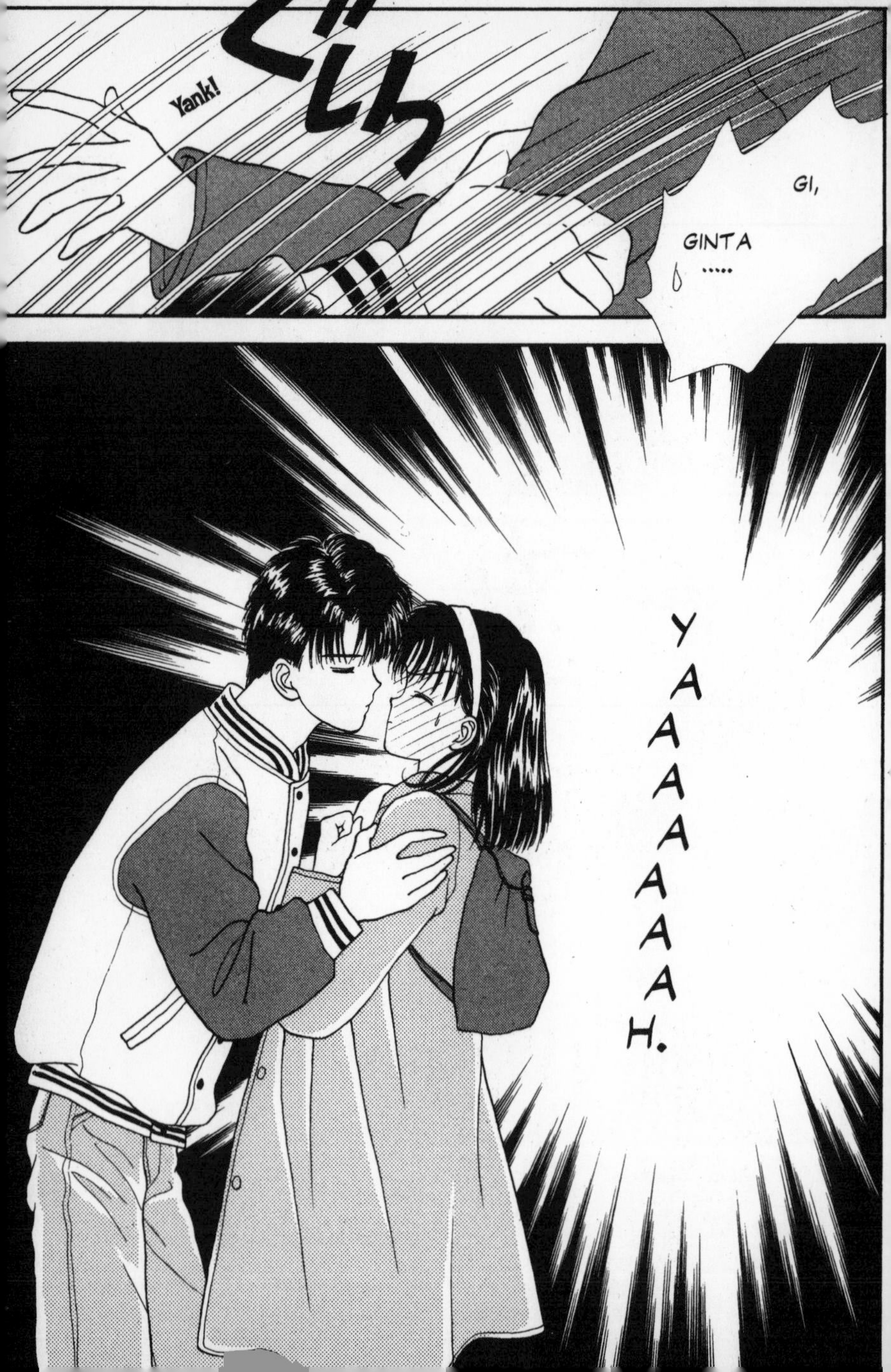
Yank!
GI,
GINTA
......
YAAAAAAAH.

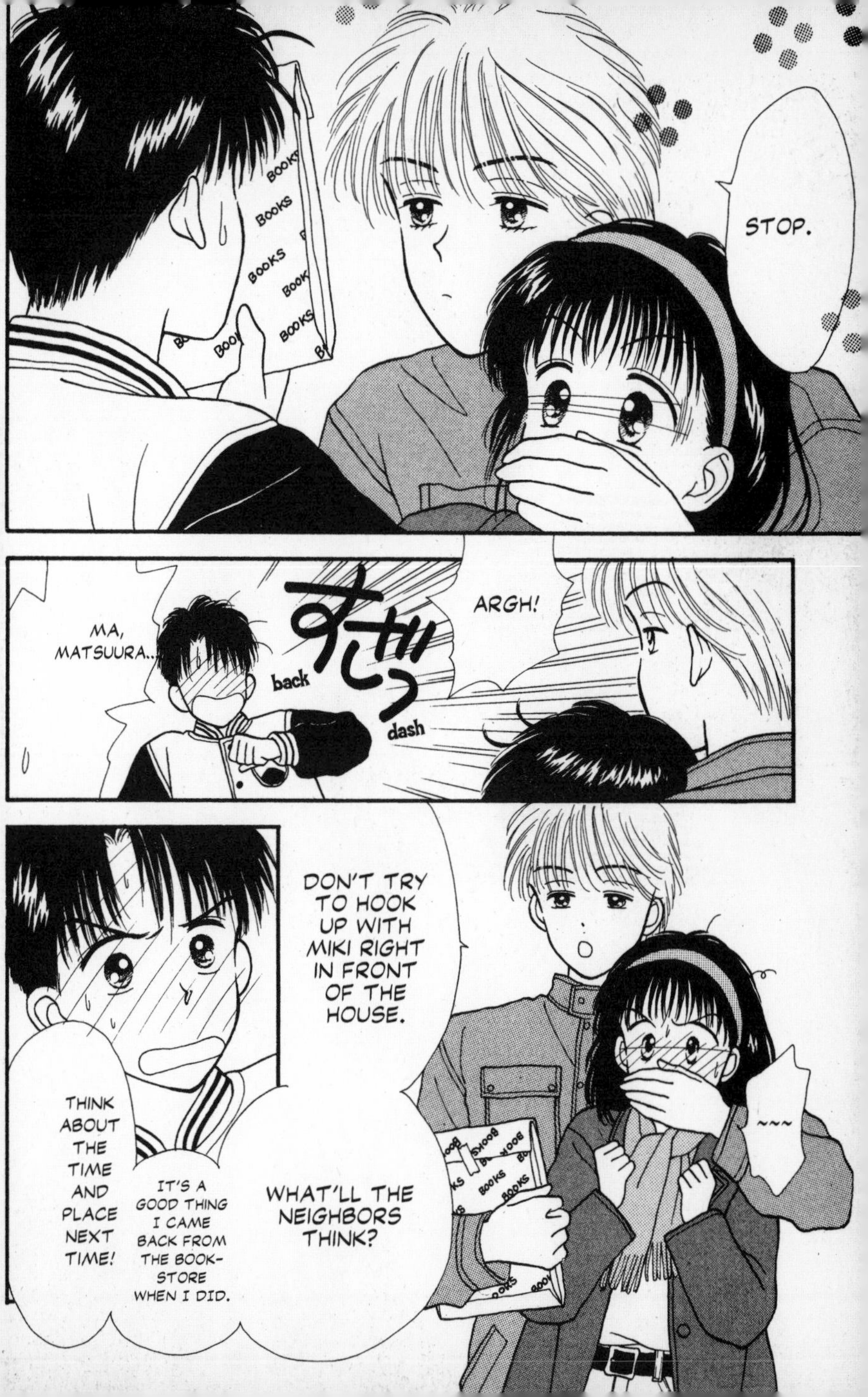
STOP.
ARGH!
back
dash
MA, MATSUURA...
~~~
DON'T TRY TO HOOK UP WITH MIKI RIGHT IN FRONT OF THE HOUSE.
WHAT'LL THE NEIGHBORS THINK?
IT'S A GOOD THING I CAME BACK FROM THE BOOK-STORE WHEN I DID.
THINK ABOUT THE TIME AND PLACE NEXT TIME!
~~~

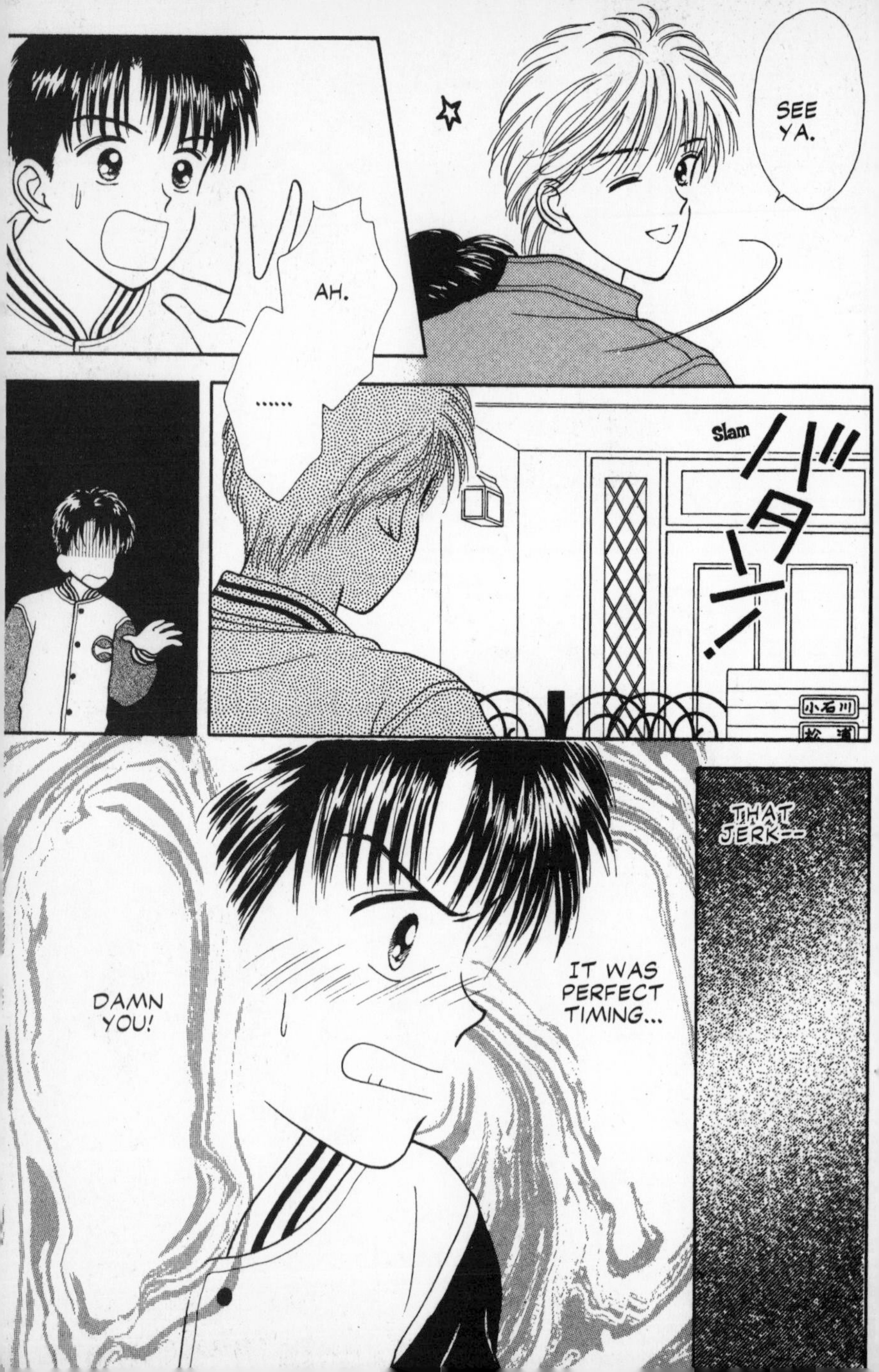

SEE YA.
AH.
Slam
バタン!
......
小石川
松浦
THAT JERK--
IT WAS PERFECT TIMING...
DAMN YOU!

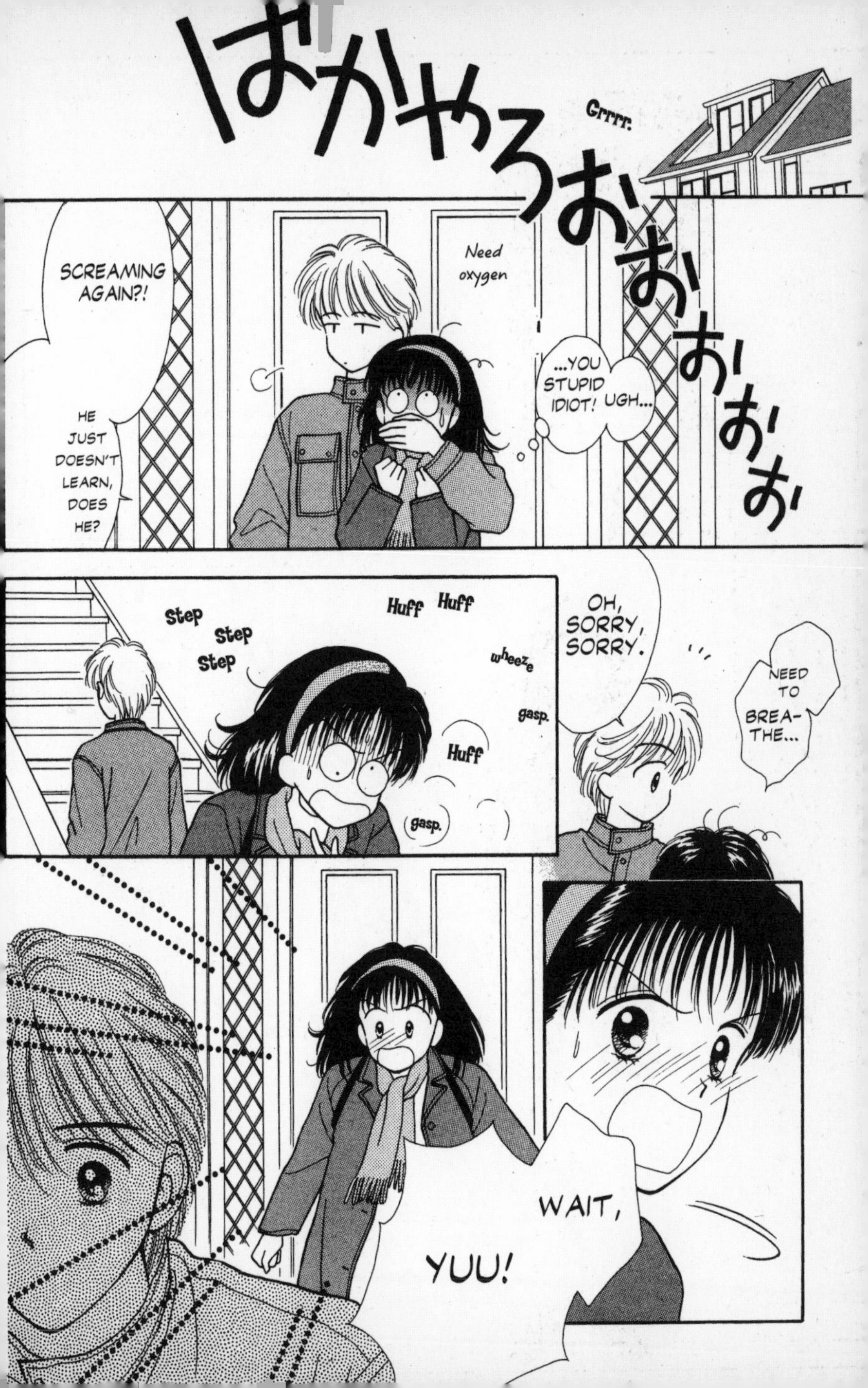
ばかやろおおおおお
Grrrr.
...YOU STUPID IDIOT! UGH...
Need oxygen
SCREAMING AGAIN?!
HE JUST DOESN'T LEARN, DOES HE?
NEED TO BREA-THE...
OH, SORRY, SORRY.
Huff Huff
wheeze
gasp.
Huff
gasp.
Step
Step
Step
WAIT, YUU!

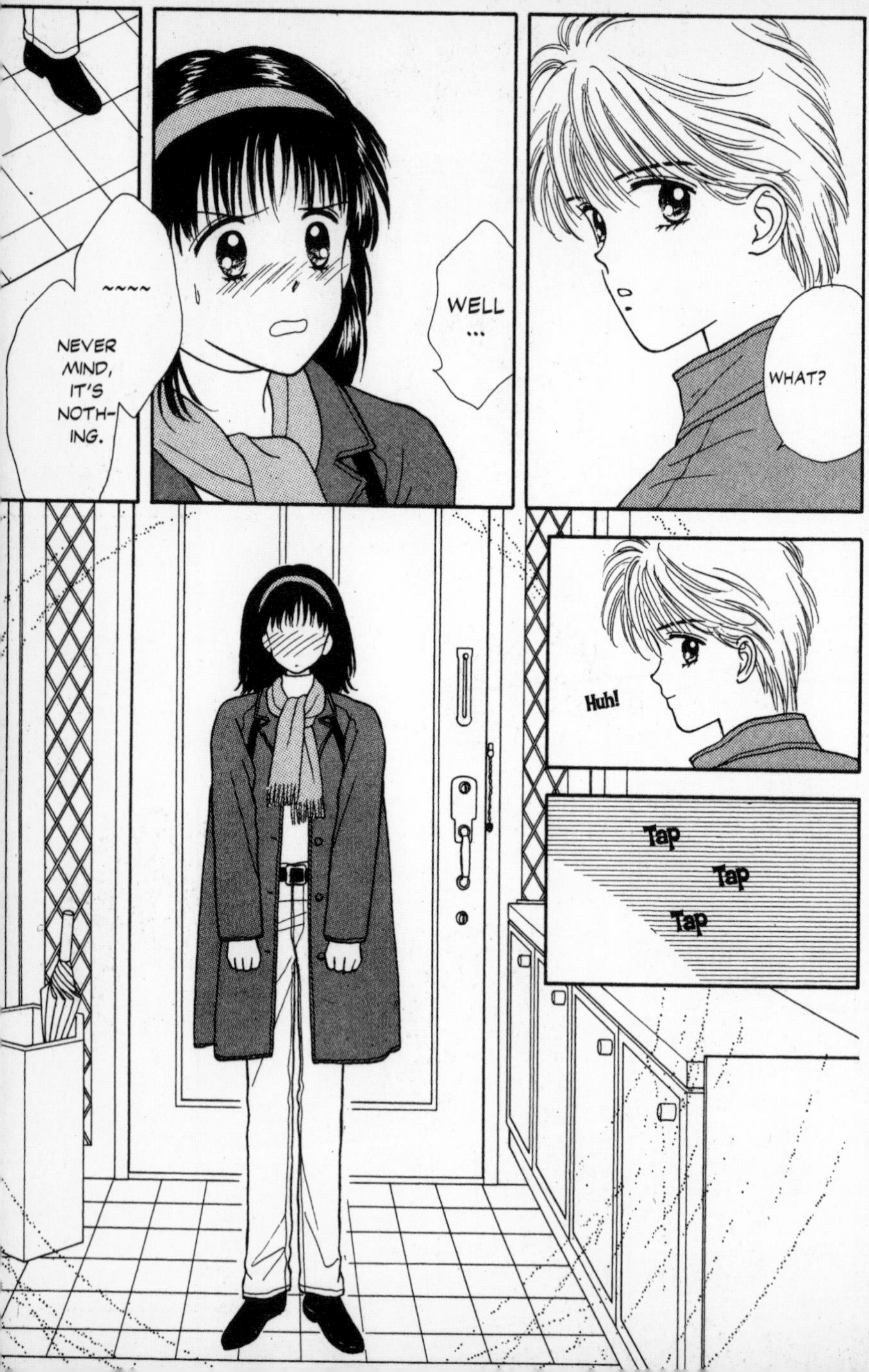
WHAT?
WELL ...
~~~~
NEVER MIND, IT'S NOTHING.
Huh!
Tap Tap Tap
~~~~

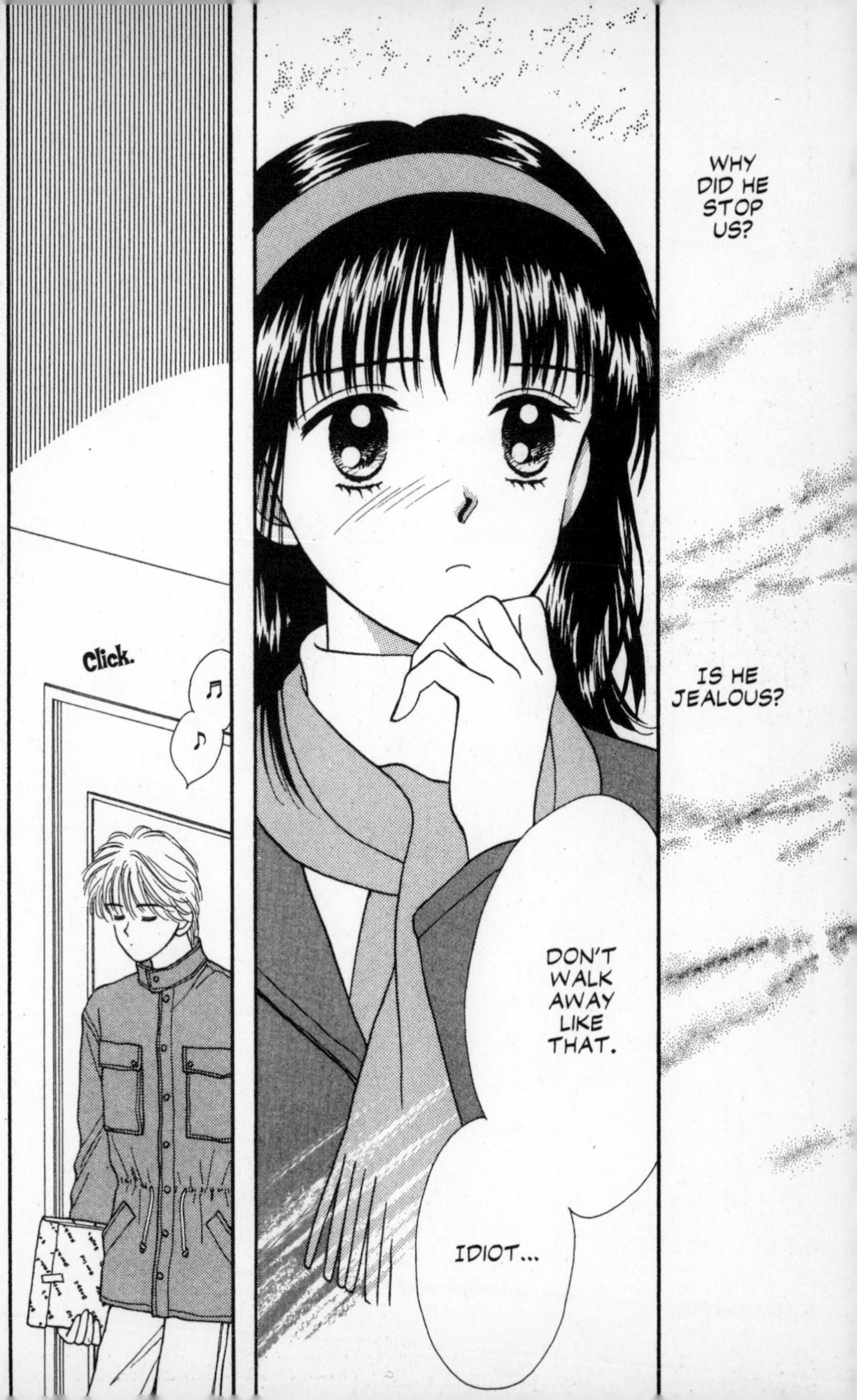
WHY DID HE STOP US?
IS HE JEALOUS?
DON'T WALK AWAY LIKE THAT.
IDIOT...
Click.
♫ ♪

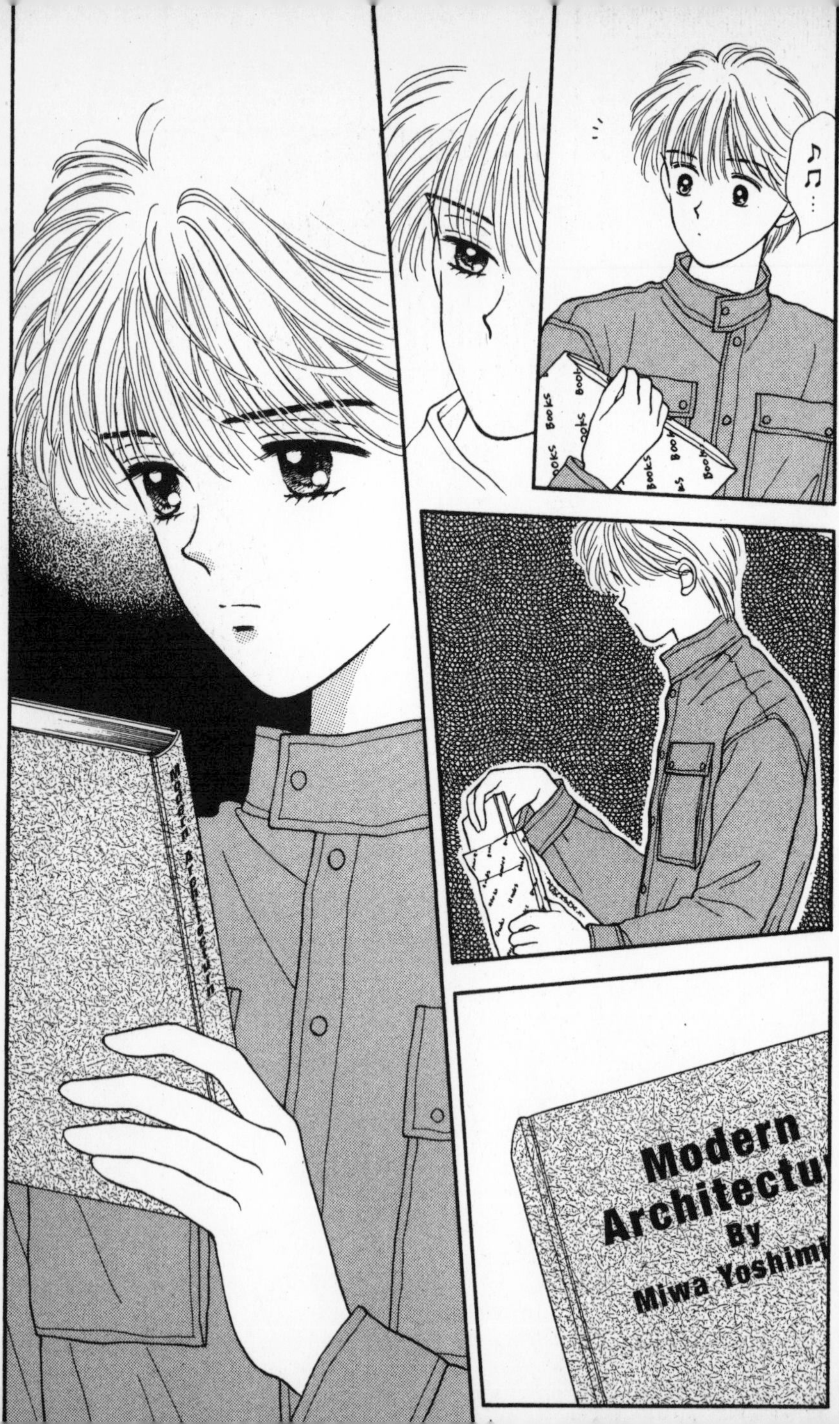

♪♫…
BOOKS
Modern
Architectu
By
Miwa Yoshimi

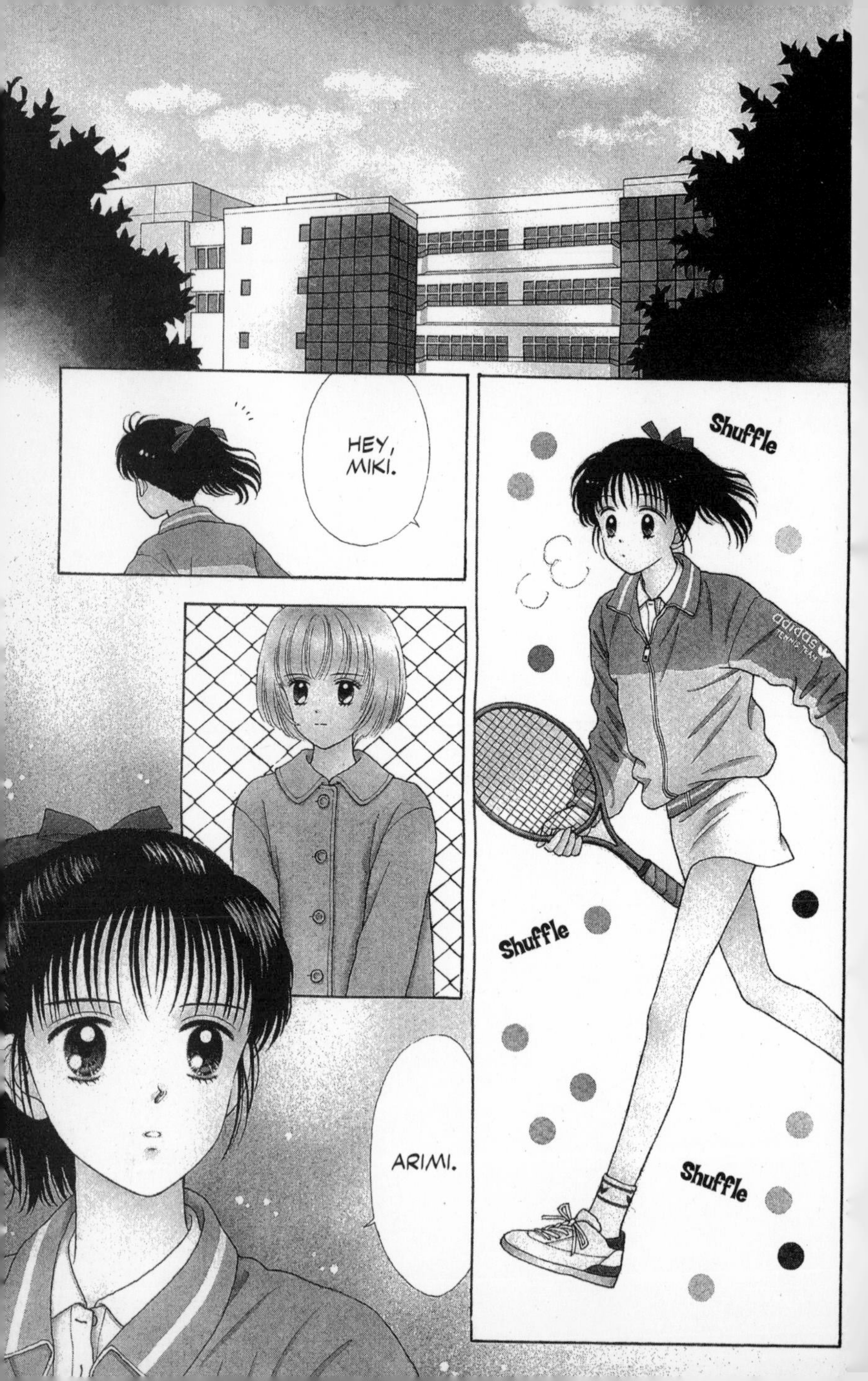
Shuffle
Shuffle
Shuffle
HEY, MIKI.
ARIMI.

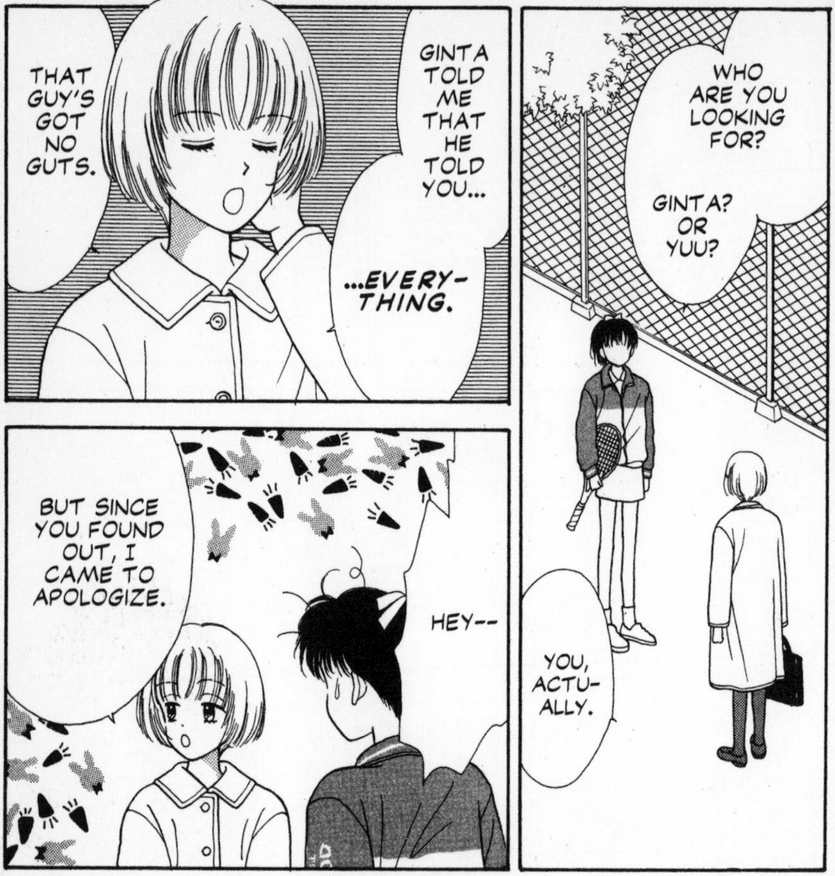
WHO ARE YOU LOOKING FOR?
GINTA? OR YUU?
YOU, ACTUALLY.
GINTA TOLD ME THAT HE TOLD YOU...
...EVERYTHING.
THAT GUY'S GOT NO GUTS.
HEY--
BUT SINCE YOU FOUND OUT, I CAME TO APOLOGIZE.

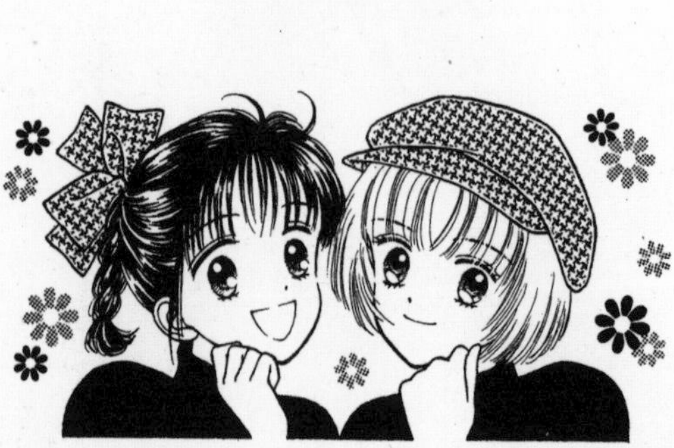

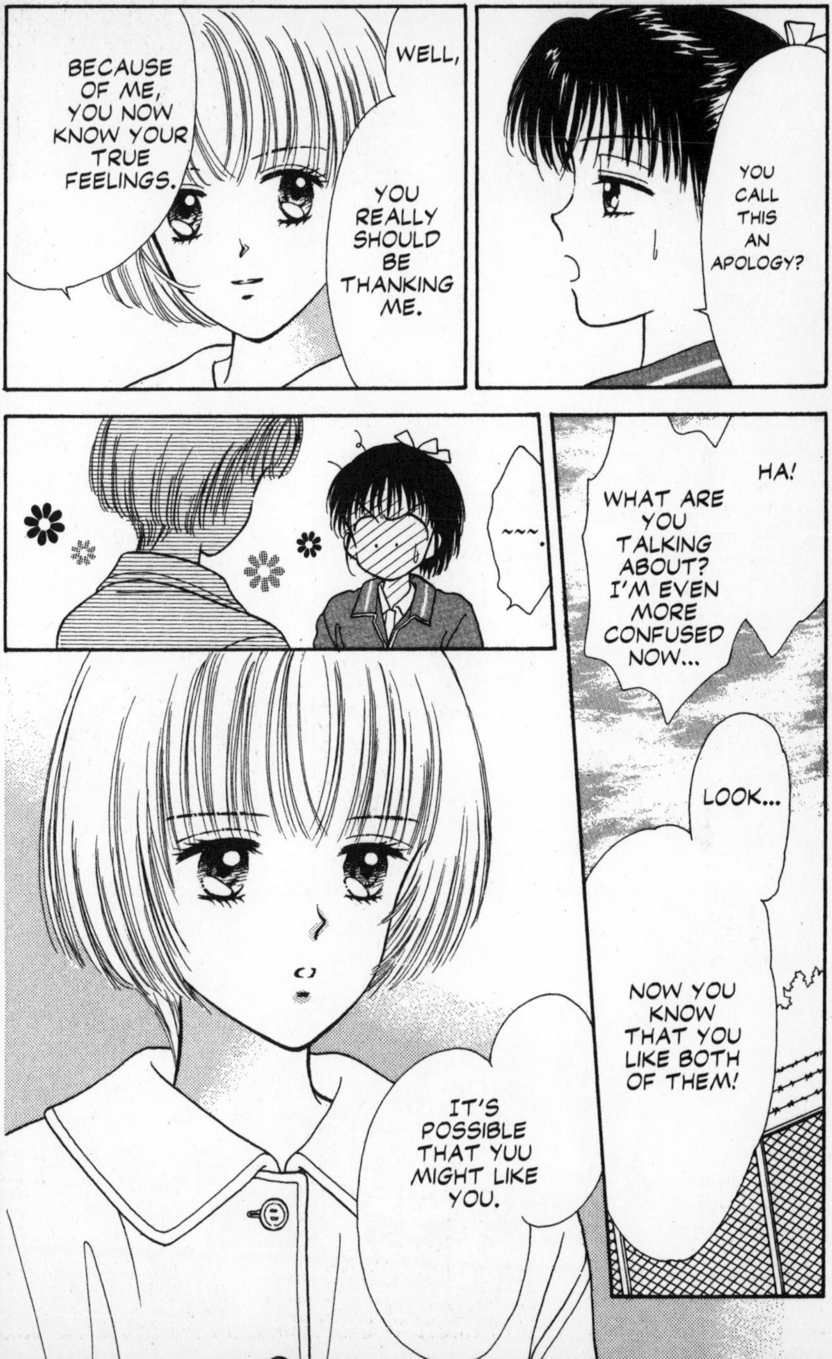
YOU CALL THIS AN APOLOGY?
WELL,
YOU REALLY SHOULD BE THANKING ME.
BECAUSE OF ME, YOU NOW KNOW YOUR TRUE FEELINGS.
HA!
WHAT ARE YOU TALKING ABOUT? I'M EVEN MORE CONFUSED NOW...
~~~.
LOOK...
NOW YOU KNOW THAT YOU LIKE BOTH OF THEM!
IT'S POSSIBLE THAT YUU MIGHT LIKE YOU.
~~~

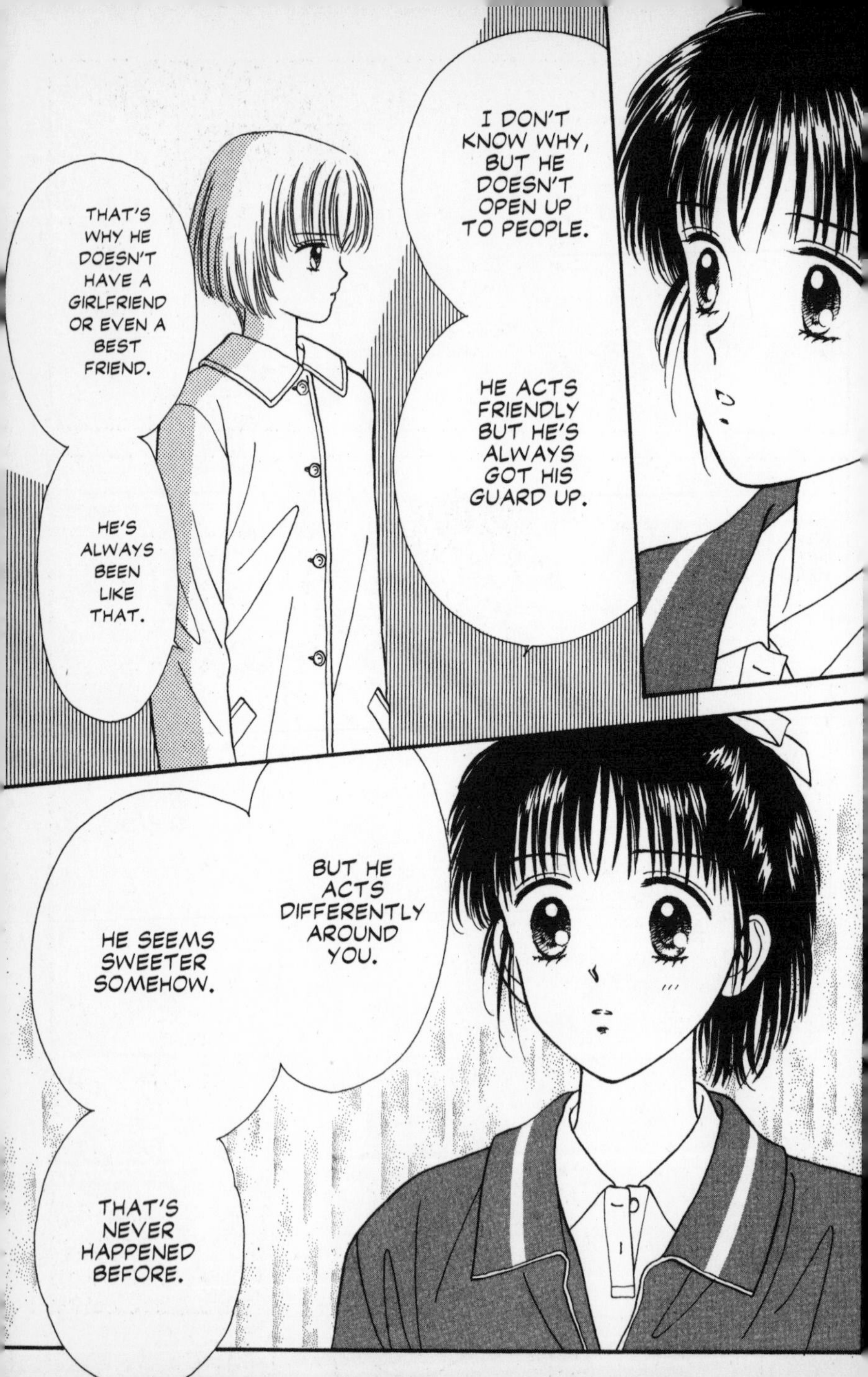
I DON'T KNOW WHY, BUT HE DOESN'T OPEN UP TO PEOPLE.
HE ACTS FRIENDLY BUT HE'S ALWAYS GOT HIS GUARD UP.
THAT'S WHY HE DOESN'T HAVE A GIRLFRIEND OR EVEN A BEST FRIEND.
HE'S ALWAYS BEEN LIKE THAT.
BUT HE ACTS DIFFERENTLY AROUND YOU.
HE SEEMS SWEETER SOMEHOW.
THAT'S NEVER HAPPENED BEFORE.

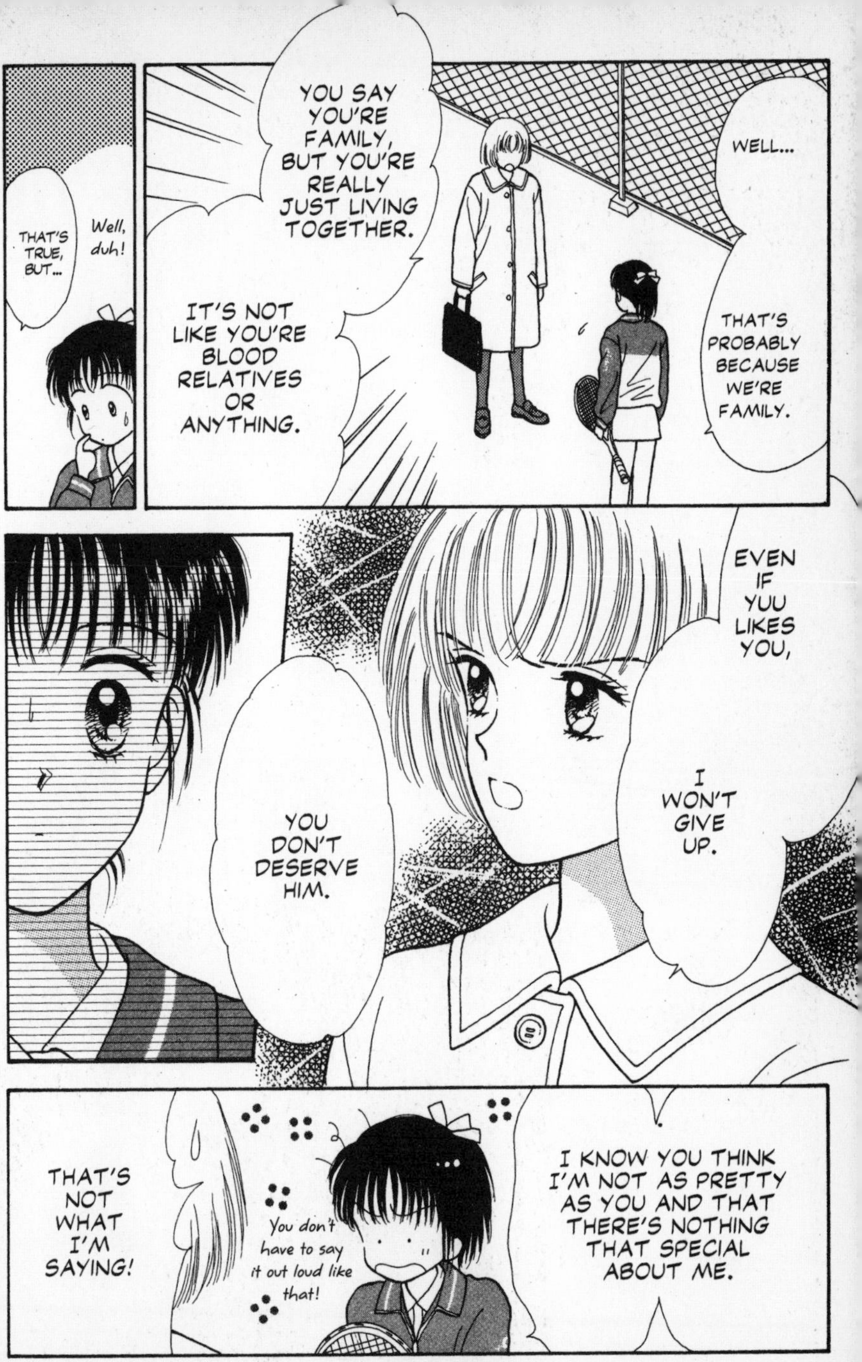
WELL...
THAT'S PROBABLY BECAUSE WE'RE FAMILY.
YOU SAY YOU'RE FAMILY, BUT YOU'RE REALLY JUST LIVING TOGETHER.
IT'S NOT LIKE YOU'RE BLOOD RELATIVES OR ANYTHING.
Well, duh!
THAT'S TRUE, BUT...
EVEN IF YUU LIKES YOU,
I WON'T GIVE UP.
YOU DON'T DESERVE HIM.
I KNOW YOU THINK I'M NOT AS PRETTY AS YOU AND THAT THERE'S NOTHING THAT SPECIAL ABOUT ME.
You don't have to say it out loud like that!
THAT'S NOT WHAT I'M SAYING!

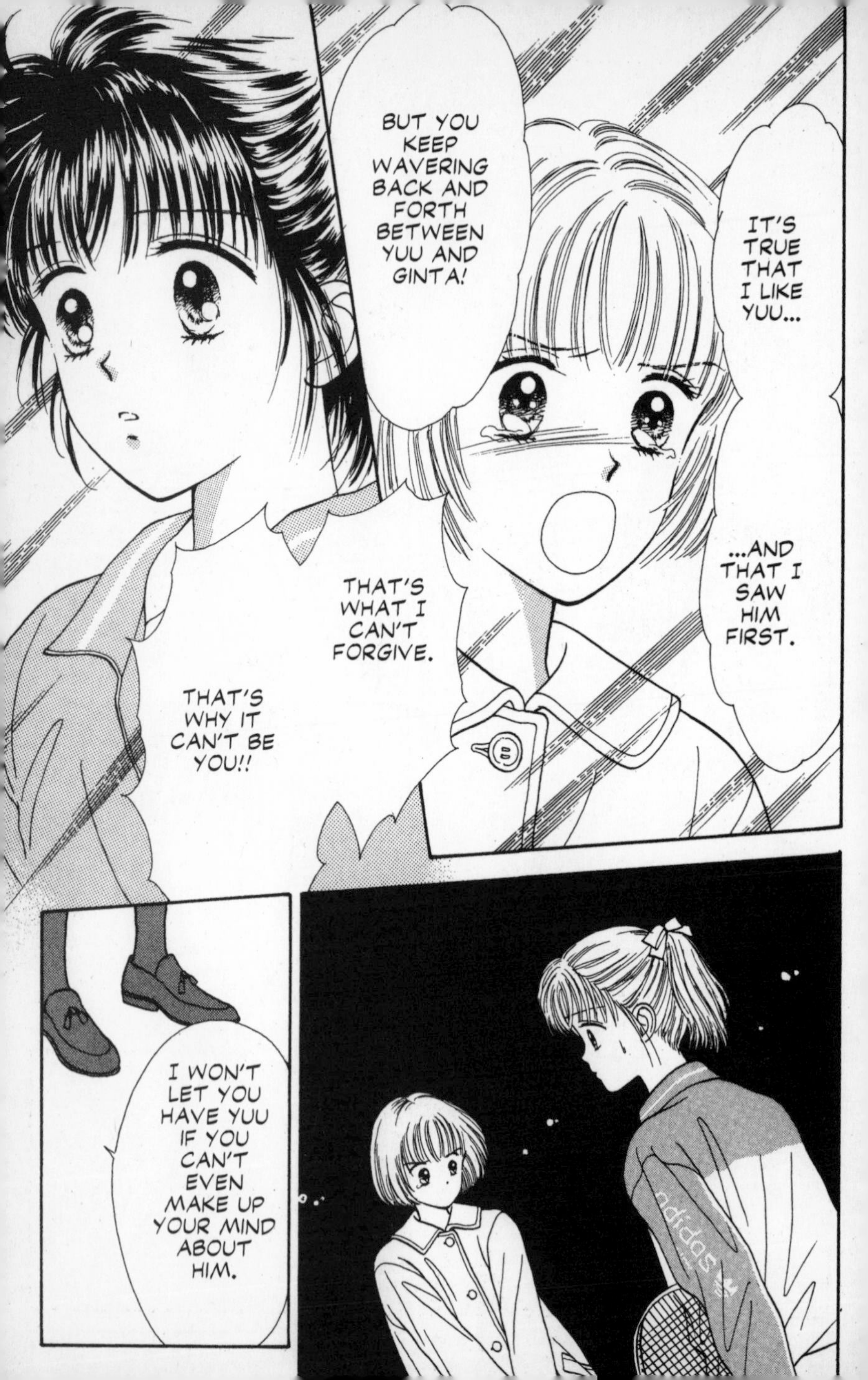
IT'S TRUE THAT I LIKE YUU...
...AND THAT I SAW HIM FIRST.
BUT YOU KEEP WAVERING BACK AND FORTH BETWEEN YUU AND GINTA!
THAT'S WHAT I CAN'T FORGIVE.
THAT'S WHY IT CAN'T BE YOU!!
adidas
I WON'T LET YOU HAVE YUU IF YOU CAN'T EVEN MAKE UP YOUR MIND ABOUT HIM.

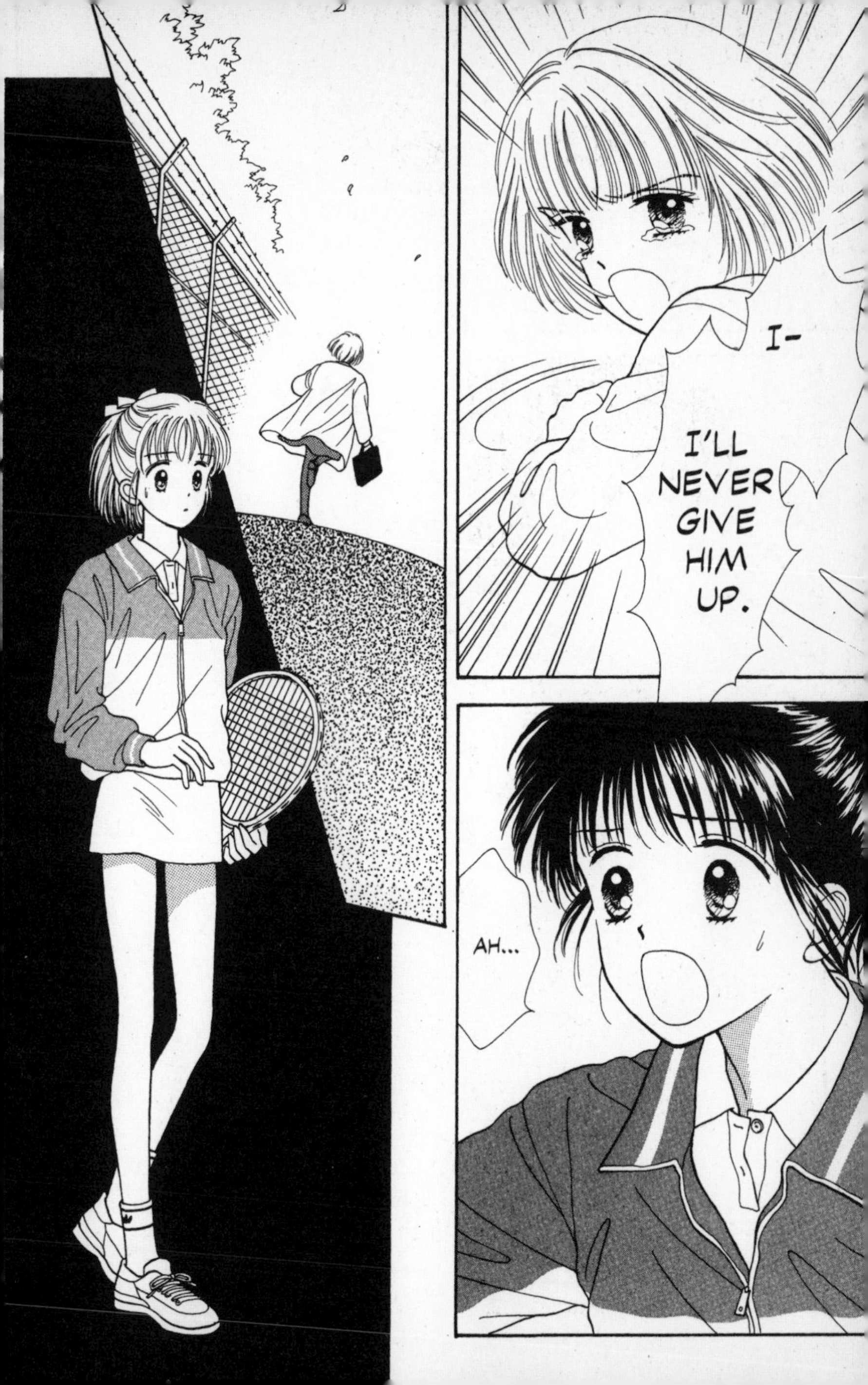
I-
I'LL NEVER GIVE HIM UP.
AH...

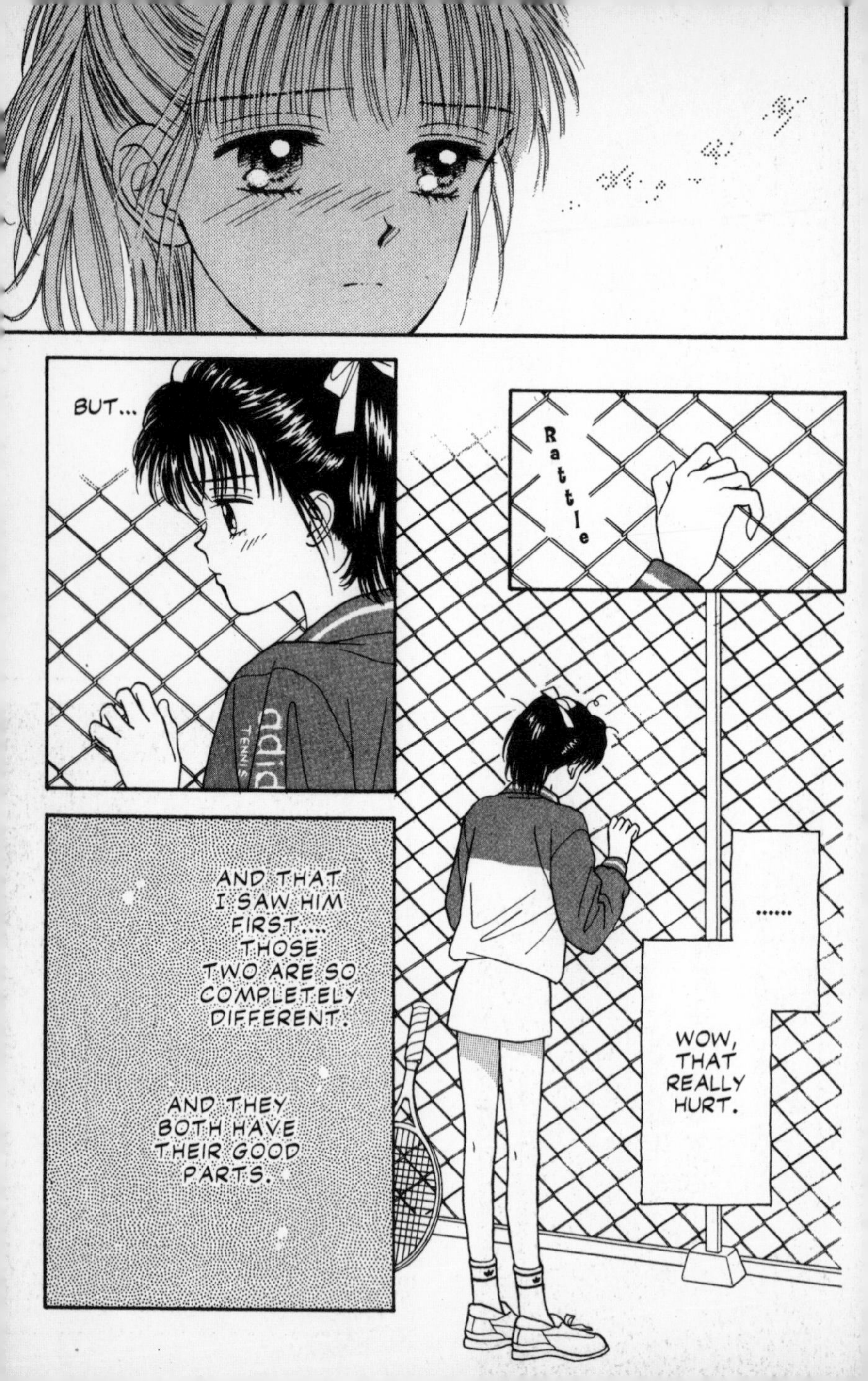
Rattle
......
WOW, THAT REALLY HURT.
BUT...
AND THAT I SAW HIM FIRST.... THOSE TWO ARE SO COMPLETELY DIFFERENT.
AND THEY BOTH HAVE THEIR GOOD PARTS.

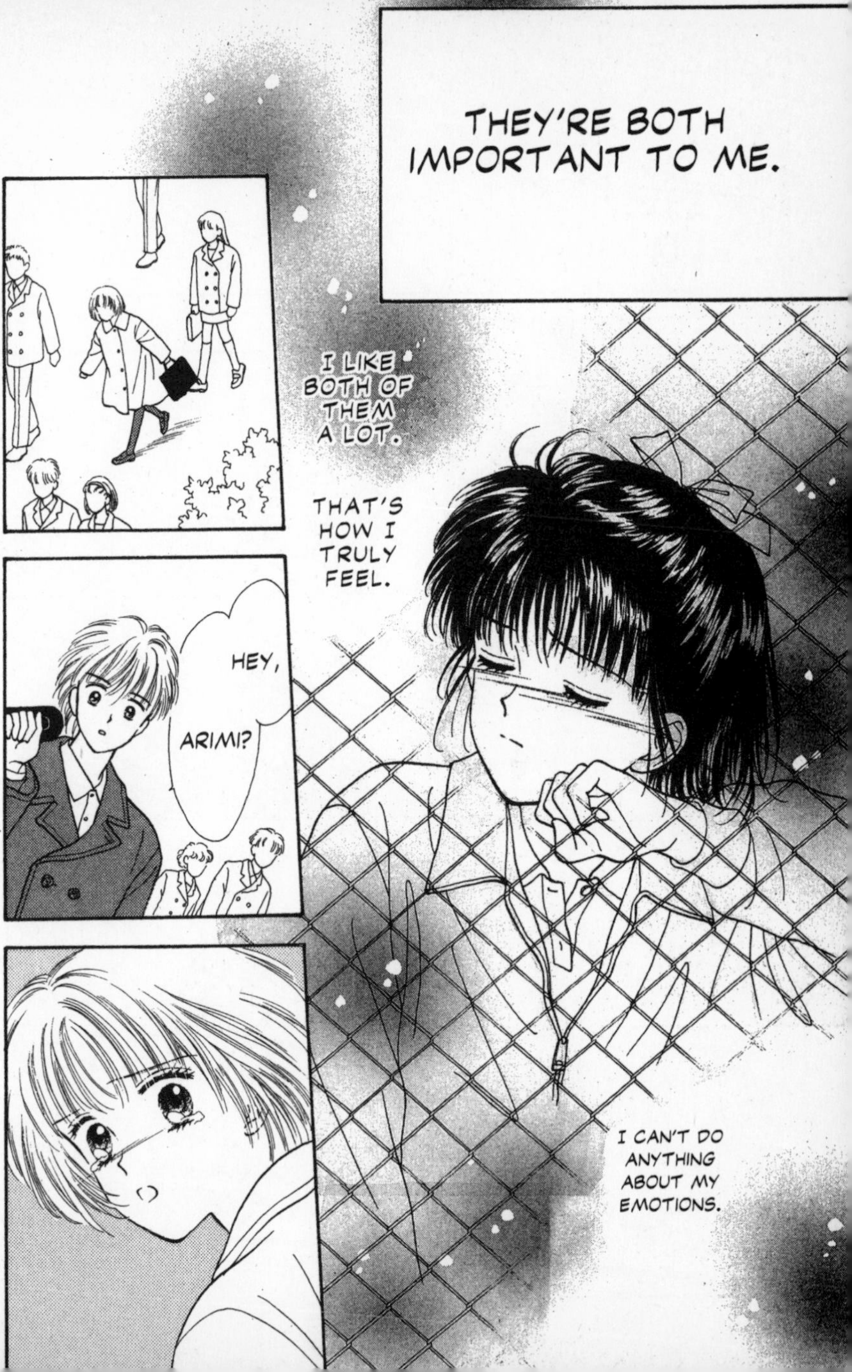
THEY'RE BOTH IMPORTANT TO ME.
I LIKE BOTH OF THEM A LOT.
THAT'S HOW I TRULY FEEL.
I CAN'T DO ANYTHING ABOUT MY EMOTIONS.
HEY,
ARIMI?

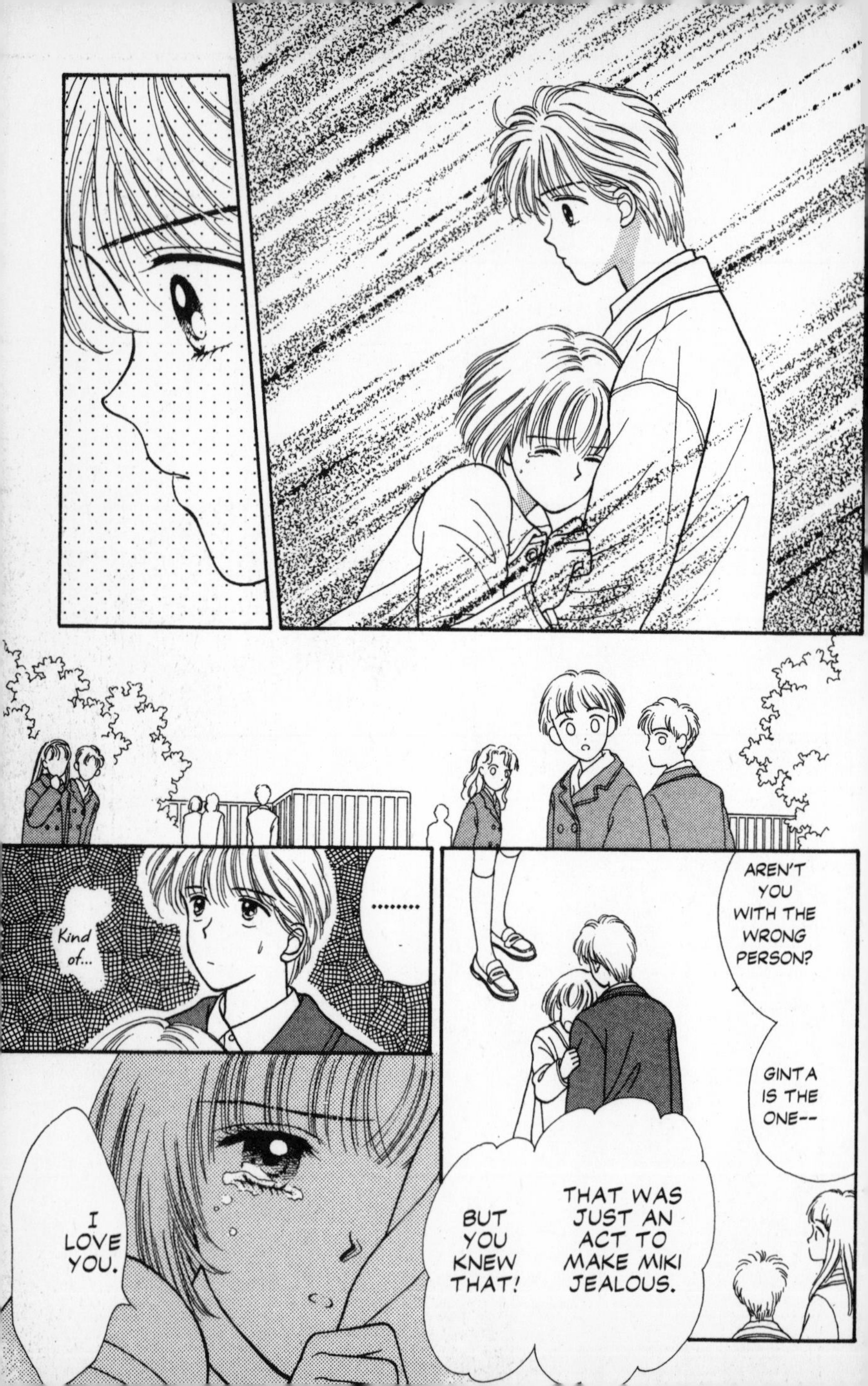
AREN'T YOU WITH THE WRONG PERSON?
GINTA IS THE ONE--
....
Kind of...
THAT WAS JUST AN ACT TO MAKE MIKI JEALOUS.
BUT YOU KNEW THAT!
I LOVE YOU.

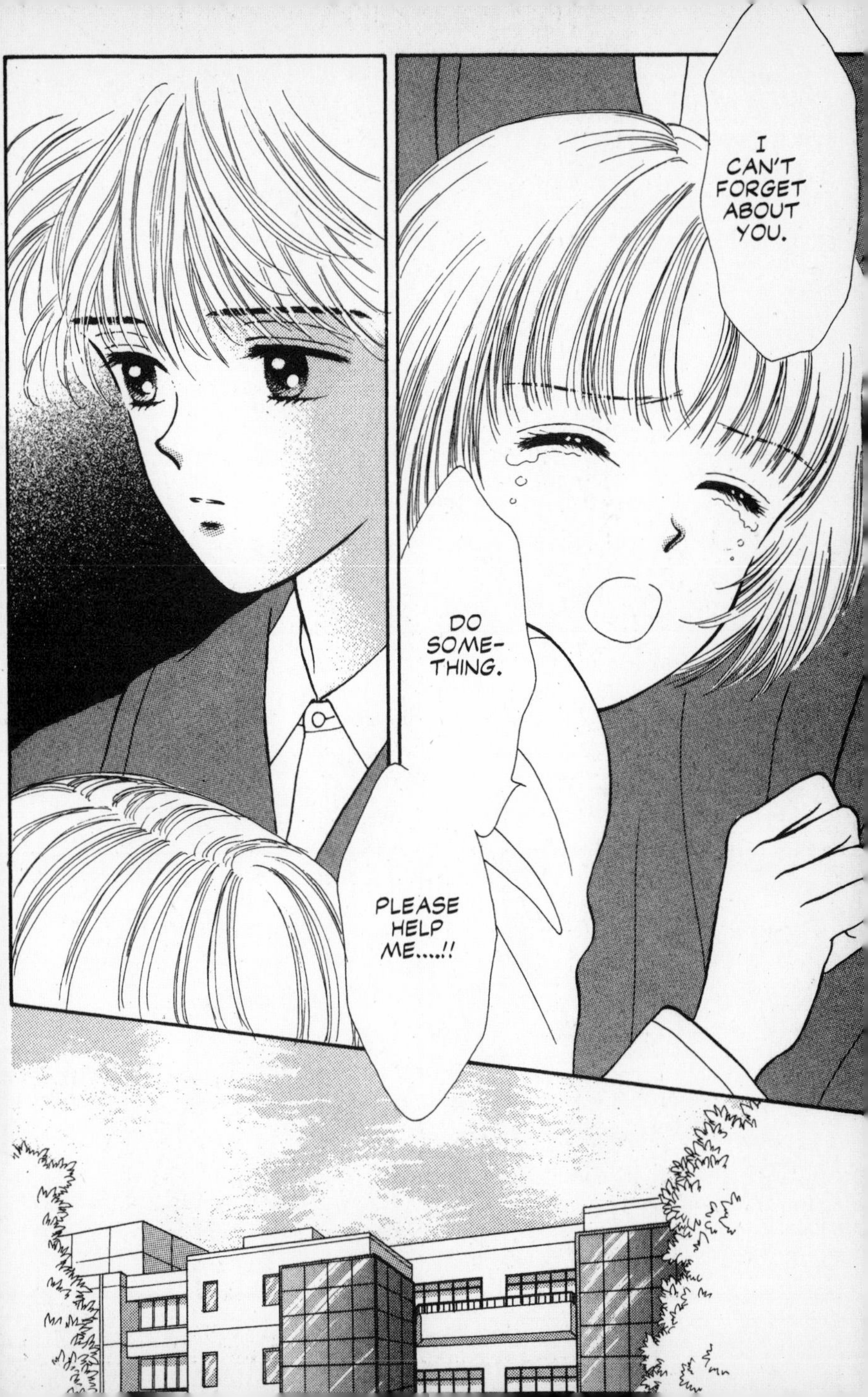
I CAN'T FORGET ABOUT YOU.
DO SOME-THING.
PLEASE HELP ME....!!

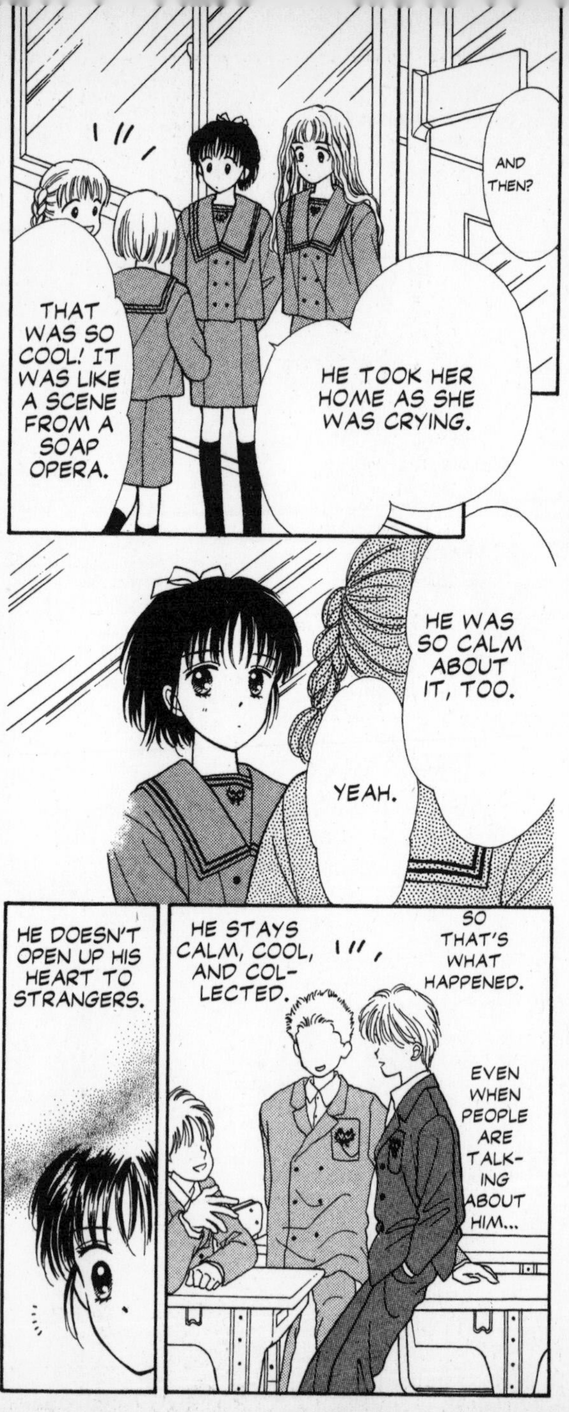
AND THEN?
HE TOOK HER HOME AS SHE WAS CRYING.
THAT WAS SO COOL! IT WAS LIKE A SCENE FROM A SOAP OPERA.
HE WAS SO CALM ABOUT IT, TOO.
YEAH.
SO THAT'S WHAT HAPPENED.
HE STAYS CALM, COOL, AND COL-LECTED.
EVEN WHEN PEOPLE ARE TALK-ING ABOUT HIM...
HE DOESN'T OPEN UP HIS HEART TO STRANGERS.

MEIKO AKIZUKI

HOROSCOPE: SCORPIO

BLOODTYPE: A

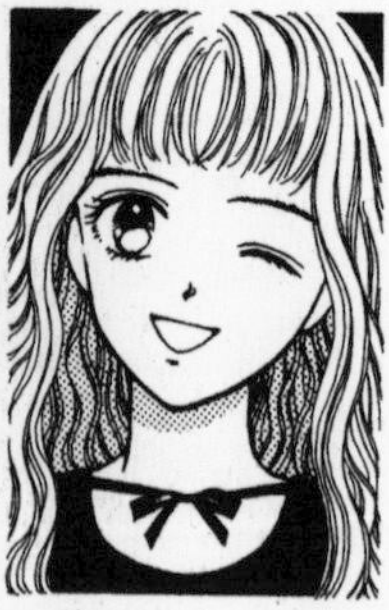

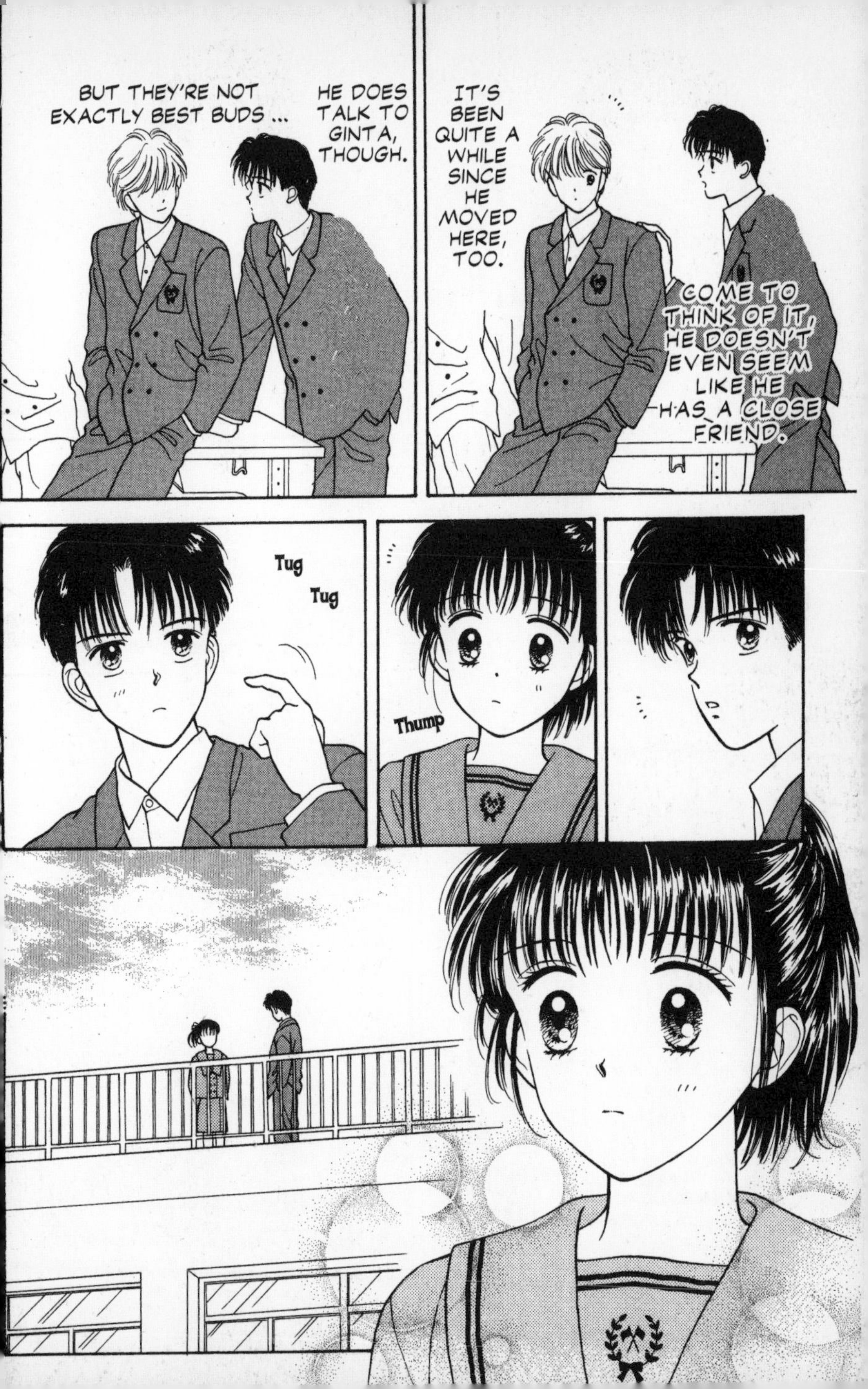
IT'S BEEN QUITE A WHILE SINCE HE MOVED HERE, TOO.
COME TO THINK OF IT, HE DOESN'T EVEN SEEM LIKE HE HAS A CLOSE FRIEND.
HE DOES TALK TO GINTA, THOUGH.
BUT THEY'RE NOT EXACTLY BEST BUDS ...
Thump
Tug
Tug

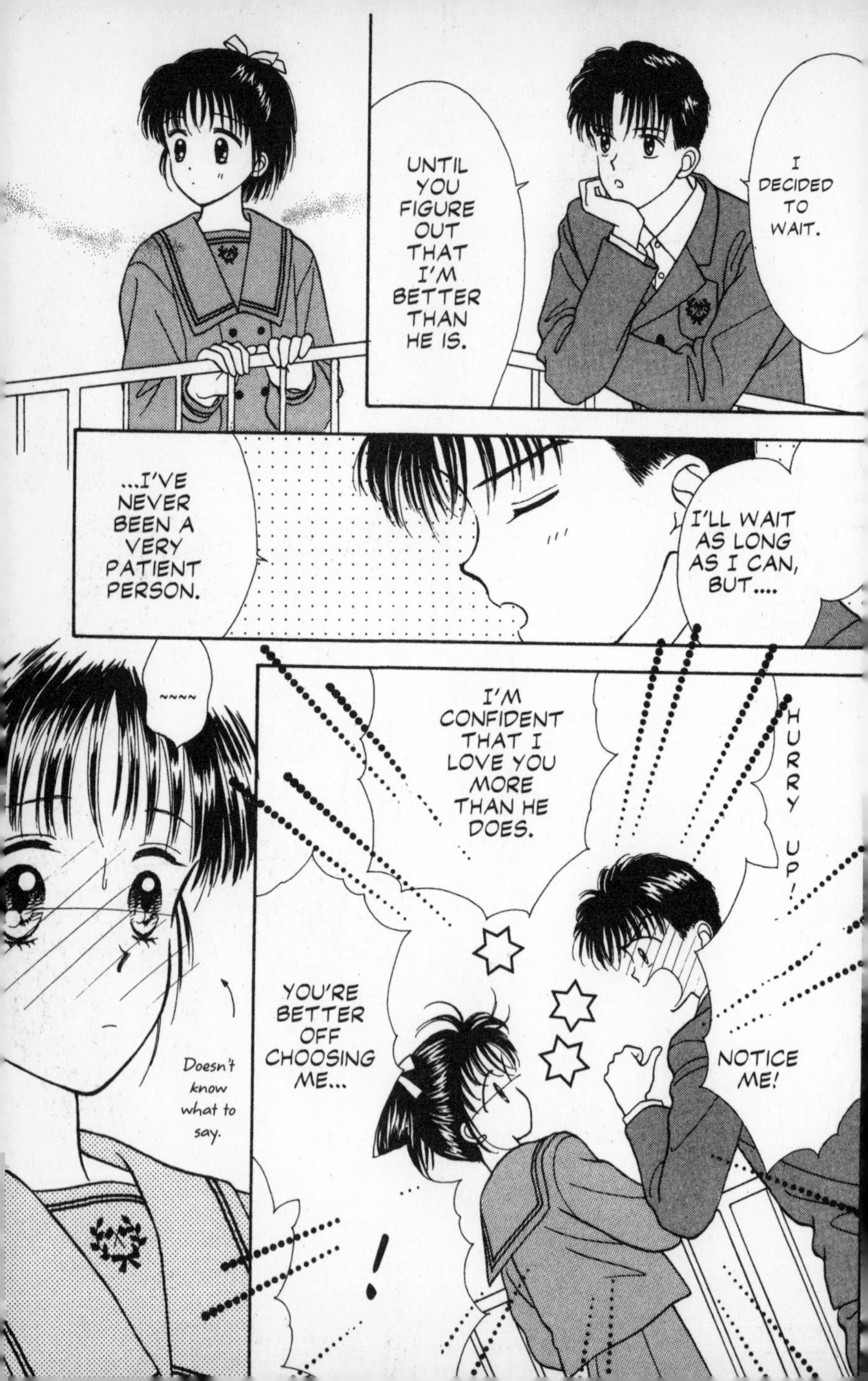
I DECIDED TO WAIT.
UNTIL YOU FIGURE OUT THAT I'M BETTER THAN HE IS.
I'LL WAIT AS LONG AS I CAN, BUT....
...I'VE NEVER BEEN A VERY PATIENT PERSON.
HURRY UP!
I'M CONFIDENT THAT I LOVE YOU MORE THAN HE DOES.
NOTICE ME!
YOU'RE BETTER OFF CHOOSING ME...
!
~~~~
Doesn't know what to say.
~~~~

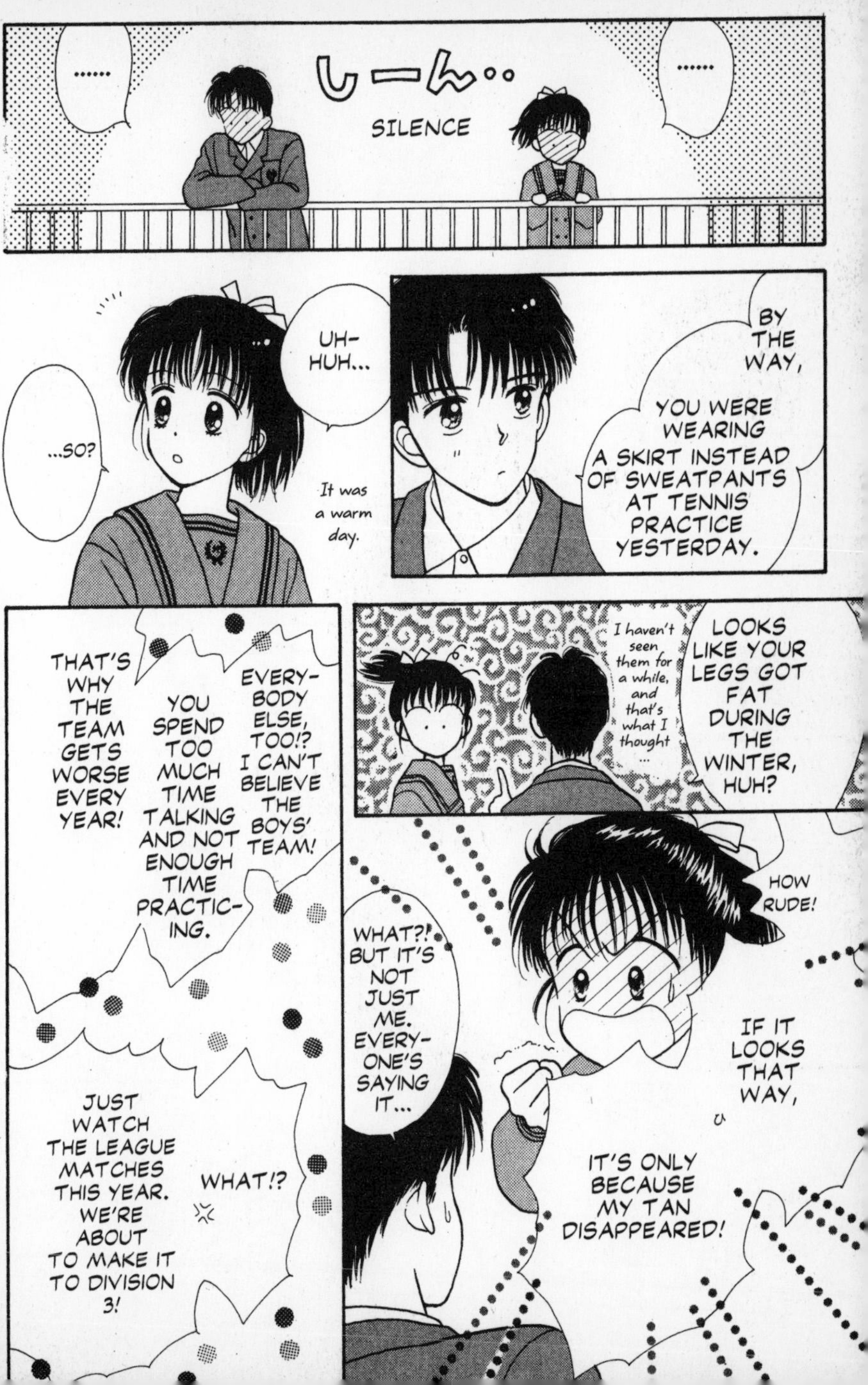
......
しーん。。
SILENCE
......
BY THE WAY, YOU WERE WEARING A SKIRT INSTEAD OF SWEATPANTS AT TENNIS PRACTICE YESTERDAY.
UH-HUH...
It was a warm day.
...SO?
LOOKS LIKE YOUR LEGS GOT FAT DURING THE WINTER, HUH?
I haven't seen them for a while, and that's what I thought...
HOW RUDE!
IF IT LOOKS THAT WAY,
IT'S ONLY BECAUSE MY TAN DISAPPEARED!
WHAT?! BUT IT'S NOT JUST ME. EVERYONE'S SAYING IT...
EVERYBODY ELSE, TOO!? I CAN'T BELIEVE THE BOYS' TEAM!
YOU SPEND TOO MUCH TIME TALKING AND NOT ENOUGH TIME PRACTICING.
THAT'S WHY THE TEAM GETS WORSE EVERY YEAR!
WHAT!?
JUST WATCH THE LEAGUE MATCHES THIS YEAR. WE'RE ABOUT TO MAKE IT TO DIVISION 3!

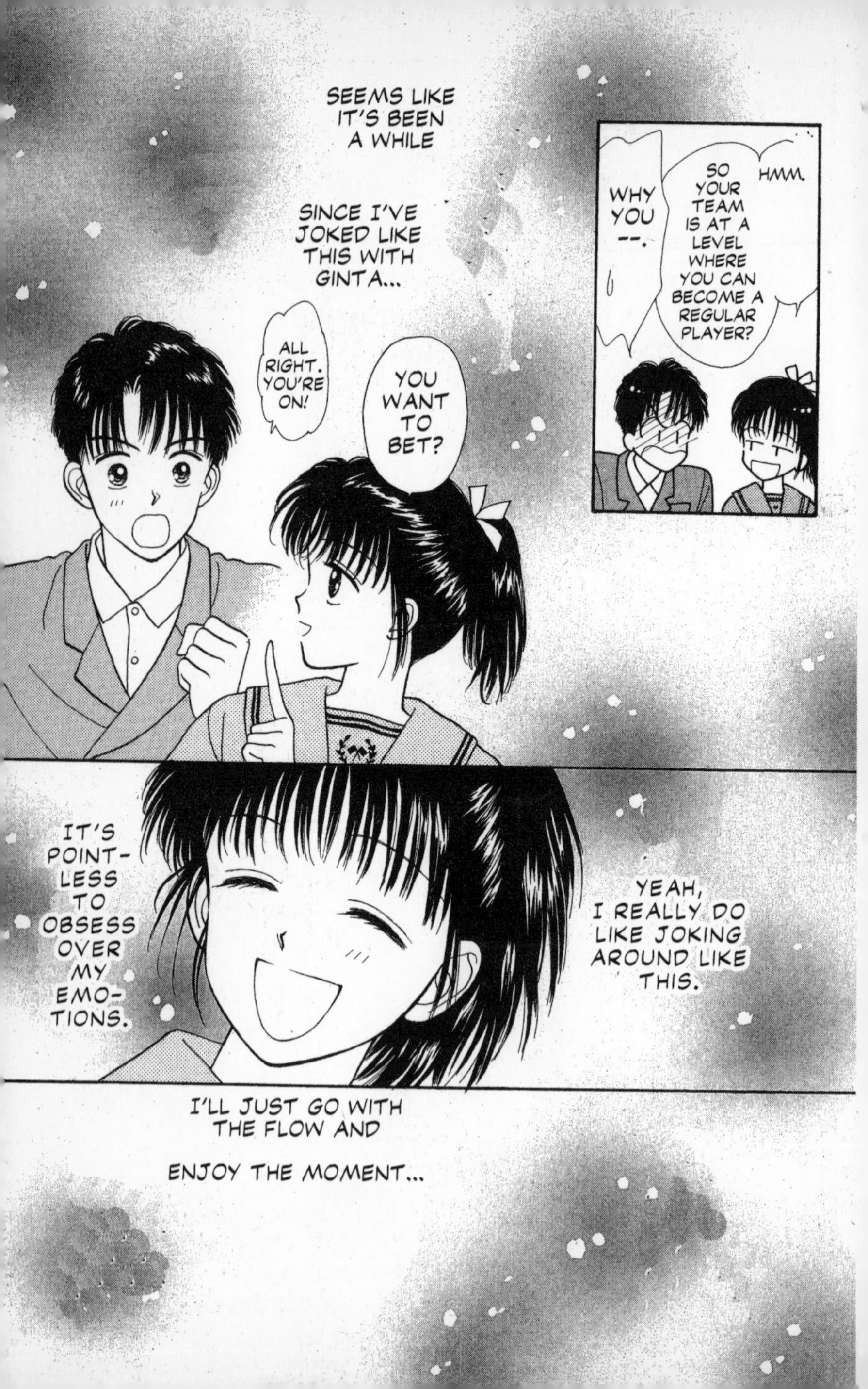
SO YOUR TEAM IS AT A LEVEL WHERE YOU CAN BECOME A REGULAR PLAYER?
HMM.
WHY YOU --.
SEEMS LIKE IT'S BEEN A WHILE
SINCE I'VE JOKED LIKE THIS WITH GINTA...
YOU WANT TO BET?
ALL RIGHT. YOU'RE ON!
YEAH, I REALLY DO LIKE JOKING AROUND LIKE THIS.
IT'S POINTLESS TO OBSESS OVER MY EMOTIONS.
I'LL JUST GO WITH THE FLOW AND
ENJOY THE MOMENT...

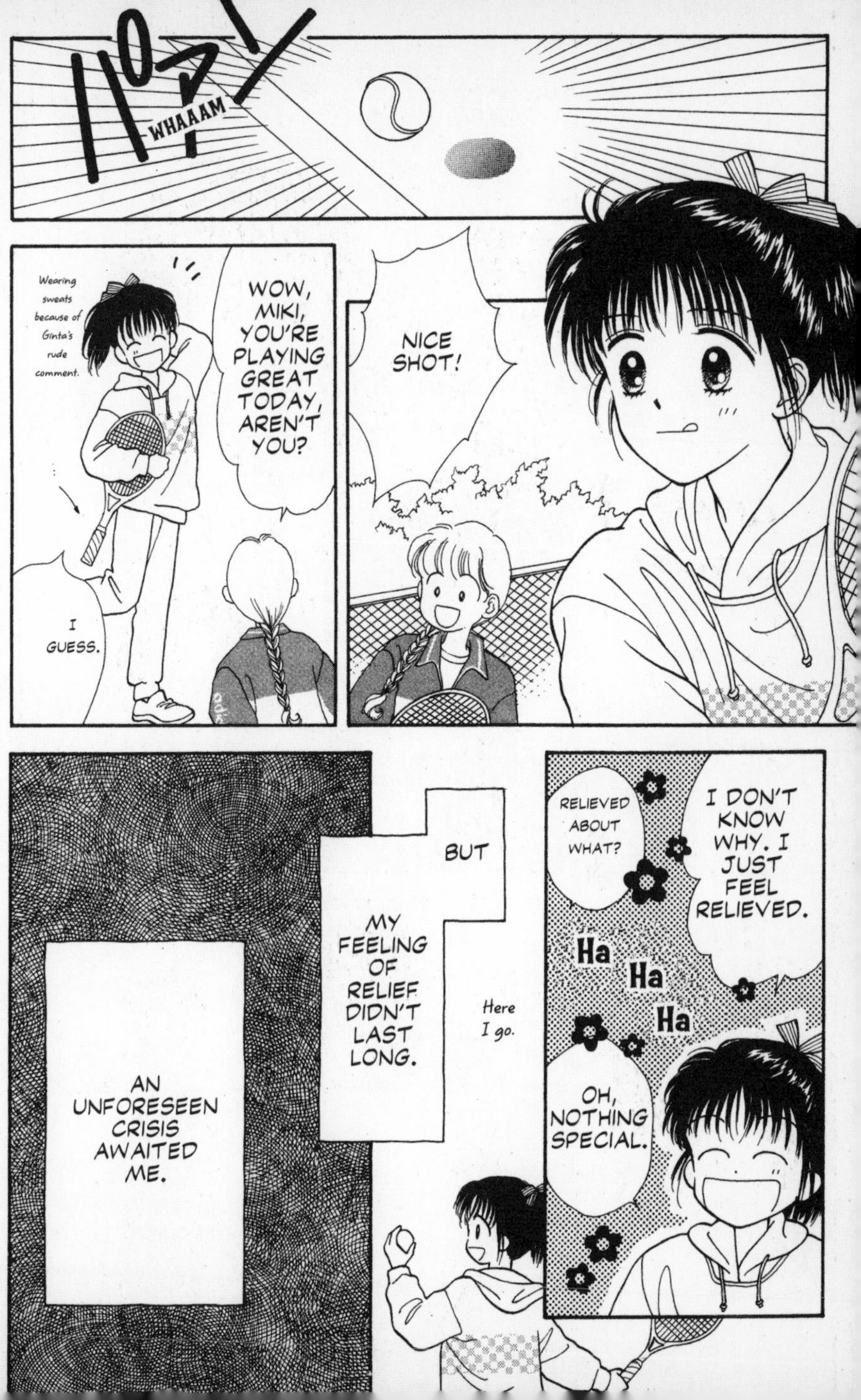
WHAAAM
NICE SHOT!
WOW, MIKI, YOU'RE PLAYING GREAT TODAY, AREN'T YOU?
Wearing sweats because of Ginta's rude comment.
I GUESS.
I DON'T KNOW WHY. I JUST FEEL RELIEVED.
RELIEVED ABOUT WHAT?
Ha Ha Ha
OH, NOTHING SPECIAL.
Here I go.
BUT
MY FEELING OF RELIEF DIDN'T LAST LONG.
AN UNFORESEEN CRISIS AWAITED ME.

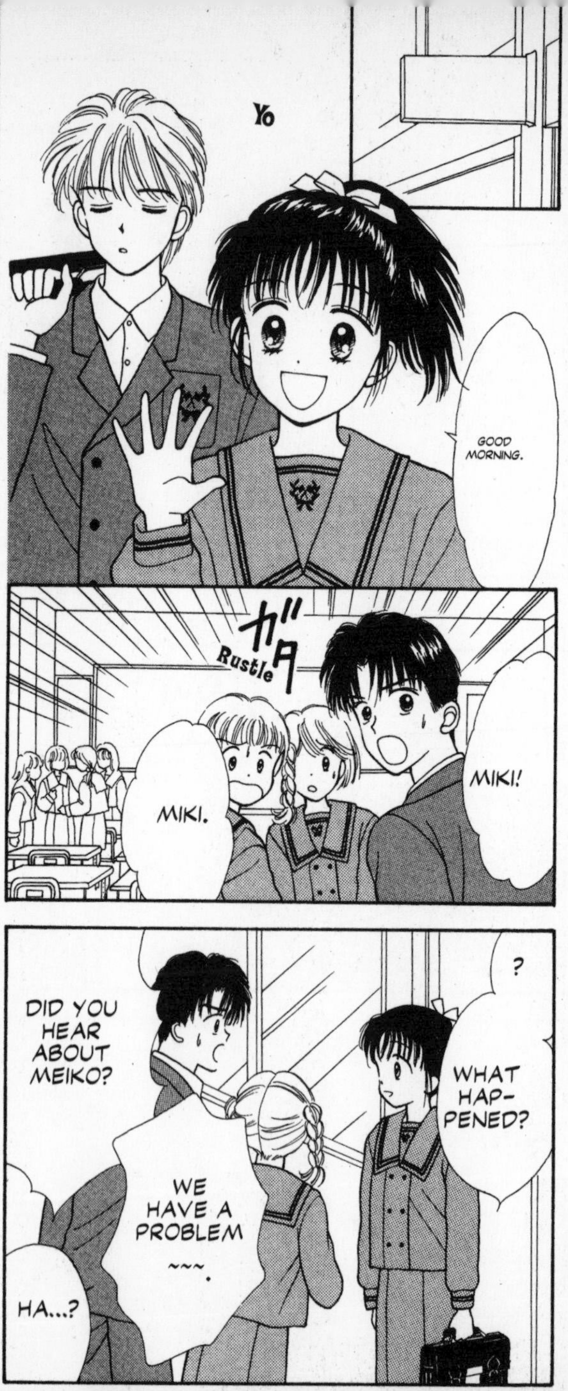
Yo
GOOD MORNING.
ガタ
Rustle
MIKI!
MIKI.
?
WHAT HAP-PENED?
DID YOU HEAR ABOUT MEIKO?
WE HAVE A PROBLEM ~~~.
HA...?

Arimi Suzuki

HOROSCOPE: LEO

BLOODTYPE: O

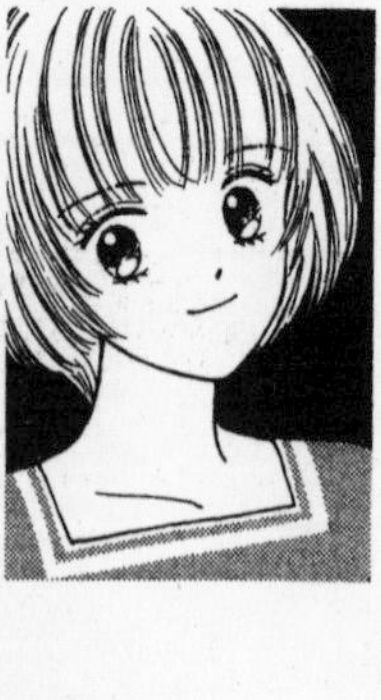

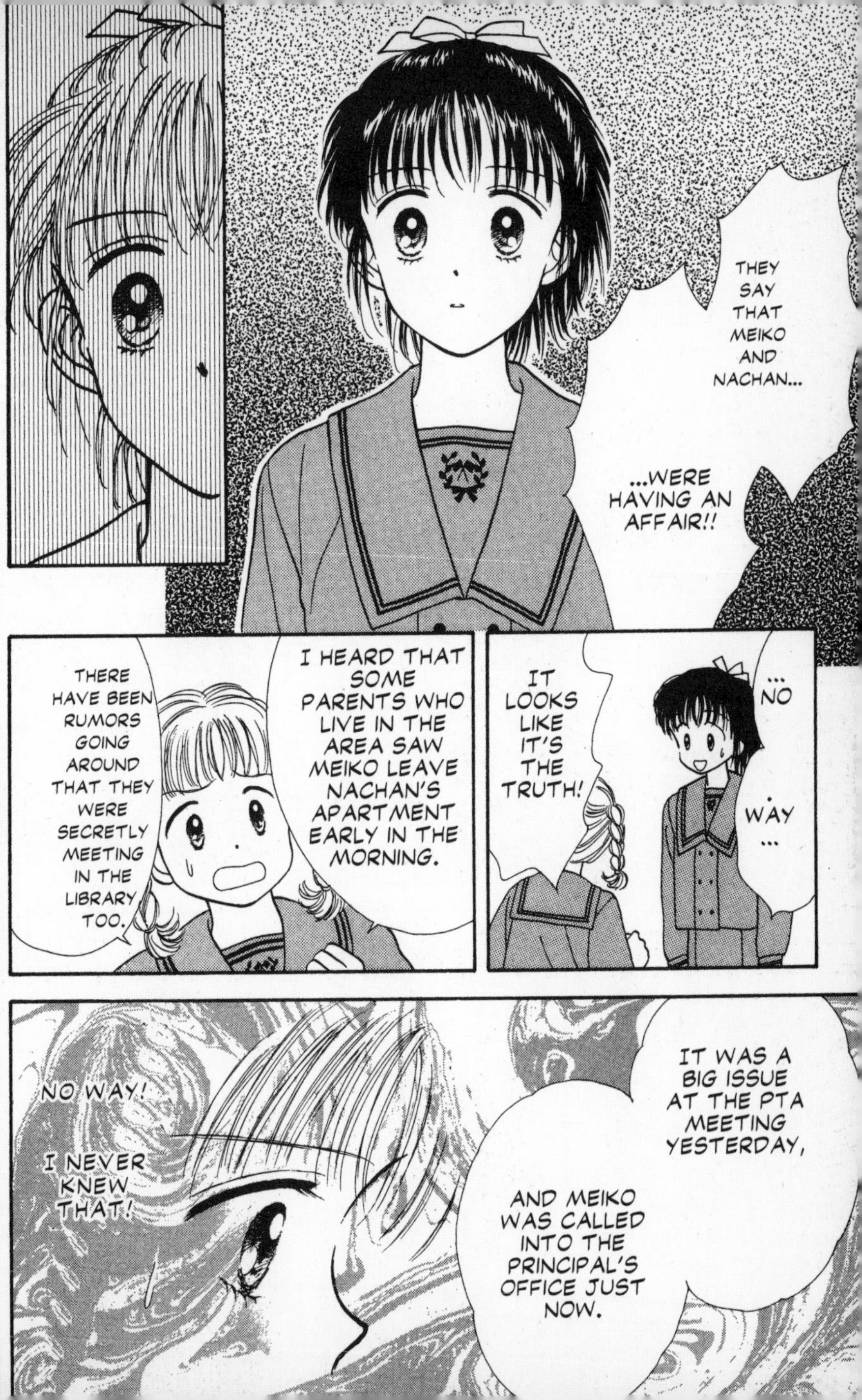
THEY SAY THAT MEIKO AND NACHAN...
...WERE HAVING AN AFFAIR!!
... NO WAY ...
IT LOOKS LIKE IT'S THE TRUTH!
I HEARD THAT SOME PARENTS WHO LIVE IN THE AREA SAW MEIKO LEAVE NACHAN'S APARTMENT EARLY IN THE MORNING.
THERE HAVE BEEN RUMORS GOING AROUND THAT THEY WERE SECRETLY MEETING IN THE LIBRARY TOO.
IT WAS A BIG ISSUE AT THE PTA MEETING YESTERDAY,
AND MEIKO WAS CALLED INTO THE PRINCIPAL'S OFFICE JUST NOW.
NO WAY!
I NEVER KNEW THAT!

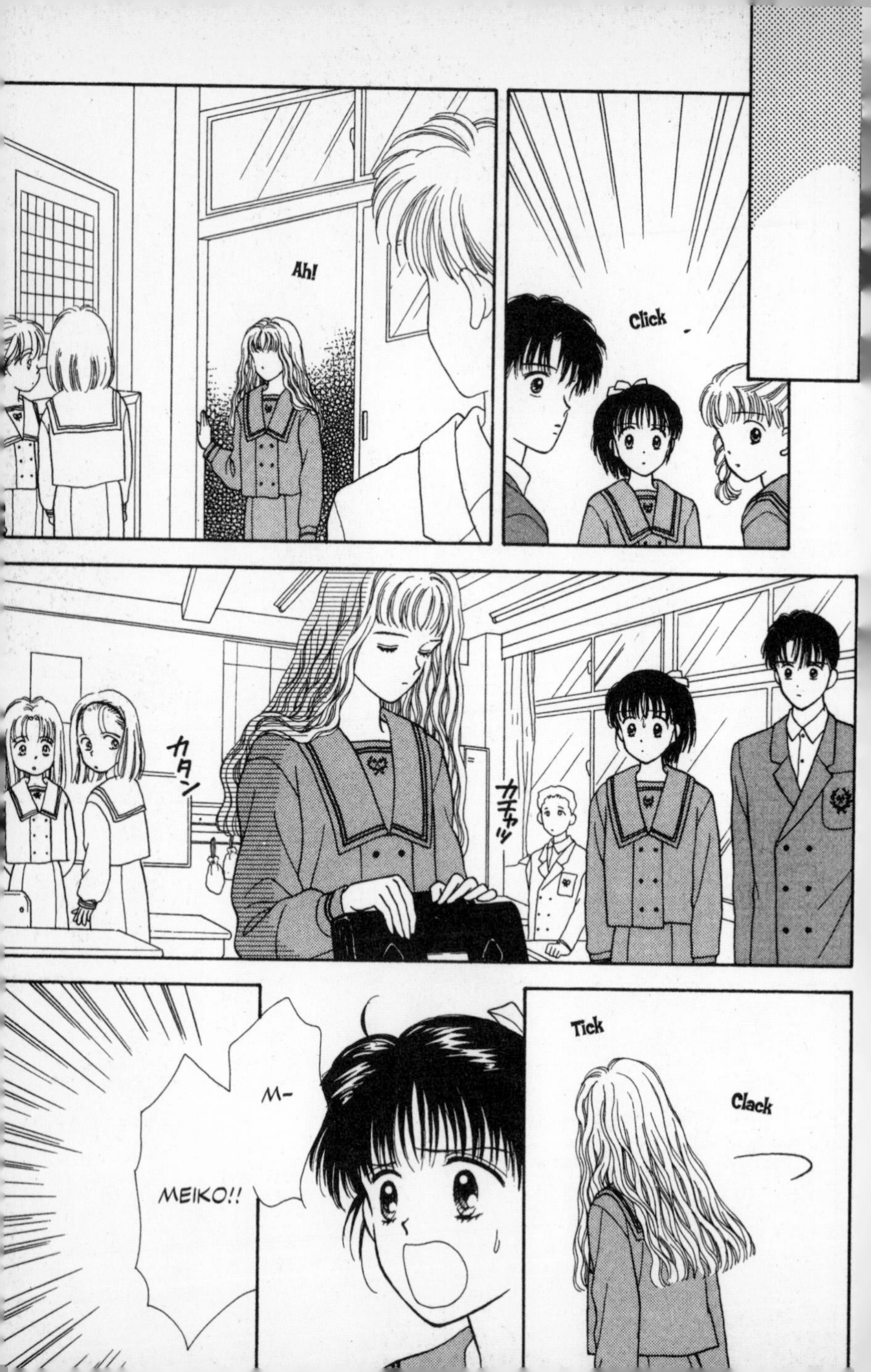

Click
Ah!
カチャッ
カタン
Tick
Clack
M-
MEIKO!!

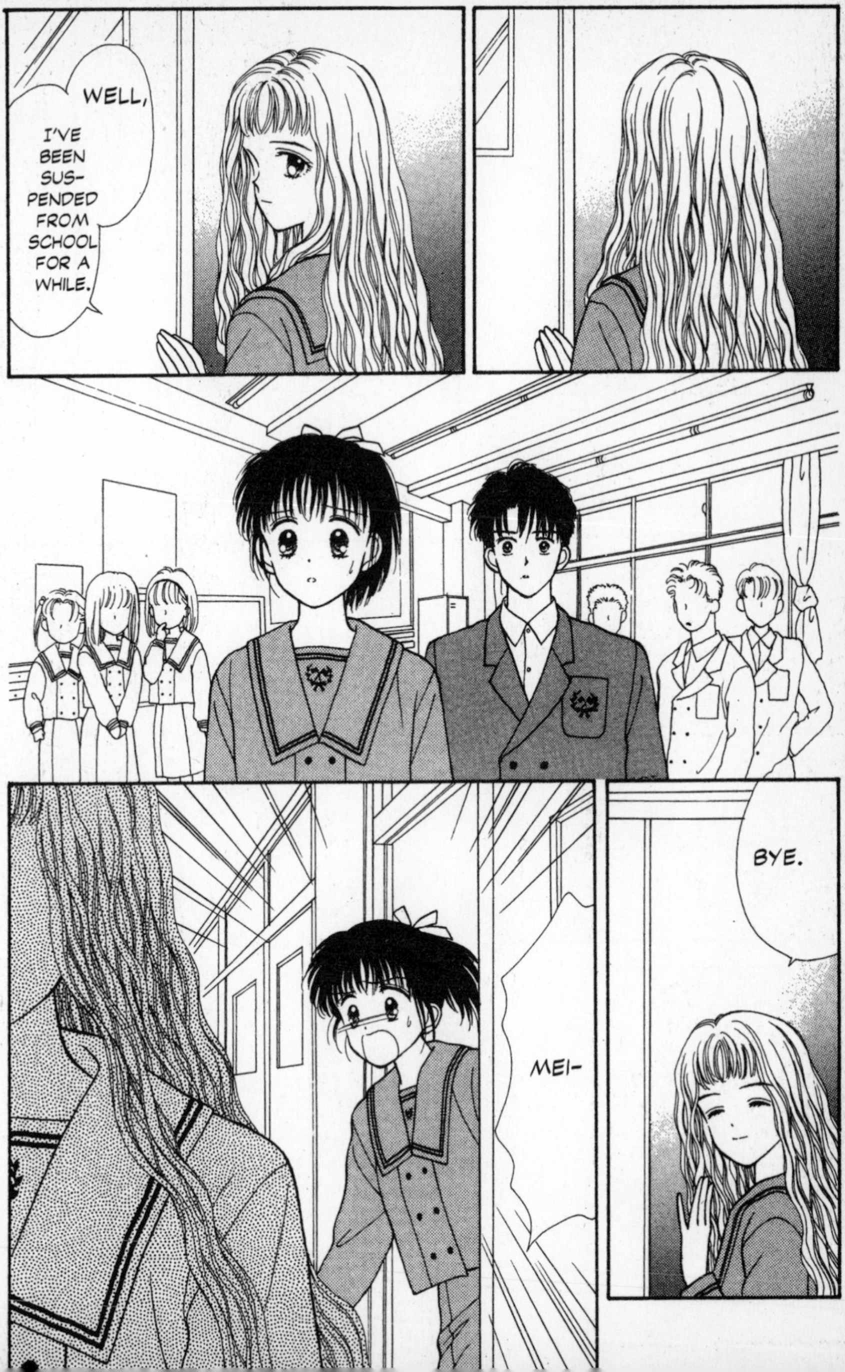
WELL, I'VE BEEN SUS-PENDED FROM SCHOOL FOR A WHILE.
BYE.
MEI-

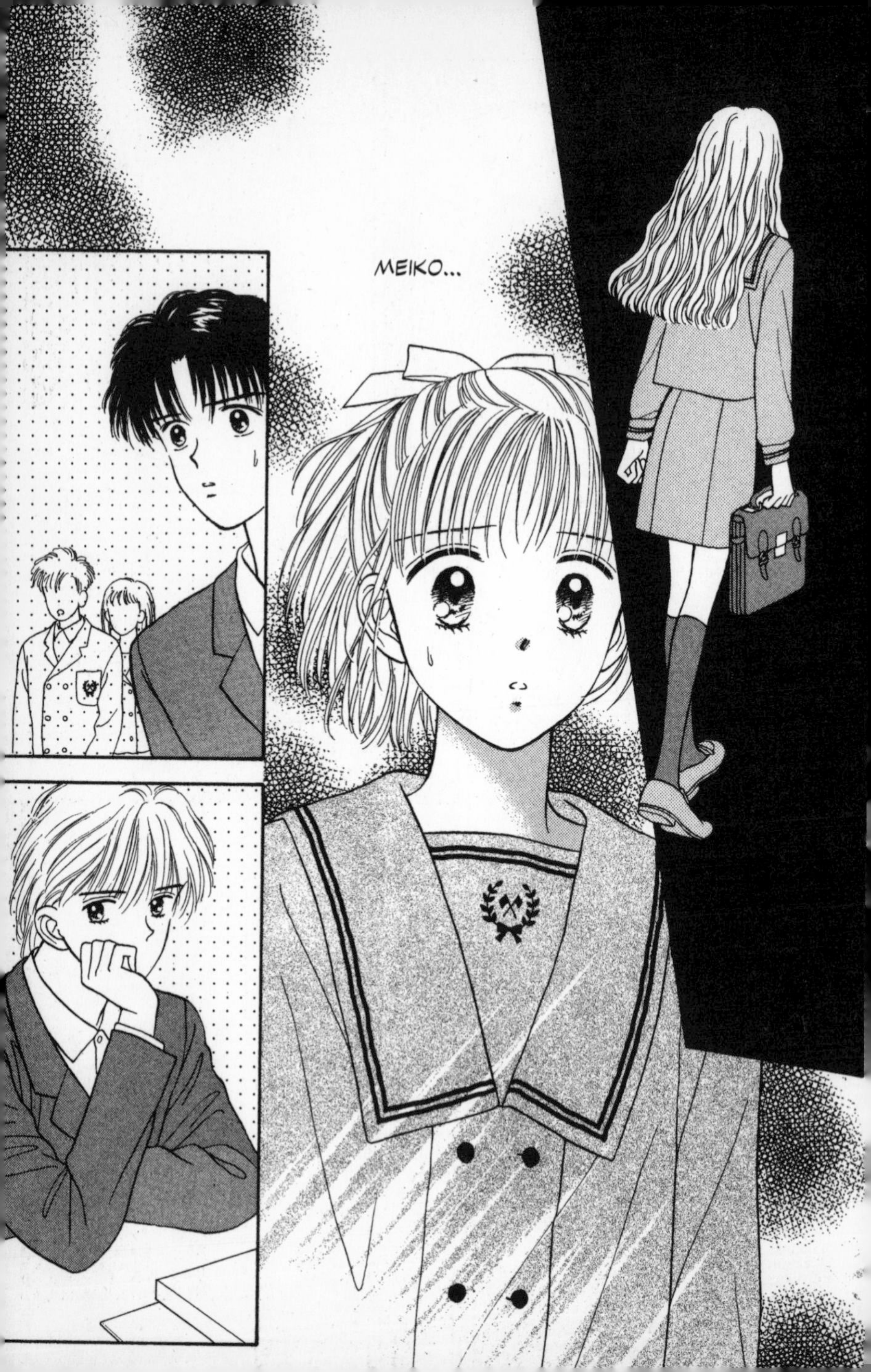
MEIKO...

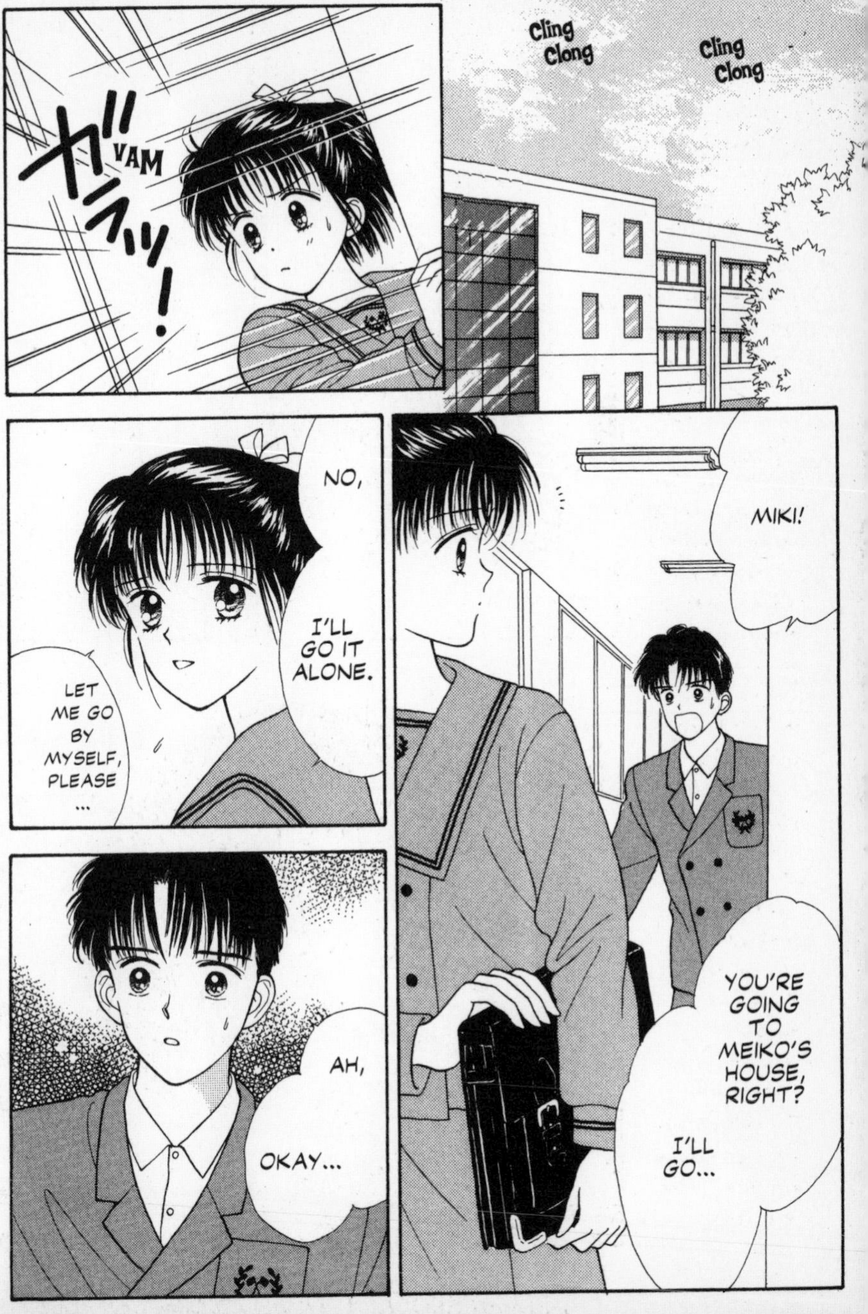
Cling Clong
Cling Clong
VAM
ガラッ!
MIKI!
YOU'RE GOING TO MEIKO'S HOUSE, RIGHT?
I'LL GO...
NO,
I'LL GO IT ALONE.
LET ME GO BY MYSELF, PLEASE ...
AH,
OKAY...

FREE TALK ④

When I'm drawing with my assistants, we sometimes watch TV or listen to CDs. But since I get easily tired of CDs, I usually turn on the radio. But oftentimes, the DJ's boring or sleep-inducing music floats out, so for a long time I'd been thinking I'd like to get cable radio, but I wasn't sure how it was installed. Just then, Yazawa Ai took the initiative. I asked her how to do it, so all that's left is the strength to carry it out. Lately, when it comes to the sort of stuff I'm listening to, I'm not interested in the en vogue Being genre. My favorite would have to be Dreams Come True, and I also often listen to Mr. Children, Bridge, B#, and the like.

I wonder when Rimiko Miura's new album is coming out. I'm hooked on her voice, y'know!

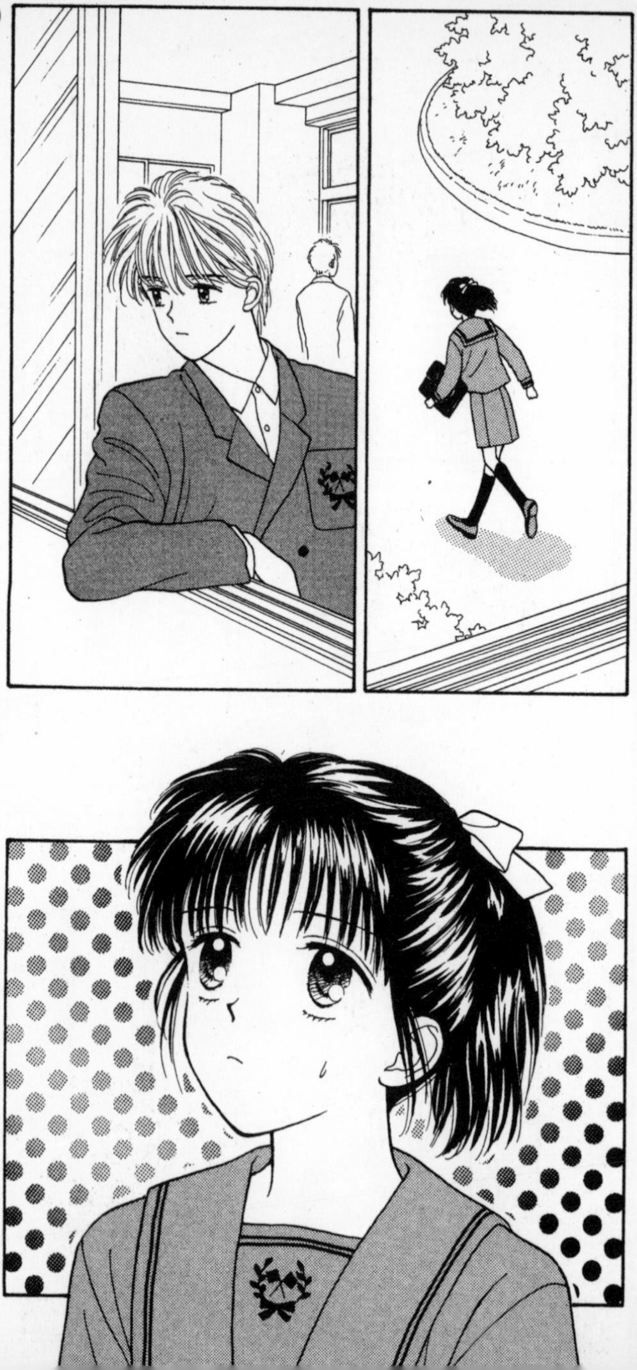

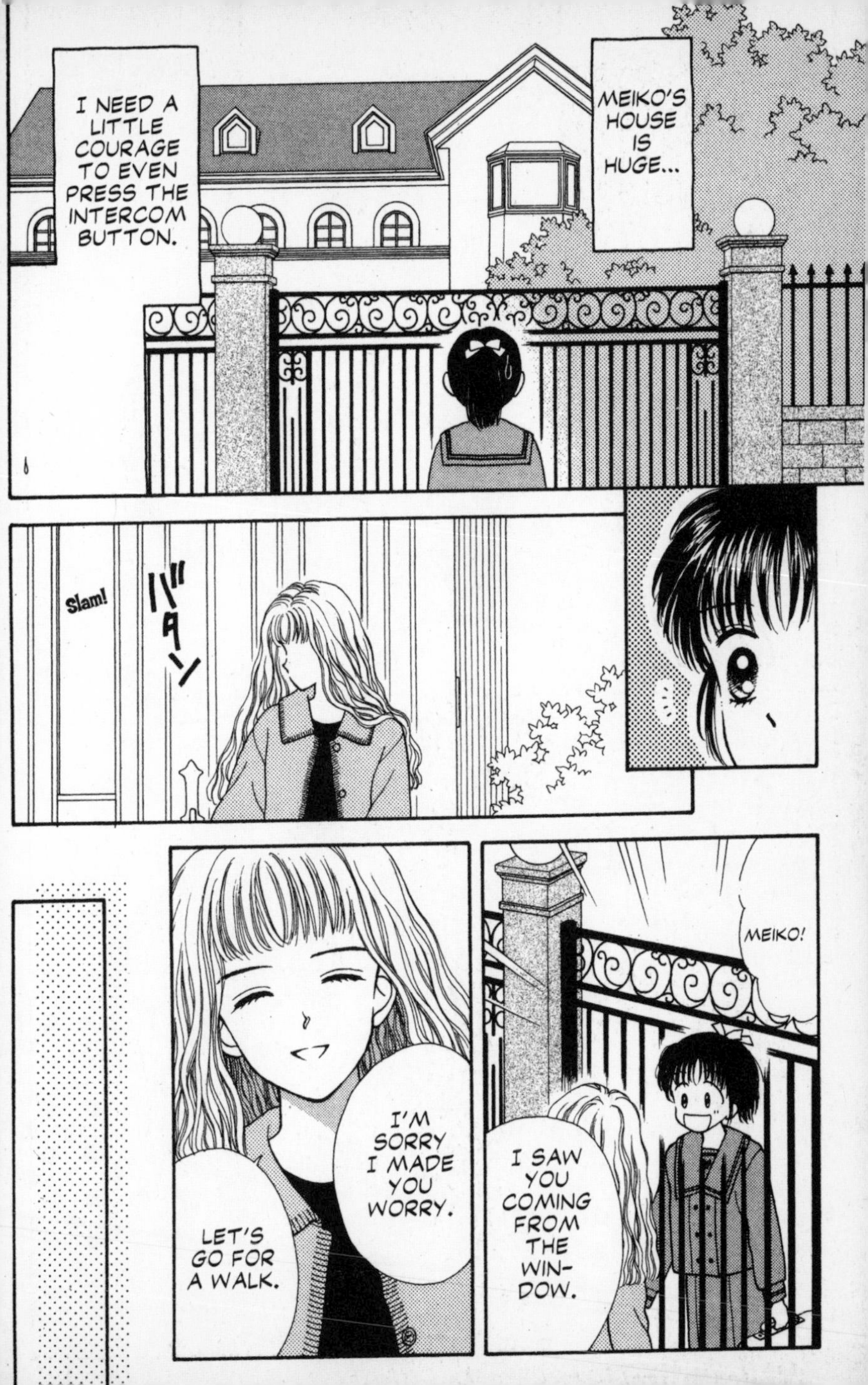
MEIKO'S HOUSE IS HUGE...
I NEED A LITTLE COURAGE TO EVEN PRESS THE INTERCOM BUTTON.
バタン
Slam!
MEIKO!
I SAW YOU COMING FROM THE WIN-DOW.
I'M SORRY I MADE YOU WORRY.
LET'S GO FOR A WALK.

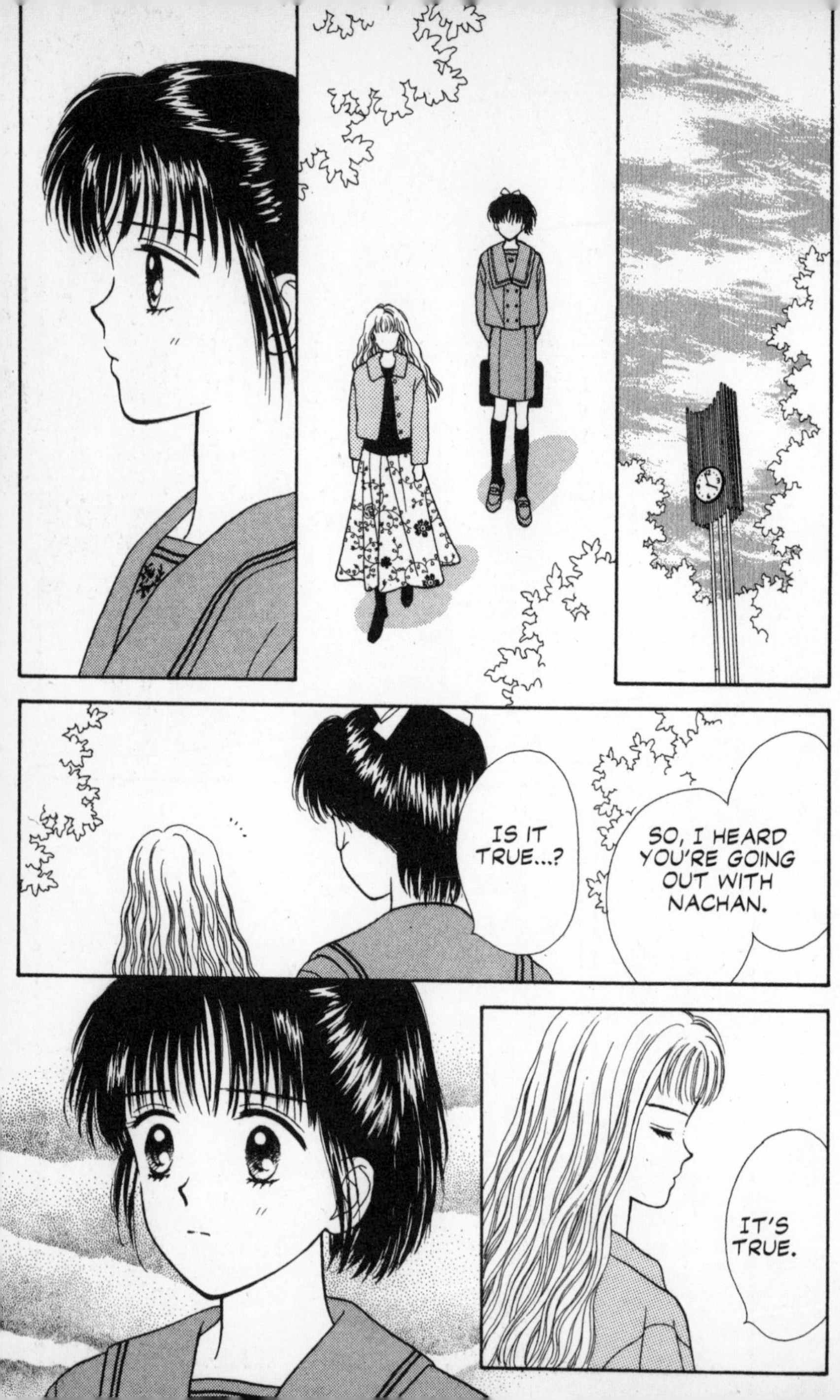
SO, I HEARD YOU'RE GOING OUT WITH NACHAN.
IS IT TRUE...?
IT'S TRUE.

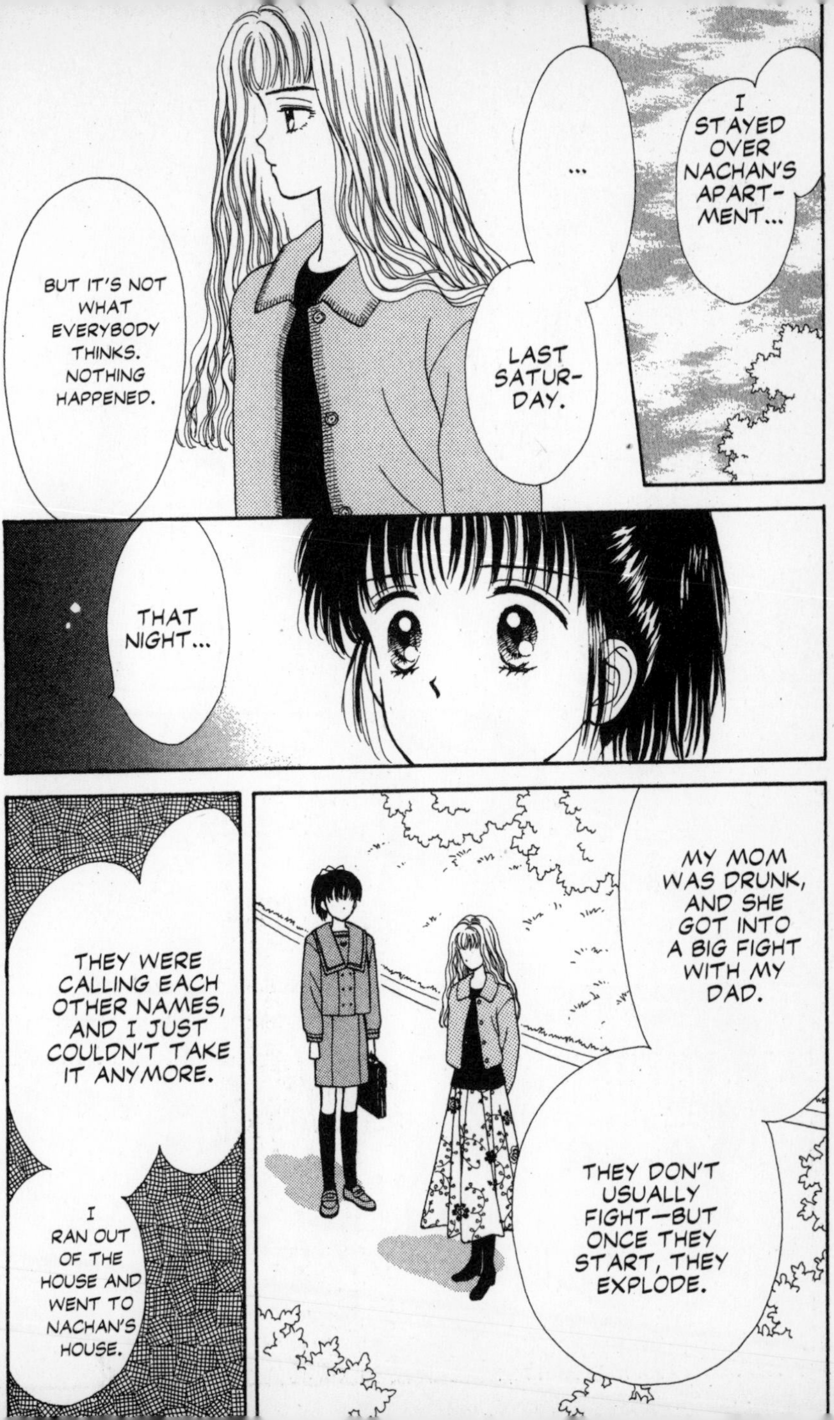
I STAYED OVER NACHAN'S APART-MENT...
...
LAST SATUR-DAY.
BUT IT'S NOT WHAT EVERYBODY THINKS. NOTHING HAPPENED.
THAT NIGHT...
MY MOM WAS DRUNK, AND SHE GOT INTO A BIG FIGHT WITH MY DAD.
THEY DON'T USUALLY FIGHT—BUT ONCE THEY START, THEY EXPLODE.
THEY WERE CALLING EACH OTHER NAMES, AND I JUST COULDN'T TAKE IT ANYMORE.
I RAN OUT OF THE HOUSE AND WENT TO NACHAN'S HOUSE.

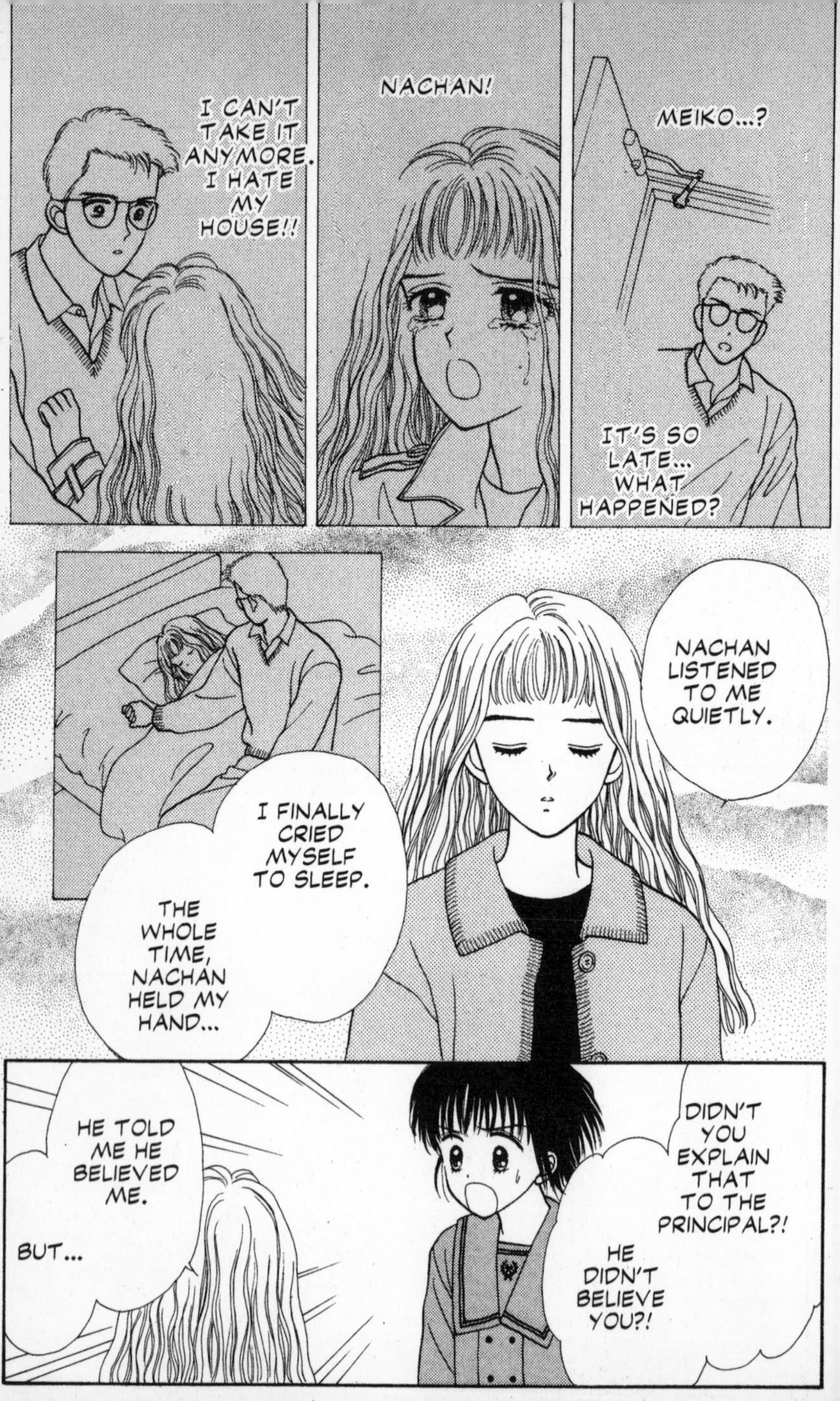
MEIKO...?
IT'S SO LATE... WHAT HAPPENED?
NACHAN!
I CAN'T TAKE IT ANYMORE. I HATE MY HOUSE!!
NACHAN LISTENED TO ME QUIETLY.
I FINALLY CRIED MYSELF TO SLEEP.
THE WHOLE TIME, NACHAN HELD MY HAND...
DIDN'T YOU EXPLAIN THAT TO THE PRINCIPAL?!
HE DIDN'T BELIEVE YOU?!
HE TOLD ME HE BELIEVED ME.
BUT...

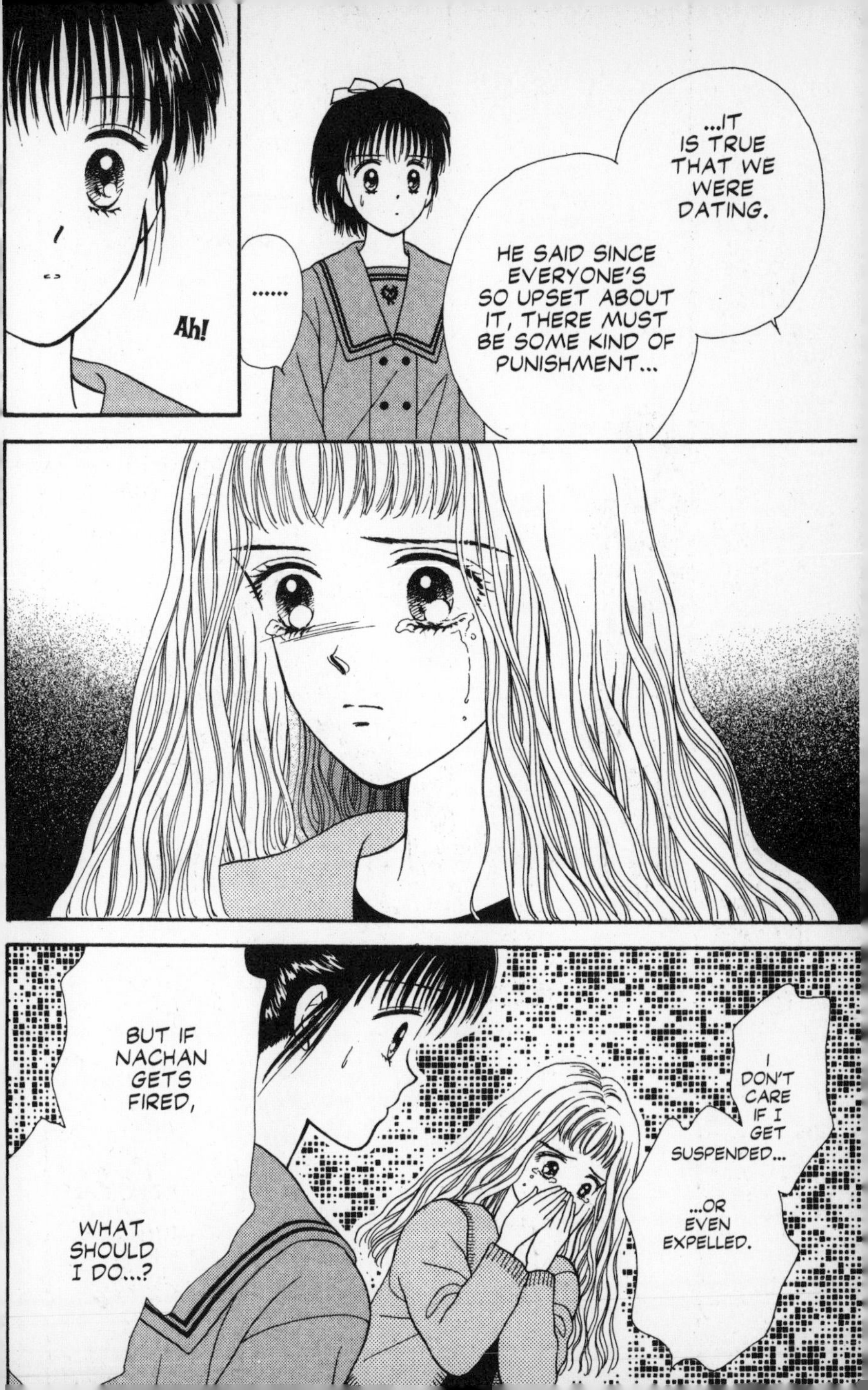
...IT IS TRUE THAT WE WERE DATING.
HE SAID SINCE EVERYONE'S SO UPSET ABOUT IT, THERE MUST BE SOME KIND OF PUNISHMENT...
......
Ah!
I DON'T CARE IF I GET SUSPENDED...
...OR EVEN EXPELLED.
BUT IF NACHAN GETS FIRED,
WHAT SHOULD I DO...?

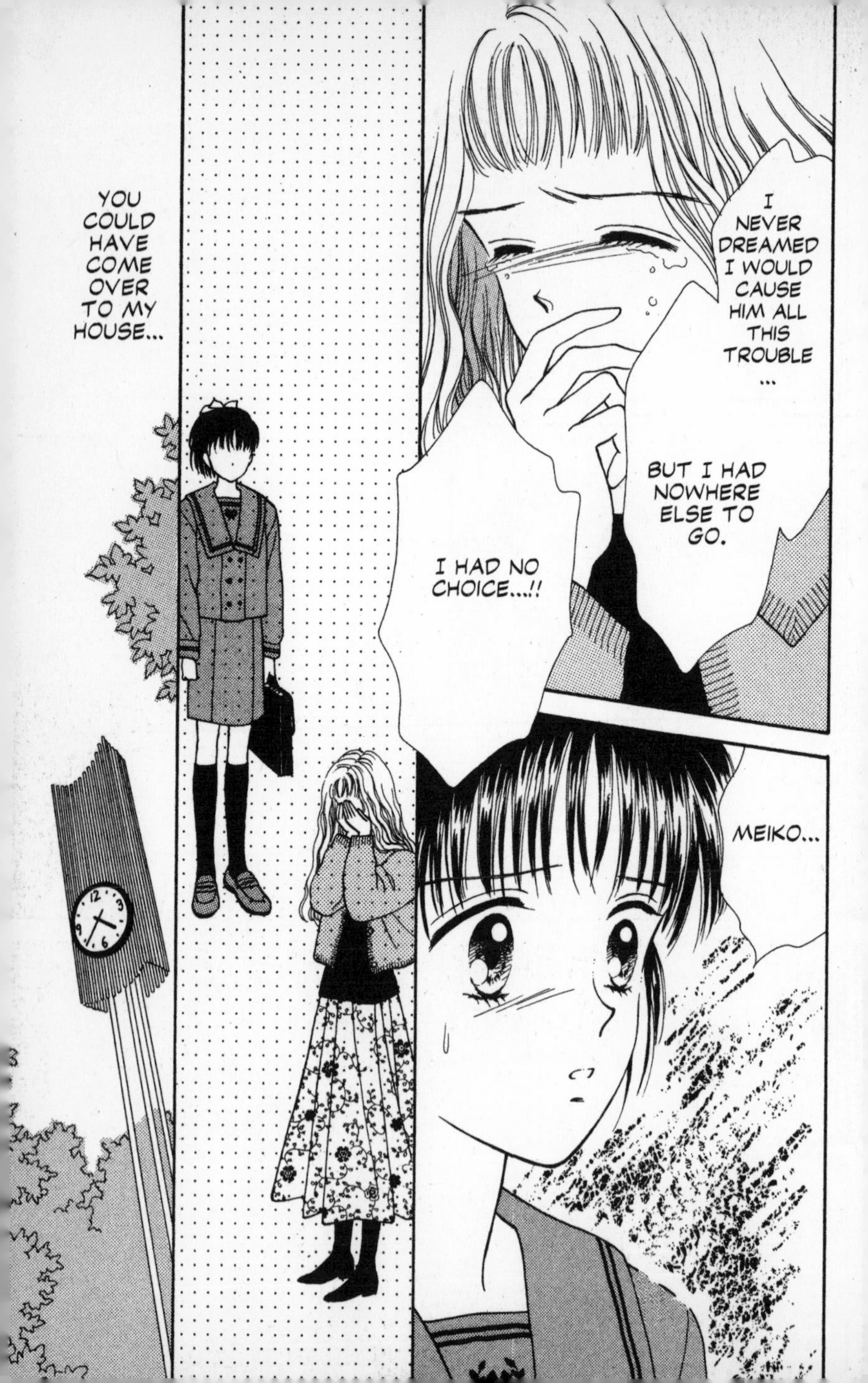
I NEVER DREAMED I WOULD CAUSE HIM ALL THIS TROUBLE ...
BUT I HAD NOWHERE ELSE TO GO.
I HAD NO CHOICE...!!
MEIKO...
YOU COULD HAVE COME OVER TO MY HOUSE...

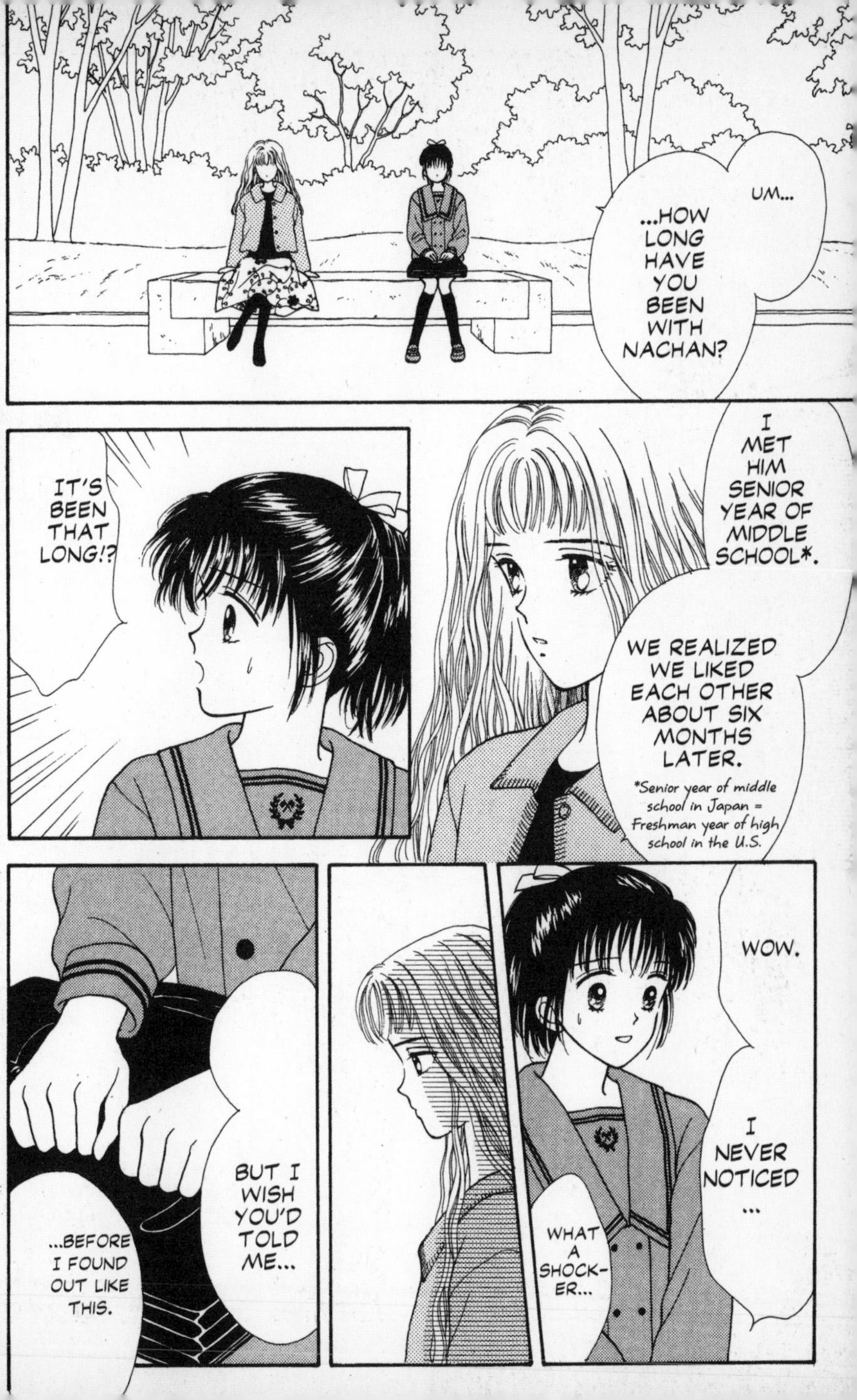
UM...
...HOW LONG HAVE YOU BEEN WITH NACHAN?
I MET HIM SENIOR YEAR OF MIDDLE SCHOOL*.
WE REALIZED WE LIKED EACH OTHER ABOUT SIX MONTHS LATER.
*Senior year of middle school in Japan = Freshman year of high school in the U.S.
IT'S BEEN THAT LONG!?
WOW.
I NEVER NOTICED ...
WHAT A SHOCKER...
BUT I WISH YOU'D TOLD ME...
...BEFORE I FOUND OUT LIKE THIS.

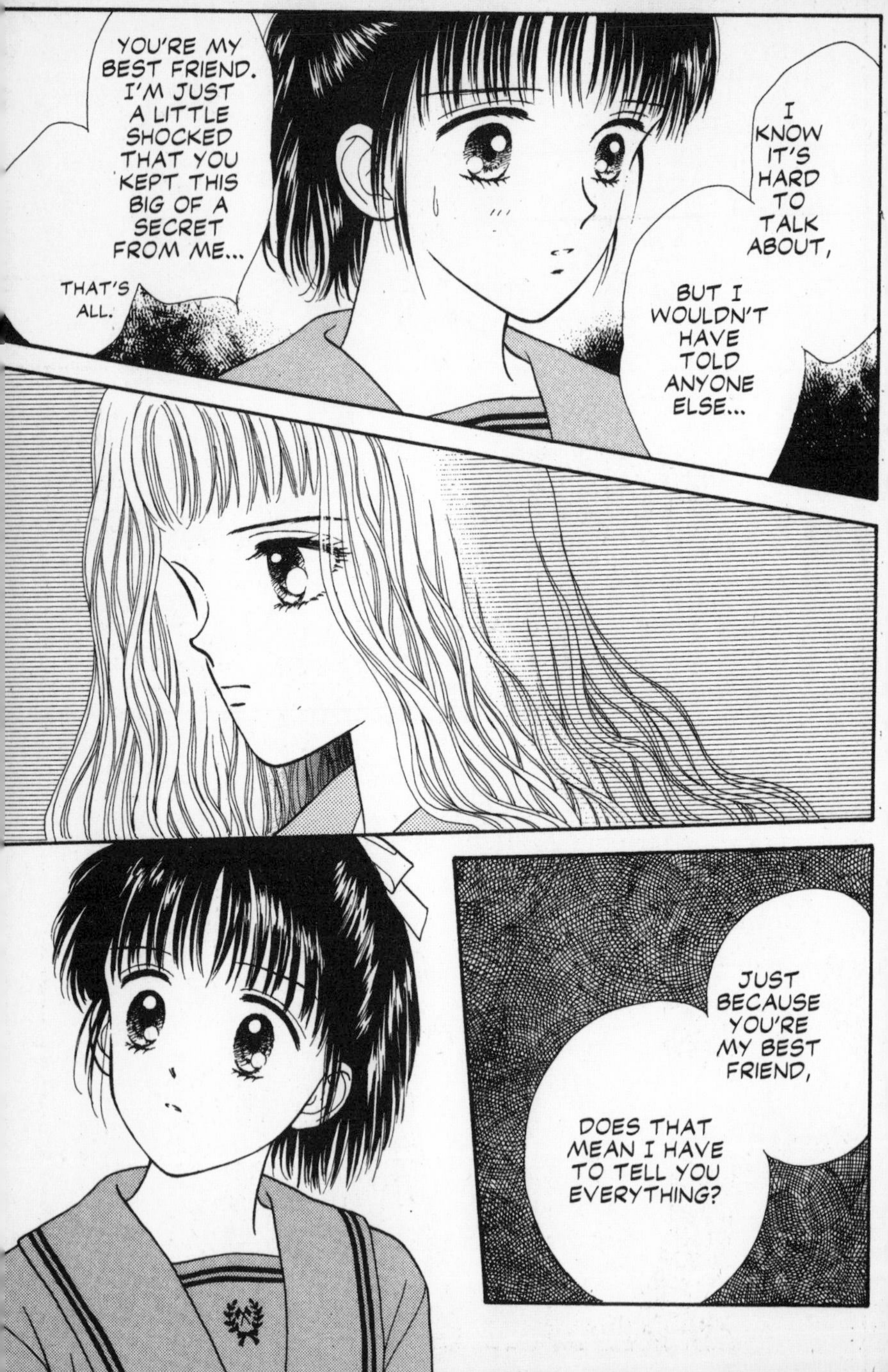
I KNOW IT'S HARD TO TALK ABOUT,
BUT I WOULDN'T HAVE TOLD ANYONE ELSE...
YOU'RE MY BEST FRIEND. I'M JUST A LITTLE SHOCKED THAT YOU KEPT THIS BIG OF A SECRET FROM ME...
THAT'S ALL.
JUST BECAUSE YOU'RE MY BEST FRIEND,
DOES THAT MEAN I HAVE TO TELL YOU EVERYTHING?

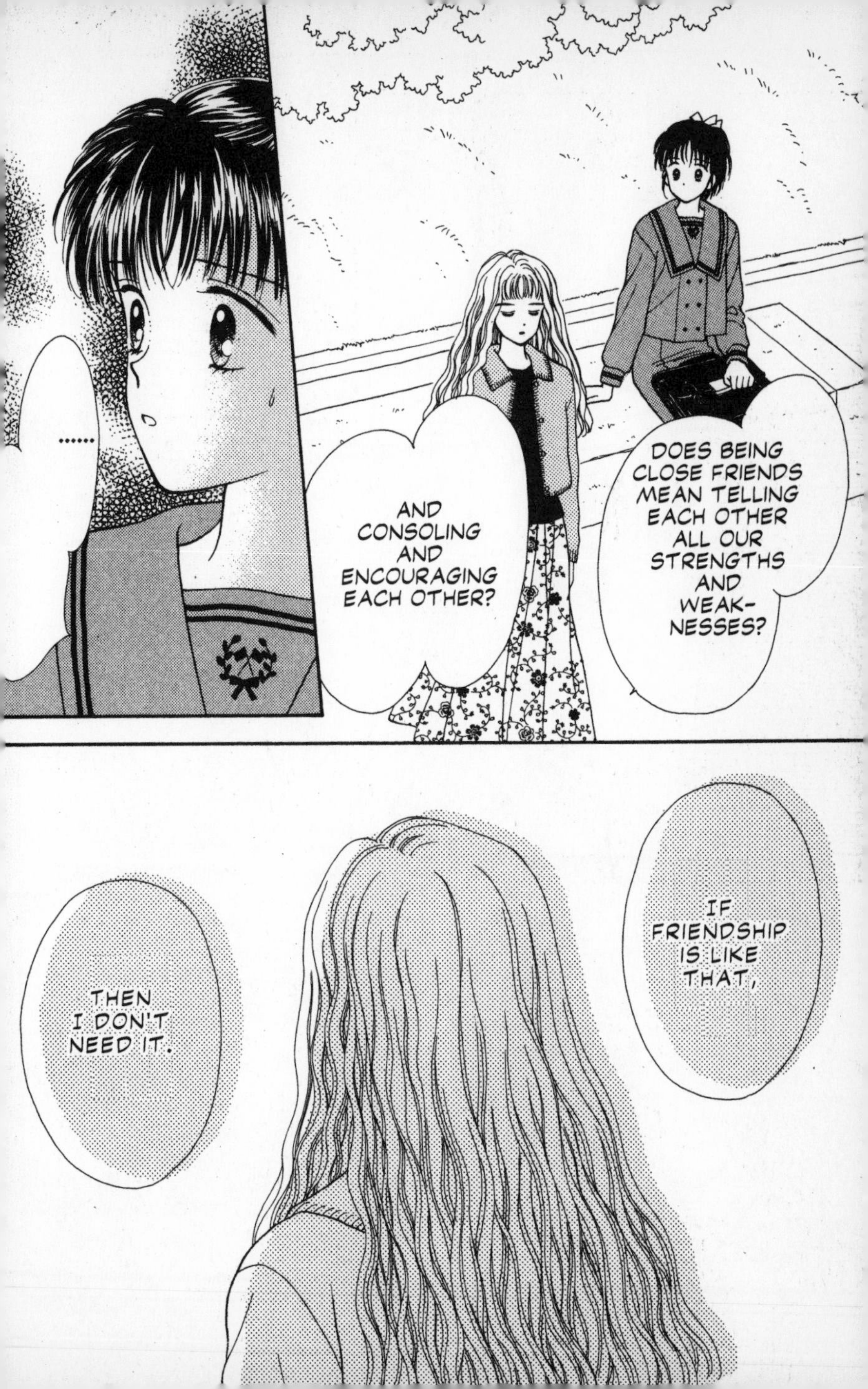
DOES BEING CLOSE FRIENDS MEAN TELLING EACH OTHER ALL OUR STRENGTHS AND WEAK-NESSES?
AND CONSOLING AND ENCOURAGING EACH OTHER?
......
IF FRIENDSHIP IS LIKE THAT,
THEN I DON'T NEED IT.

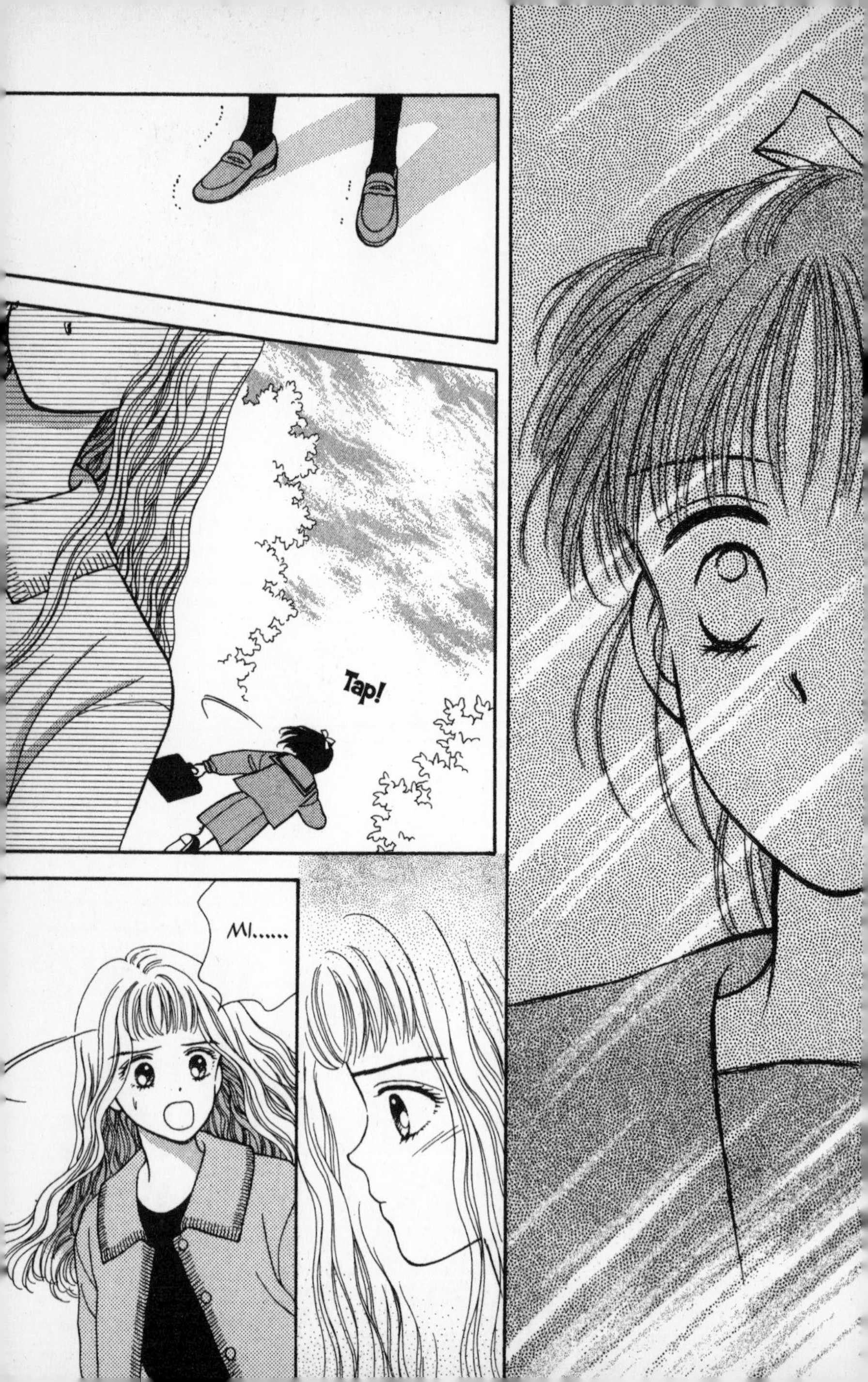
Tap!
MI......

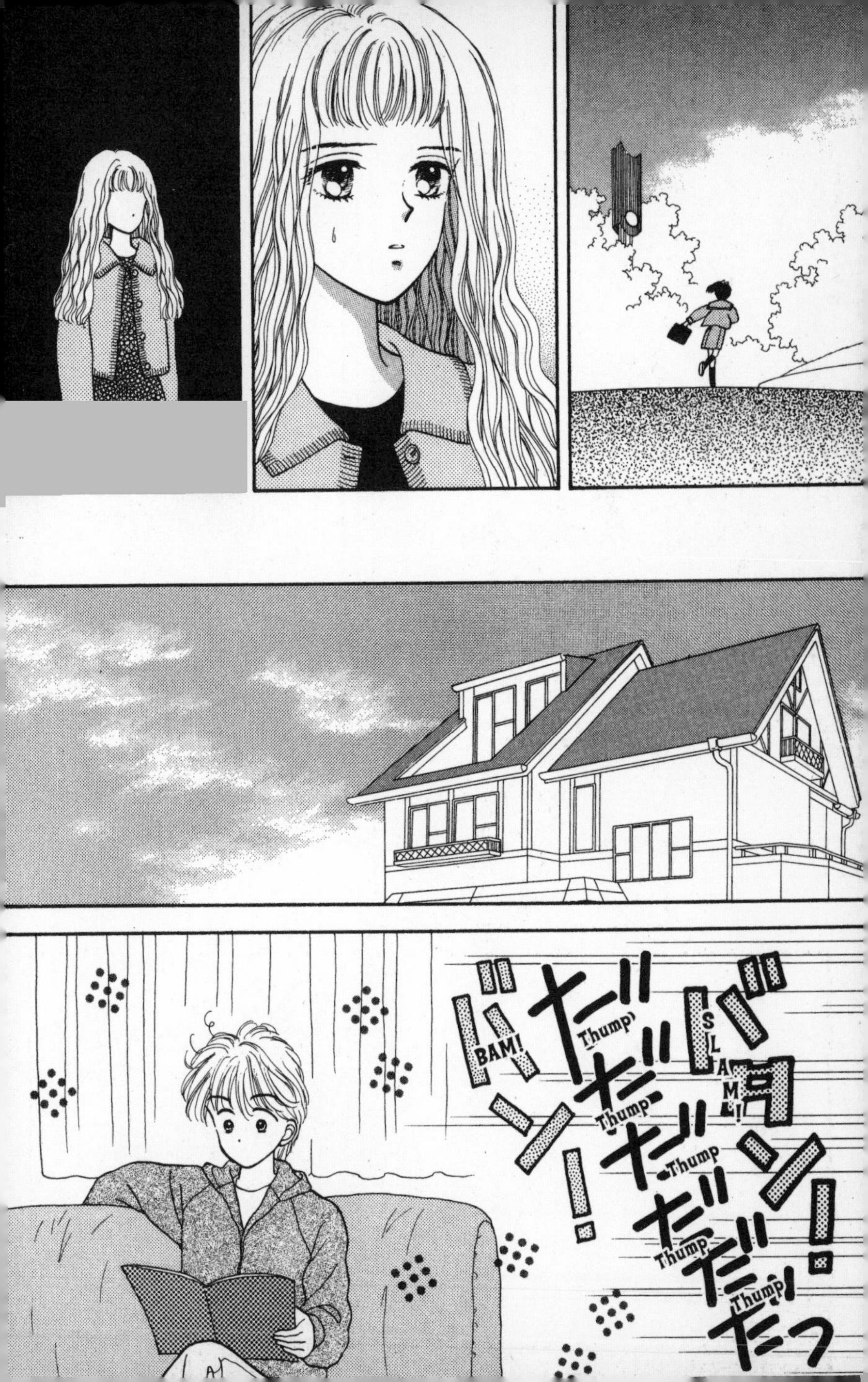
バタン!
SLAM!
ダダダダダッ
Thump Thump Thump Thump Thump
バン!
BAM!

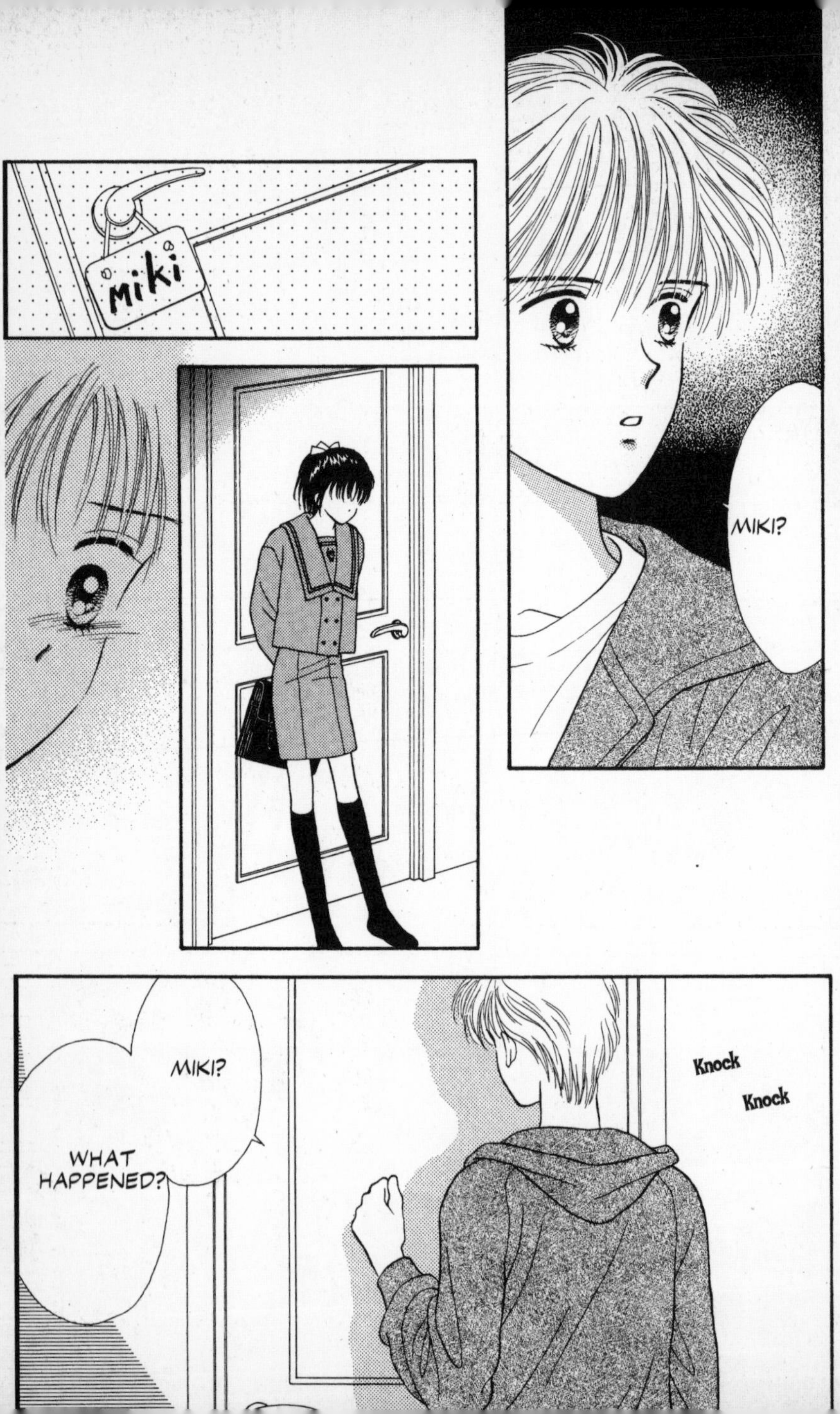
MIKI?
Miki
Knock
Knock
MIKI?
WHAT HAPPENED?

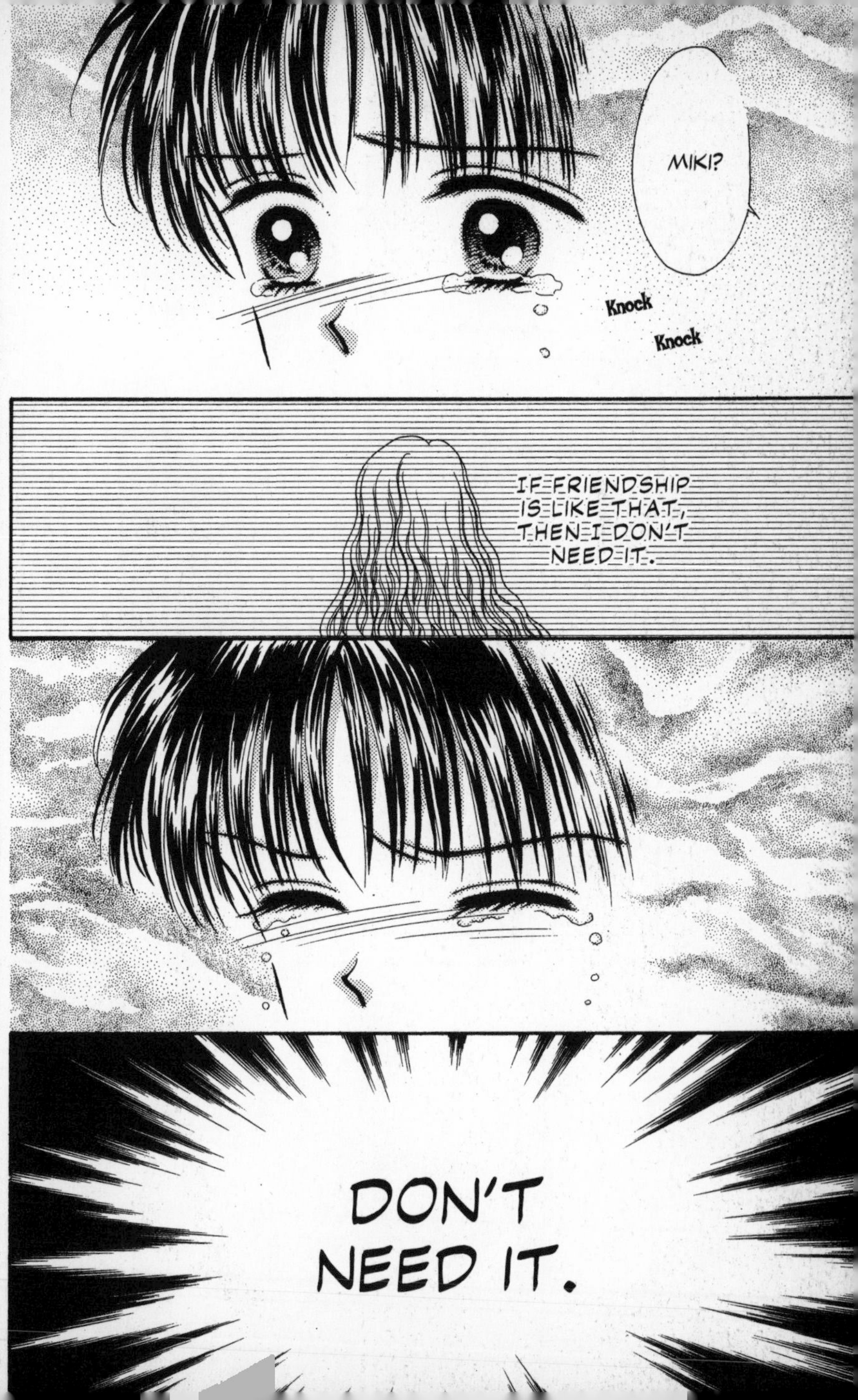
MIKI?
Knock
Knock
IF FRIENDSHIP IS LIKE THAT, THEN I DON'T NEED IT.
DON'T NEED IT.

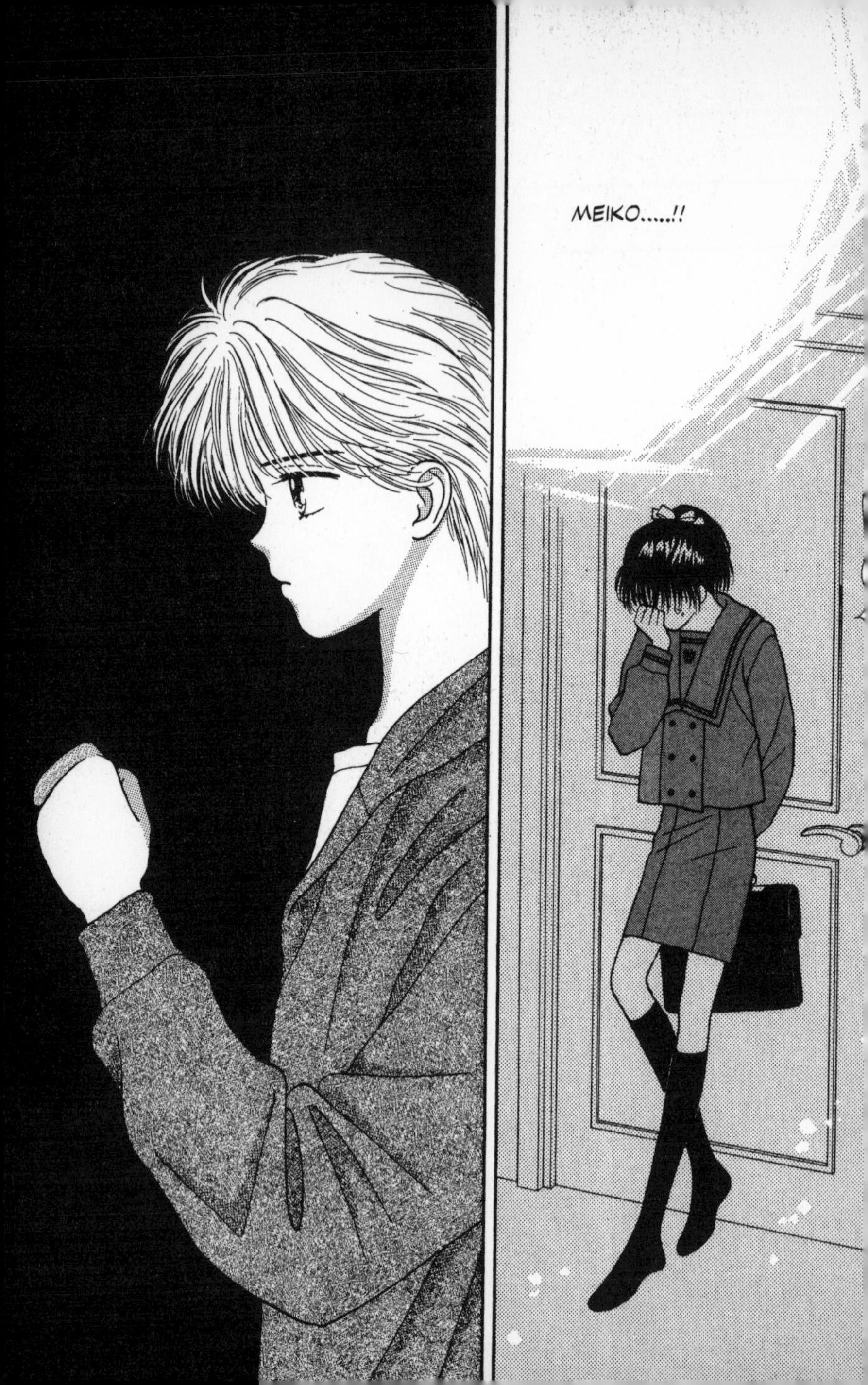
MEIKO.....!!

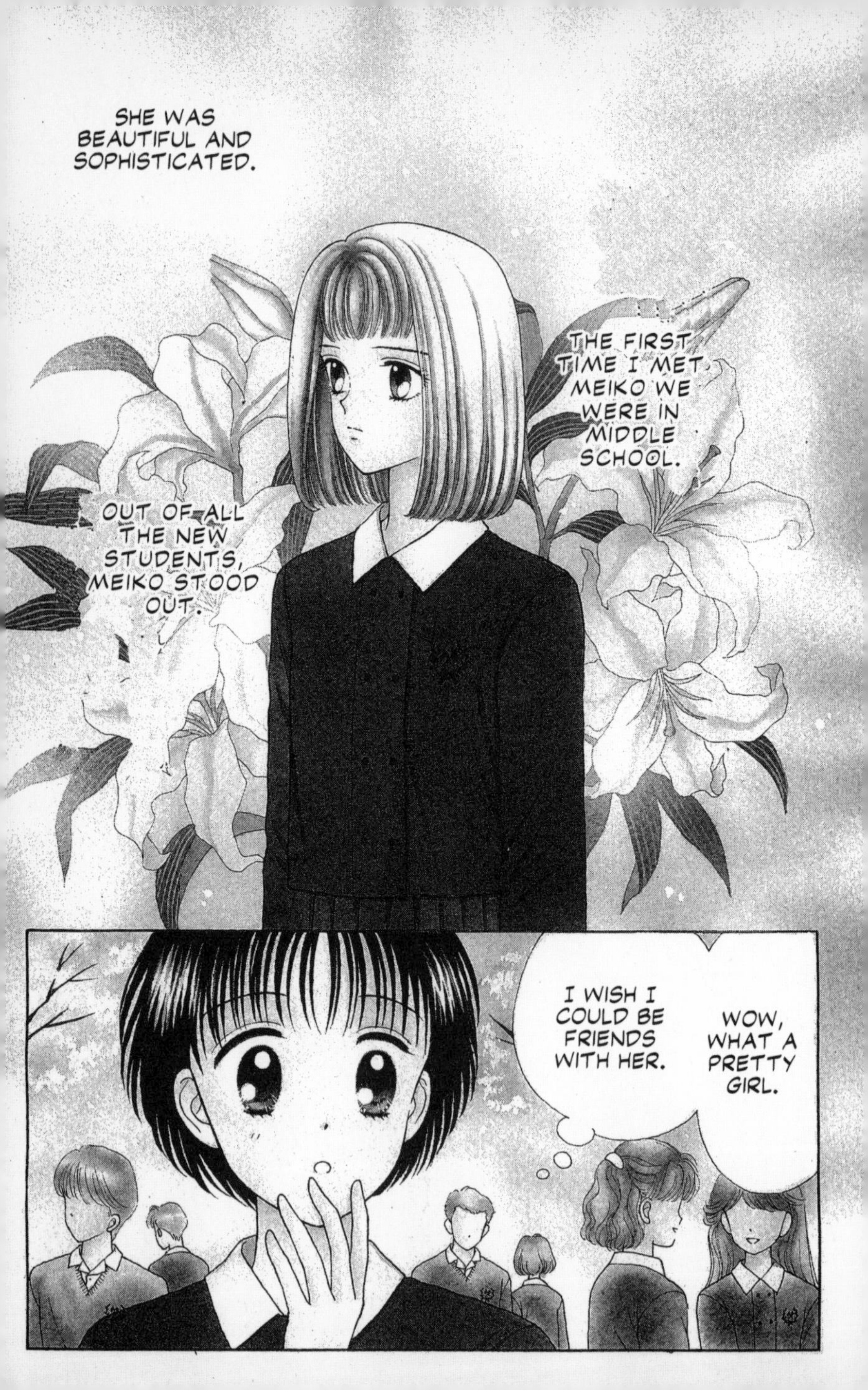
SHE WAS BEAUTIFUL AND SOPHISTICATED.
THE FIRST TIME I MET MEIKO WE WERE IN MIDDLE SCHOOL.
OUT OF ALL THE NEW STUDENTS, MEIKO STOOD OUT.
WOW, WHAT A PRETTY GIRL.
I WISH I COULD BE FRIENDS WITH HER.

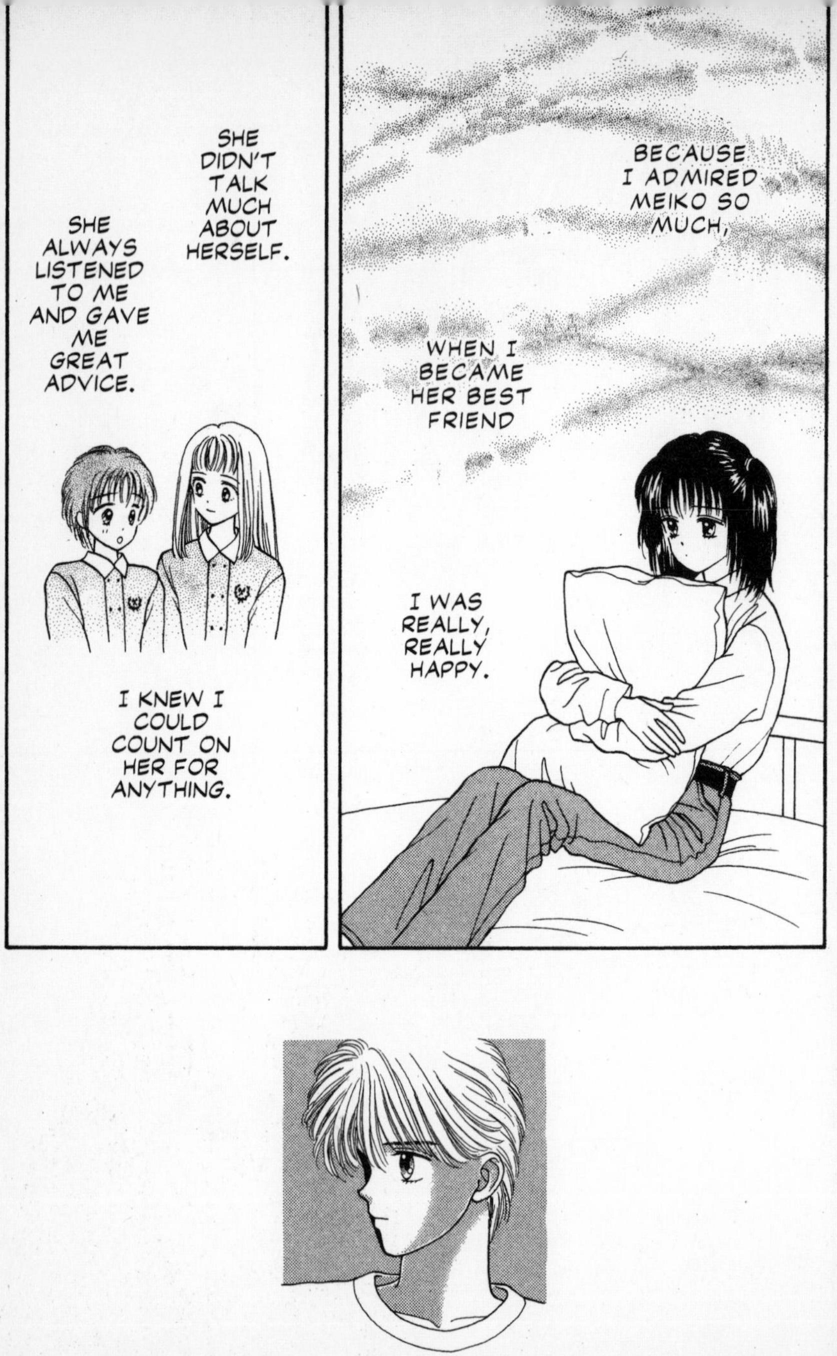
BECAUSE I ADMIRED MEIKO SO MUCH,
WHEN I BECAME HER BEST FRIEND
I WAS REALLY, REALLY HAPPY.
SHE DIDN'T TALK MUCH ABOUT HERSELF.
SHE ALWAYS LISTENED TO ME AND GAVE ME GREAT ADVICE.
I KNEW I COULD COUNT ON HER FOR ANYTHING.

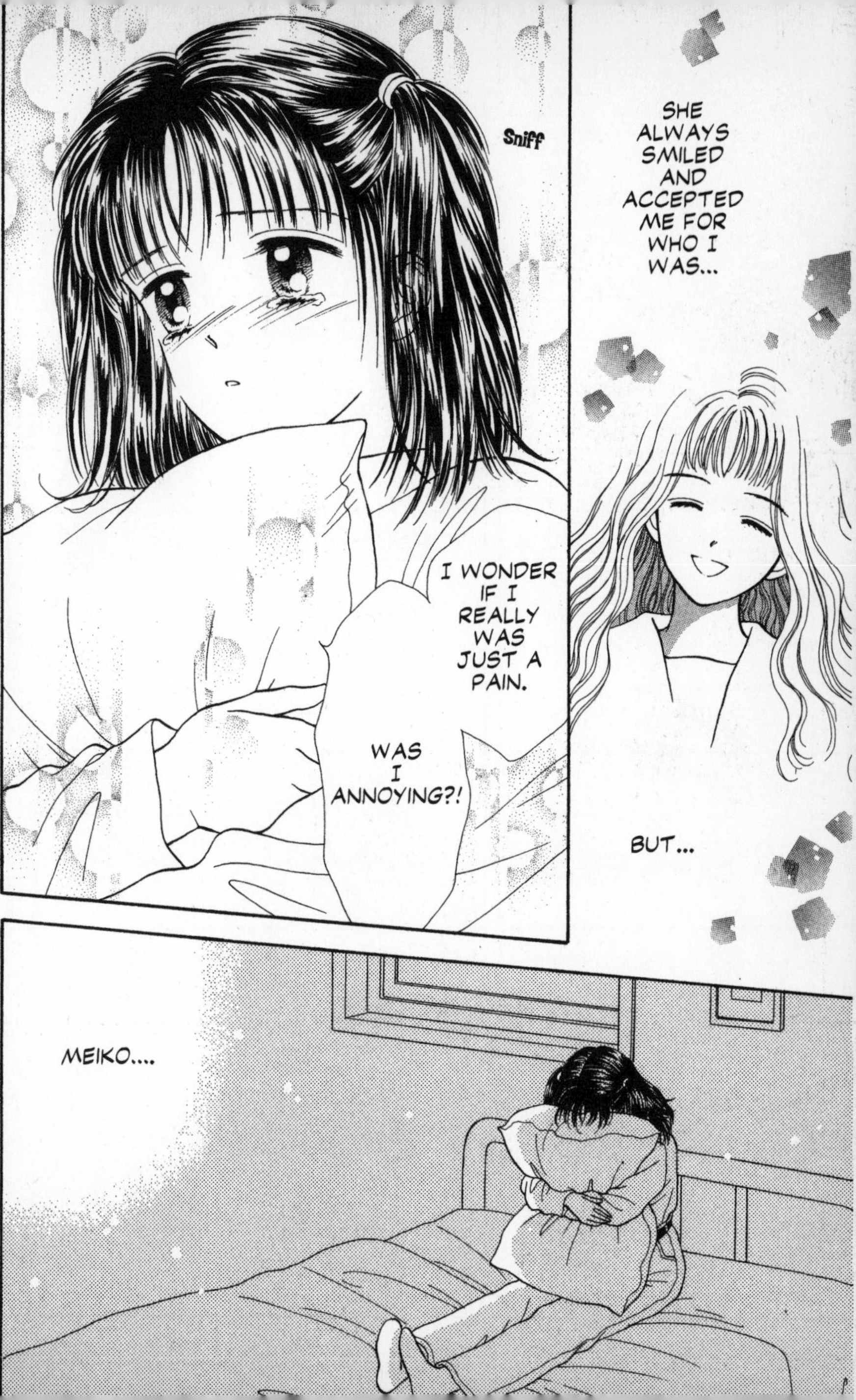
SHE ALWAYS SMILED AND ACCEPTED ME FOR WHO I WAS...
BUT...
Sniff
I WONDER IF I REALLY WAS JUST A PAIN.
WAS I ANNOYING?!
MEIKO....

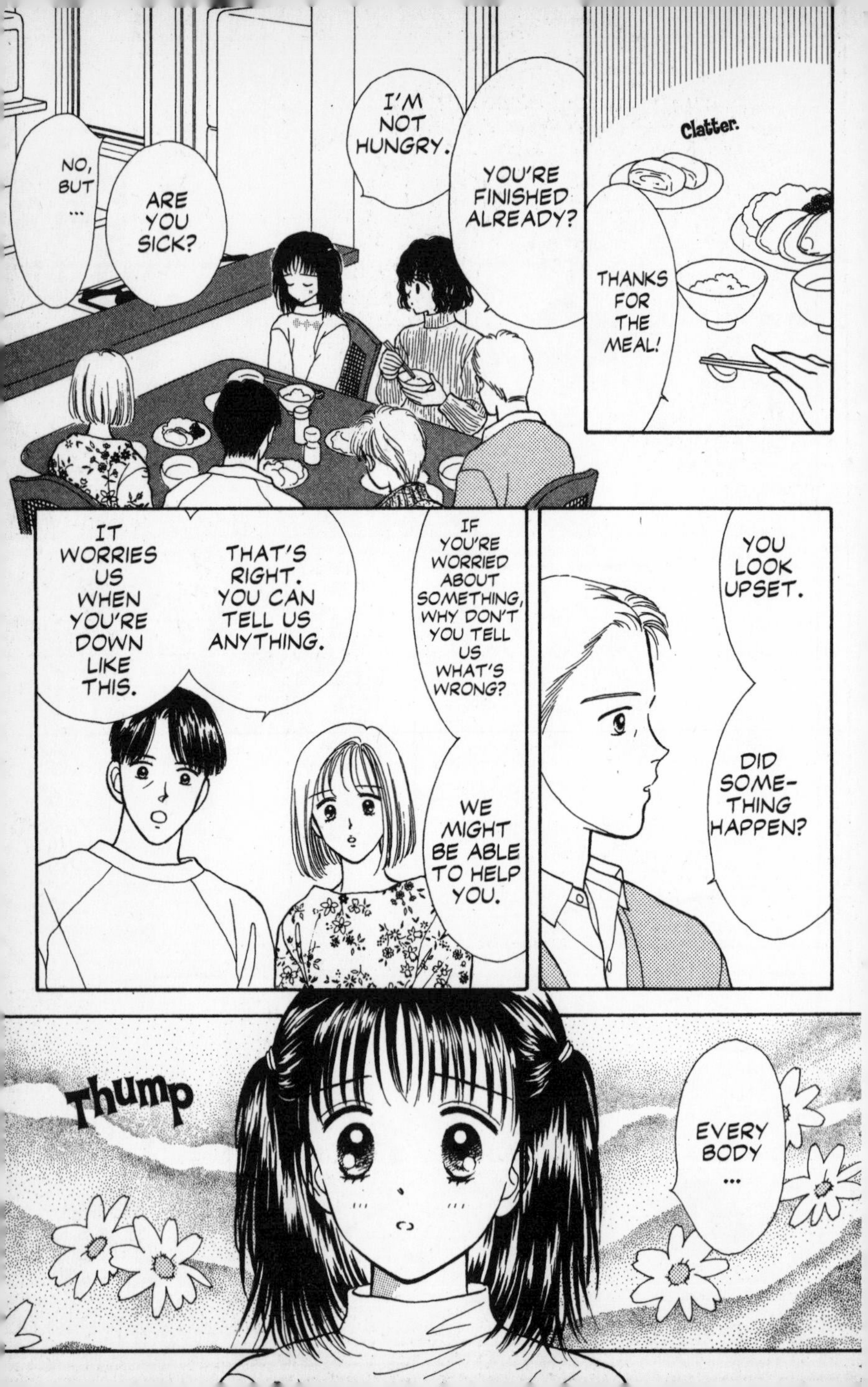

Clatter.
THANKS FOR THE MEAL!
YOU'RE FINISHED ALREADY?
I'M NOT HUNGRY.
ARE YOU SICK?
NO, BUT ...
YOU LOOK UPSET.
DID SOME-THING HAPPEN?
IF YOU'RE WORRIED ABOUT SOMETHING, WHY DON'T YOU TELL US WHAT'S WRONG?
WE MIGHT BE ABLE TO HELP YOU.
THAT'S RIGHT. YOU CAN TELL US ANYTHING.
IT WORRIES US WHEN YOU'RE DOWN LIKE THIS.
EVERY BODY ...
Thump

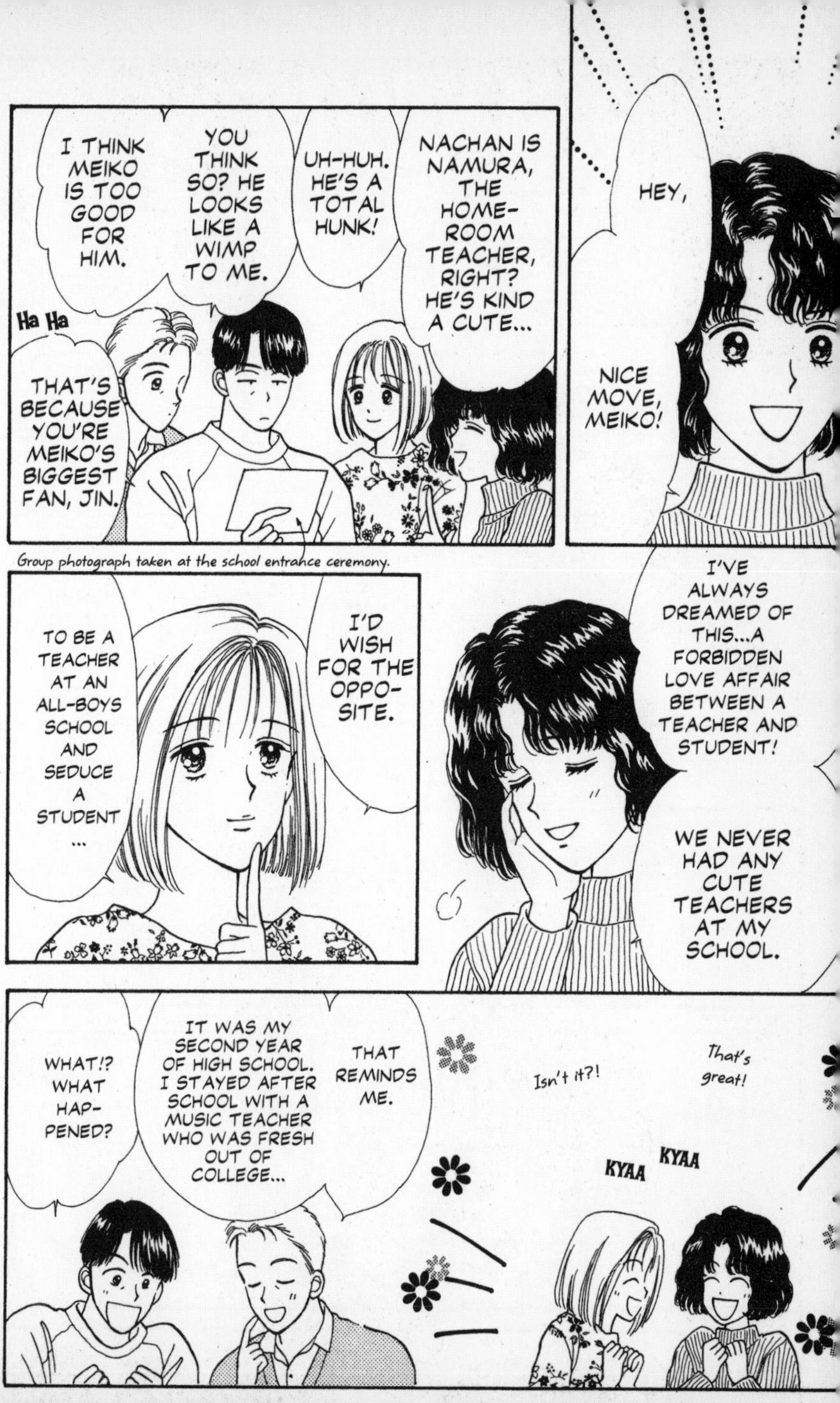
HEY,
NICE MOVE, MEIKO!
NACHAN IS NAMURA, THE HOMEROOM TEACHER, RIGHT? HE'S KIND A CUTE...
UH-HUH. HE'S A TOTAL HUNK!
YOU THINK SO? HE LOOKS LIKE A WIMP TO ME.
I THINK MEIKO IS TOO GOOD FOR HIM.
Ha Ha
THAT'S BECAUSE YOU'RE MEIKO'S BIGGEST FAN, JIN.
Group photograph taken at the school entrance ceremony.
I'VE ALWAYS DREAMED OF THIS...A FORBIDDEN LOVE AFFAIR BETWEEN A TEACHER AND STUDENT!
WE NEVER HAD ANY CUTE TEACHERS AT MY SCHOOL.
I'D WISH FOR THE OPPOSITE.
TO BE A TEACHER AT AN ALL-BOYS SCHOOL AND SEDUCE A STUDENT...
That's great!
Isn't it?!
KYAA
KYAA
THAT REMINDS ME.
IT WAS MY SECOND YEAR OF HIGH SCHOOL. I STAYED AFTER SCHOOL WITH A MUSIC TEACHER WHO WAS FRESH OUT OF COLLEGE...
WHAT!? WHAT HAPPENED?

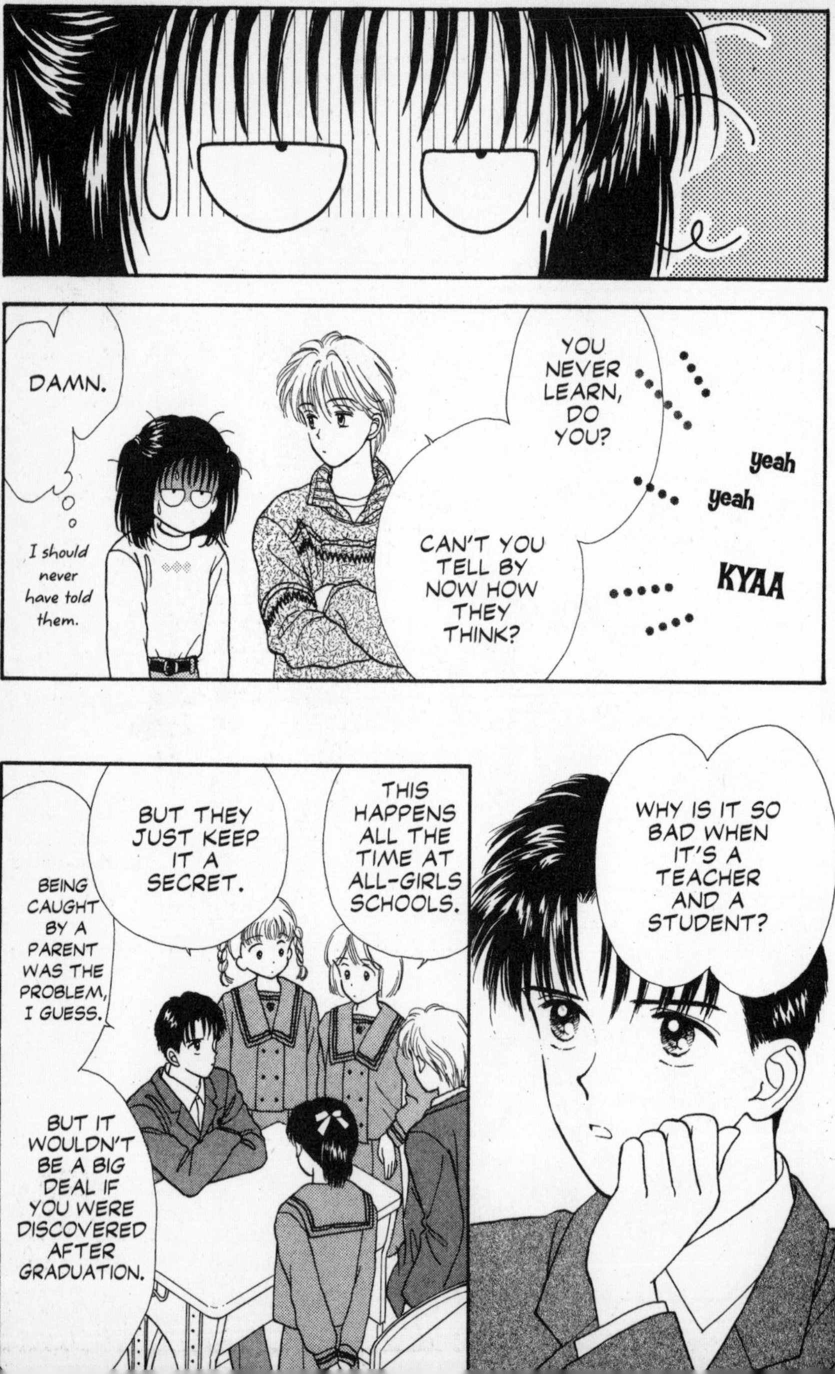
YOU NEVER LEARN, DO YOU?
CAN'T YOU TELL BY NOW HOW THEY THINK?
yeah
yeah
KYAA
DAMN.
I should never have told them.
WHY IS IT SO BAD WHEN IT'S A TEACHER AND A STUDENT?
THIS HAPPENS ALL THE TIME AT ALL-GIRLS SCHOOLS.
BUT THEY JUST KEEP IT A SECRET.
BEING CAUGHT BY A PARENT WAS THE PROBLEM, I GUESS.
BUT IT WOULDN'T BE A BIG DEAL IF YOU WERE DISCOVERED AFTER GRADUATION.

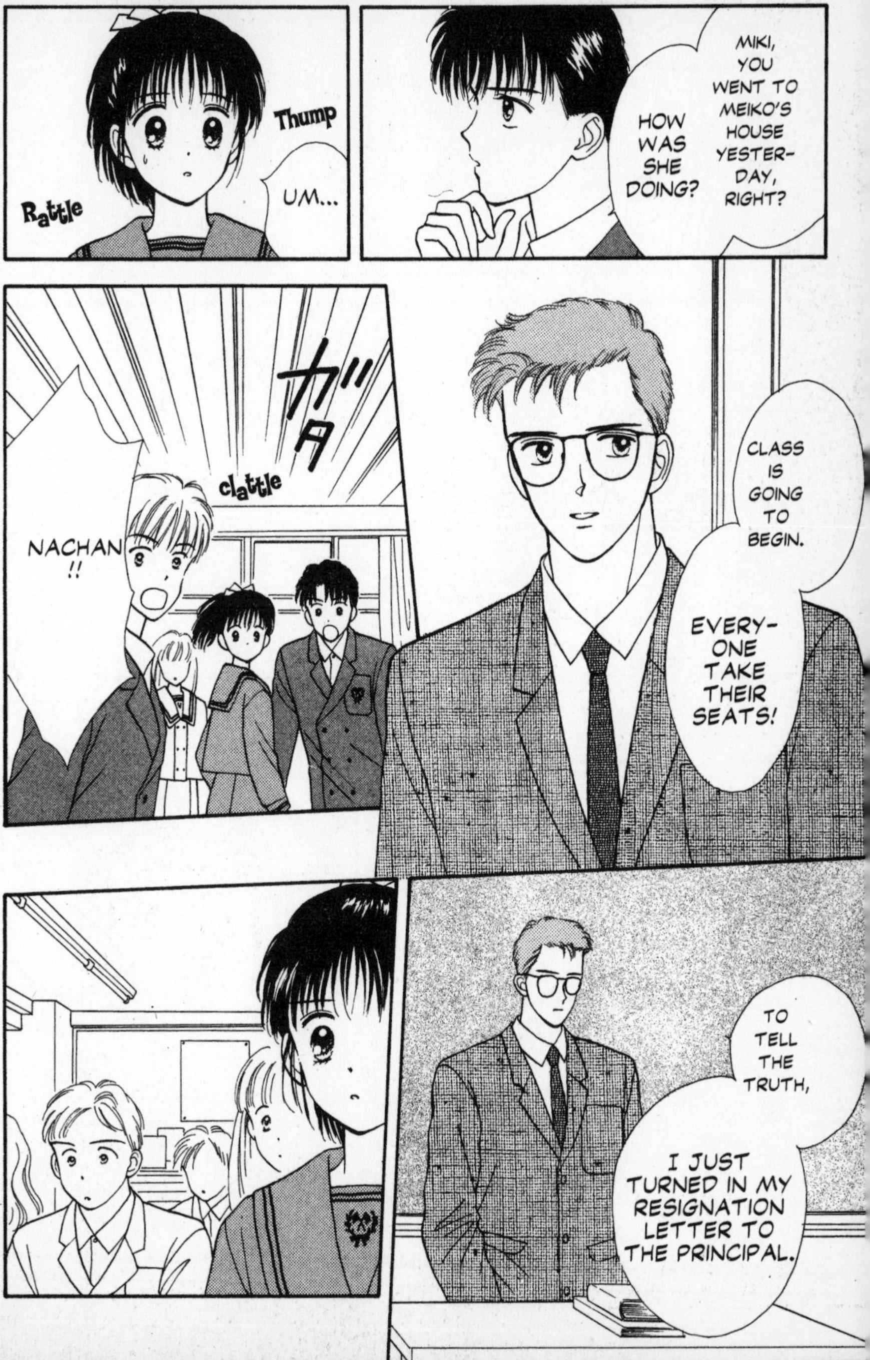

MIKI, YOU WENT TO MEIKO'S HOUSE YESTER-DAY, RIGHT?
HOW WAS SHE DOING?
Thump
UM...
Rattle
CLASS IS GOING TO BEGIN.
EVERY-ONE TAKE THEIR SEATS!
ガタ
clattle
NACHAN !!
TO TELL THE TRUTH,
I JUST TURNED IN MY RESIGNATION LETTER TO THE PRINCIPAL.

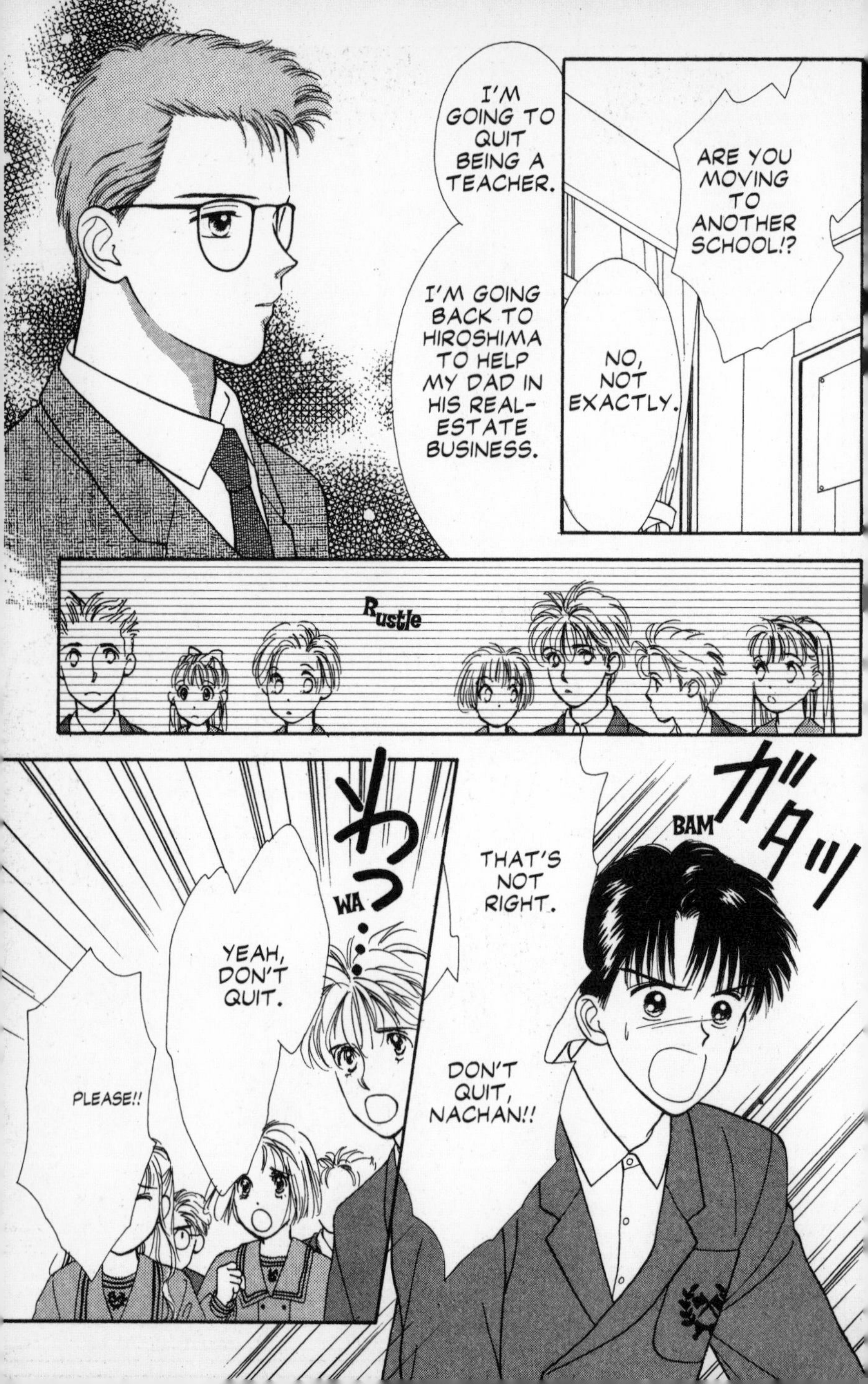
ARE YOU MOVING TO ANOTHER SCHOOL!?
NO, NOT EXACTLY.
I'M GOING TO QUIT BEING A TEACHER.
I'M GOING BACK TO HIROSHIMA TO HELP MY DAD IN HIS REAL-ESTATE BUSINESS.
Rustle
ガタッ
BAM
THAT'S NOT RIGHT.
DON'T QUIT, NACHAN!!
わっ
WA...
YEAH, DON'T QUIT.
PLEASE!!

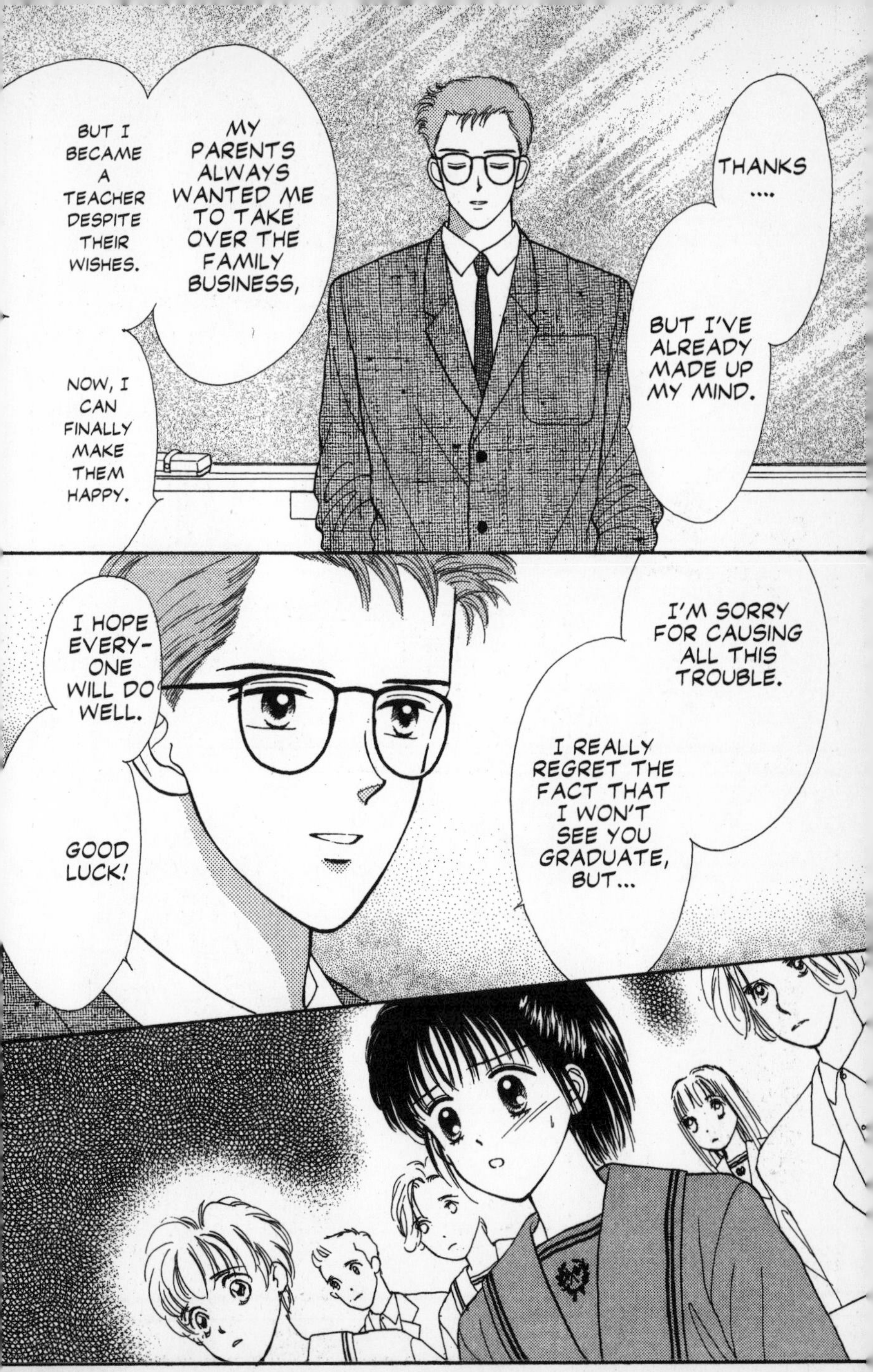
THANKS ....
BUT I'VE ALREADY MADE UP MY MIND.
MY PARENTS ALWAYS WANTED ME TO TAKE OVER THE FAMILY BUSINESS,
BUT I BECAME A TEACHER DESPITE THEIR WISHES.
NOW, I CAN FINALLY MAKE THEM HAPPY.
I'M SORRY FOR CAUSING ALL THIS TROUBLE.
I REALLY REGRET THE FACT THAT I WON'T SEE YOU GRADUATE, BUT...
I HOPE EVERYONE WILL DO WELL.
GOOD LUCK!

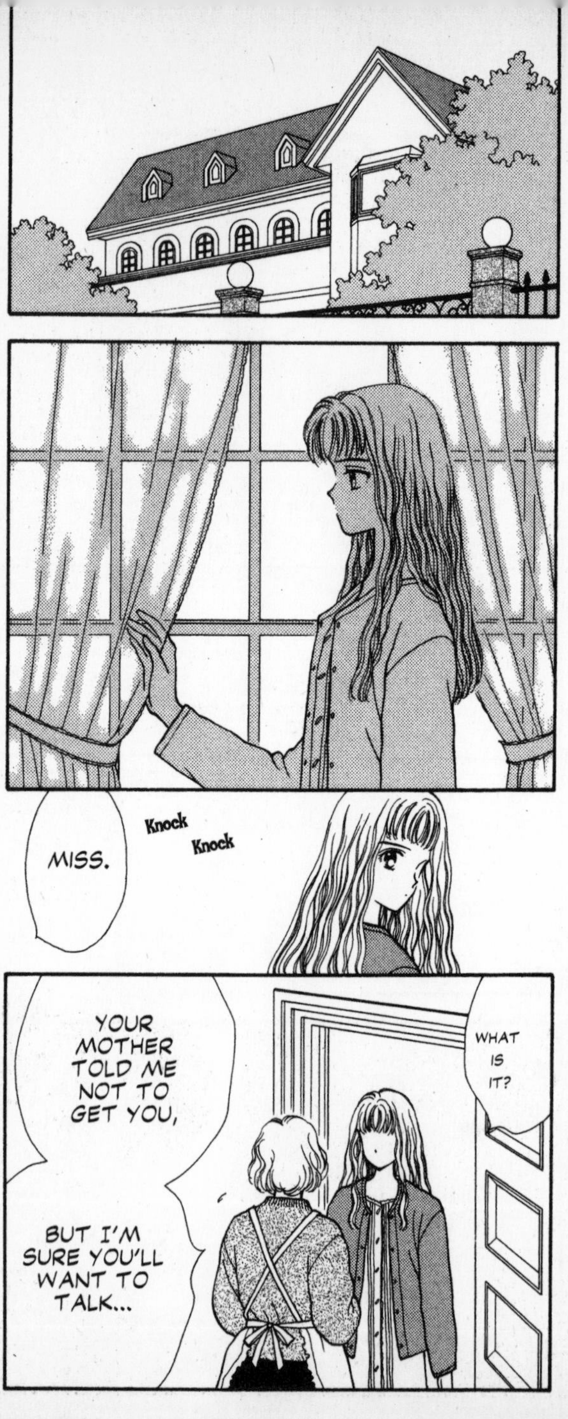
Knock
Knock
MISS.
WHAT IS IT?
YOUR MOTHER TOLD ME NOT TO GET YOU,
BUT I'M SURE YOU'LL WANT TO TALK...

Shin ichi Namura

HOROSCOPE: PISCES

BLOODTYPE: A

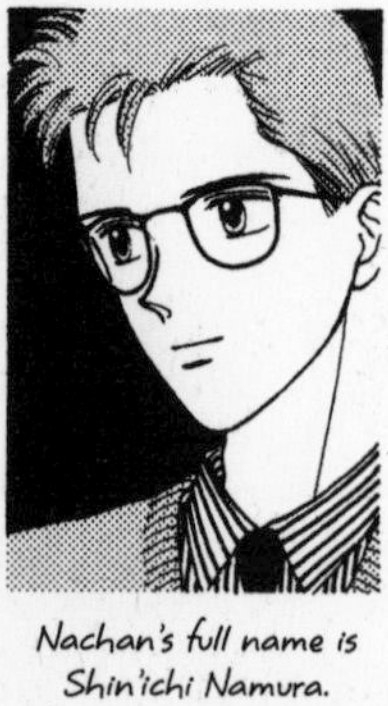

Nachan's full name is Shin'ichi Namura. (I just decided now!)

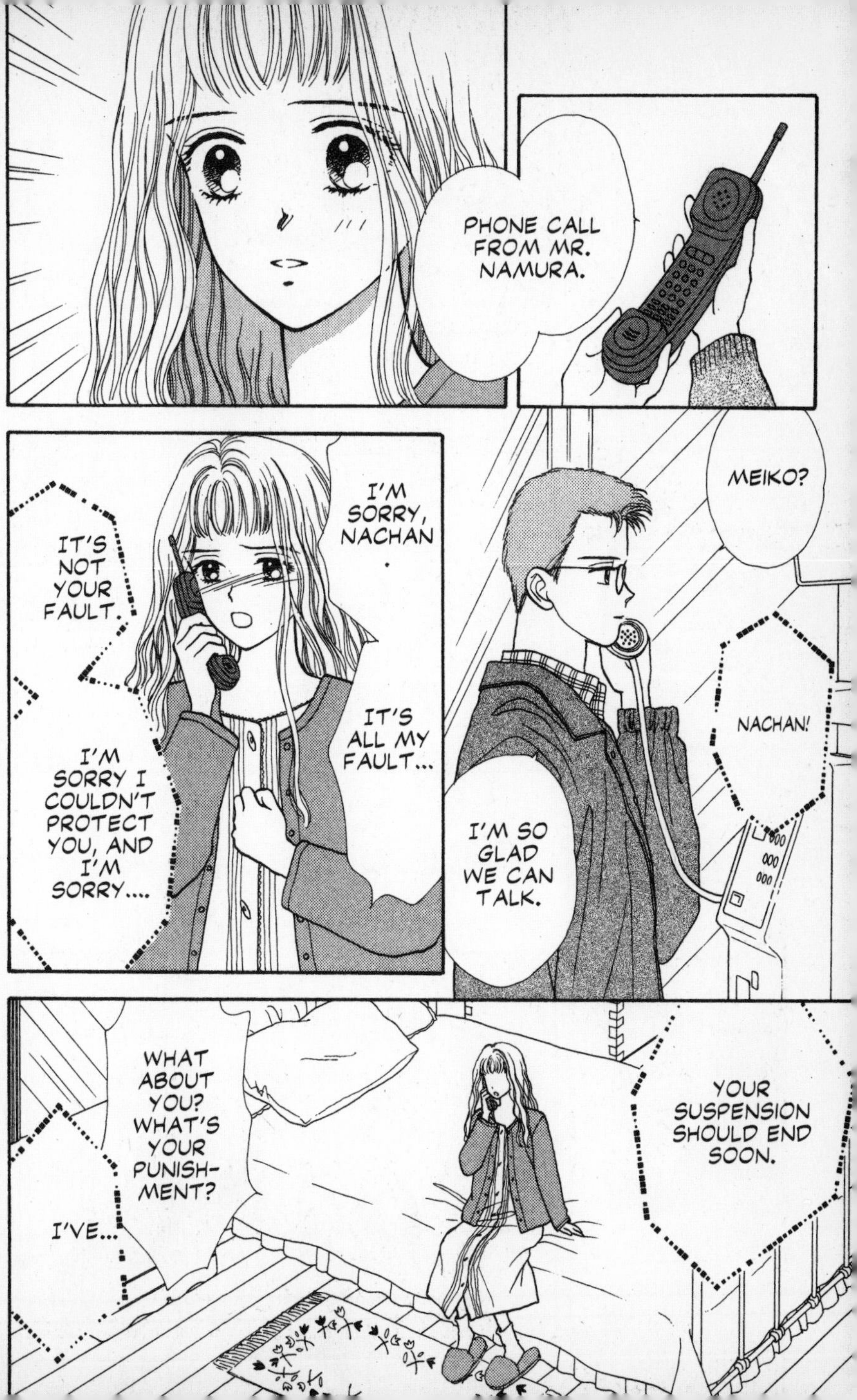
PHONE CALL FROM MR. NAMURA.
MEIKO?
NACHAN!
I'M SO GLAD WE CAN TALK.
I'M SORRY, NACHAN.
IT'S ALL MY FAULT...
IT'S NOT YOUR FAULT.
I'M SORRY I COULDN'T PROTECT YOU, AND I'M SORRY....
YOUR SUSPENSION SHOULD END SOON.
WHAT ABOUT YOU? WHAT'S YOUR PUNISHMENT?
I'VE...

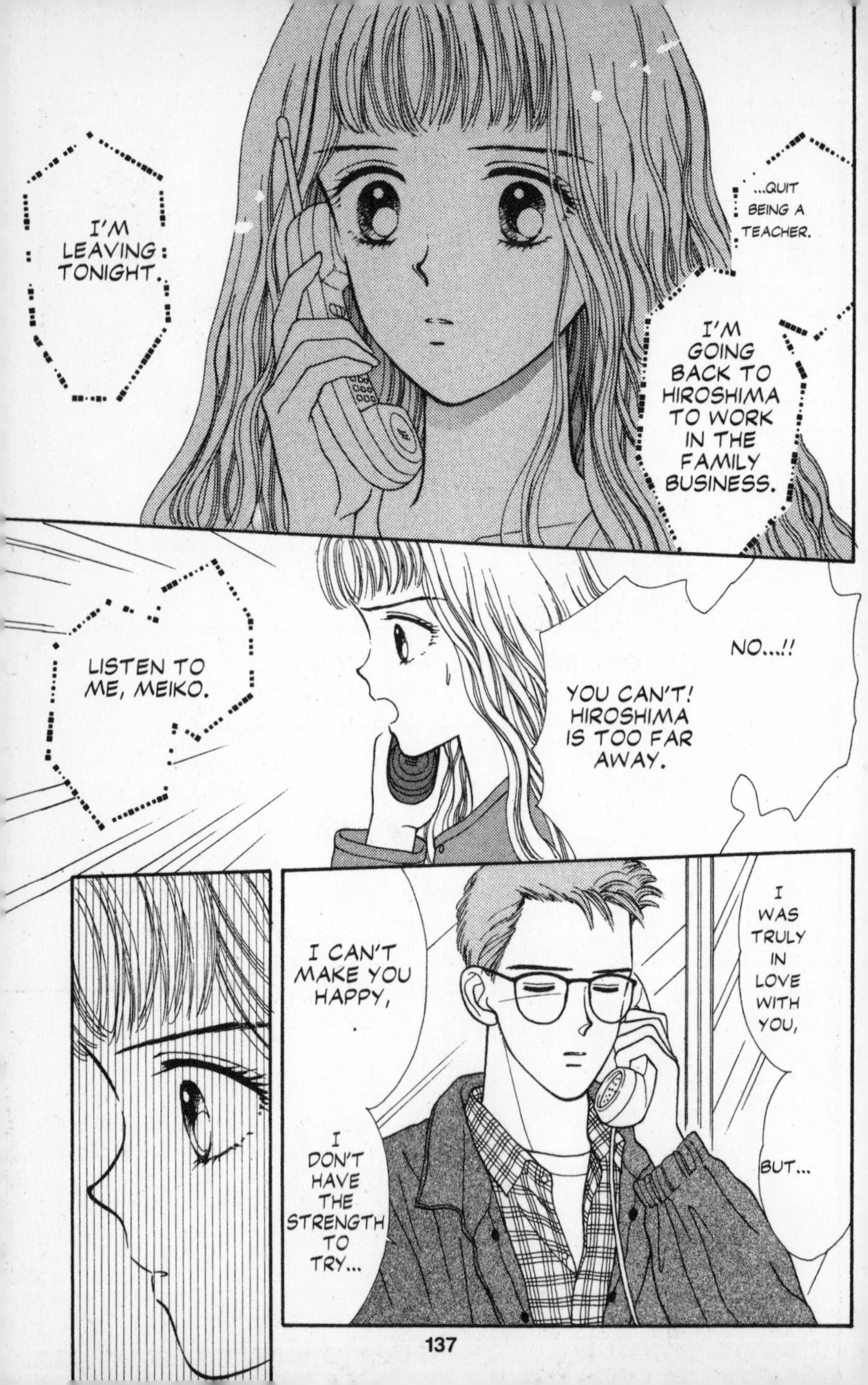
...QUIT BEING A TEACHER.
I'M GOING BACK TO HIROSHIMA TO WORK IN THE FAMILY BUSINESS.
I'M LEAVING TONIGHT.
NO...!!
YOU CAN'T! HIROSHIMA IS TOO FAR AWAY.
LISTEN TO ME, MEIKO.
I WAS TRULY IN LOVE WITH YOU,
BUT...
I CAN'T MAKE YOU HAPPY,
I DON'T HAVE THE STRENGTH TO TRY...

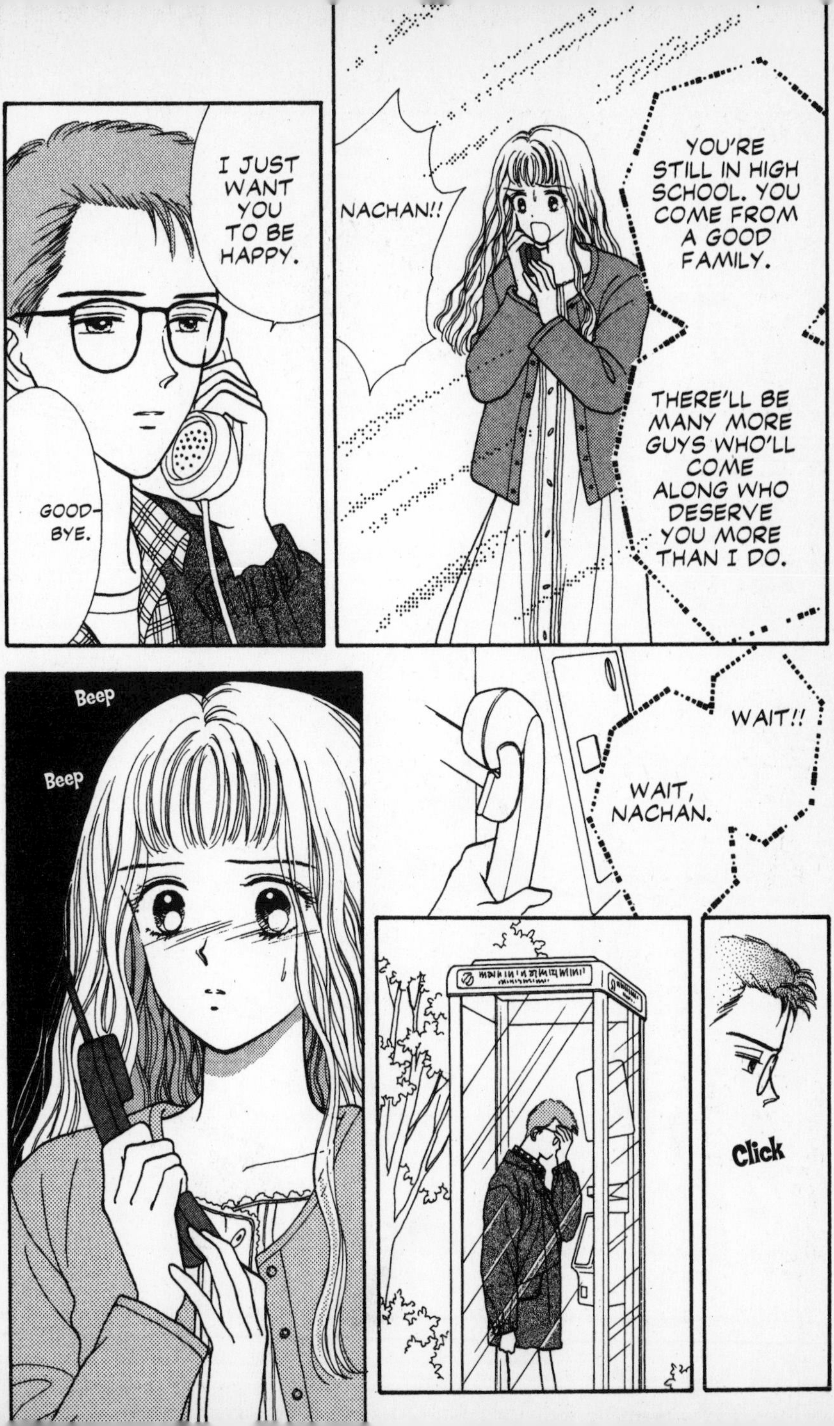
YOU'RE STILL IN HIGH SCHOOL. YOU COME FROM A GOOD FAMILY.
NACHAN!!
THERE'LL BE MANY MORE GUYS WHO'LL COME ALONG WHO DESERVE YOU MORE THAN I DO.
I JUST WANT YOU TO BE HAPPY.
GOOD-BYE.
WAIT!!
WAIT, NACHAN.
Click
Beep
Beep

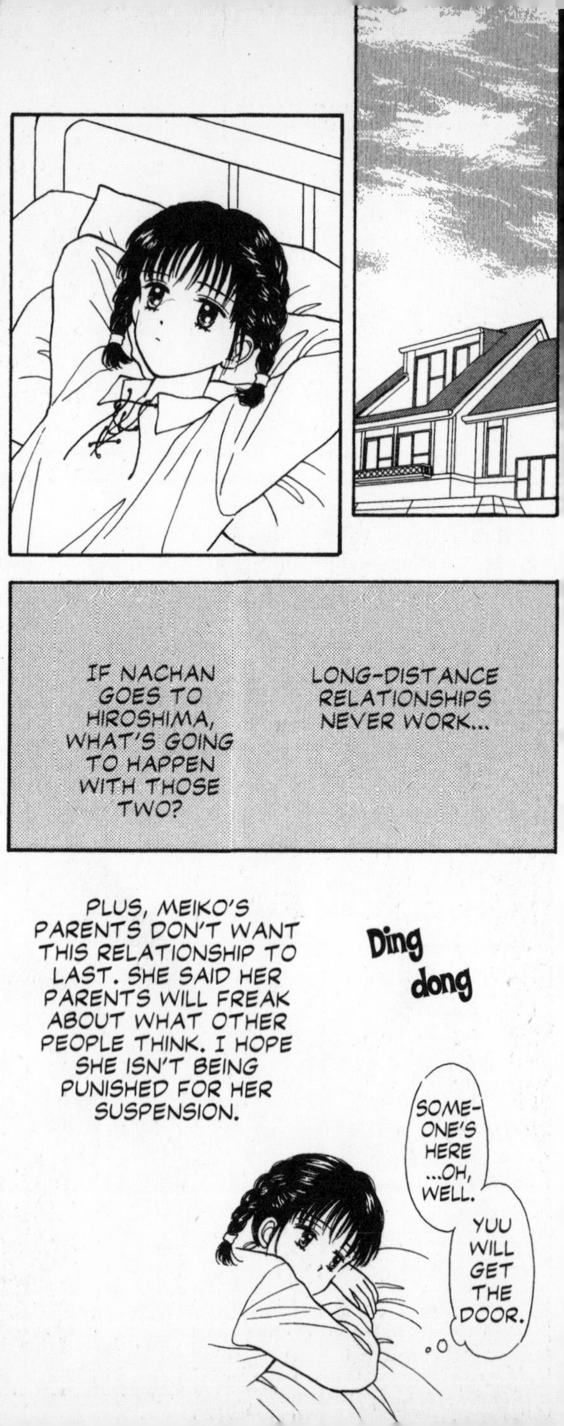
LONG-DISTANCE RELATIONSHIPS NEVER WORK...
IF NACHAN GOES TO HIROSHIMA, WHAT'S GOING TO HAPPEN WITH THOSE TWO?
PLUS, MEIKO'S PARENTS DON'T WANT THIS RELATIONSHIP TO LAST. SHE SAID HER PARENTS WILL FREAK ABOUT WHAT OTHER PEOPLE THINK. I HOPE SHE ISN'T BEING PUNISHED FOR HER SUSPENSION.
Ding dong
SOME-ONE'S HERE ...OH, WELL.
YUU WILL GET THE DOOR.

FREE TALK ⑤

June 21-28, 1993

I went on a trip to Switzerland and France with my parents. What I liked most about the trip was shopping. I wasn't really searching for brand -name stuff. In fact, I like finding lots of cute things at stationary shops, general stores, bookstores, art supply stores, post offices, and supermarkets. Any store will do!

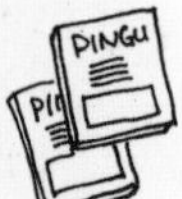
PINGU

Pingu book

Bought this at a Swiss bookstore

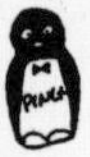

Pingu chocolate

(The real one looks cuter)

I found it at a Swiss kiosk. I thought it was so cute, I bought 10 and handed them out to my friends.

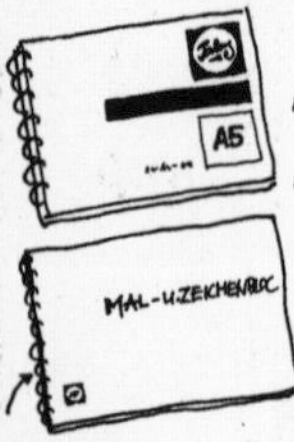
A5
MAL-UZEKHENBLOC

Sketch book

Purchased at a Swiss art store. What should I draw? The colors are beautiful. The top one is white with sky-blue letters. The bottom one is peppermint-green with red letters.

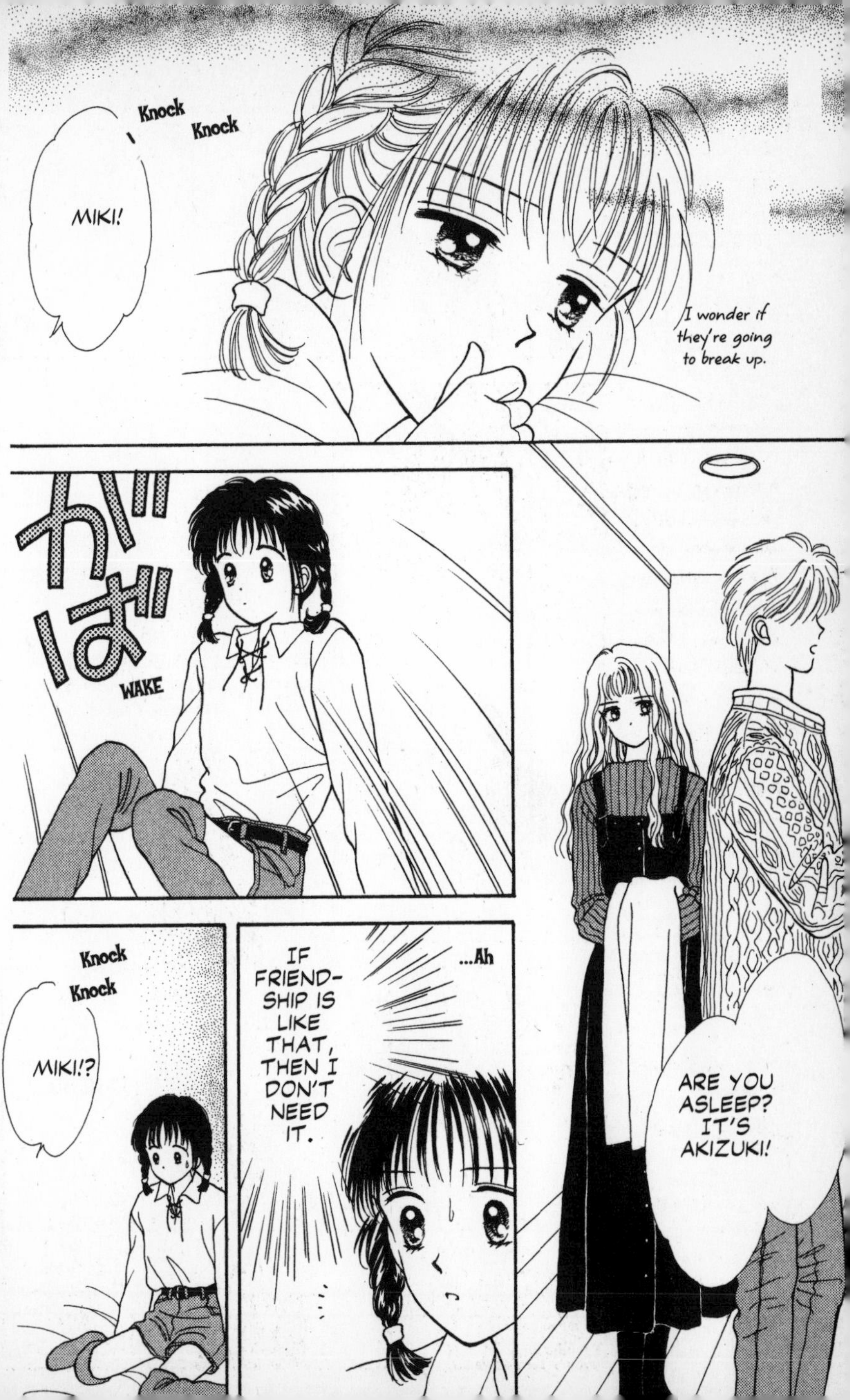
I wonder if they're going to break up.
Knock
Knock
MIKI!
わばっ
WAKE
IF FRIENDSHIP IS LIKE THAT, THEN I DON'T NEED IT.
...Ah
Knock
Knock
MIKI!?
ARE YOU ASLEEP? IT'S AKIZUKI!

FREE TALK ⑥

At the Swiss post office, I bought postage stamps with amazing illustrations of animals. A lot of post offices sell nice-looking envelopes and things, so it was fun. Envelopes designed for American express mail had a Hershey's Kiss design on them and I thought those were super cute. Even at stationary stores, Japan has a way bigger selection of beautiful letter sets and stationary. But foreign countries have better-looking business envelopes and notebooks. They're so cute and stylish!

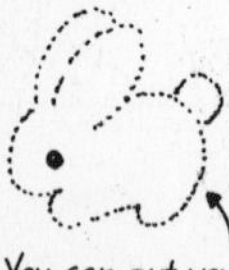

I bought this stuffed bunny in Paris.

You can put your hands in and move its front paws and face.

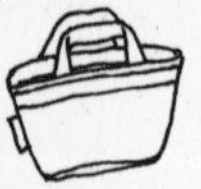

Designer mini tote bag.

I bought a lot of these as gifts for my friends.

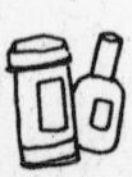

The illustration on Jacadi's baby cologne is cute.

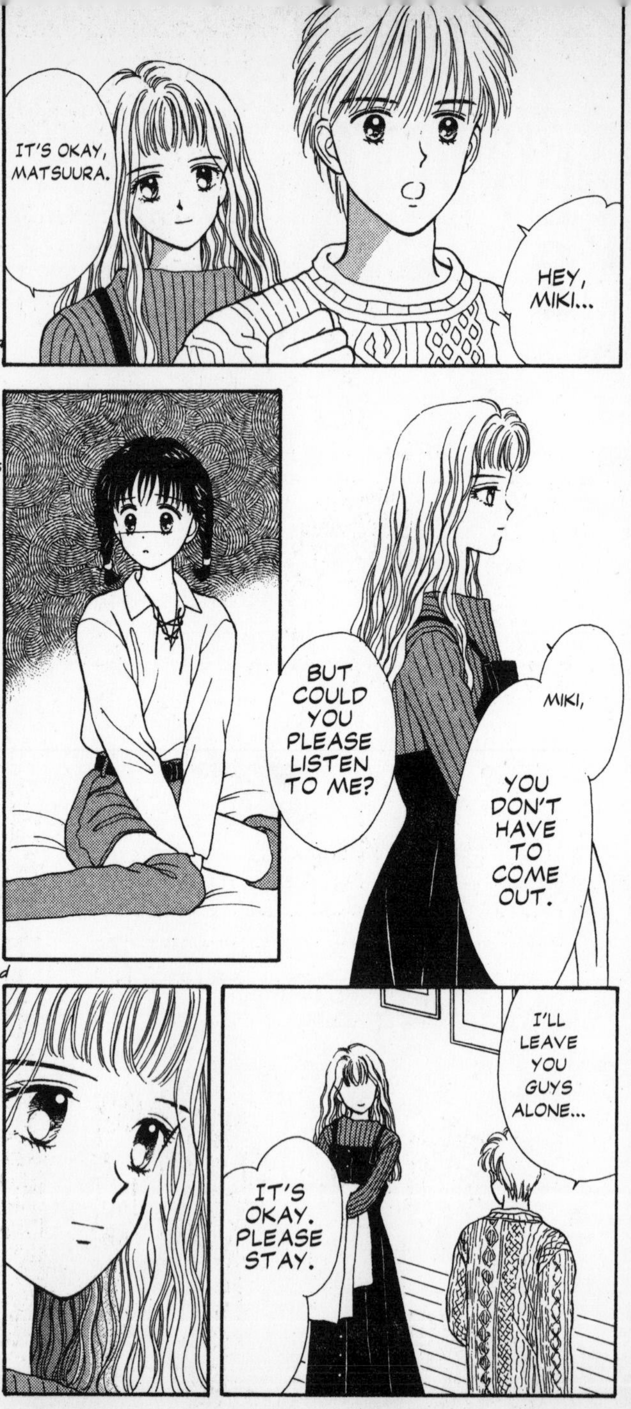
HEY, MIKI...
IT'S OKAY, MATSUURA.
MIKI,
YOU DON'T HAVE TO COME OUT.
BUT COULD YOU PLEASE LISTEN TO ME?
I'LL LEAVE YOU GUYS ALONE...
IT'S OKAY. PLEASE STAY.

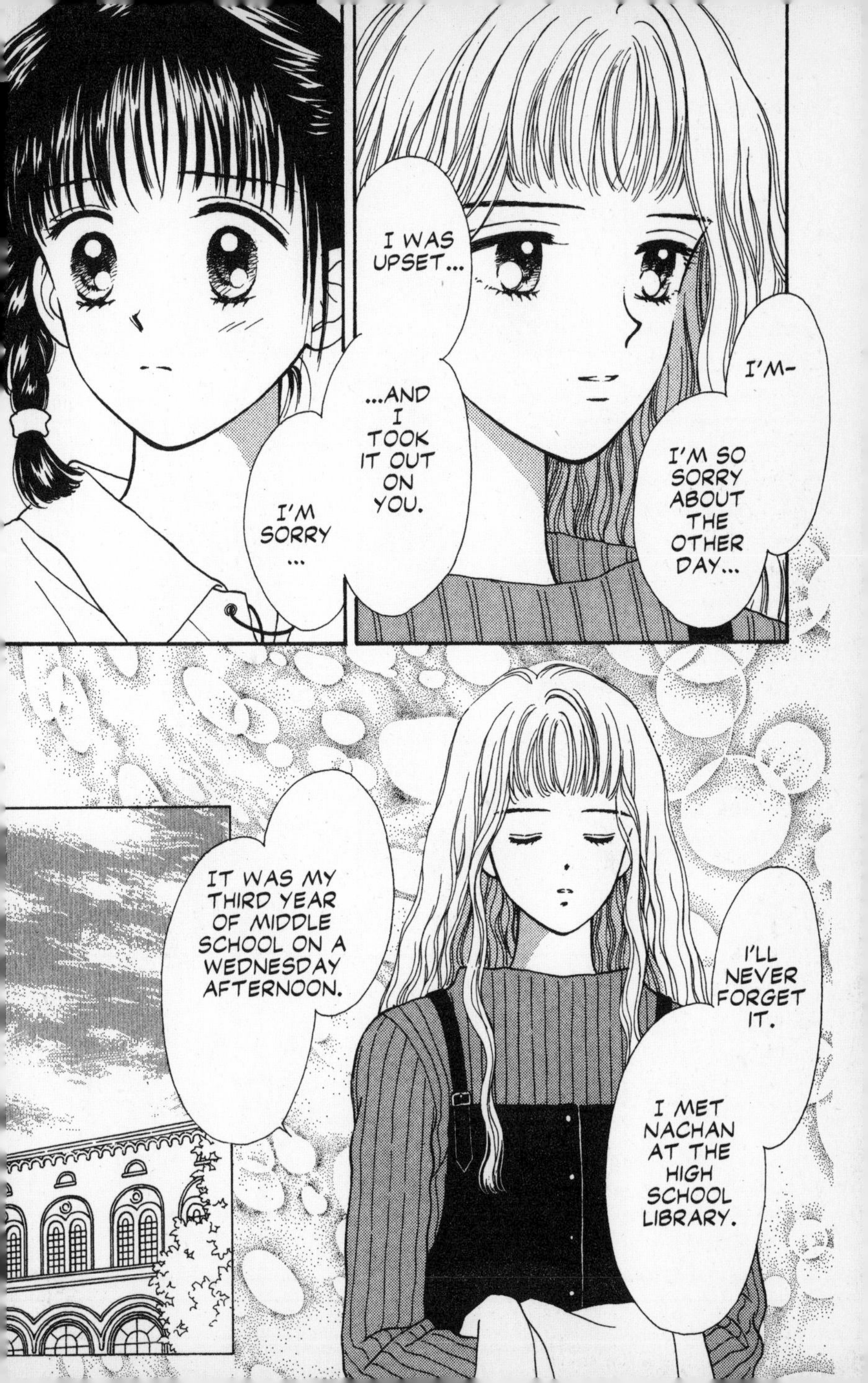
I'M-
I'M SO SORRY ABOUT THE OTHER DAY...
I WAS UPSET...
...AND I TOOK IT OUT ON YOU.
I'M SORRY ...
I'LL NEVER FORGET IT.
I MET NACHAN AT THE HIGH SCHOOL LIBRARY.
IT WAS MY THIRD YEAR OF MIDDLE SCHOOL ON A WEDNESDAY AFTERNOON.

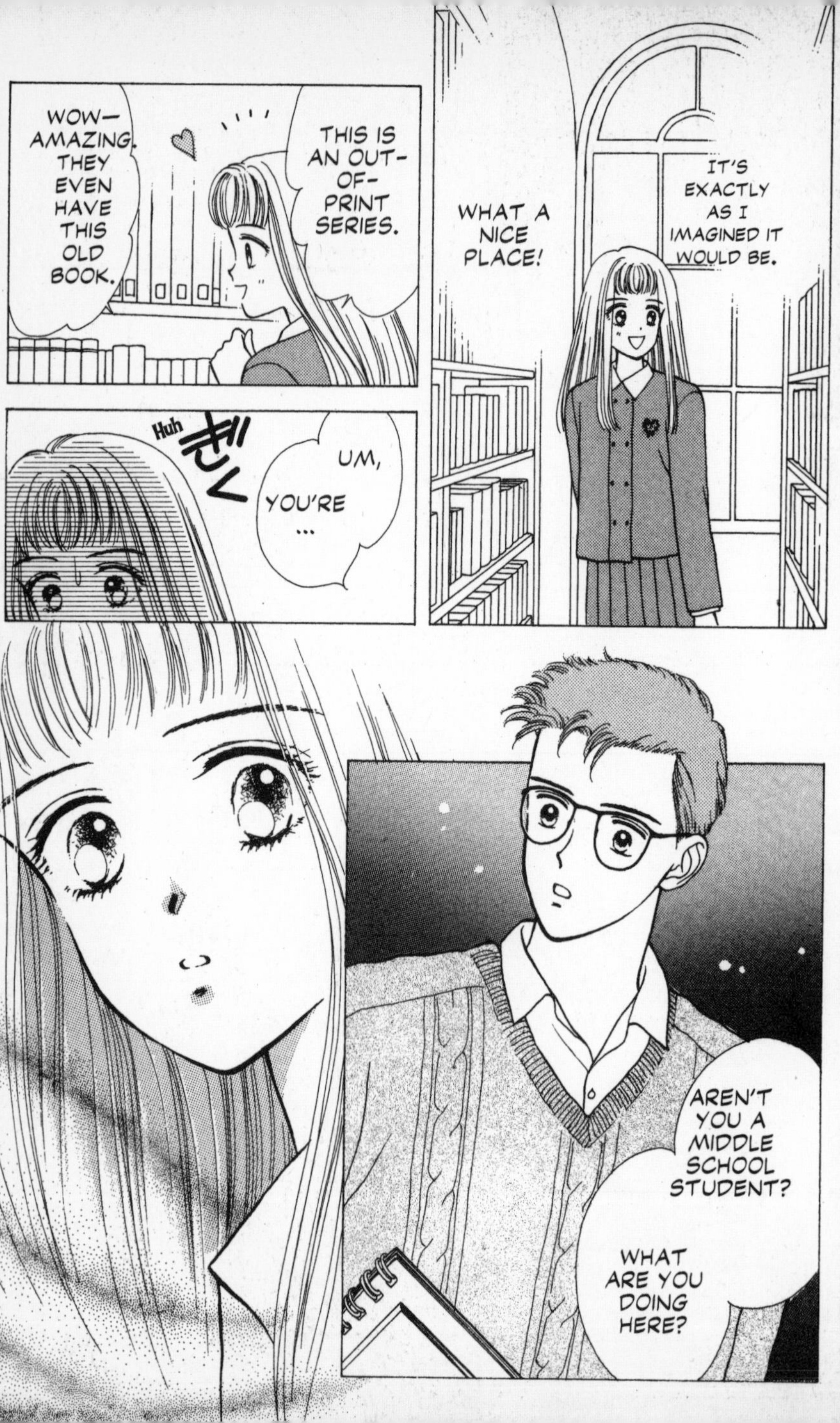
IT'S EXACTLY AS I IMAGINED IT WOULD BE.
WHAT A NICE PLACE!
THIS IS AN OUT-OF-PRINT SERIES.
WOW—AMAZING. THEY EVEN HAVE THIS OLD BOOK.
UM, YOU'RE ...
Huh
ぎく
AREN'T YOU A MIDDLE SCHOOL STUDENT?
WHAT ARE YOU DOING HERE?

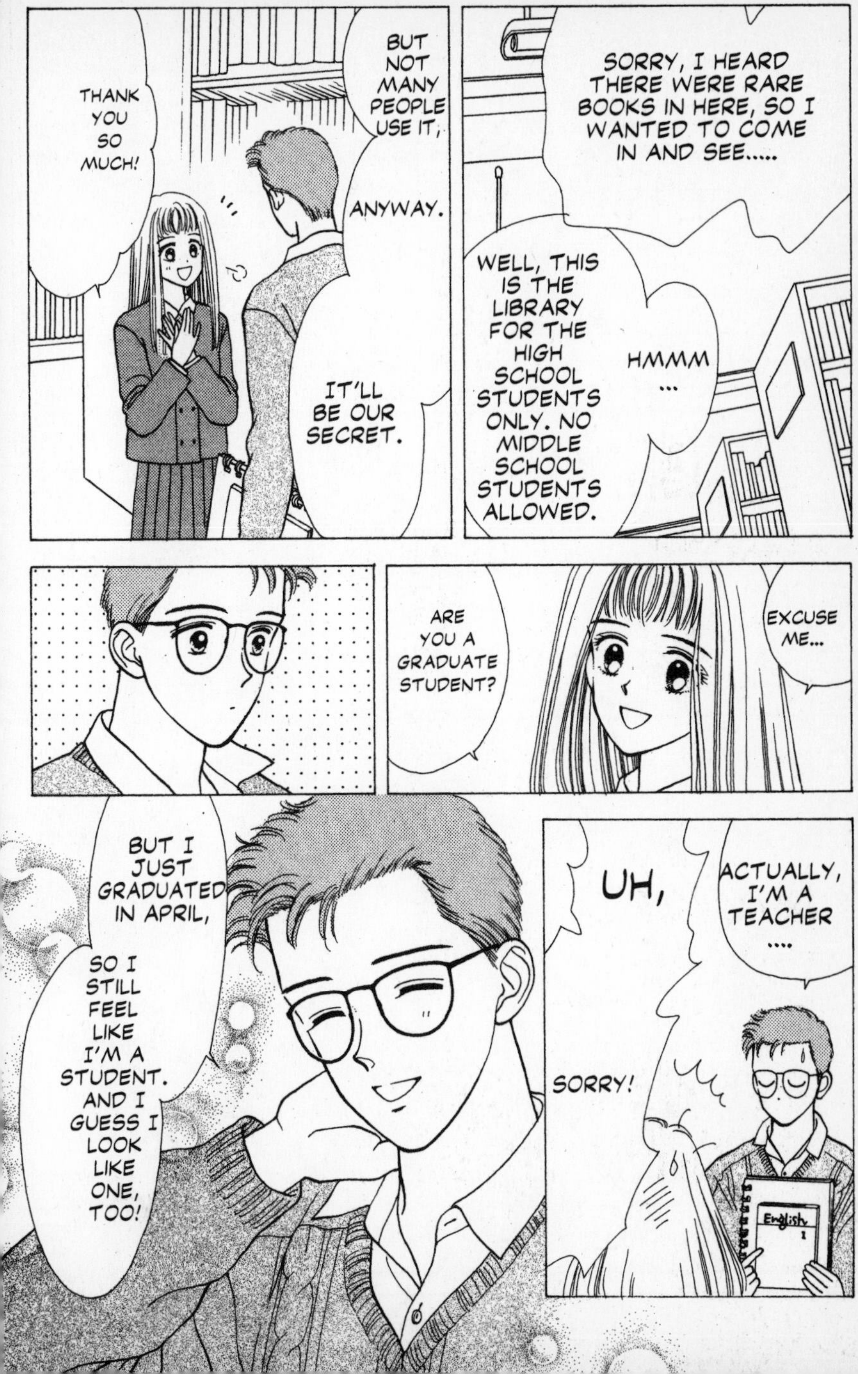
SORRY, I HEARD THERE WERE RARE BOOKS IN HERE, SO I WANTED TO COME IN AND SEE.....
HMMM ...
WELL, THIS IS THE LIBRARY FOR THE HIGH SCHOOL STUDENTS ONLY. NO MIDDLE SCHOOL STUDENTS ALLOWED.
BUT NOT MANY PEOPLE USE IT, ANYWAY.
IT'LL BE OUR SECRET.
THANK YOU SO MUCH!
EXCUSE ME...
ARE YOU A GRADUATE STUDENT?
ACTUALLY, I'M A TEACHER ....
UH,
SORRY!
English 1
BUT I JUST GRADUATED IN APRIL,
SO I STILL FEEL LIKE I'M A STUDENT. AND I GUESS I LOOK LIKE ONE, TOO!

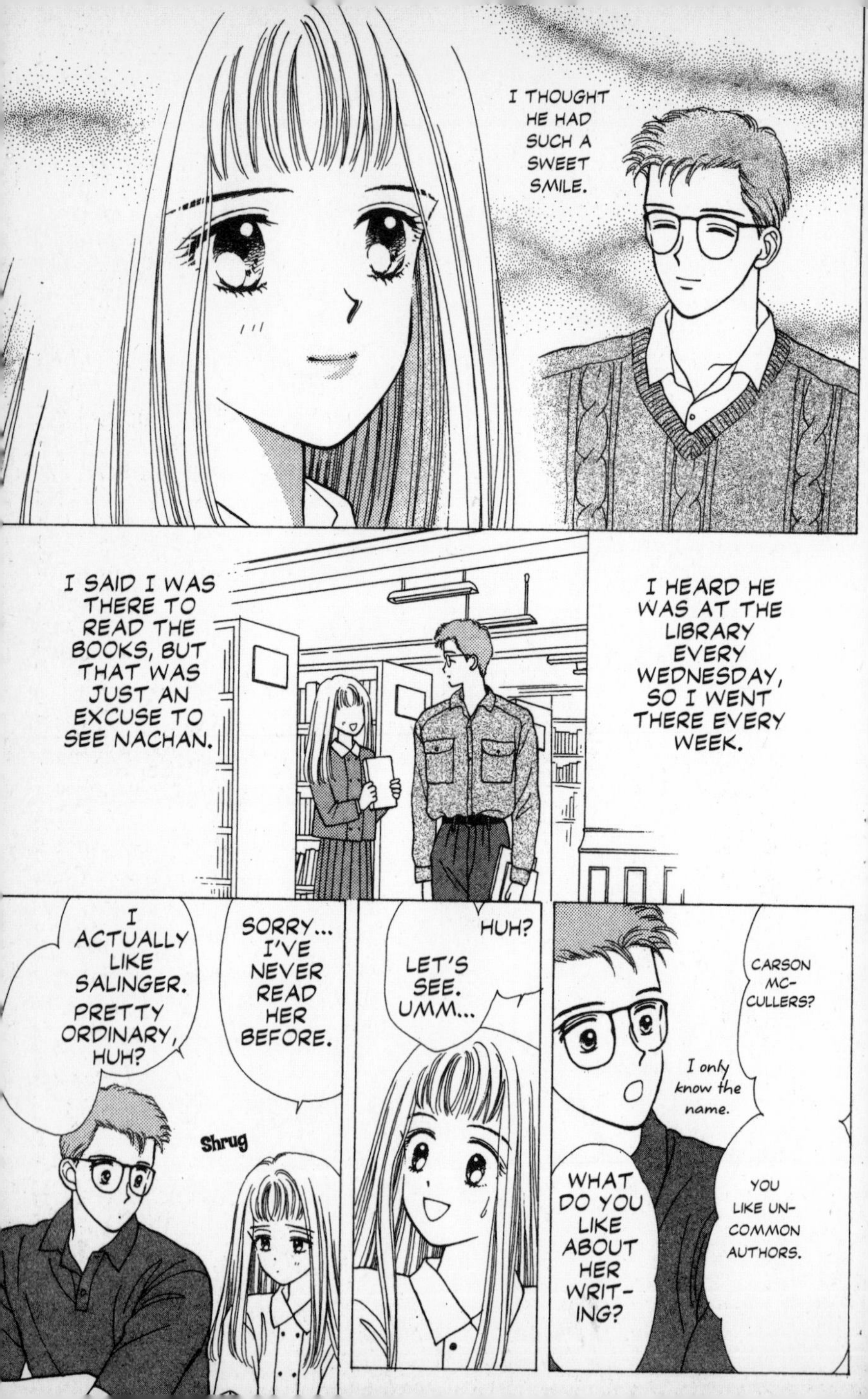
I THOUGHT HE HAD SUCH A SWEET SMILE.
I HEARD HE WAS AT THE LIBRARY EVERY WEDNESDAY, SO I WENT THERE EVERY WEEK.
I SAID I WAS THERE TO READ THE BOOKS, BUT THAT WAS JUST AN EXCUSE TO SEE NACHAN.
CARSON MC-CULLERS?
I only know the name.
YOU LIKE UN-COMMON AUTHORS.
WHAT DO YOU LIKE ABOUT HER WRIT-ING?
HUH?
LET'S SEE. UMM...
SORRY... I'VE NEVER READ HER BEFORE.
I ACTUALLY LIKE SALINGER. PRETTY ORDINARY, HUH?
Shrug

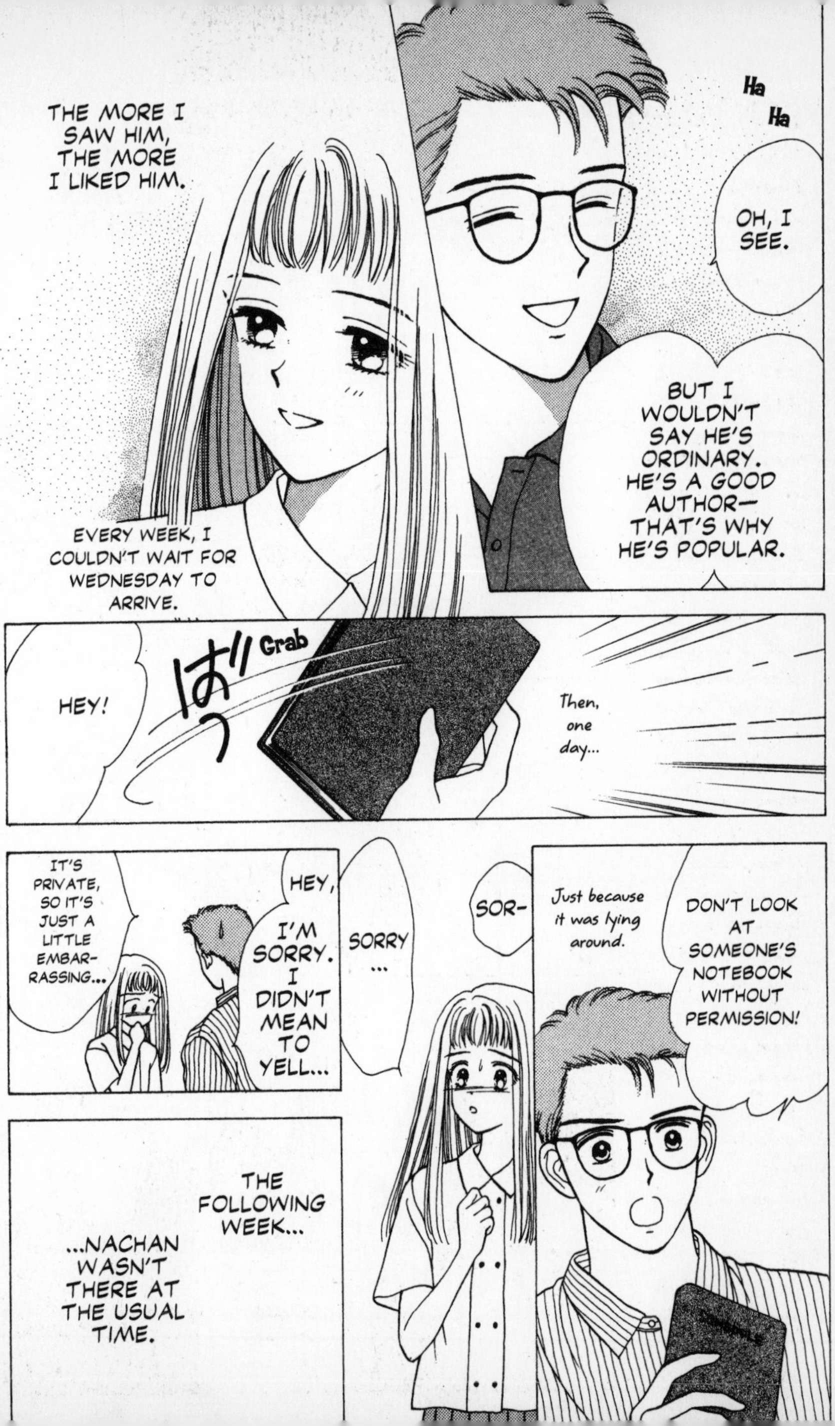
Ha
Ha
OH, I SEE.
BUT I WOULDN'T SAY HE'S ORDINARY. HE'S A GOOD AUTHOR—THAT'S WHY HE'S POPULAR.
THE MORE I SAW HIM, THE MORE I LIKED HIM.
EVERY WEEK, I COULDN'T WAIT FOR WEDNESDAY TO ARRIVE.
Then, one day...
Grab
はッ
HEY!
DON'T LOOK AT SOMEONE'S NOTEBOOK WITHOUT PERMISSION!
Just because it was lying around.
SOR-
SORRY...
HEY, I'M SORRY. I DIDN'T MEAN TO YELL...
IT'S PRIVATE, SO IT'S JUST A LITTLE EMBARRASSING...
THE FOLLOWING WEEK...
...NACHAN WASN'T THERE AT THE USUAL TIME.

FREE TALK ⑦

7/20-22/93
I went to Hokkaido with Yazawa Ai. It was our goal to see the lavender gardens of Furano.

7/20
We both were working until the last minute before we left, so we were extremely tired. During the train ride from Chitose to Sapporo, we had lunch. We ate the salmon and salmon roe rice box lunch that our Ribon editor, Miss U., recommended so highly. It was so delicious. After we got to Sapporo, we stopped by Daitsu Park and ate sugar cane. Once we got back to the hotel, we called up Takada Emi and we all went out to a sushi bar. The uni came in a small champagne glass, and we were really impressed.

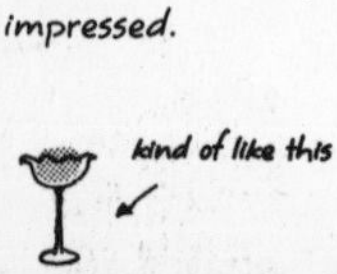
kind of like this

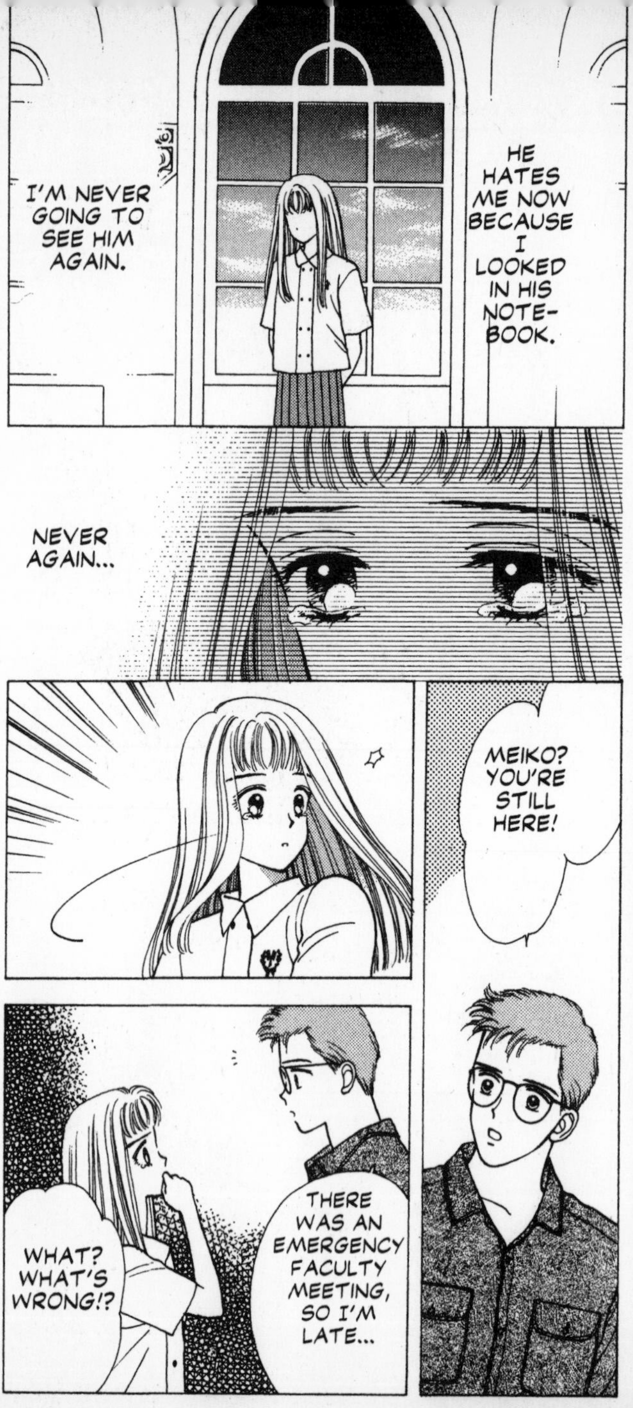
HE HATES ME NOW BECAUSE I LOOKED IN HIS NOTEBOOK.
I'M NEVER GOING TO SEE HIM AGAIN.
NEVER AGAIN...
MEIKO? YOU'RE STILL HERE!
THERE WAS AN EMERGENCY FACULTY MEETING, SO I'M LATE...
WHAT? WHAT'S WRONG!?

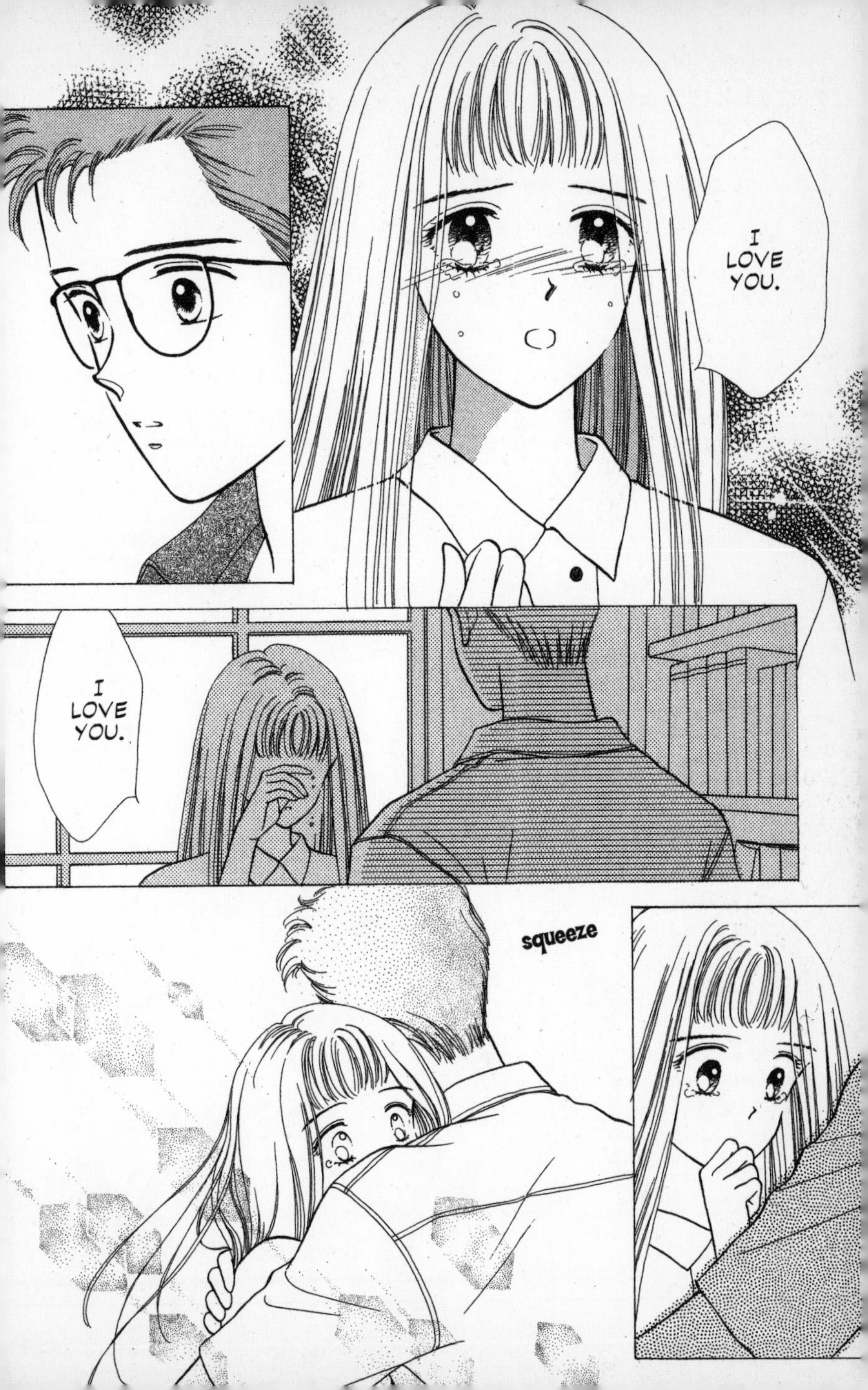
I LOVE YOU.
I LOVE YOU.
squeeze

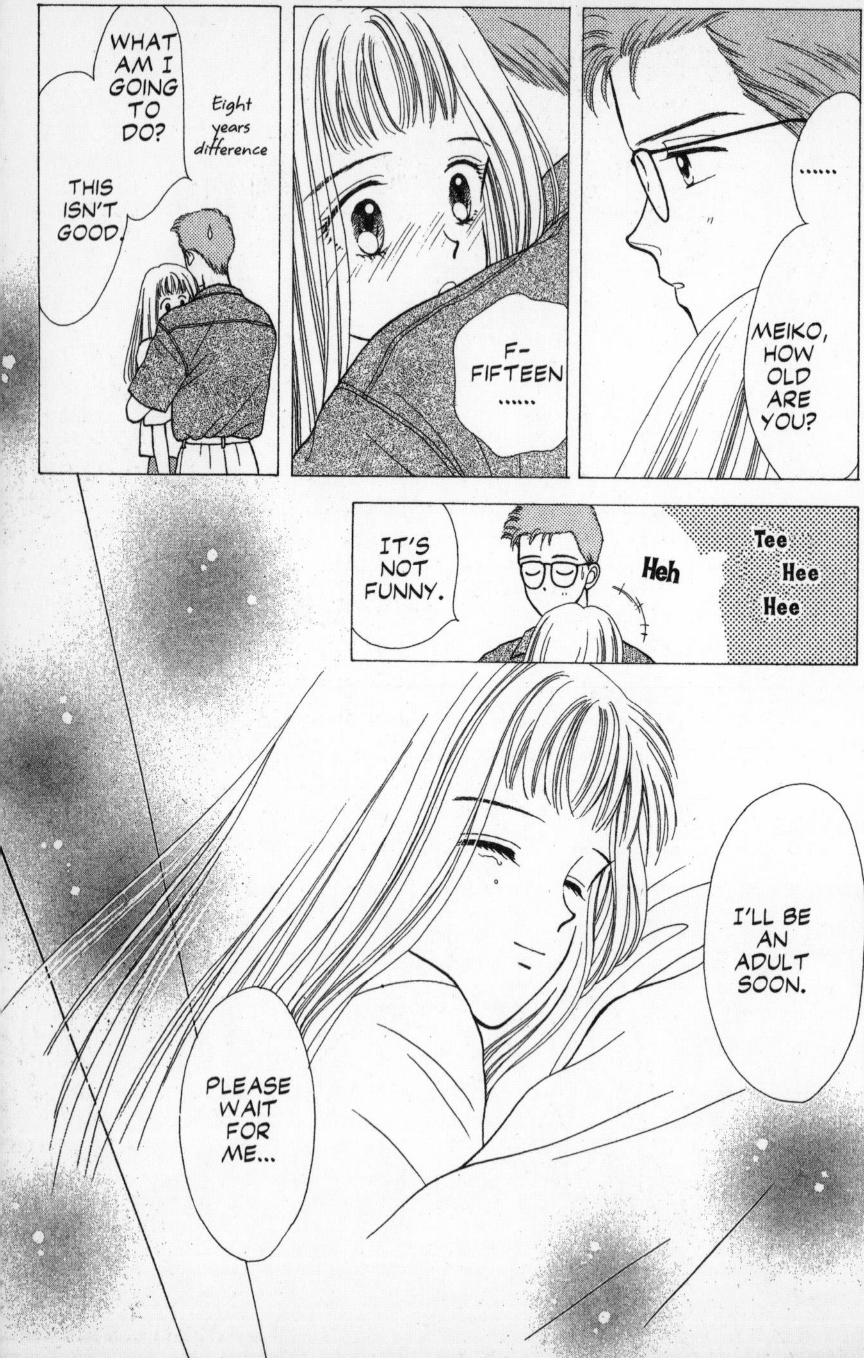
......
MEIKO, HOW OLD ARE YOU?
F- FIFTEEN ......
WHAT AM I GOING TO DO?
Eight years difference
THIS ISN'T GOOD.
Tee Hee Hee
Heh
IT'S NOT FUNNY.
I'LL BE AN ADULT SOON.
PLEASE WAIT FOR ME...

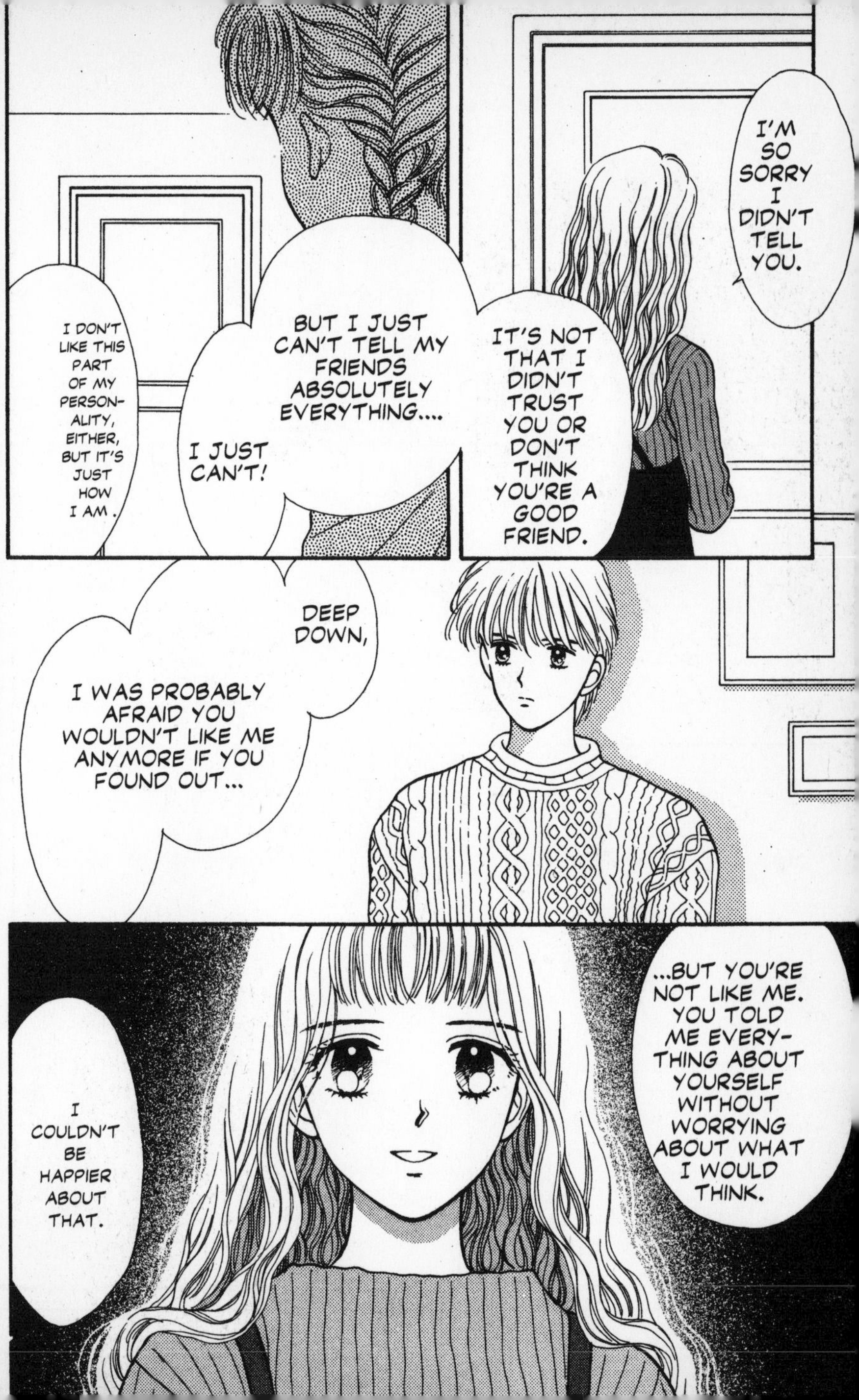
I'M SO SORRY I DIDN'T TELL YOU.
IT'S NOT THAT I DIDN'T TRUST YOU OR DON'T THINK YOU'RE A GOOD FRIEND.
BUT I JUST CAN'T TELL MY FRIENDS ABSOLUTELY EVERYTHING....
I JUST CAN'T!
I DON'T LIKE THIS PART OF MY PERSON-ALITY, EITHER, BUT IT'S JUST HOW I AM.
DEEP DOWN,
I WAS PROBABLY AFRAID YOU WOULDN'T LIKE ME ANYMORE IF YOU FOUND OUT...
...BUT YOU'RE NOT LIKE ME. YOU TOLD ME EVERY-THING ABOUT YOURSELF WITHOUT WORRYING ABOUT WHAT I WOULD THINK.
I COULDN'T BE HAPPIER ABOUT THAT.

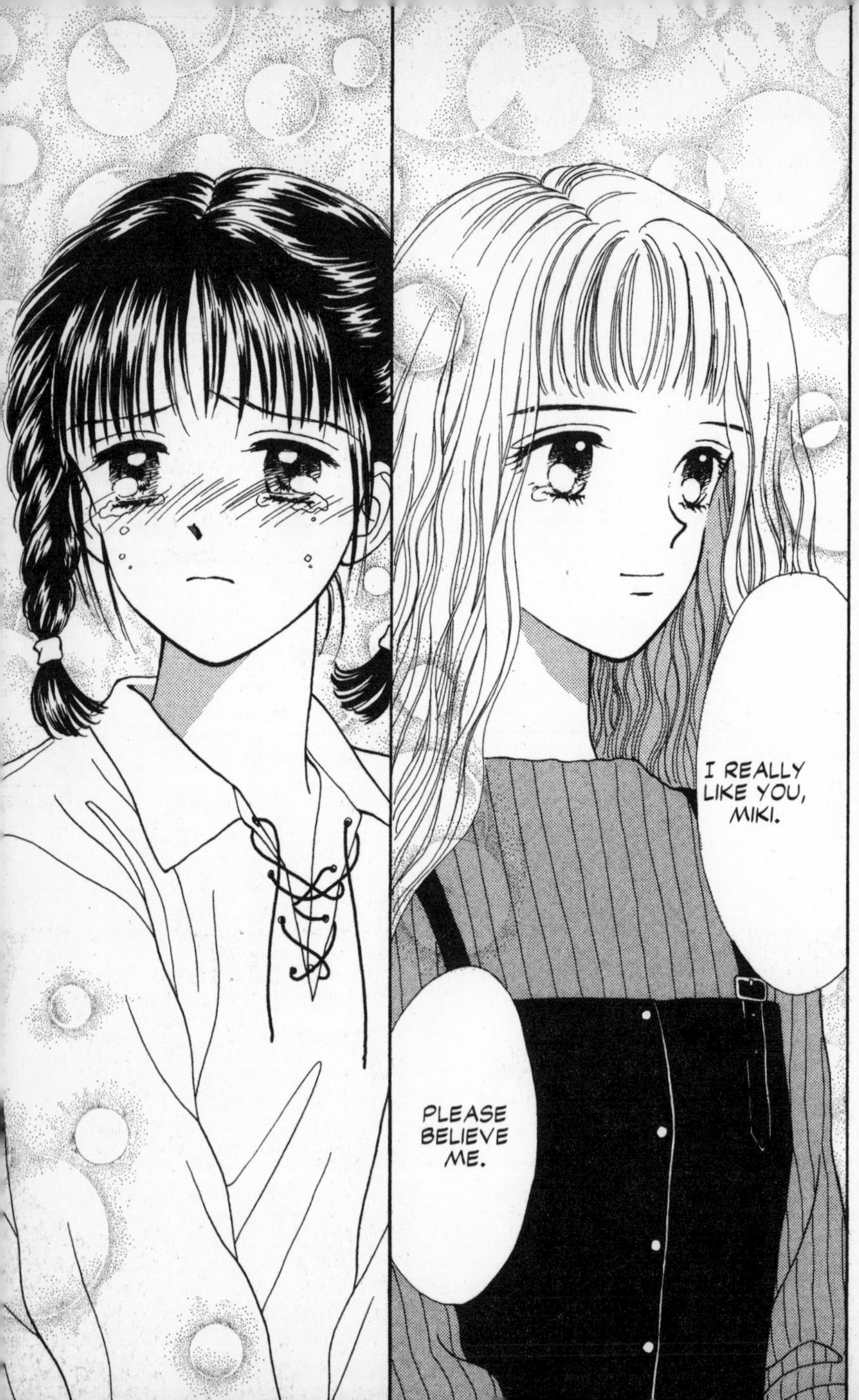
I REALLY LIKE YOU, MIKI.
PLEASE BELIEVE ME.

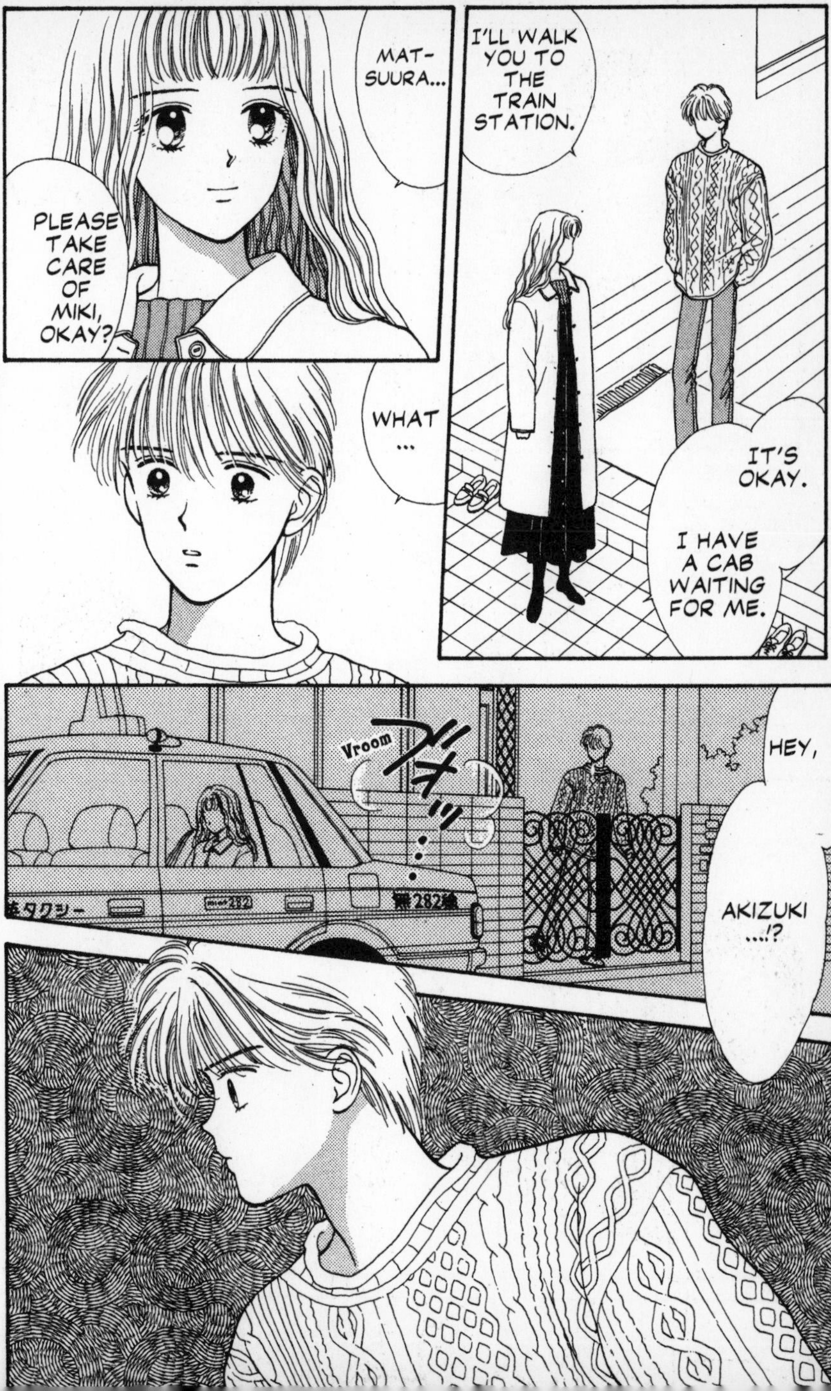
I'LL WALK YOU TO THE TRAIN STATION.
IT'S OKAY.
I HAVE A CAB WAITING FOR ME.
MAT-SUURA...
PLEASE TAKE CARE OF MIKI, OKAY?
WHAT ...
HEY,
AKIZUKI ...!?
Vroom

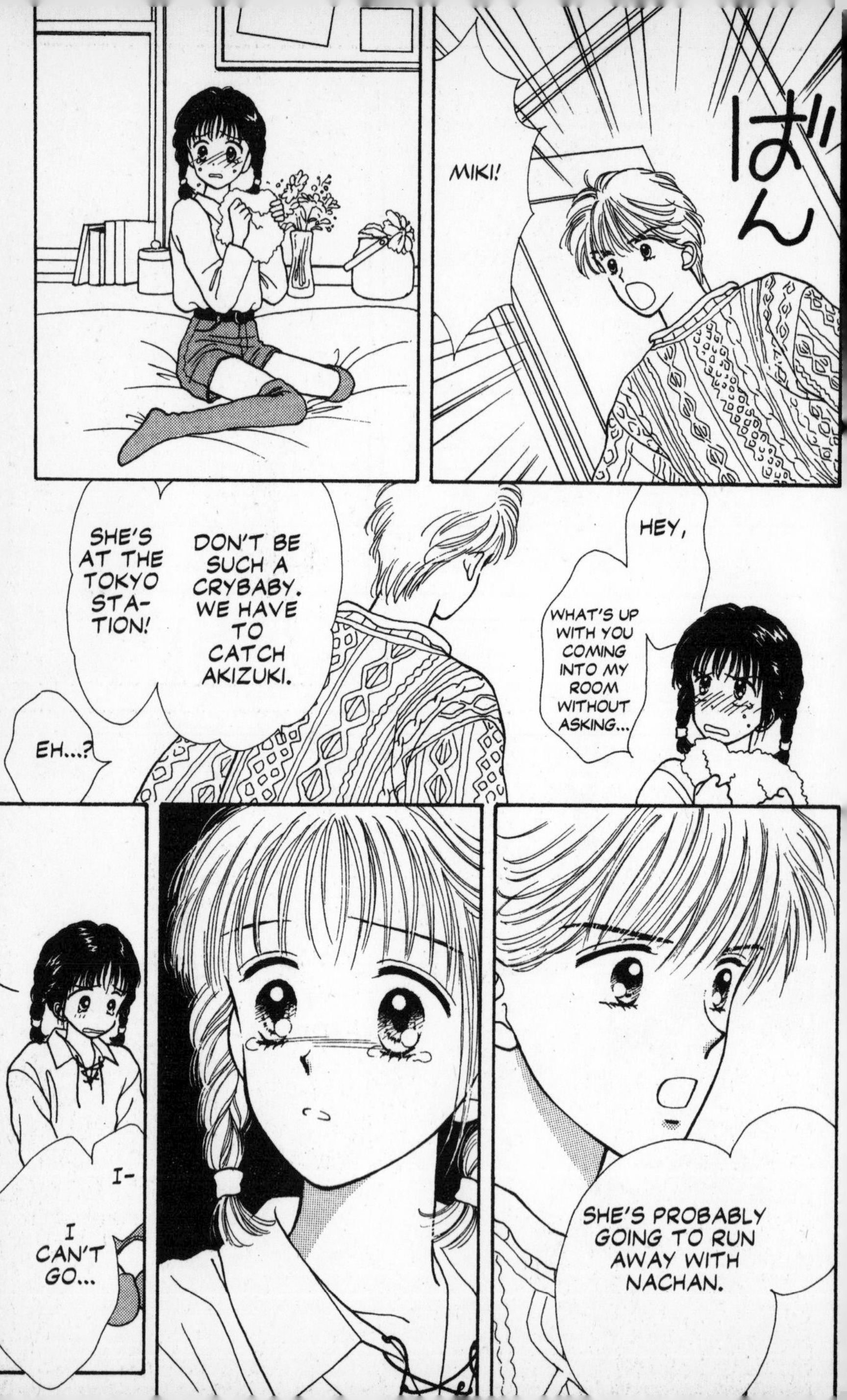
ばん
MIKI!
HEY,
WHAT'S UP WITH YOU COMING INTO MY ROOM WITHOUT ASKING...
DON'T BE SUCH A CRYBABY. WE HAVE TO CATCH AKIZUKI.
SHE'S AT THE TOKYO STA-TION!
EH...?
SHE'S PROBABLY GOING TO RUN AWAY WITH NACHAN.
I-
I CAN'T GO...

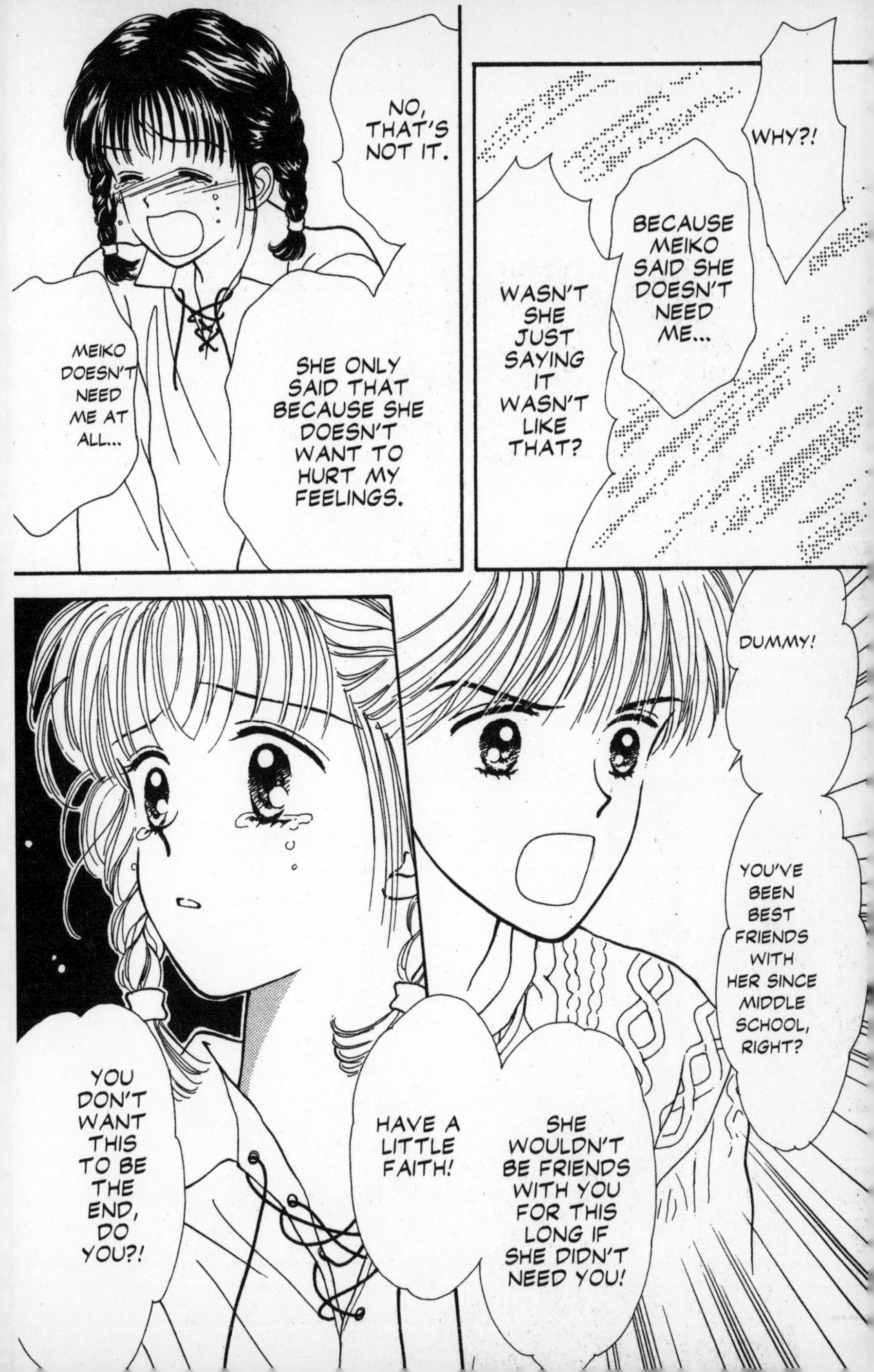
WHY?!
BECAUSE MEIKO SAID SHE DOESN'T NEED ME...
WASN'T SHE JUST SAYING IT WASN'T LIKE THAT?
NO, THAT'S NOT IT.
SHE ONLY SAID THAT BECAUSE SHE DOESN'T WANT TO HURT MY FEELINGS.
MEIKO DOESN'T NEED ME AT ALL...
DUMMY!
YOU'VE BEEN BEST FRIENDS WITH HER SINCE MIDDLE SCHOOL, RIGHT?
SHE WOULDN'T BE FRIENDS WITH YOU FOR THIS LONG IF SHE DIDN'T NEED YOU!
HAVE A LITTLE FAITH!
YOU DON'T WANT THIS TO BE THE END, DO YOU?!

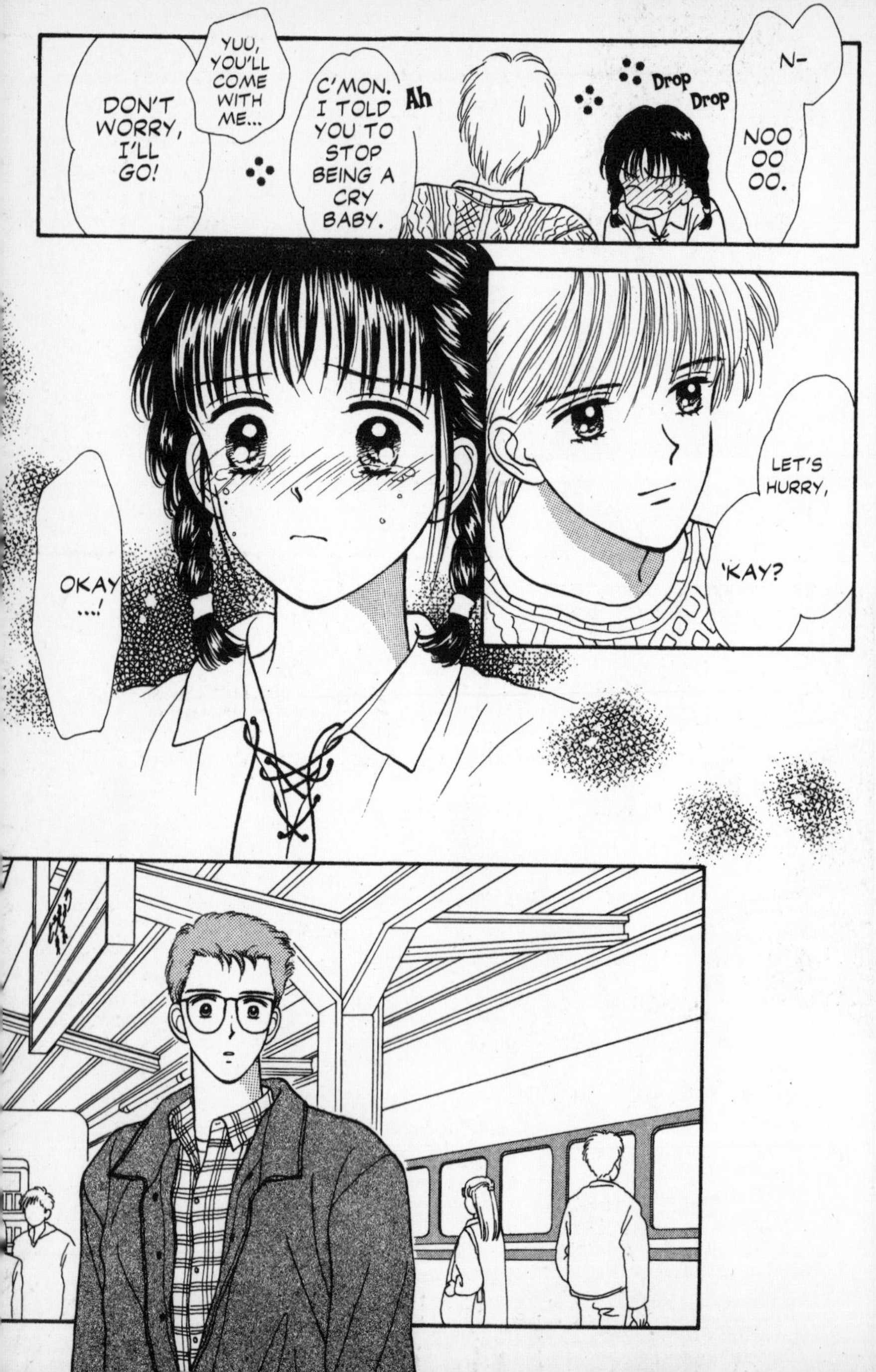
N-
NOOOOOOO.
Drop
Drop
Ah
C'MON. I TOLD YOU TO STOP BEING A CRY BABY.
YUU, YOU'LL COME WITH ME...
DON'T WORRY, I'LL GO!
LET'S HURRY,
'KAY?
OKAY ...!

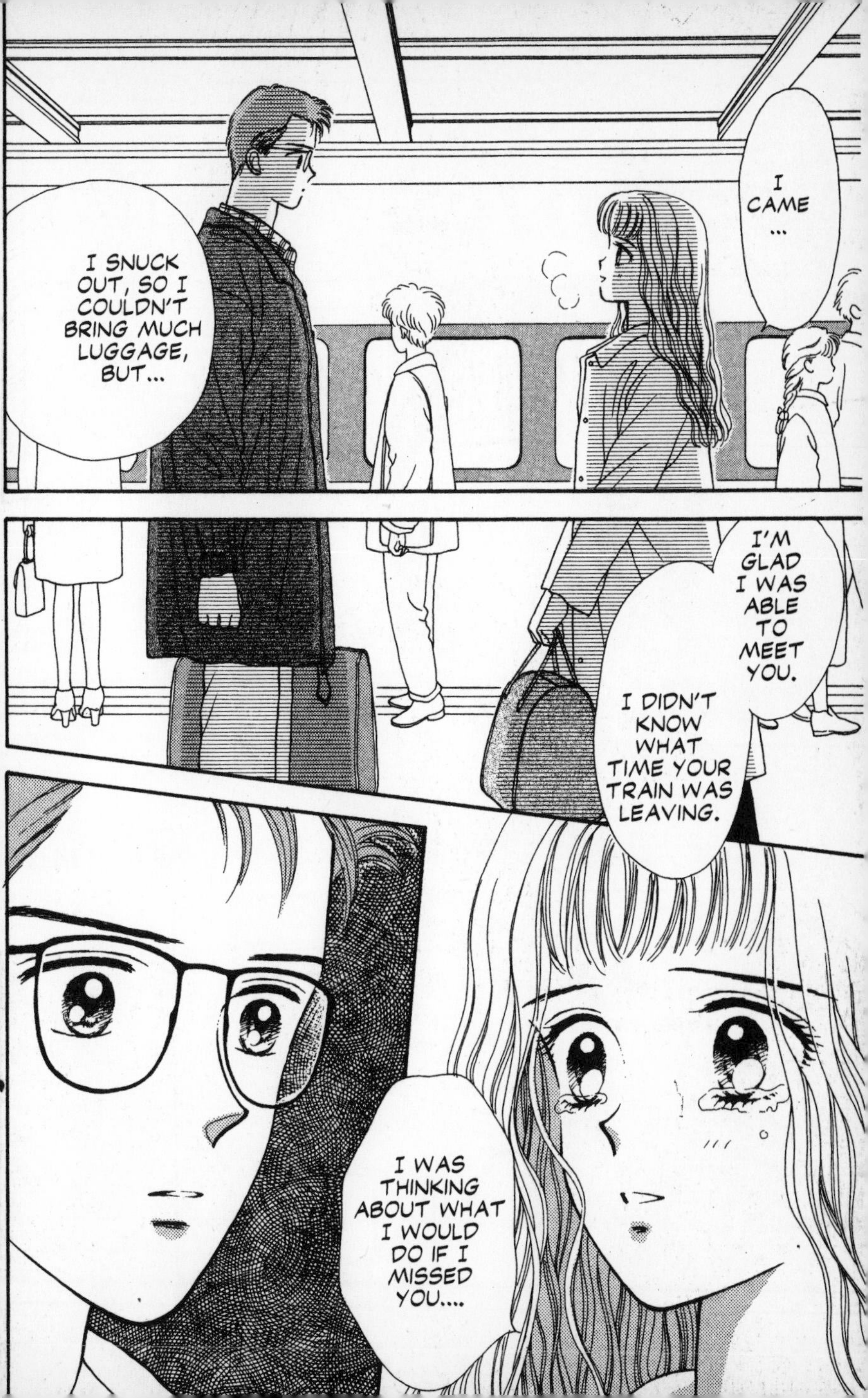
I CAME ...
I SNUCK OUT, SO I COULDN'T BRING MUCH LUGGAGE, BUT...
I'M GLAD I WAS ABLE TO MEET YOU.
I DIDN'T KNOW WHAT TIME YOUR TRAIN WAS LEAVING.
I WAS THINKING ABOUT WHAT I WOULD DO IF I MISSED YOU....

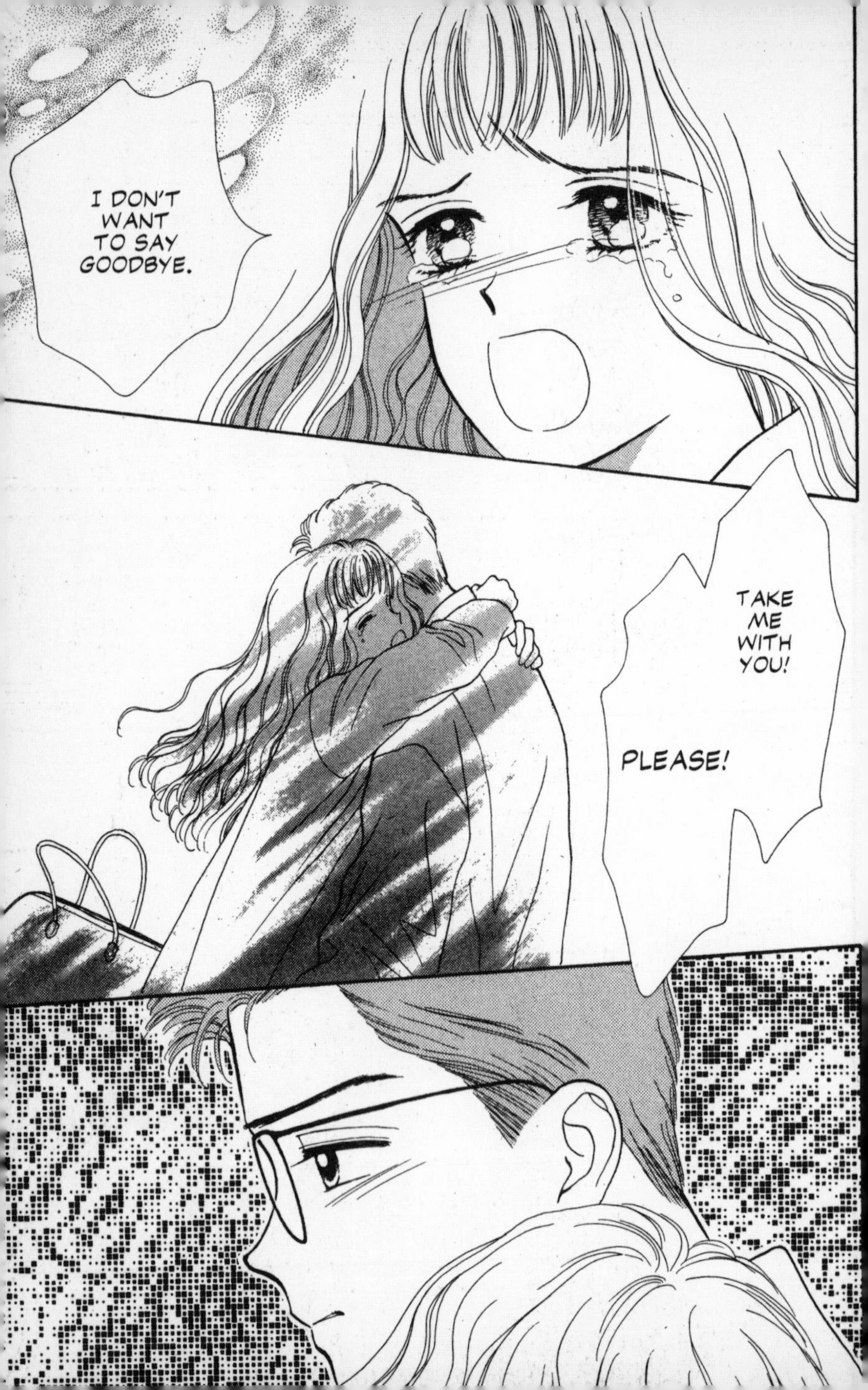
I DON'T WANT TO SAY GOODBYE.
TAKE ME WITH YOU!
PLEASE!

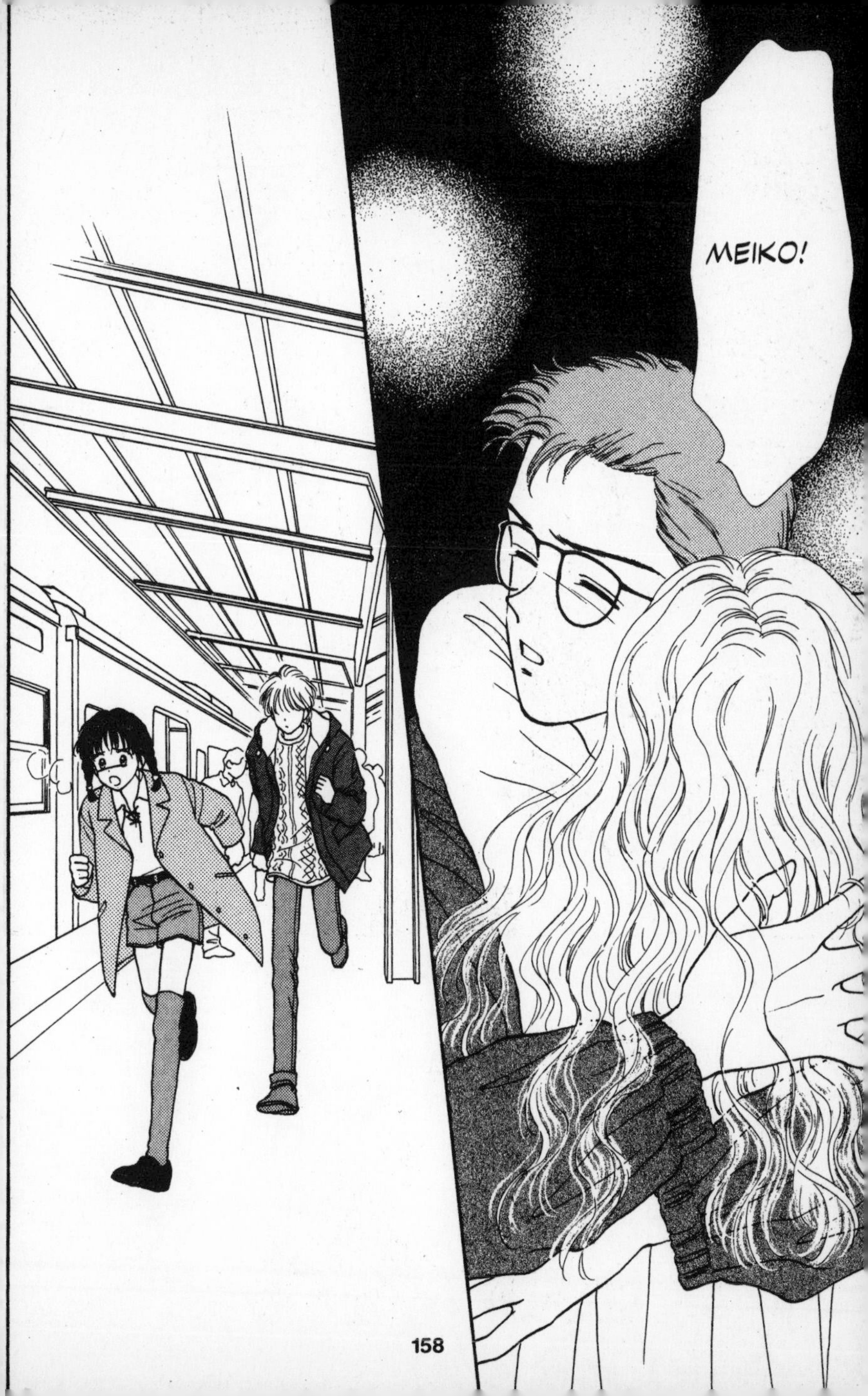
MEIKO!

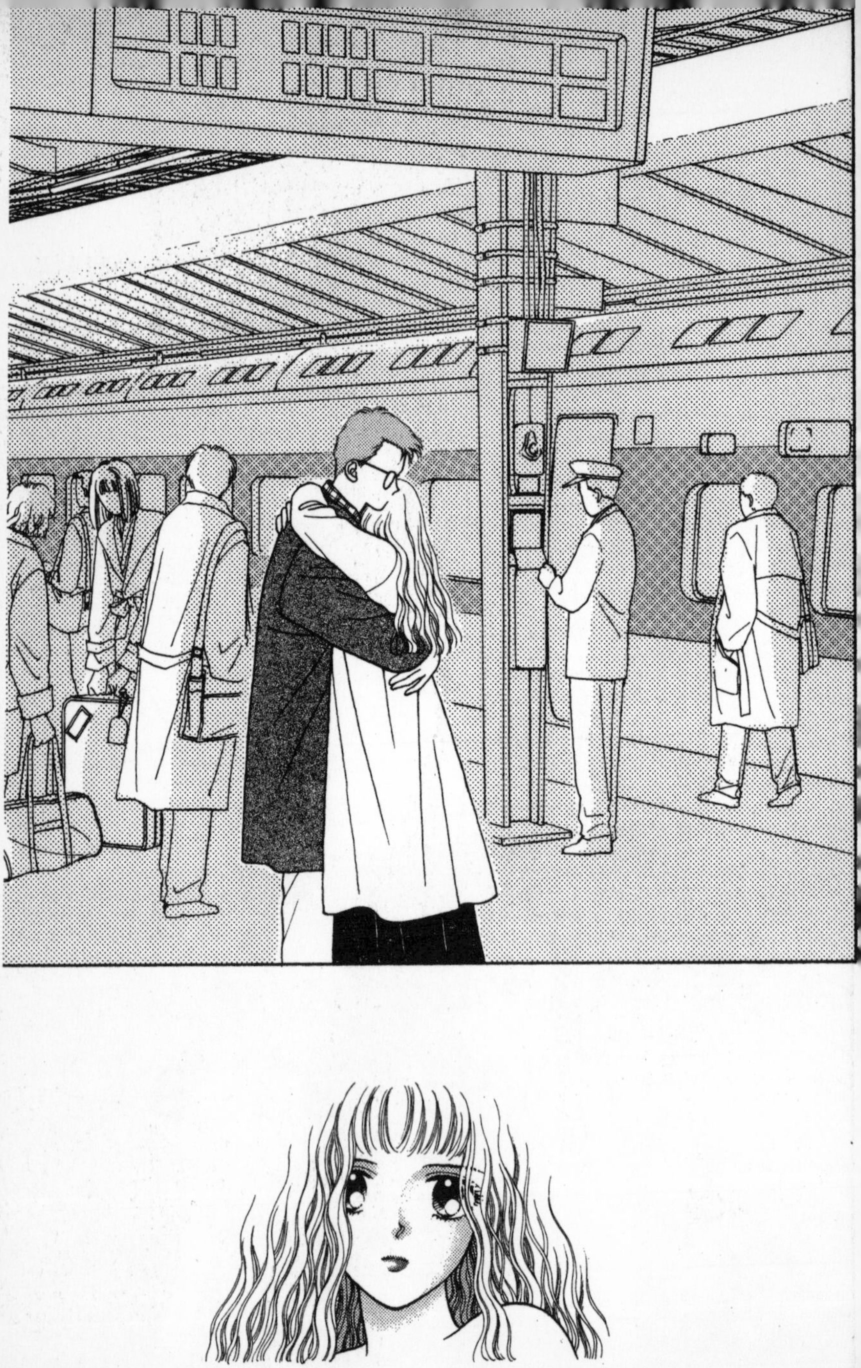

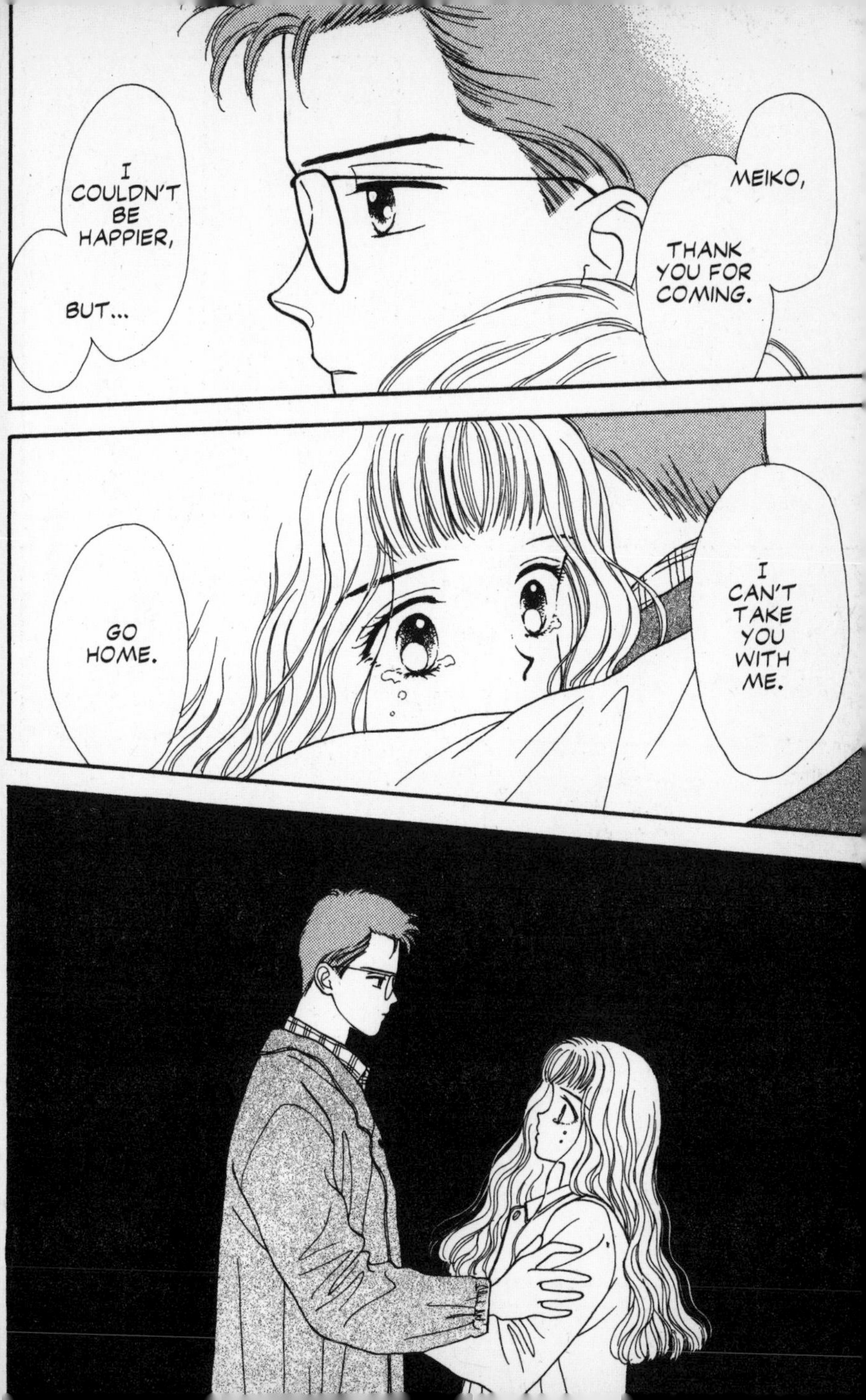
MEIKO,
THANK YOU FOR COMING.
I COULDN'T BE HAPPIER,
BUT...
I CAN'T TAKE YOU WITH ME.
GO HOME.

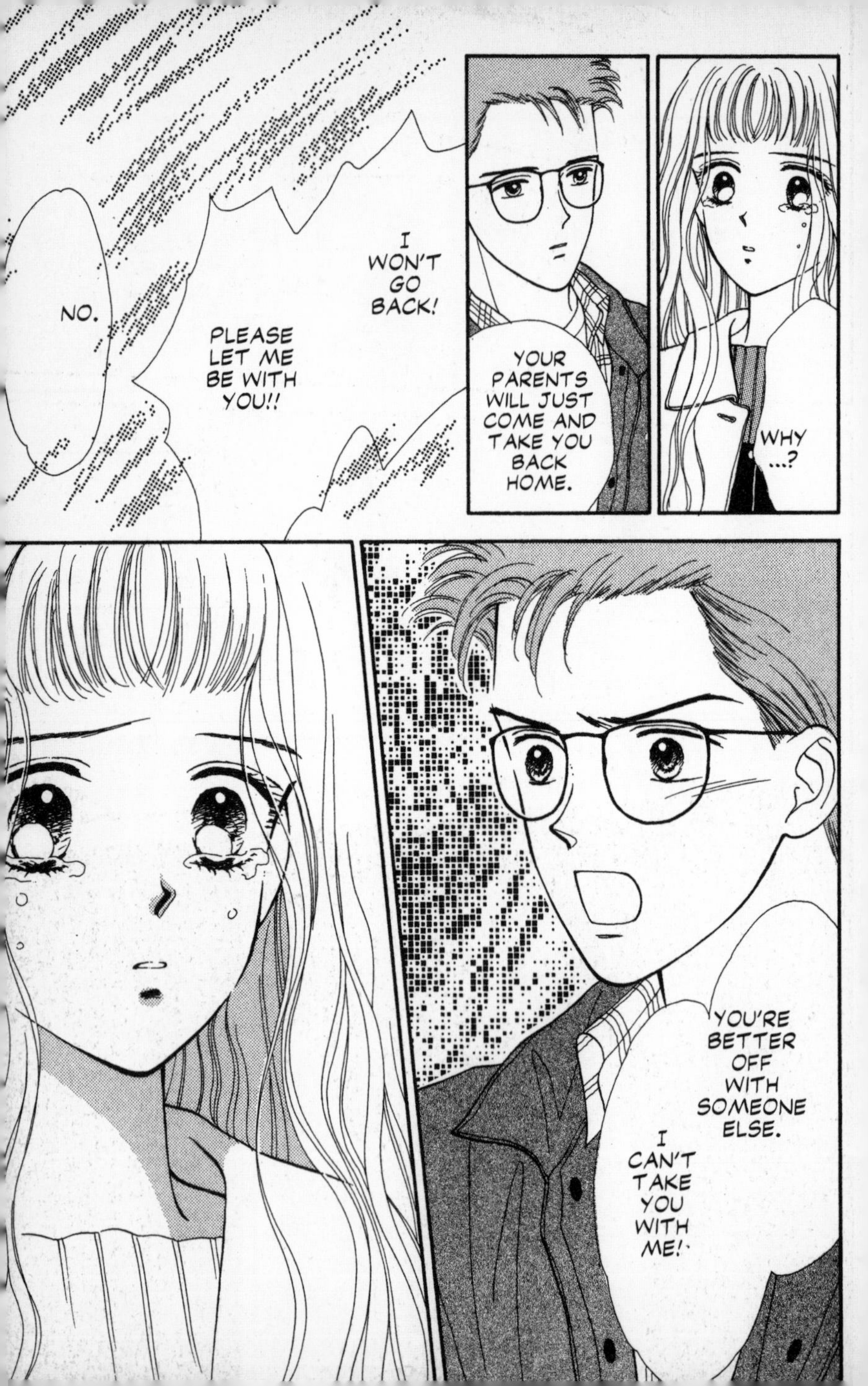
WHY ...?
YOUR PARENTS WILL JUST COME AND TAKE YOU BACK HOME.
I WON'T GO BACK!
PLEASE LET ME BE WITH YOU!!
NO.
YOU'RE BETTER OFF WITH SOMEONE ELSE.
I CAN'T TAKE YOU WITH ME!

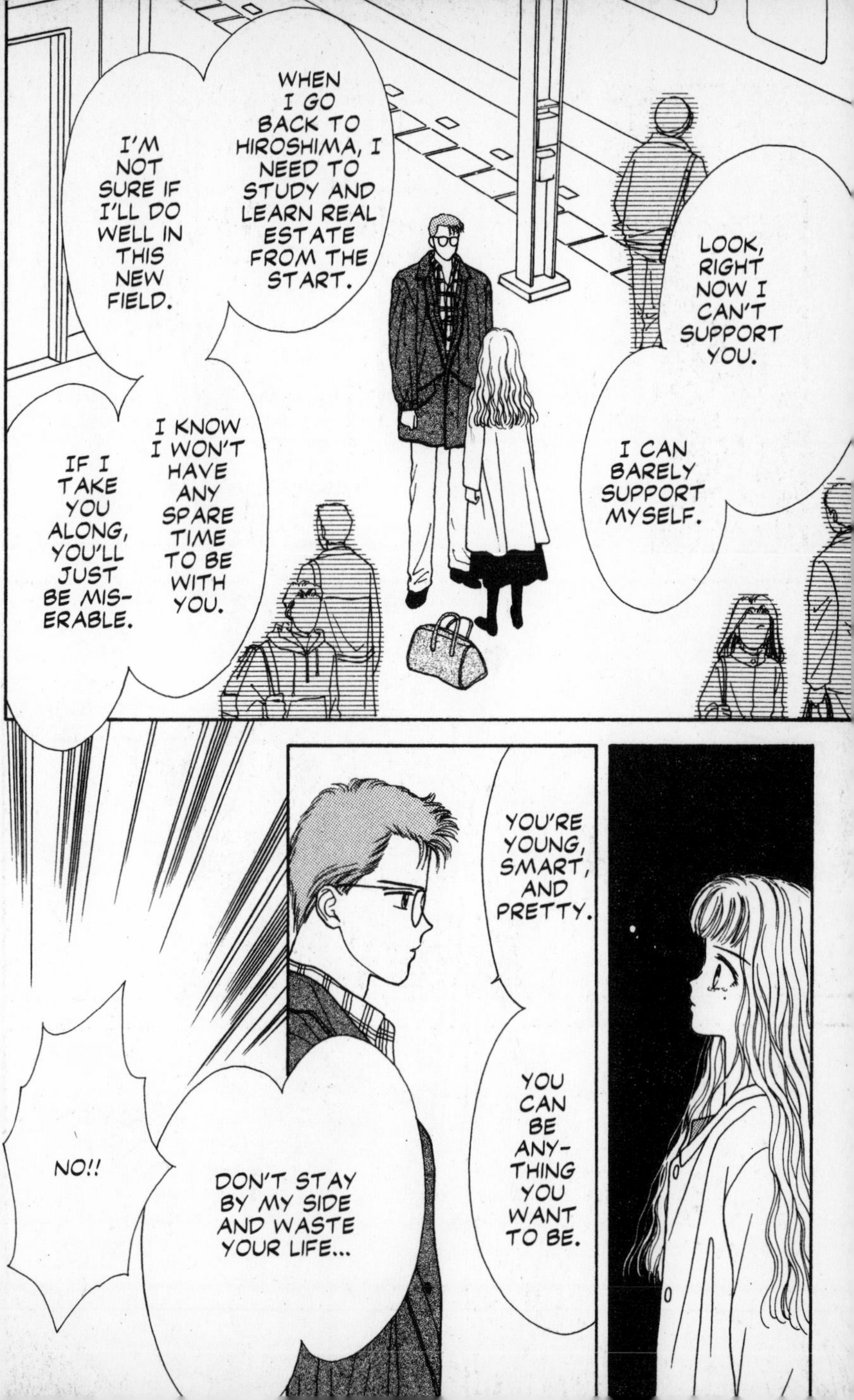
LOOK, RIGHT NOW I CAN'T SUPPORT YOU.
I CAN BARELY SUPPORT MYSELF.
WHEN I GO BACK TO HIROSHIMA, I NEED TO STUDY AND LEARN REAL ESTATE FROM THE START.
I'M NOT SURE IF I'LL DO WELL IN THIS NEW FIELD.
I KNOW I WON'T HAVE ANY SPARE TIME TO BE WITH YOU.
IF I TAKE YOU ALONG, YOU'LL JUST BE MIS-ERABLE.
YOU'RE YOUNG, SMART, AND PRETTY.
YOU CAN BE ANY-THING YOU WANT TO BE.
DON'T STAY BY MY SIDE AND WASTE YOUR LIFE...
NO!!

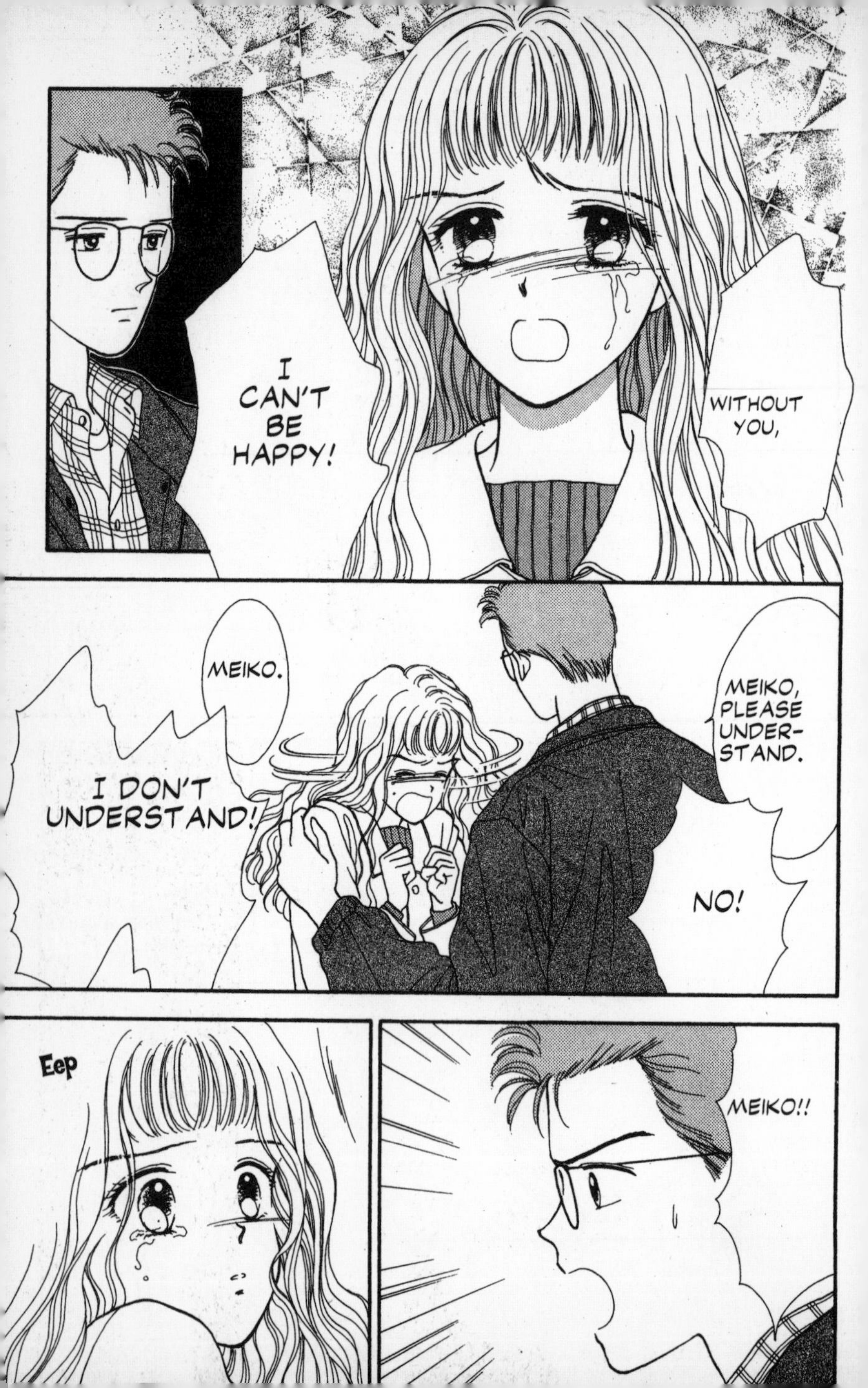
WITHOUT YOU,
I CAN'T BE HAPPY!
MEIKO, PLEASE UNDER-STAND.
MEIKO.
I DON'T UNDERSTAND!
NO!
MEIKO!!
Eep

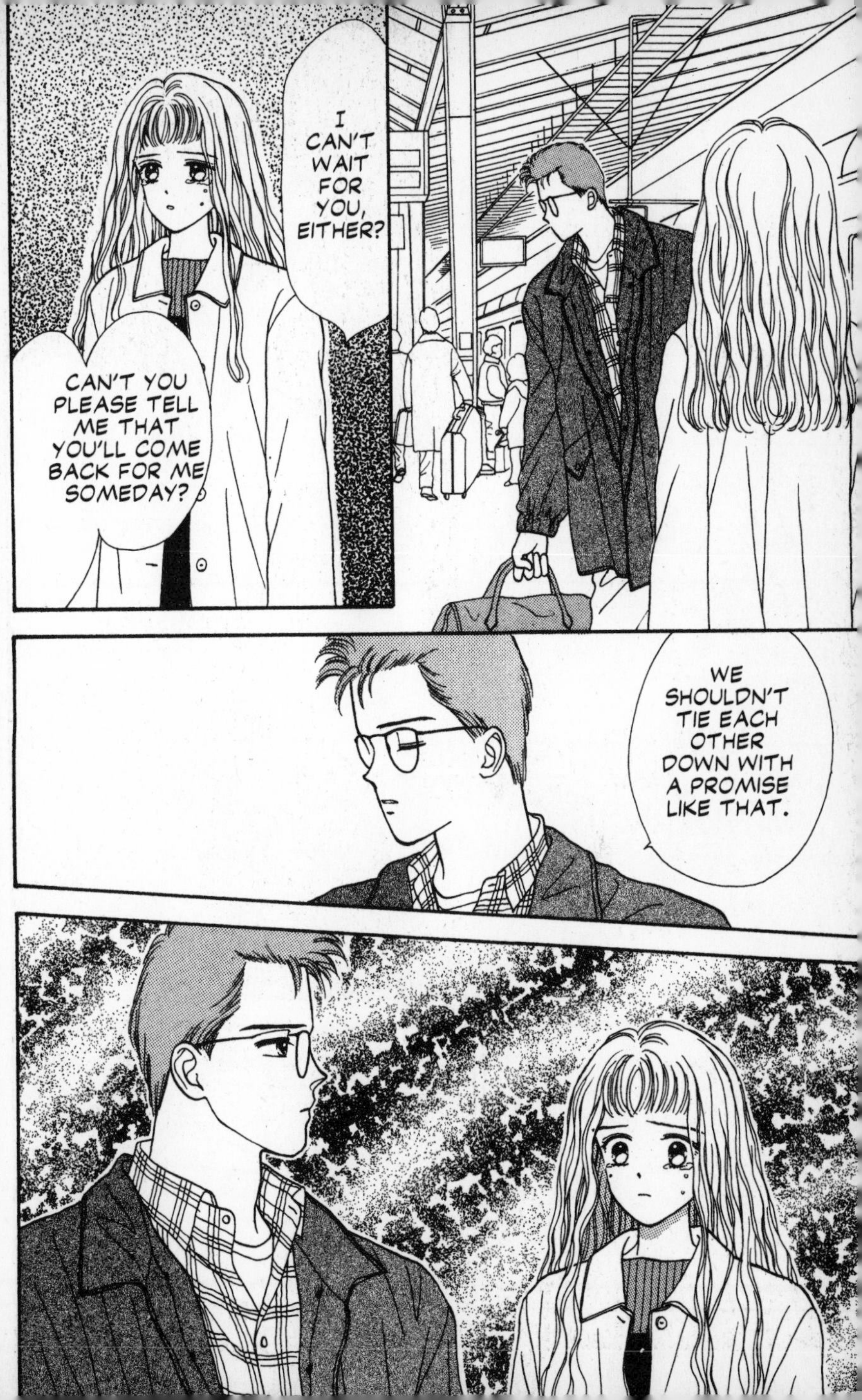
I CAN'T WAIT FOR YOU, EITHER?
CAN'T YOU PLEASE TELL ME THAT YOU'LL COME BACK FOR ME SOMEDAY?
WE SHOULDN'T TIE EACH OTHER DOWN WITH A PROMISE LIKE THAT.

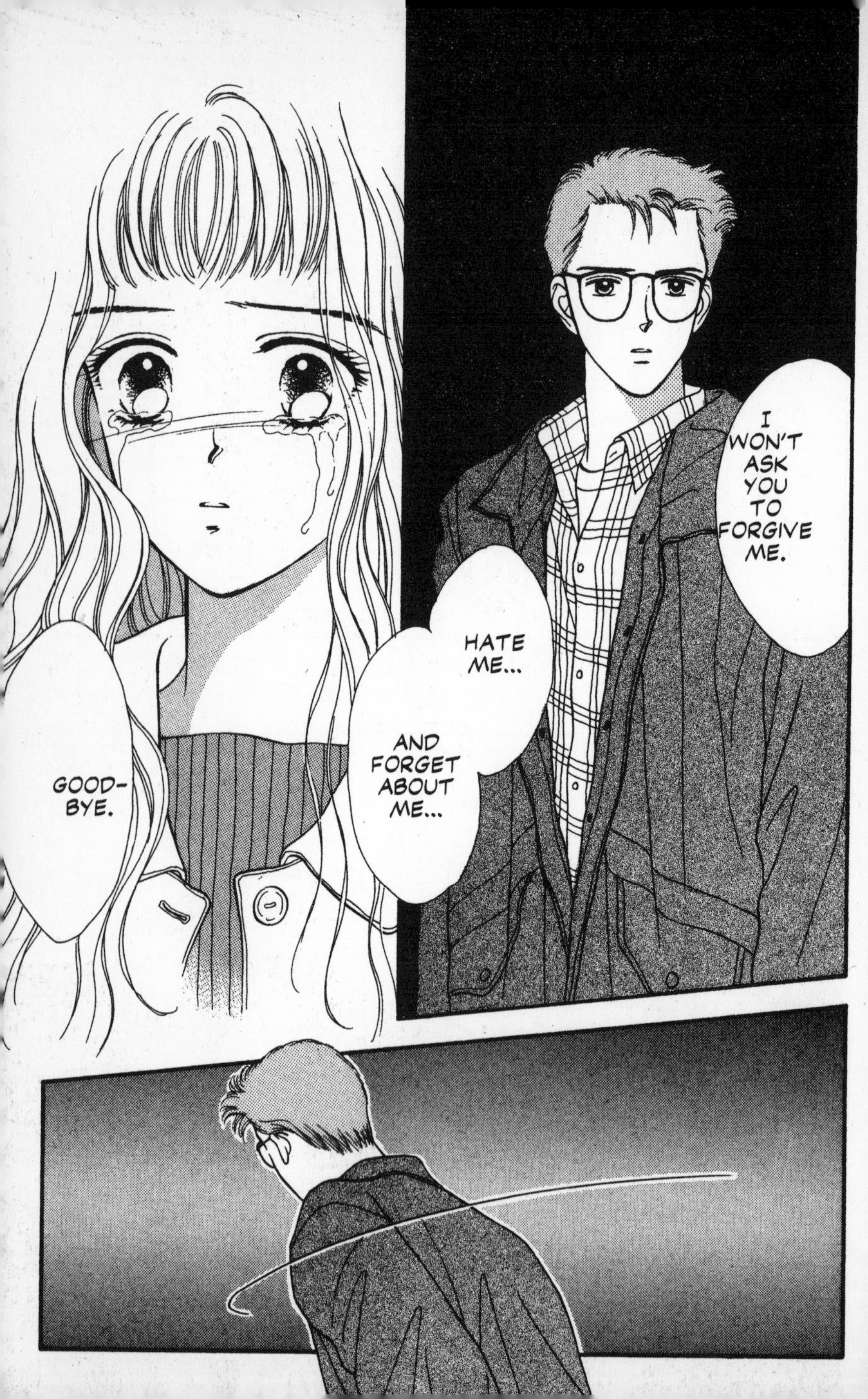
I WON'T ASK YOU TO FORGIVE ME.
HATE ME...
AND FORGET ABOUT ME...
GOOD-BYE.

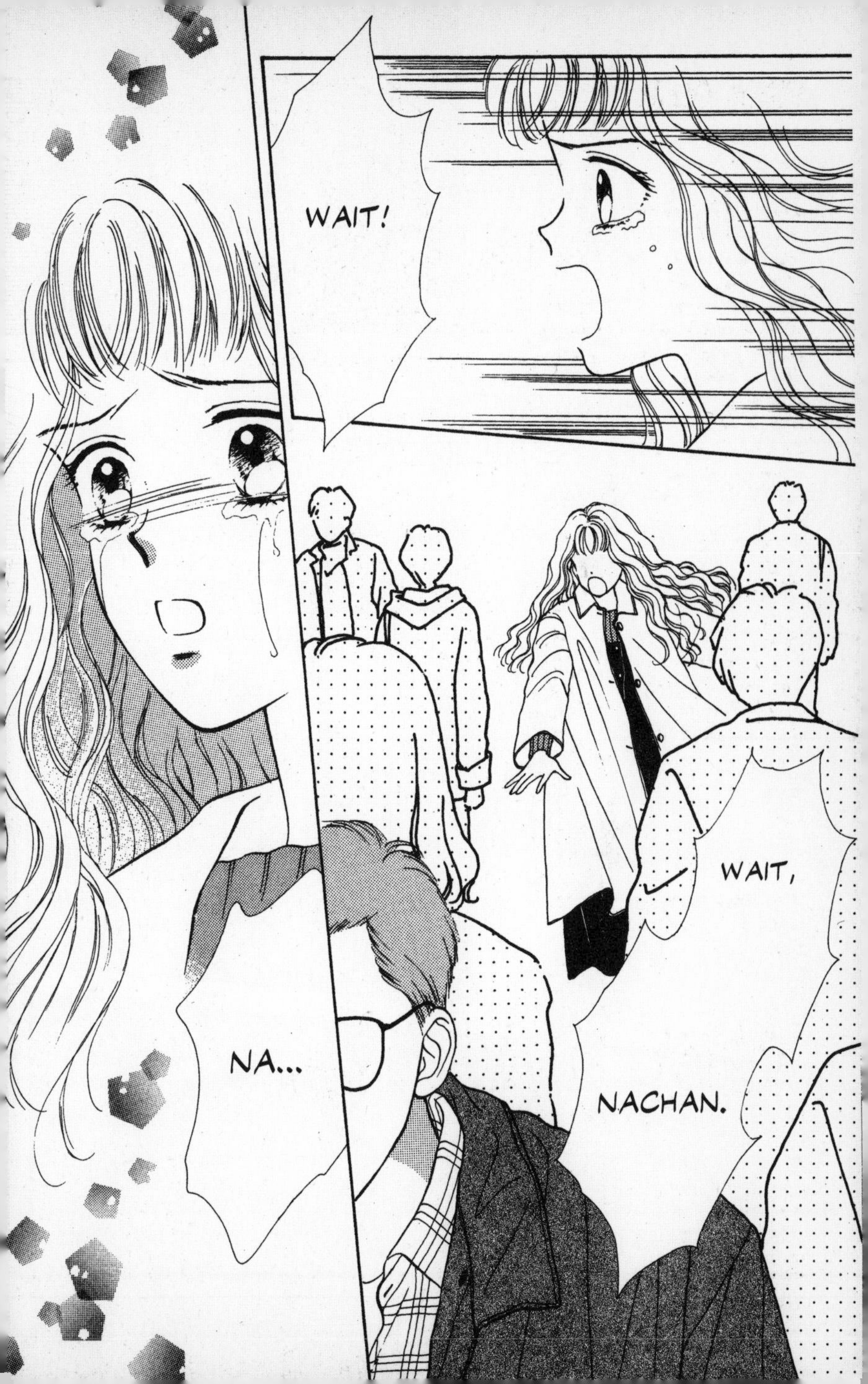
WAIT!
WAIT, NACHAN.
NA...

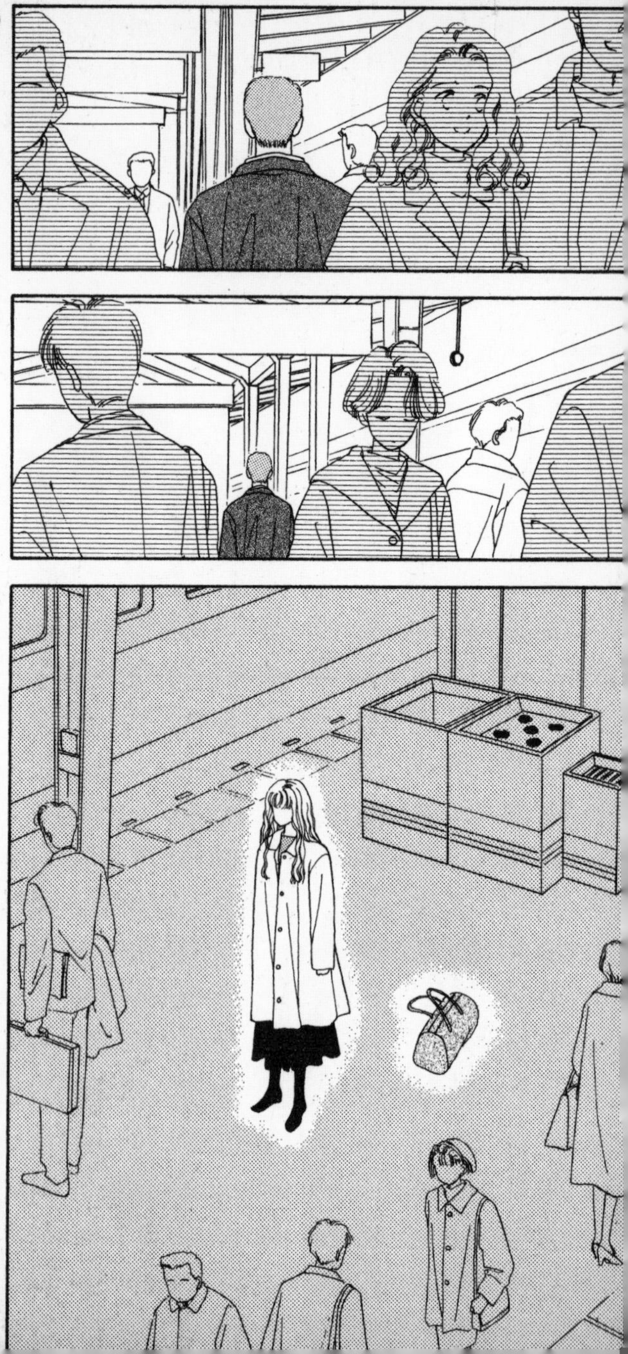

FREE TALK⑧

7/21
(Wed.)

I went to Furano on the Furano Express. We took a taxi to a lot of Furano's sightseeing spots. There were so many flower gardens--it was beautiful. The path in the garden of Tomita Farm was wonderful because it had such an incredible view. I hope I can go again next year.

7/22
(Thurs.)

After we ate crab for lunch, we went to Sapporo's Fine Arts Forest. The outdoor art class was a lot of fun!

A sculpture titled, "Let's Be a Chair and Rest."

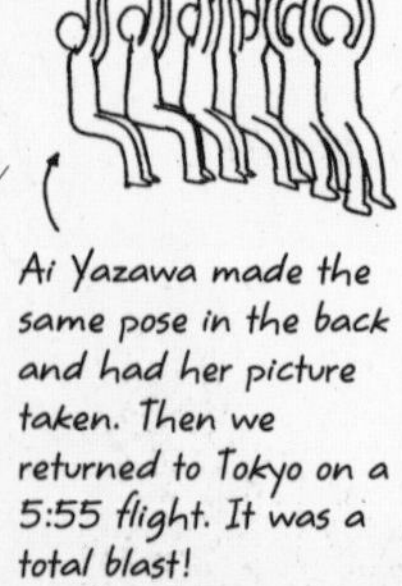

Ai Yazawa made the same pose in the back and had her picture taken. Then we returned to Tokyo on a 5:55 flight. It was a total blast!

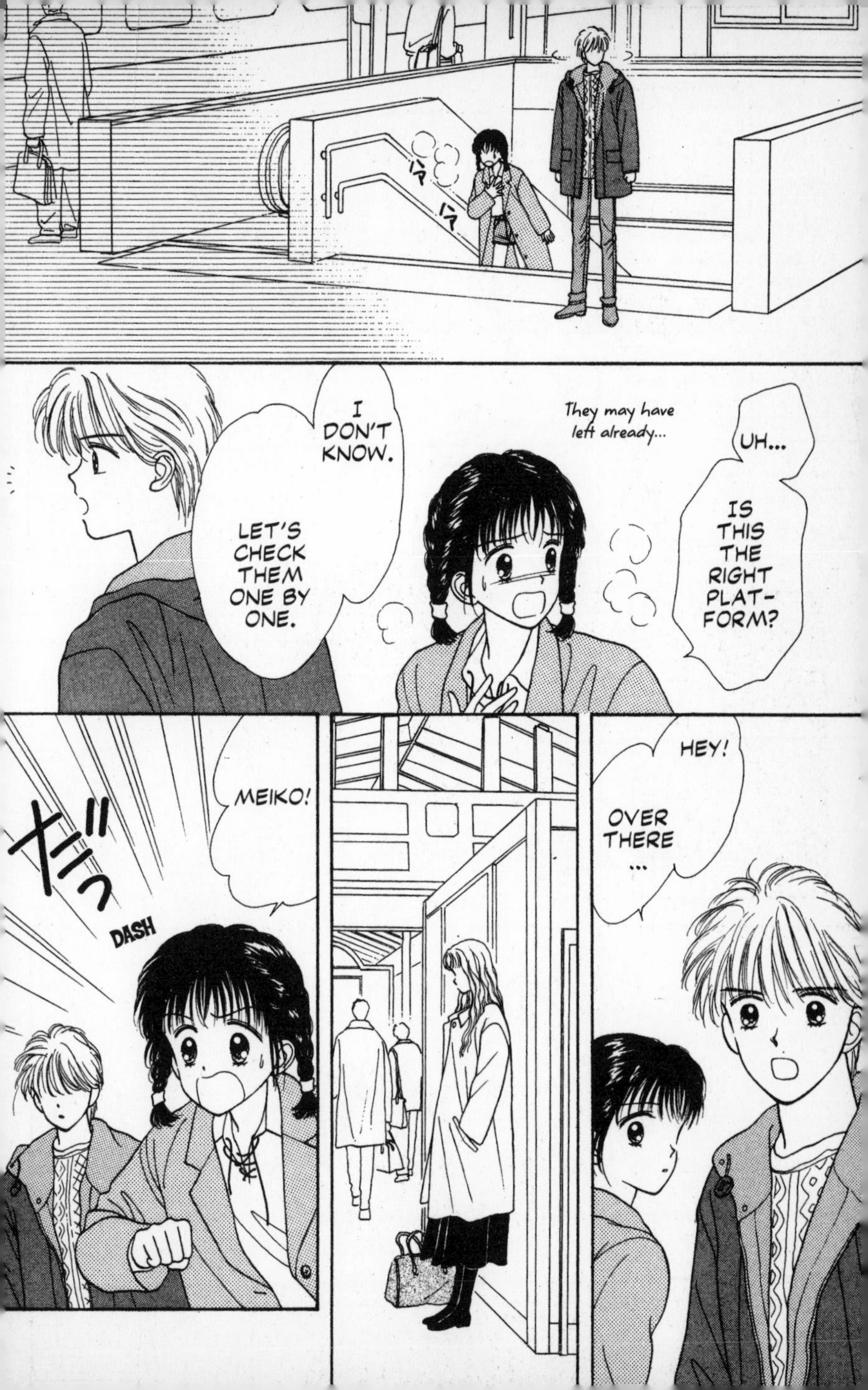

ハァ
ハァ
UH...
IS THIS THE RIGHT PLATFORM?
They may have left already...
I DON'T KNOW.
LET'S CHECK THEM ONE BY ONE.
HEY!
OVER THERE ...
MEIKO!
ダッ
DASH

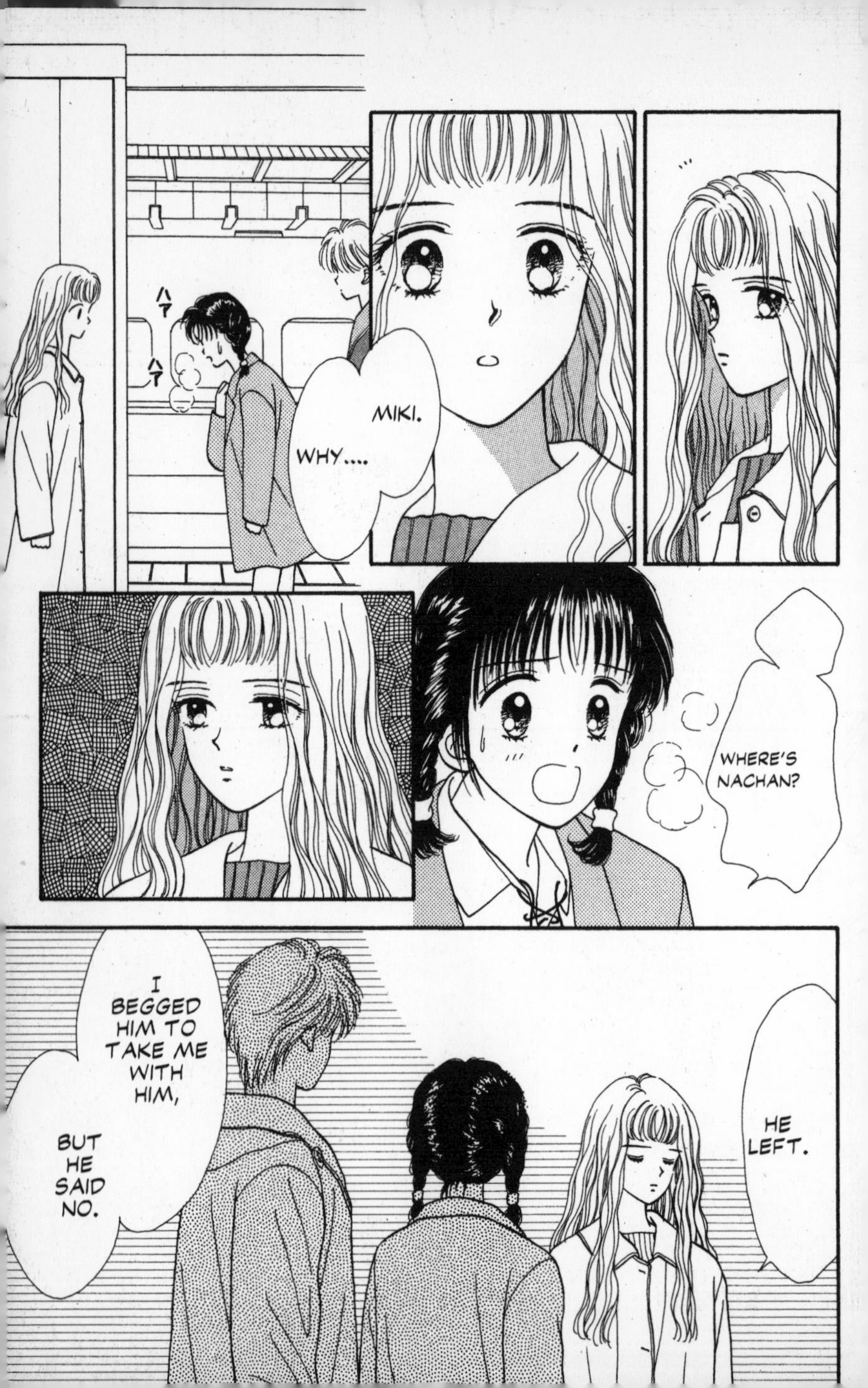
...
MIKI. WHY....
ハァ
ハァ
WHERE'S NACHAN?
HE LEFT.
I BEGGED HIM TO TAKE ME WITH HIM,
BUT HE SAID NO.

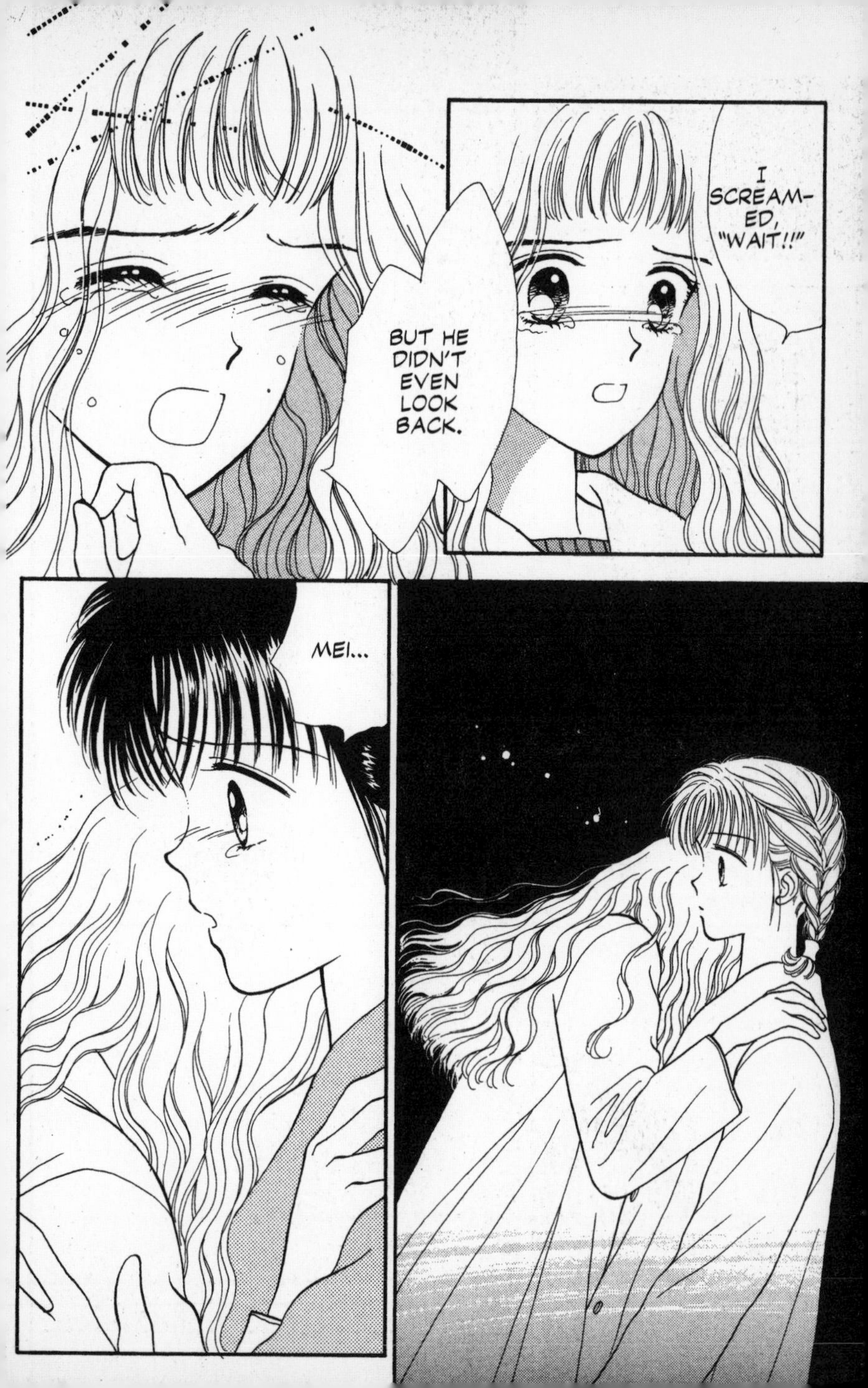
I SCREAM-ED, "WAIT!!"
BUT HE DIDN'T EVEN LOOK BACK.
MEI...

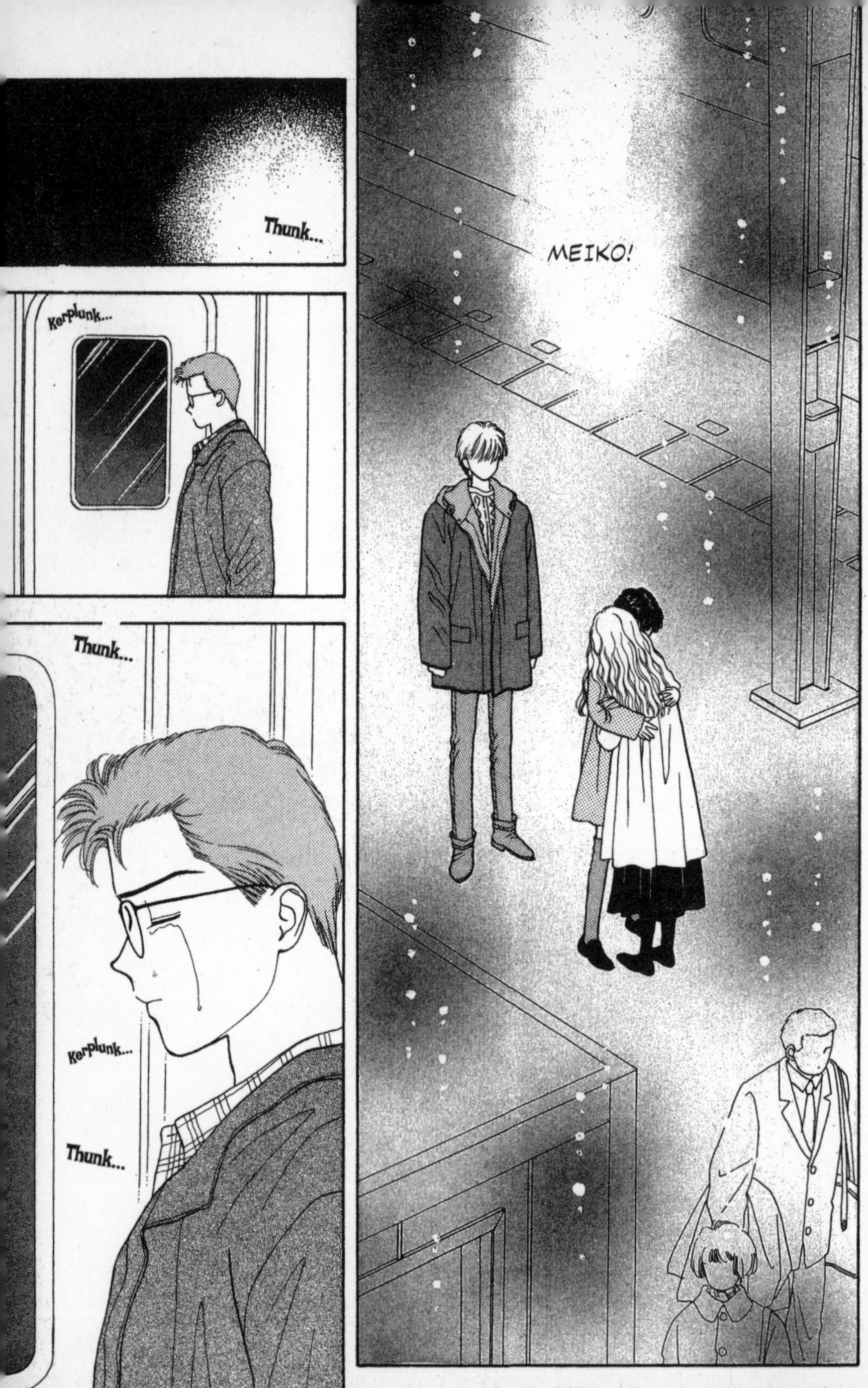
MEIKO!
Thunk...
Kerplunk...
Thunk...
Kerplunk...
Thunk...

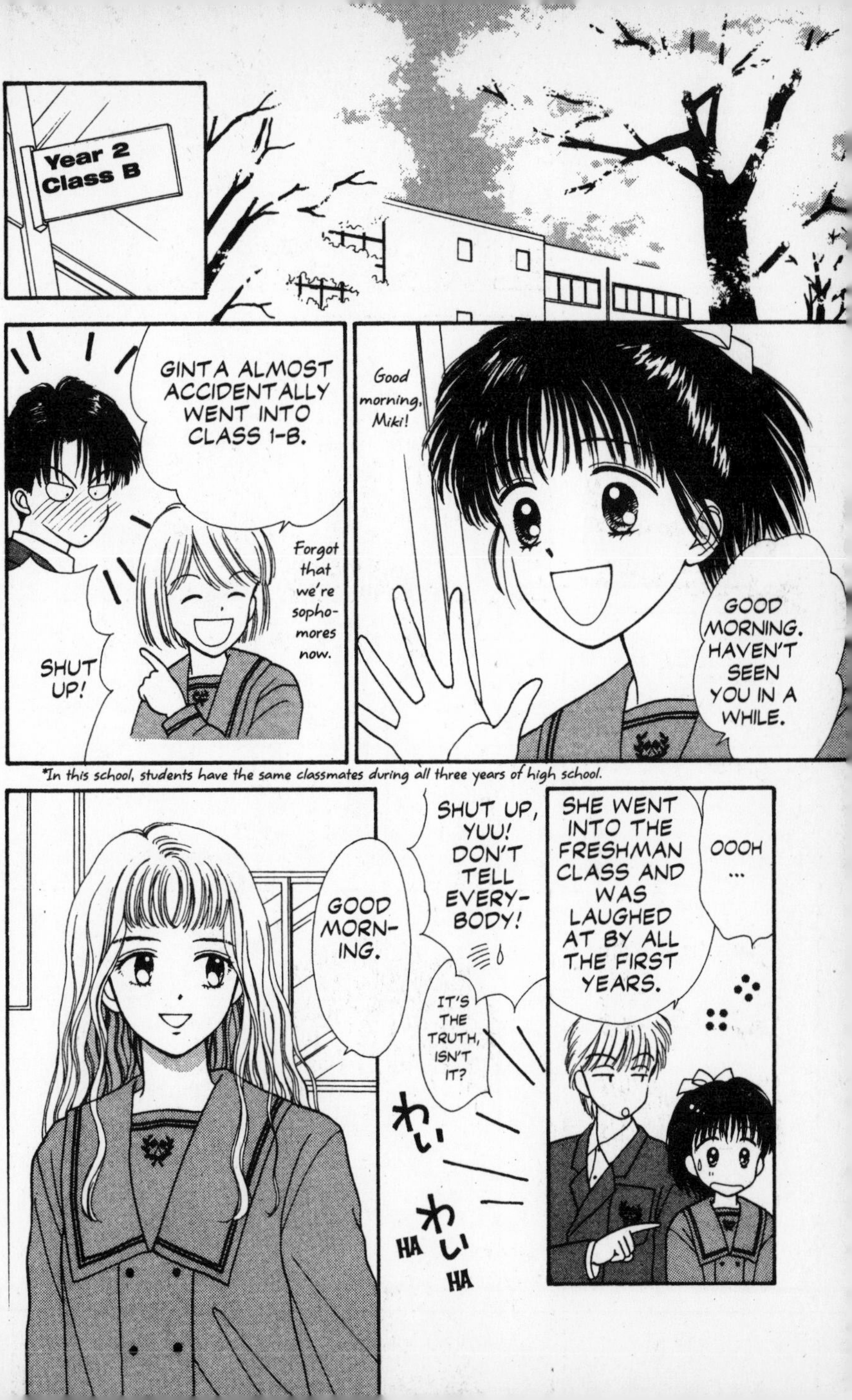
Year 2
Class B
Good morning, Miki!
GOOD MORNING. HAVEN'T SEEN YOU IN A WHILE.
GINTA ALMOST ACCIDENTALLY WENT INTO CLASS 1-B.
Forgot that we're sopho-mores now.
SHUT UP!
OOOH ...
SHE WENT INTO THE FRESHMAN CLASS AND WAS LAUGHED AT BY ALL THE FIRST YEARS.
SHUT UP, YUU! DON'T TELL EVERY-BODY!
IT'S THE TRUTH, ISN'T IT?
GOOD MORN-ING.
わい
わい
HA
HA

*In this school, students have the same classmates during all three years of high school.

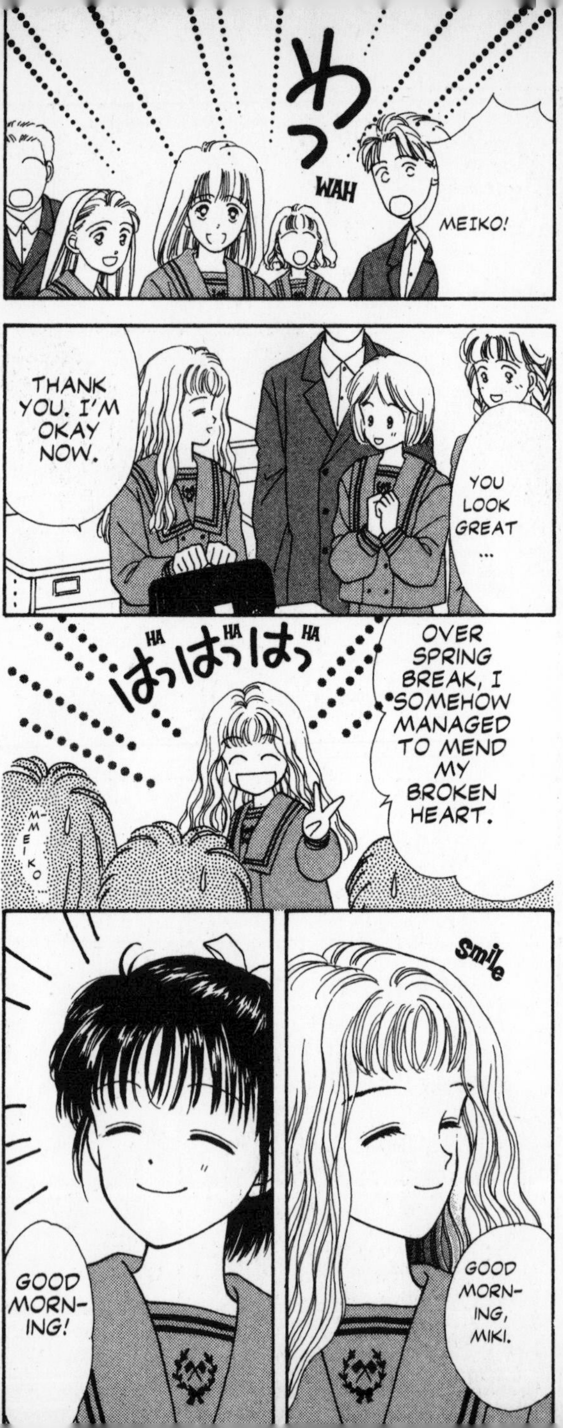
わっ
WAH
MEIKO!
YOU LOOK GREAT ...
THANK YOU. I'M OKAY NOW.
はっはっはっ
HA HA HA
OVER SPRING BREAK, I SOMEHOW MANAGED TO MEND MY BROKEN HEART.
M-MEIKO...
Smile
GOOD MORNING, MIKI.
GOOD MORNING!

Tsutomu Rokutanda

HOROSCOPE: CANCER

BLOODTYPE: B

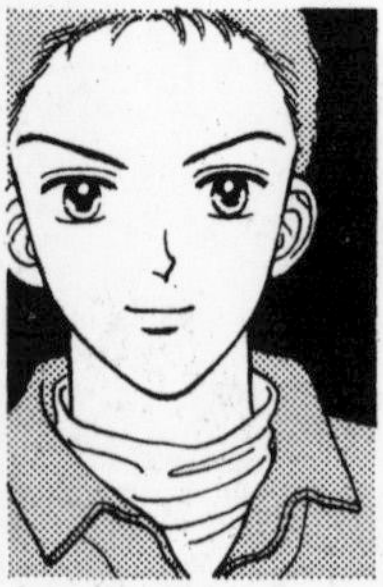

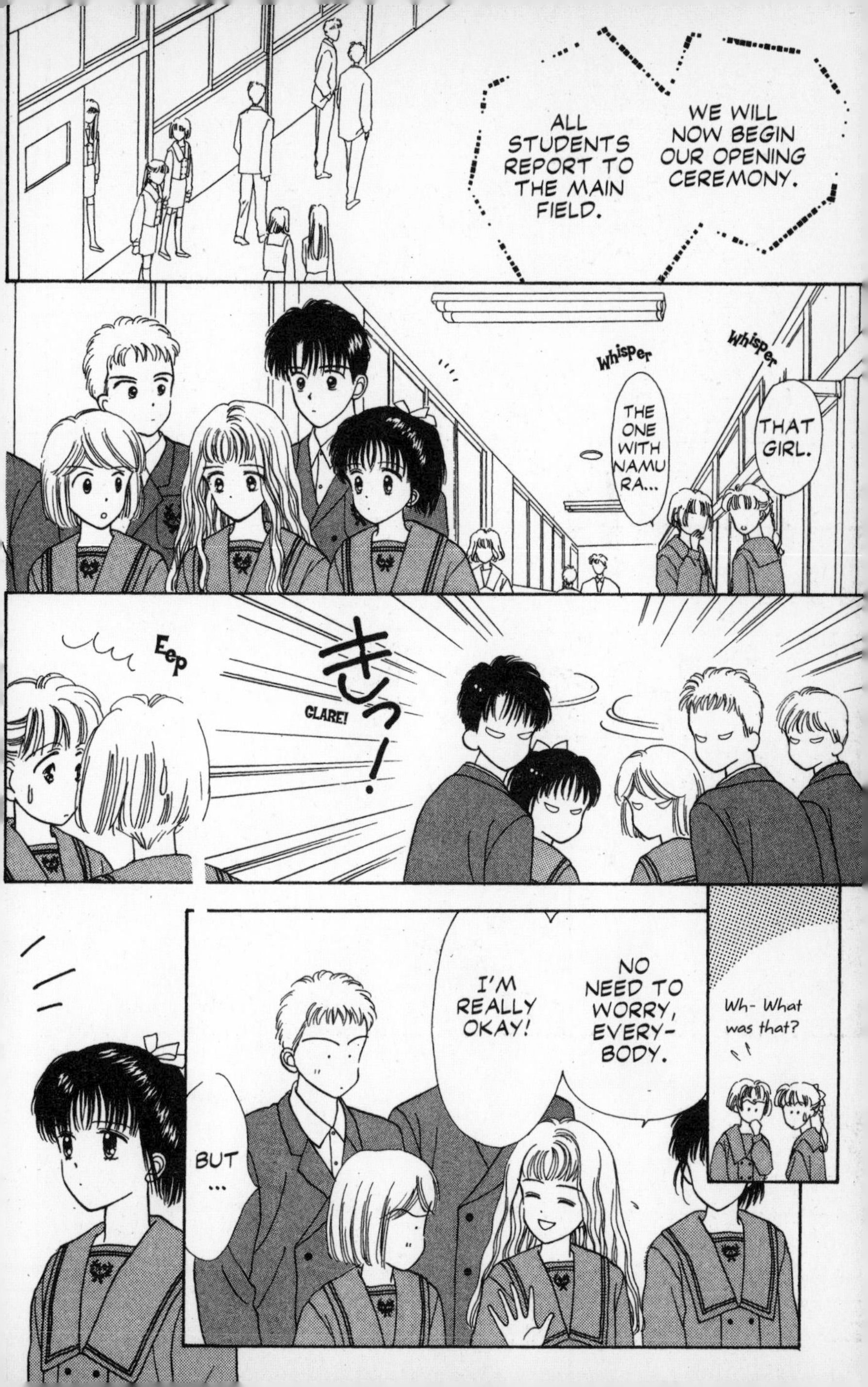
WE WILL NOW BEGIN OUR OPENING CEREMONY.
ALL STUDENTS REPORT TO THE MAIN FIELD.
Whisper
THAT GIRL.
Whisper
THE ONE WITH NAMURA...
きっ!
GLARE!
Eep
Wh- What was that?
NO NEED TO WORRY, EVERYBODY.
I'M REALLY OKAY!
BUT ...

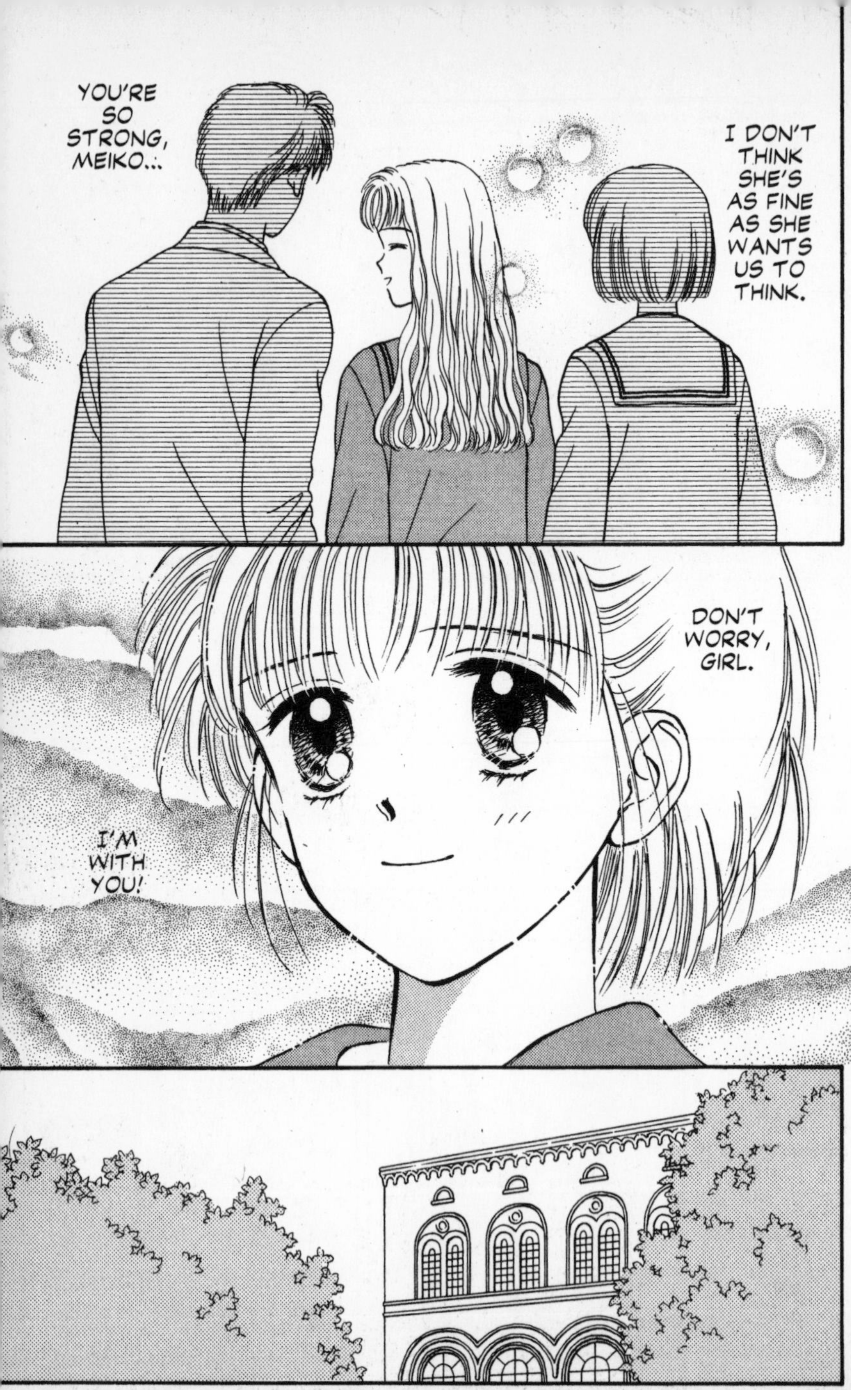
I DON'T THINK SHE'S AS FINE AS SHE WANTS US TO THINK.
YOU'RE SO STRONG, MEIKO...
DON'T WORRY, GIRL.
I'M WITH YOU!

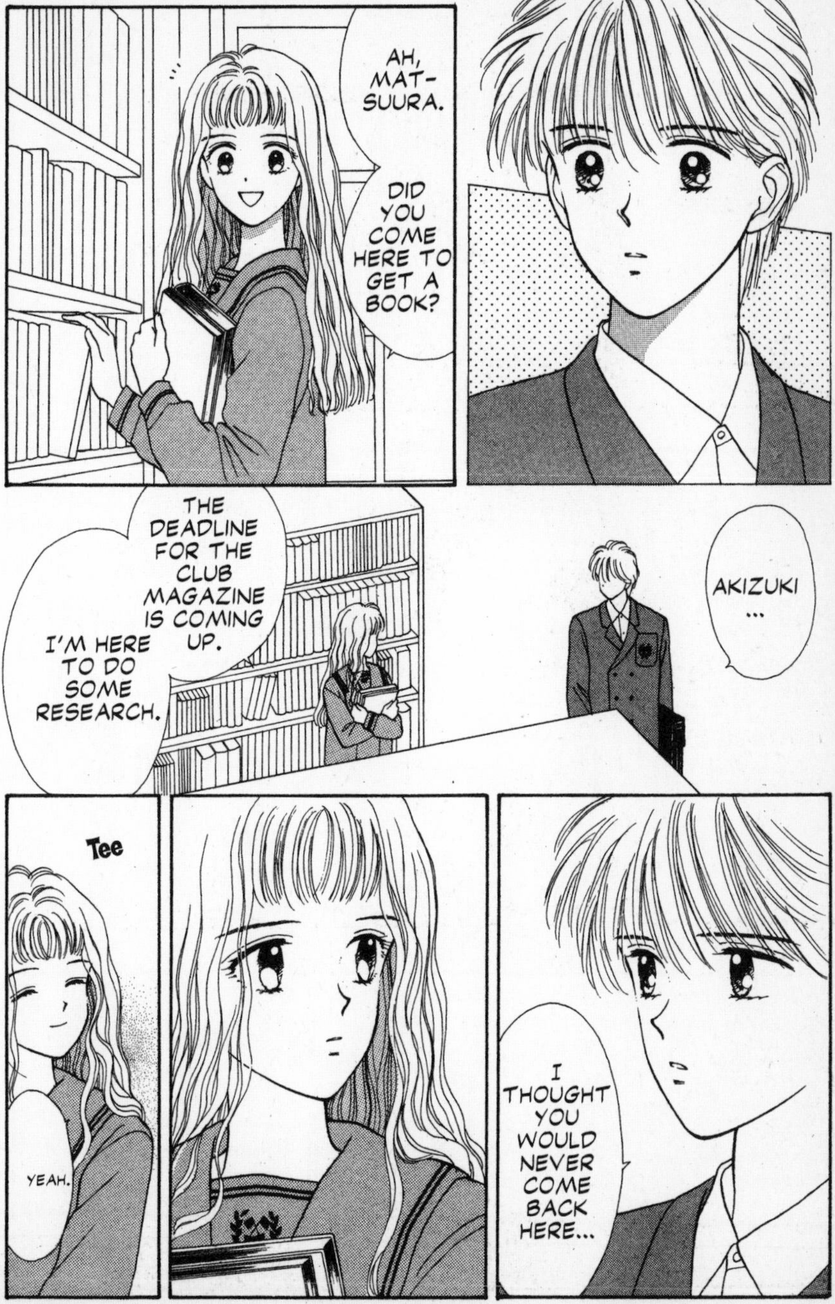
AH, MAT-SUURA.
DID YOU COME HERE TO GET A BOOK?
AKIZUKI ...
THE DEADLINE FOR THE CLUB MAGAZINE IS COMING UP.
I'M HERE TO DO SOME RESEARCH.
I THOUGHT YOU WOULD NEVER COME BACK HERE...
Tee
YEAH.

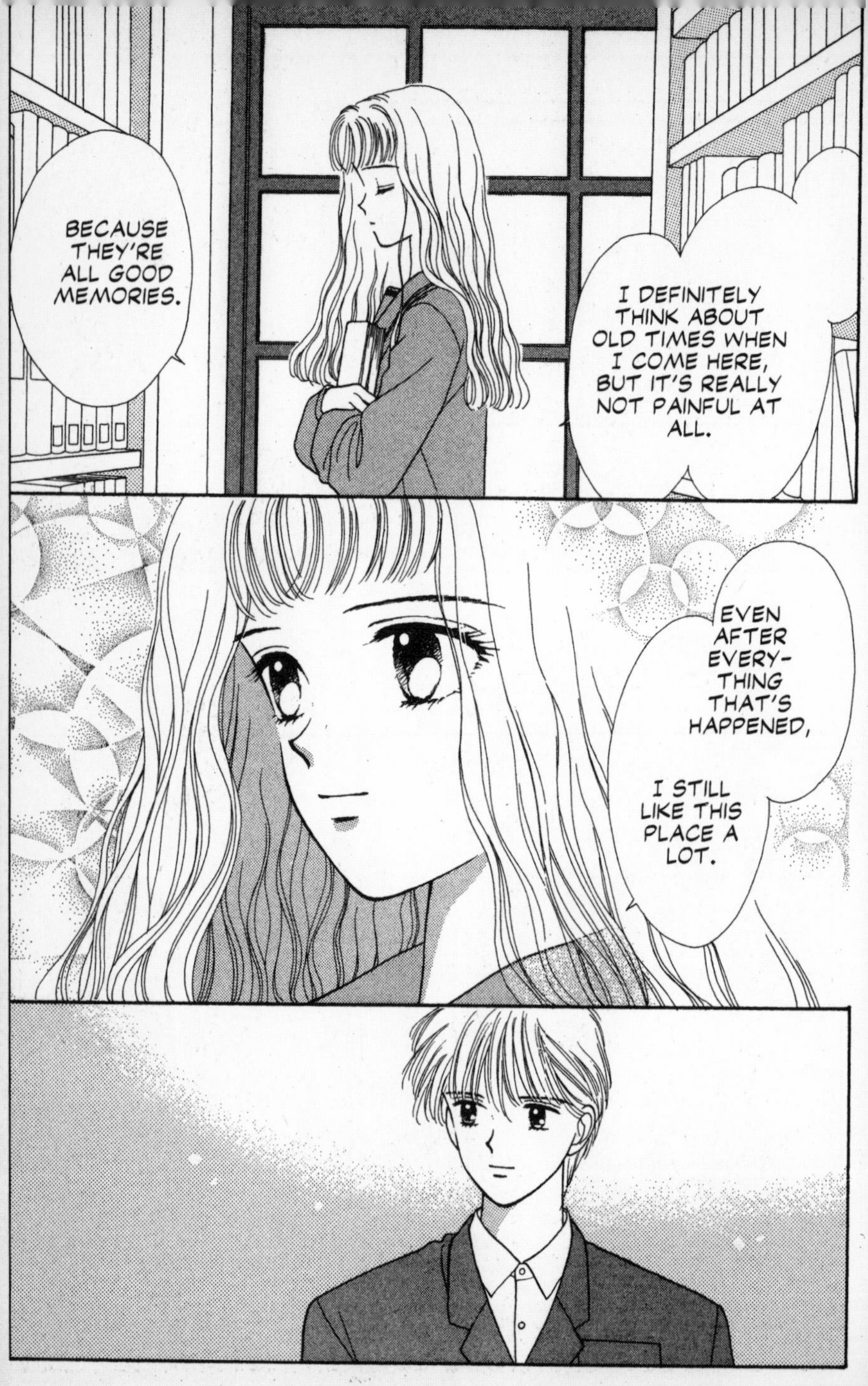
I DEFINITELY THINK ABOUT OLD TIMES WHEN I COME HERE, BUT IT'S REALLY NOT PAINFUL AT ALL.
BECAUSE THEY'RE ALL GOOD MEMORIES.
EVEN AFTER EVERY-THING THAT'S HAPPENED,
I STILL LIKE THIS PLACE A LOT.

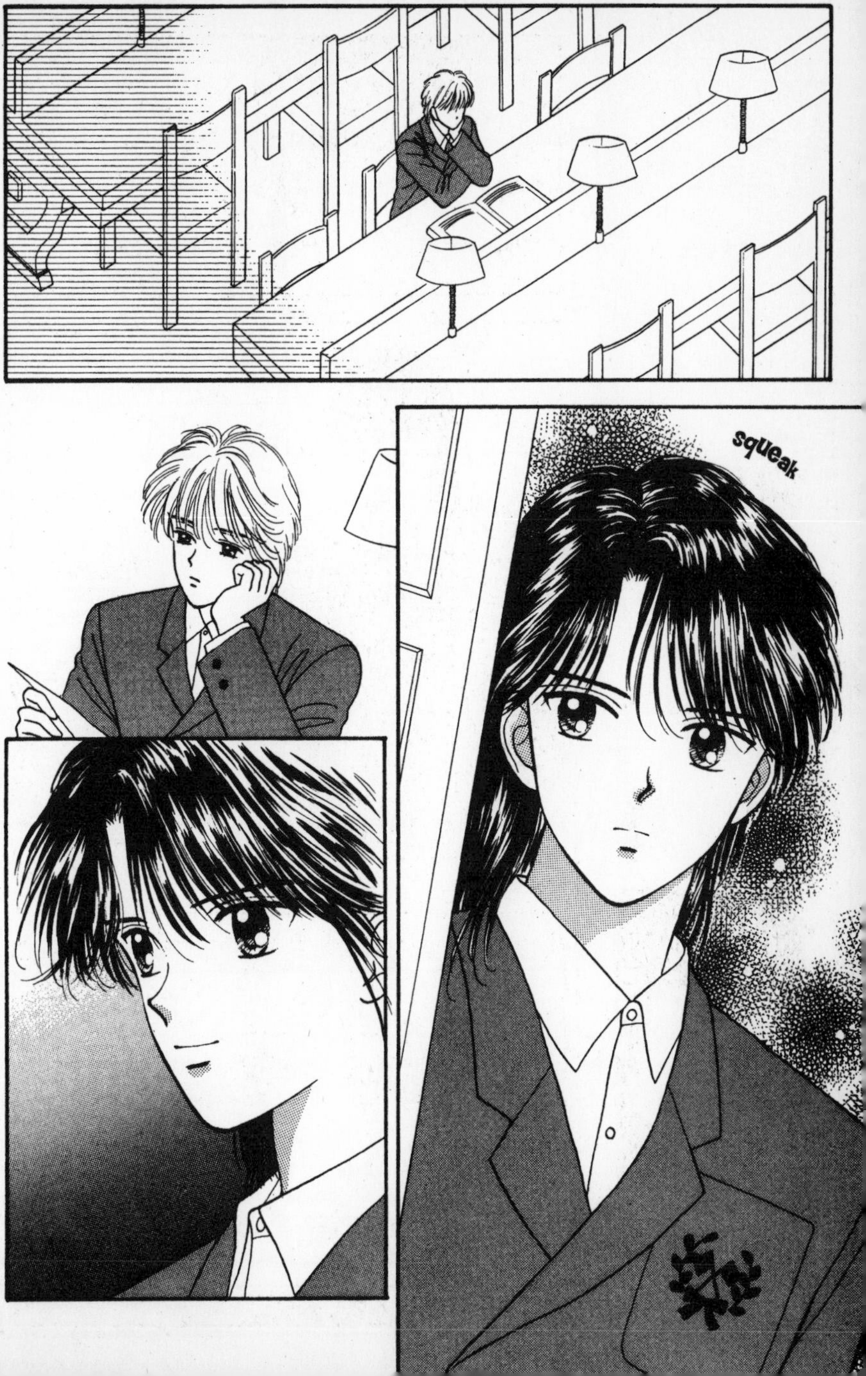
squeak

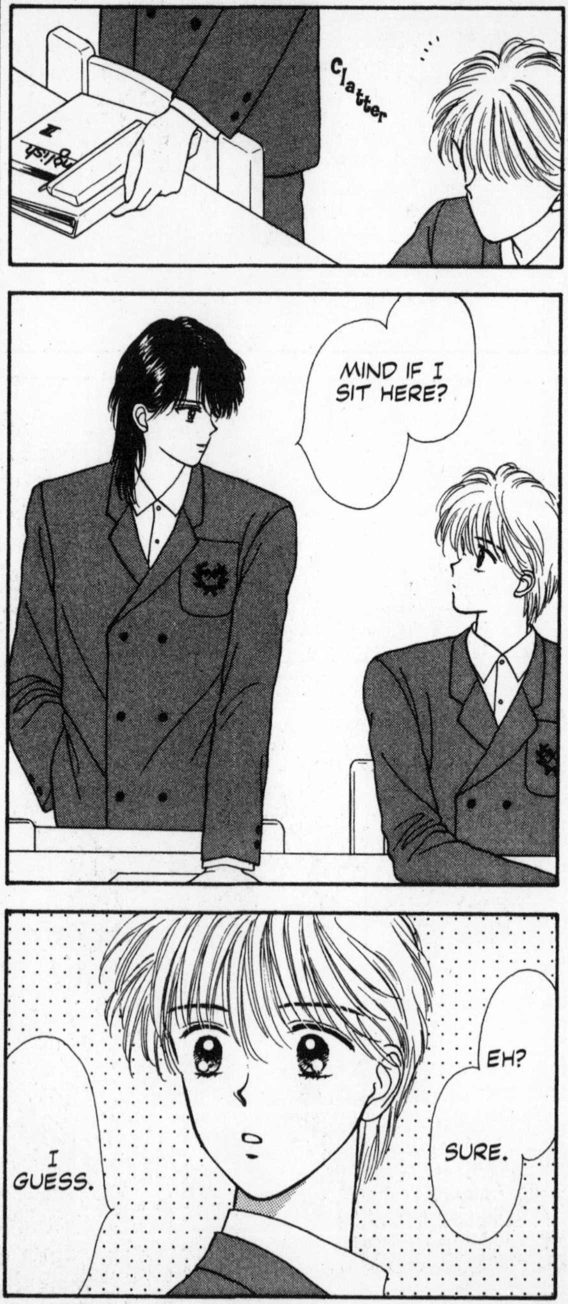
Clatter
MIND IF I SIT HERE?
EH?
SURE.
I GUESS.

Satoshi Miwa

HOROSCOPE: SAGITTARIUS

BLOODTYPE: AB

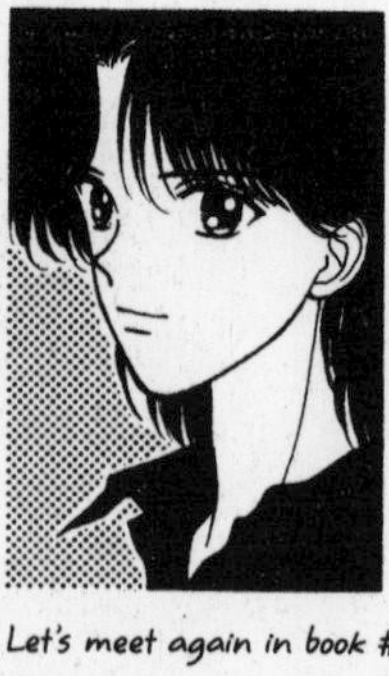

Let's meet again in book #4.

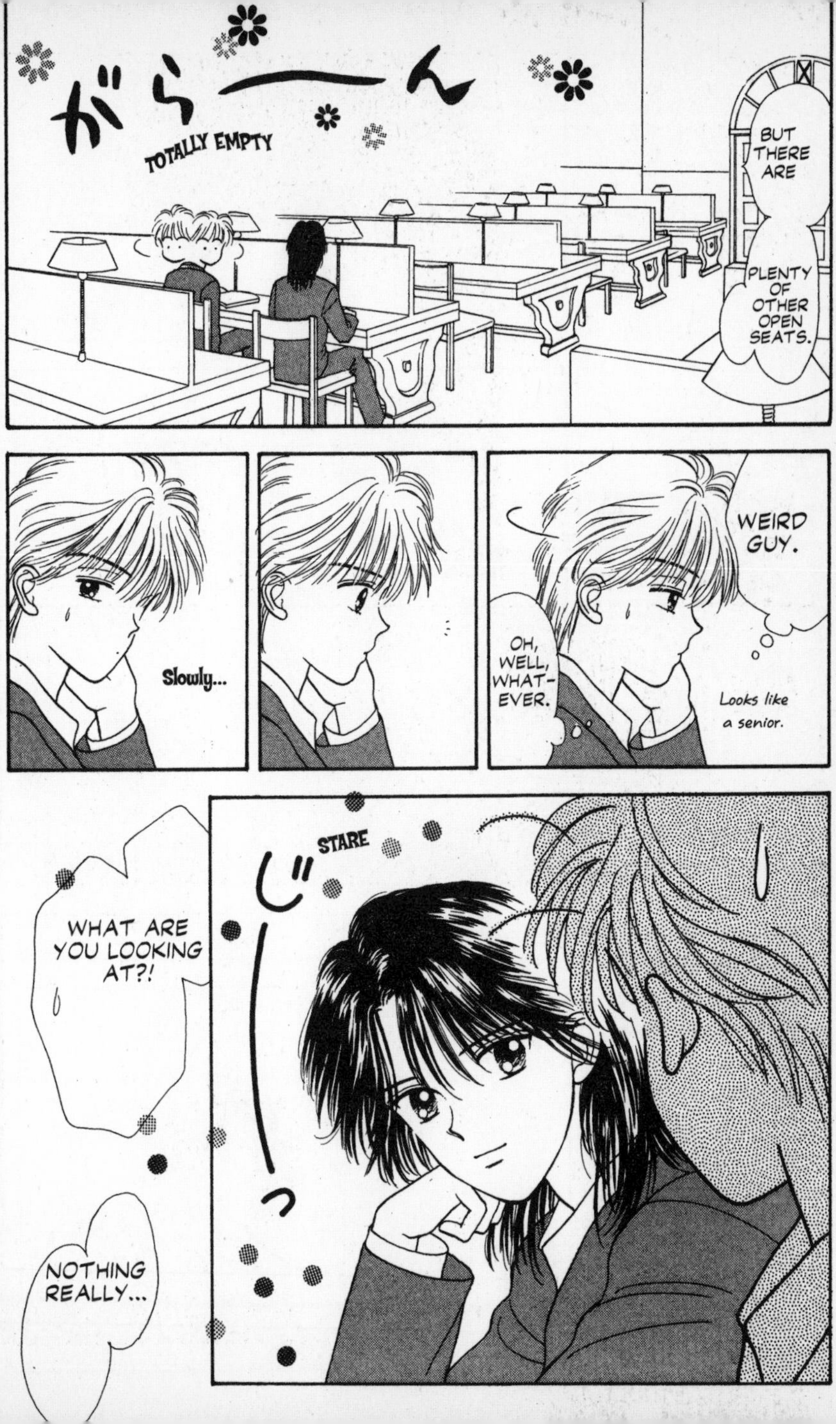
がらーーん
TOTALLY EMPTY
BUT THERE ARE
PLENTY OF OTHER OPEN SEATS.
WEIRD GUY.
Looks like a senior.
OH, WELL, WHAT-EVER.
Slowly...
じーっ
STARE
WHAT ARE YOU LOOKING AT?!
NOTHING REALLY...

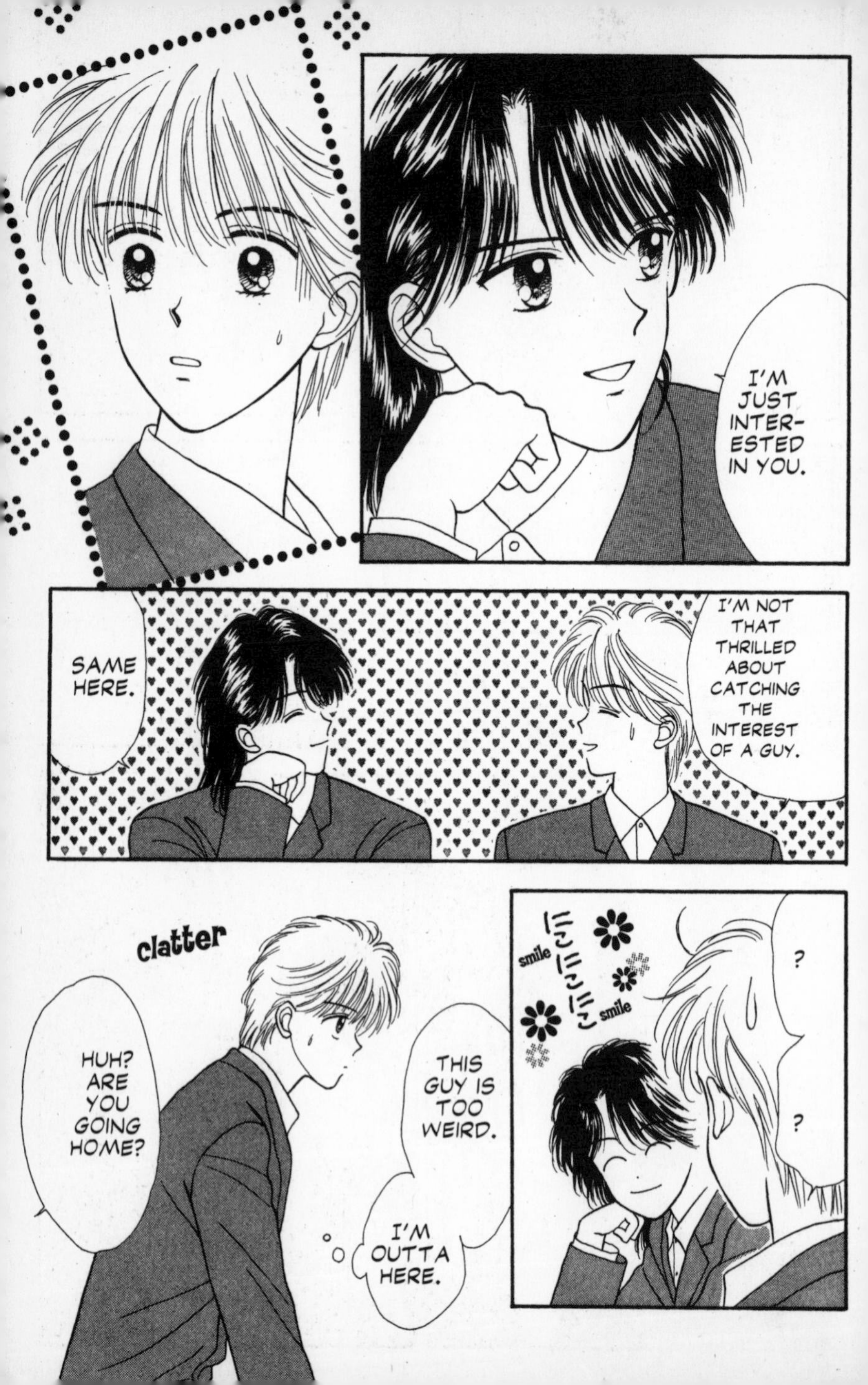
I'M JUST INTERESTED IN YOU.
I'M NOT THAT THRILLED ABOUT CATCHING THE INTEREST OF A GUY.
SAME HERE.
?
?
にこにこ
smile
smile
THIS GUY IS TOO WEIRD.
I'M OUTTA HERE.
clatter
HUH? ARE YOU GOING HOME?

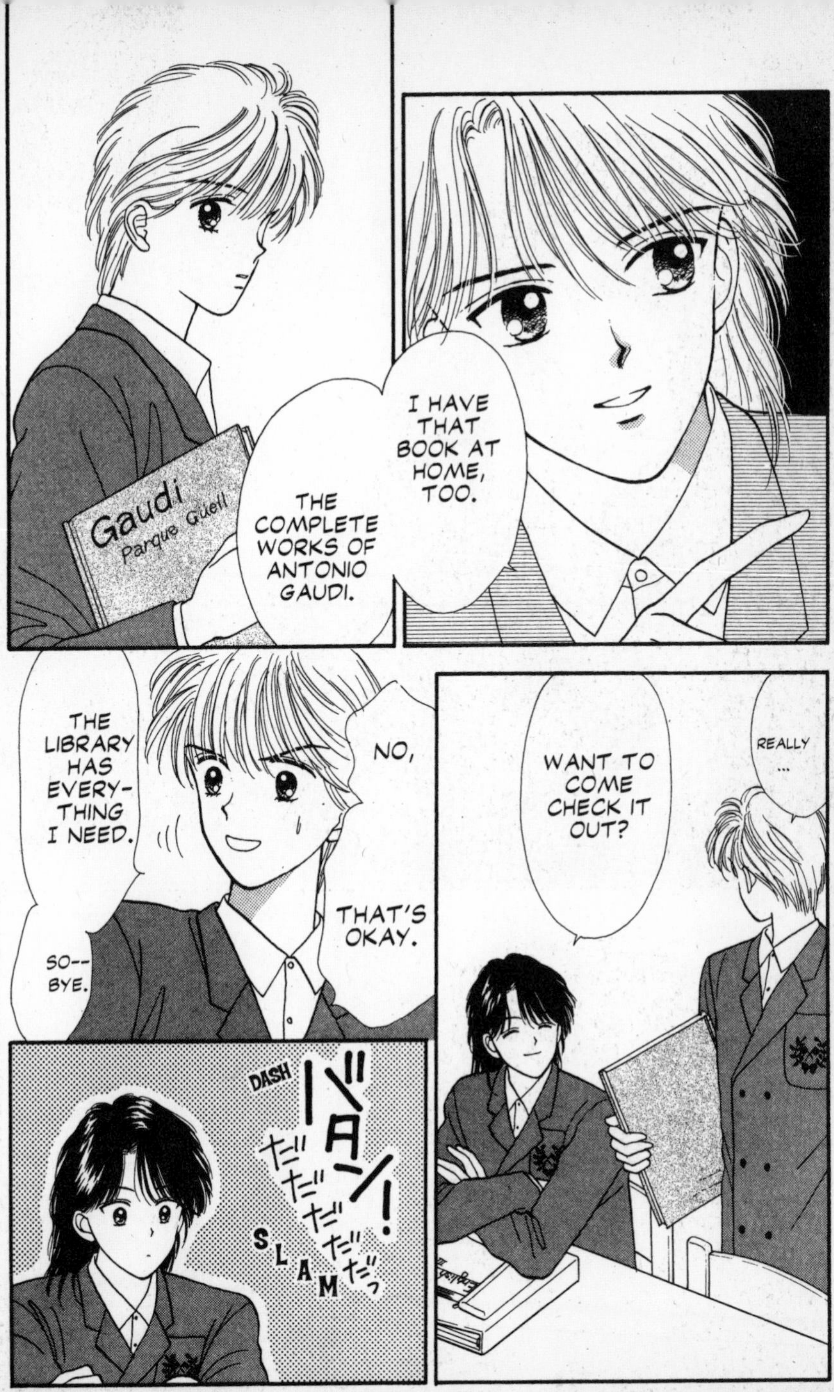
I HAVE THAT BOOK AT HOME, TOO.
THE COMPLETE WORKS OF ANTONIO GAUDI.
Gaudi
Parque Güell
REALLY ...
WANT TO COME CHECK IT OUT?
NO,
THAT'S OKAY.
THE LIBRARY HAS EVERY-THING I NEED.
SO-- BYE.
DASH
バタン!
SLAM
だだだだっ

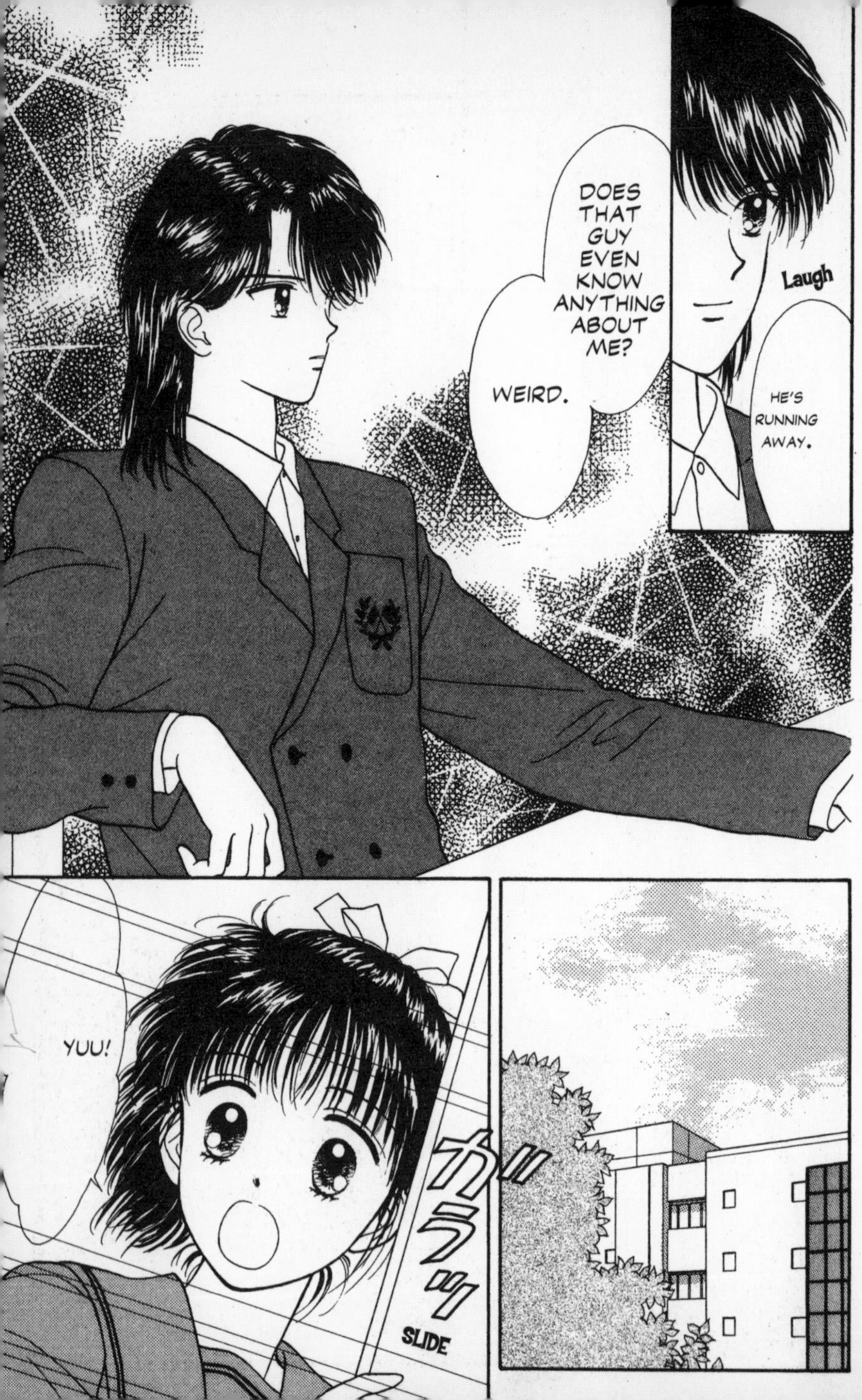
Laugh
HE'S RUNNING AWAY.
DOES THAT GUY EVEN KNOW ANYTHING ABOUT ME?
WEIRD.
YUU!
カラッ
SLIDE

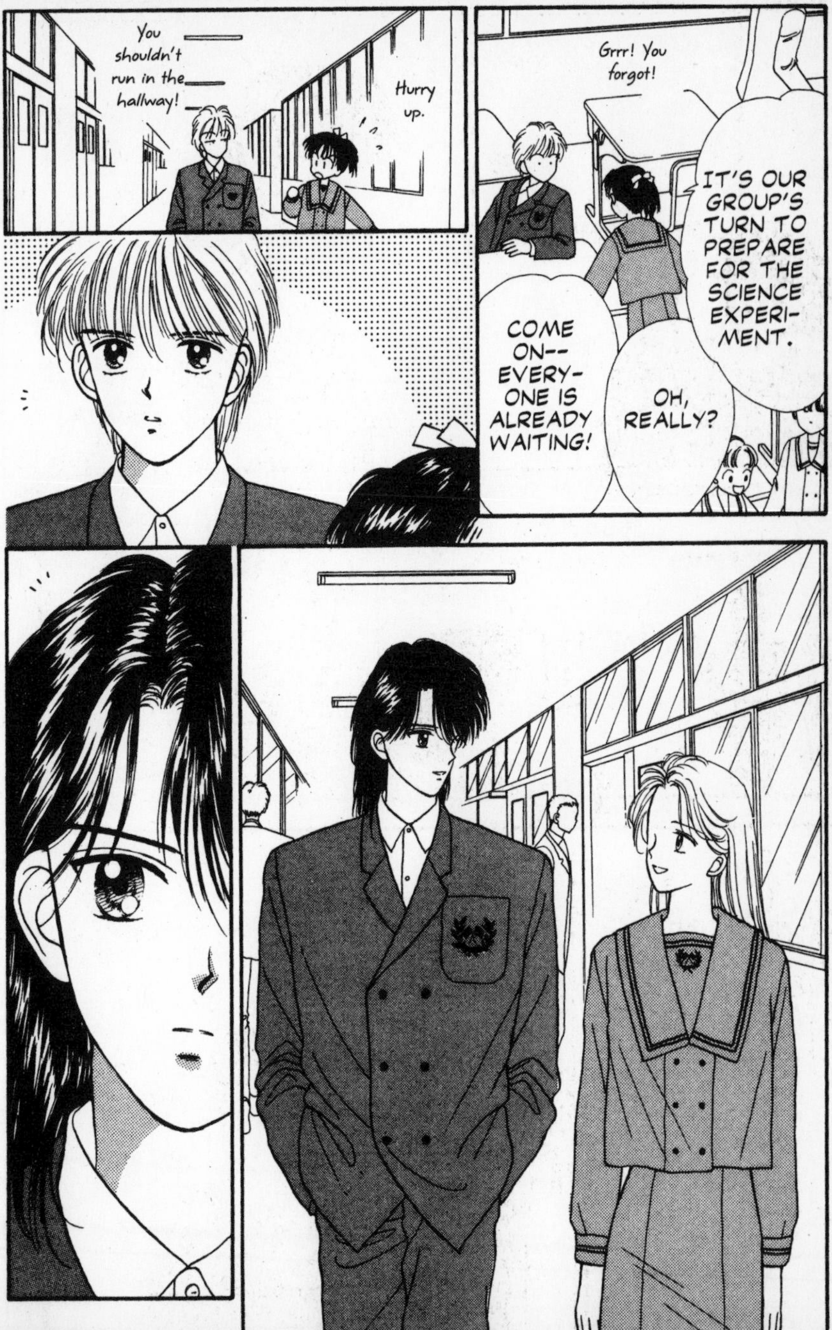
Grrr! You forgot!
IT'S OUR GROUP'S TURN TO PREPARE FOR THE SCIENCE EXPERIMENT.
OH, REALLY?
COME ON-- EVERYONE IS ALREADY WAITING!
Hurry up.
You shouldn't run in the hallway!

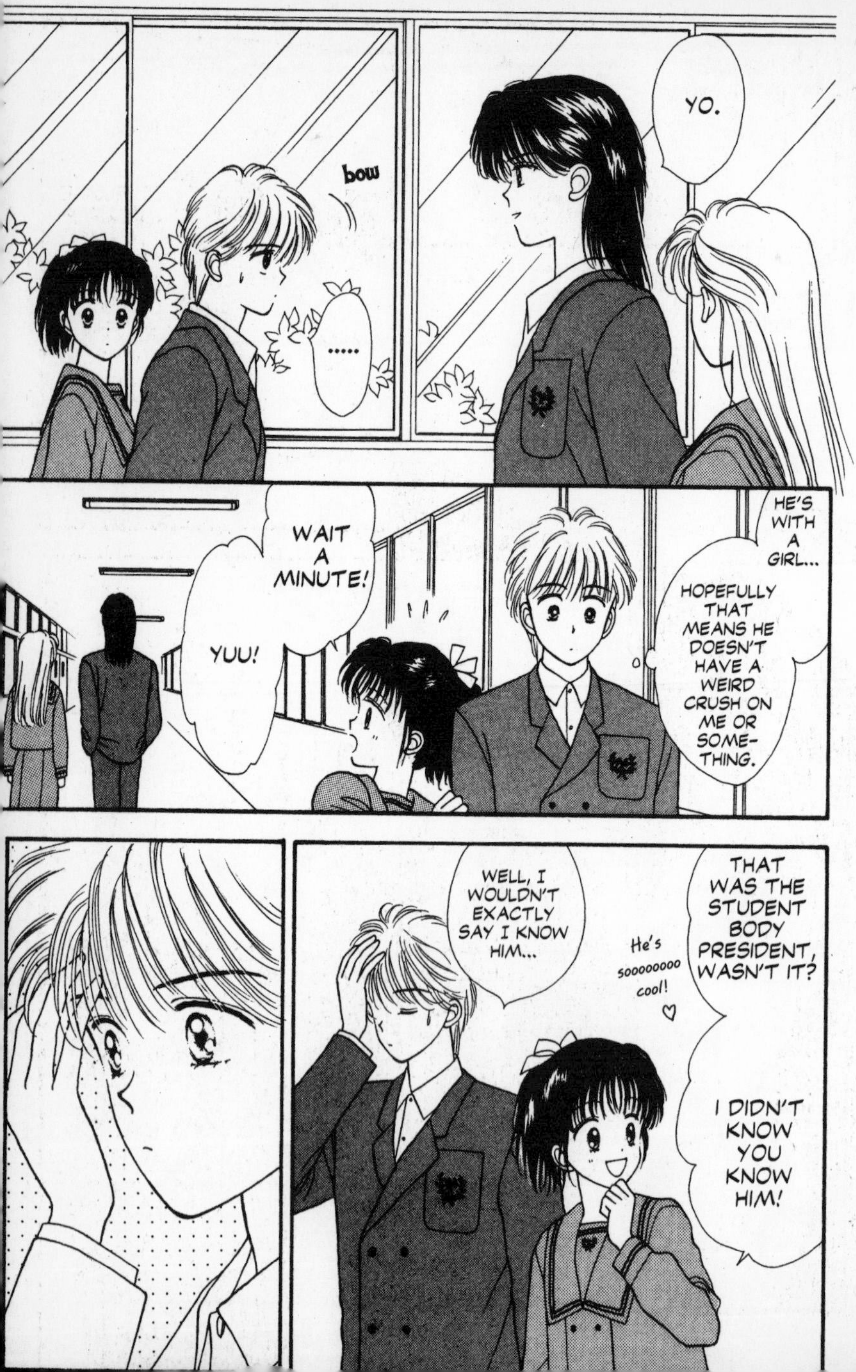
YO.
bow
......
HE'S WITH A GIRL...
HOPEFULLY THAT MEANS HE DOESN'T HAVE A WEIRD CRUSH ON ME OR SOME-THING.
WAIT A MINUTE!
YUU!
THAT WAS THE STUDENT BODY PRESIDENT, WASN'T IT?
I DIDN'T KNOW YOU KNOW HIM!
He's soooooooo cool! ♥
WELL, I WOULDN'T EXACTLY SAY I KNOW HIM...

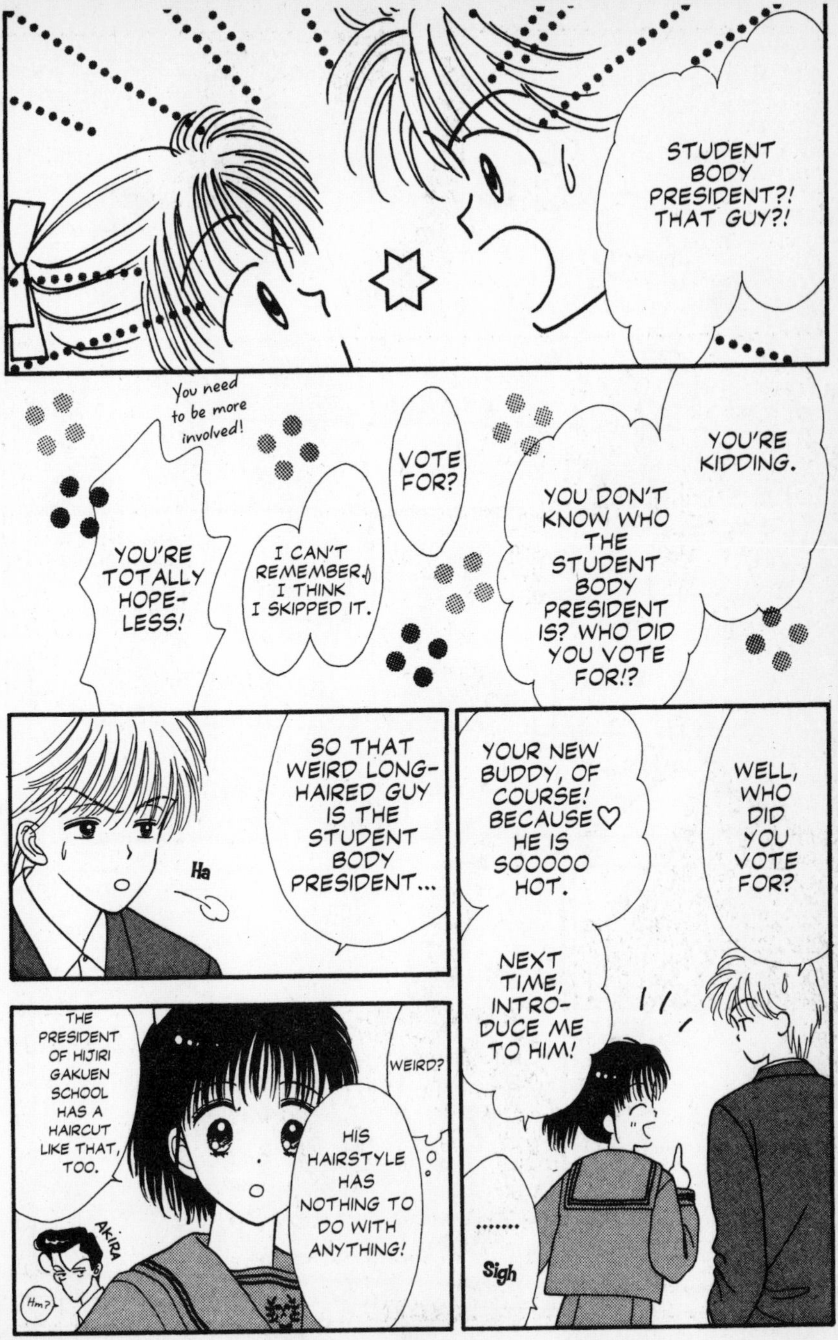
STUDENT BODY PRESIDENT?! THAT GUY?!
YOU'RE KIDDING.
YOU DON'T KNOW WHO THE STUDENT BODY PRESIDENT IS? WHO DID YOU VOTE FOR!?
VOTE FOR?
I CAN'T REMEMBER. I THINK I SKIPPED IT.
YOU'RE TOTALLY HOPE-LESS!
You need to be more involved!
WELL, WHO DID YOU VOTE FOR?
YOUR NEW BUDDY, OF COURSE! BECAUSE ♡ HE IS SOOOOO HOT.
NEXT TIME, INTRO-DUCE ME TO HIM!
....
Sigh
SO THAT WEIRD LONG-HAIRED GUY IS THE STUDENT BODY PRESIDENT...
Ha
WEIRD?
HIS HAIRSTYLE HAS NOTHING TO DO WITH ANYTHING!
THE PRESIDENT OF HIJIRI GAKUEN SCHOOL HAS A HAIRCUT LIKE THAT, TOO.
AKIRA
Hm?

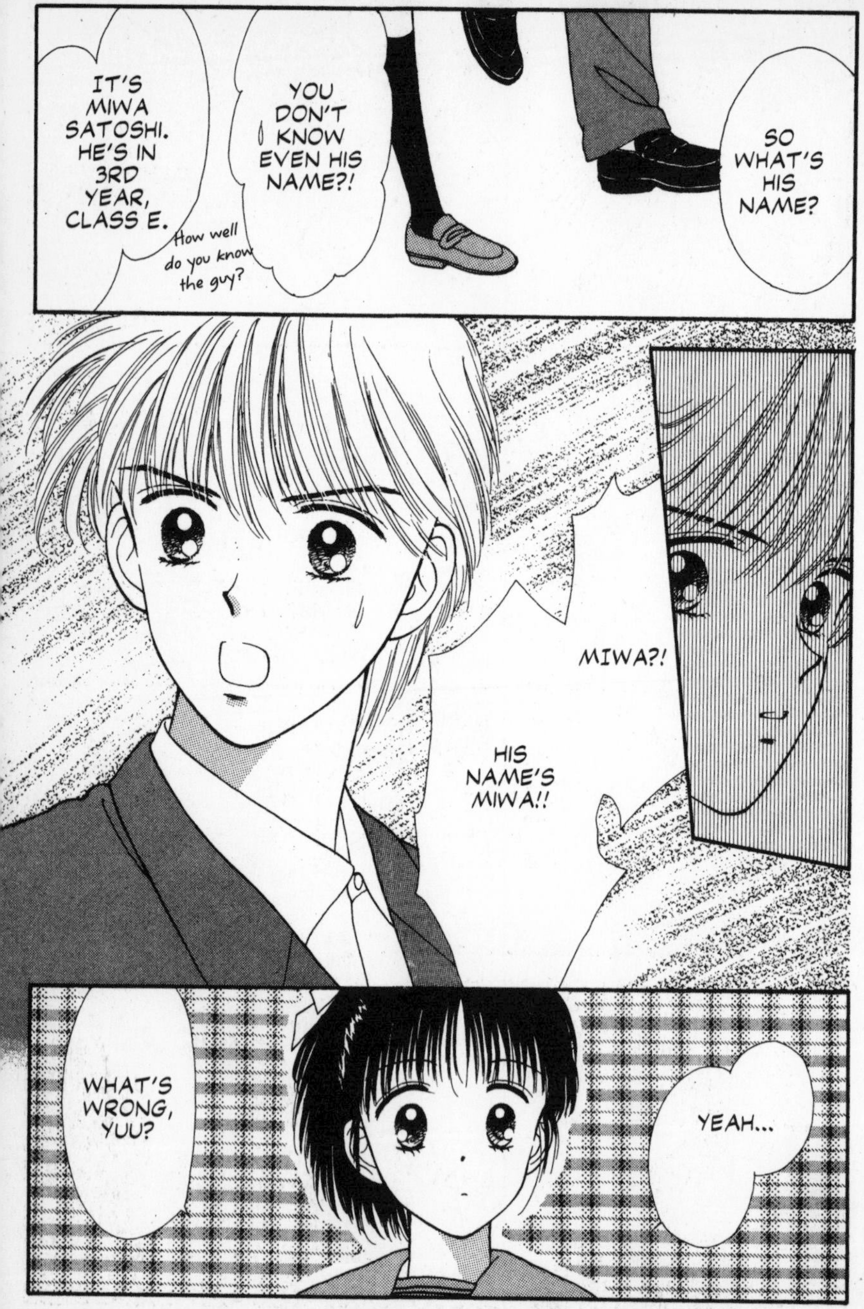
SO WHAT'S HIS NAME?
YOU DON'T KNOW EVEN HIS NAME?!
How well do you know the guy?
IT'S MIWA SATOSHI. HE'S IN 3RD YEAR, CLASS E.
MIWA?!
HIS NAME'S MIWA!!
YEAH...
WHAT'S WRONG, YUU?

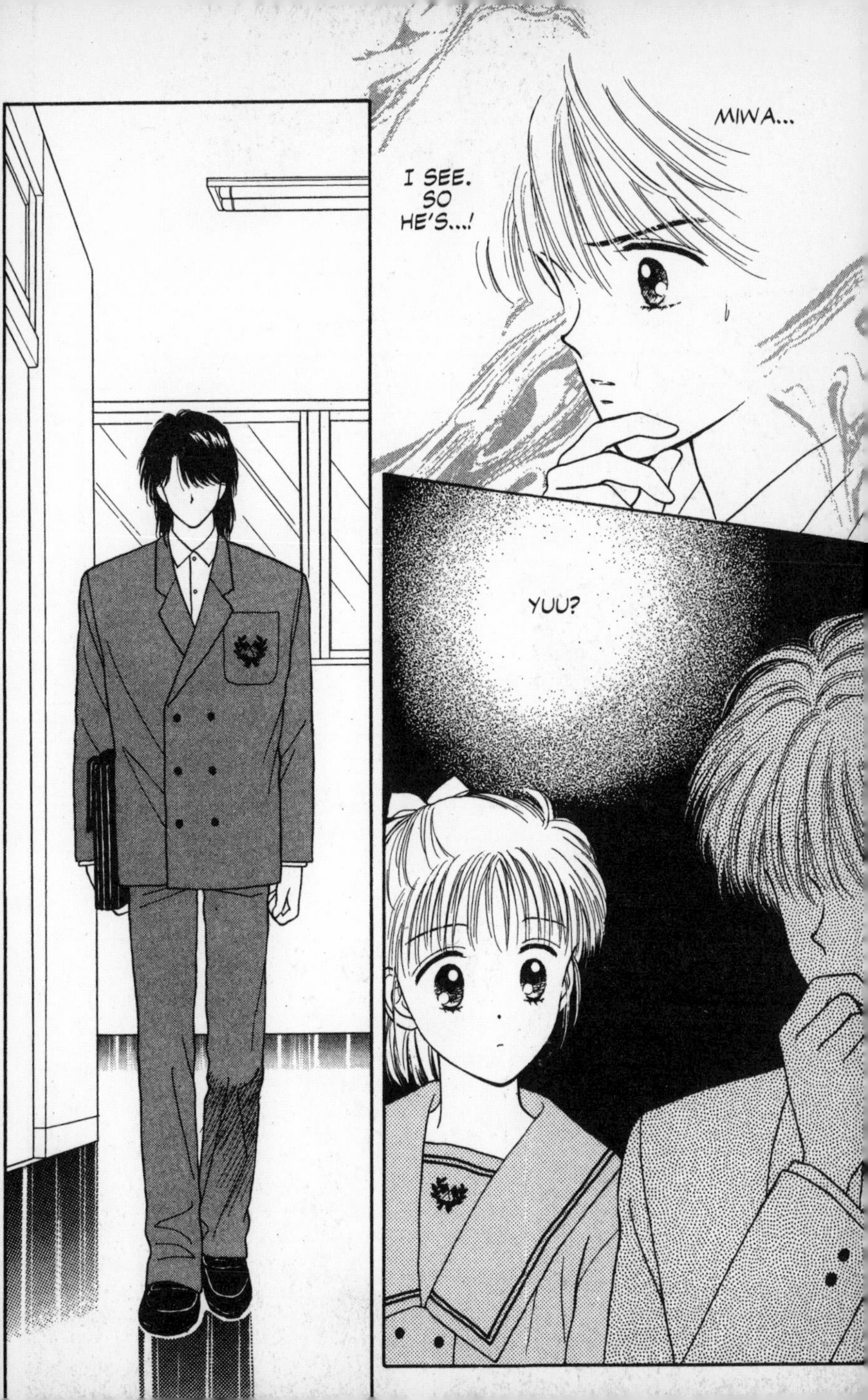
MIWA...
I SEE. SO HE'S...!
YUU?

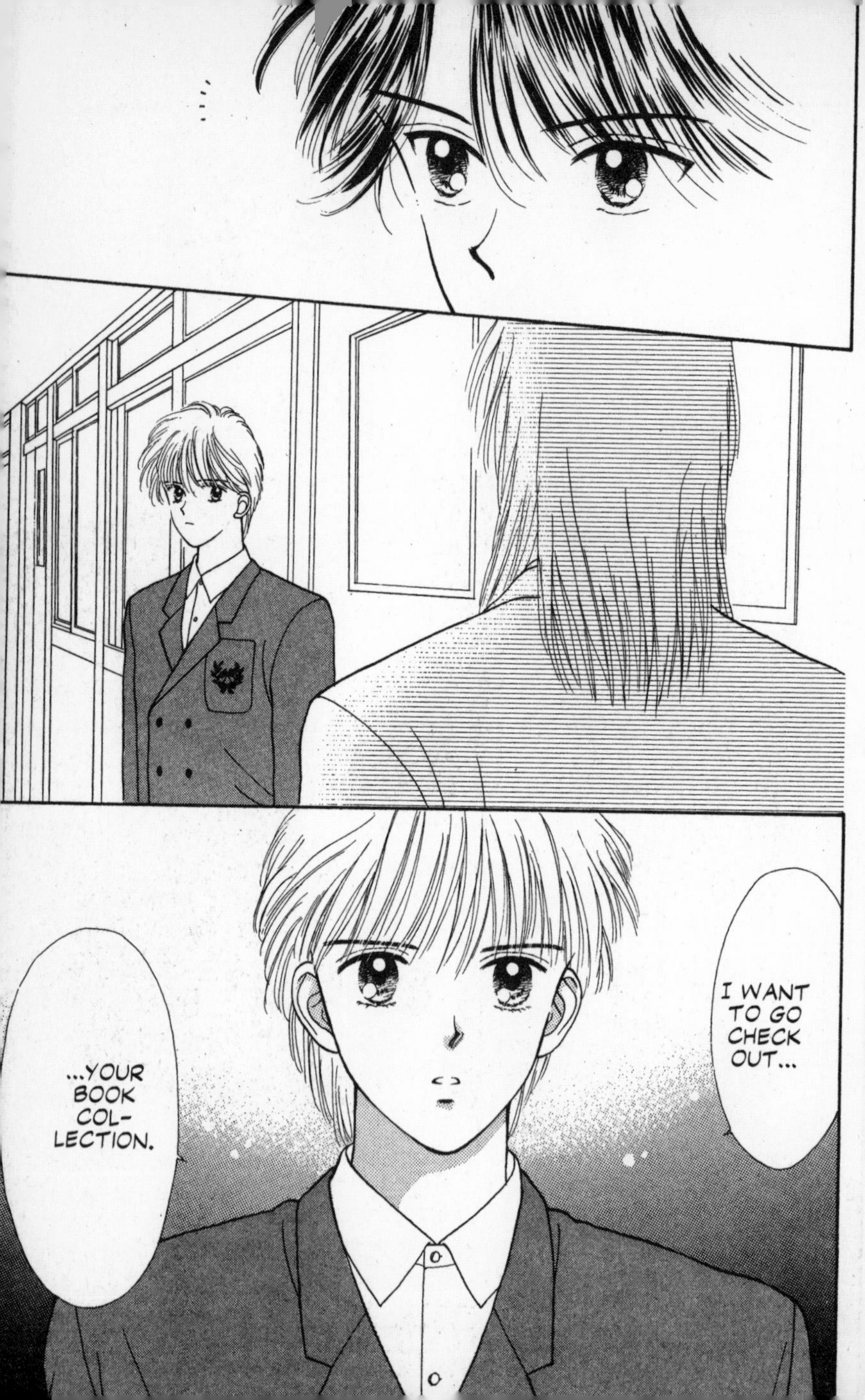
I WANT TO GO CHECK OUT...
...YOUR BOOK COL-LECTION.

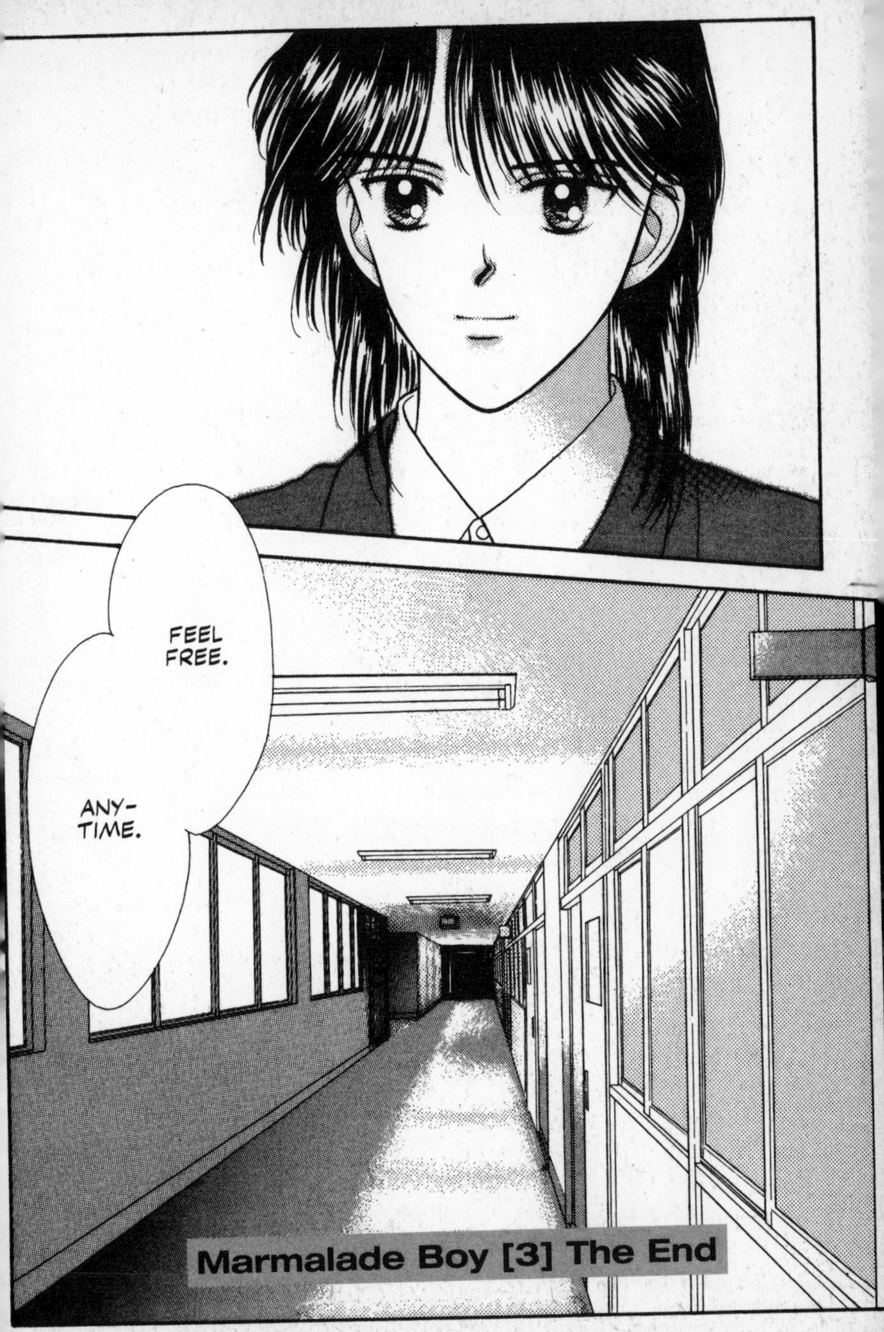
FEEL FREE.
ANY-TIME.
Marmalade Boy [3] The End

 S0-BAW-579

STOP!

This is the back of the book
You wouldn't want to spoil a great ending!

This book is printed "manga-style," the authentic Japanese right-to-left format. Since none of the artwork has been flipped or altered, readers get to experience the story just as the creator intended. You've been asking for it, so TOKYOPOP® delivered: authentic, hot-off-the-press, and far more fun.

DIRECTIONS

If this is your first time reading manga-style, here's a quick guide to help you understand how it works.

It's easy... just start in the top right panel and follow the numbers. Have fun, and look for more manga-style comics from TOKYOPOP® coming soon!

MANGA BOOKS